THE STORY OF A NATION

THE

NEW

KOREANS

MICHAEL BREEN

THOMAS DUNNE BOOKS ST. MARTIN'S PRESS NEW YORK

THOMAS DUNNE BOOKS.
An imprint of St. Martin's Press.

THE NEW KOREANS. Copyright © 2017 by Michael Breen.
All rights reserved. Printed in the United States of America. For information,
address St. Martin's Press, 175 Fifth Avenue, New York, N.Y. 10010.

www.thomasdunnebooks.com
www.stmartins.com

Designed by Anna Gorovoy

Map by Cameron Jones

The Library of Congress Cataloging-in-Publication
Data is available upon request.

ISBN 978-1-250-06505-6 (hardcover)
ISBN 978-1-250-14656-4 (international, sold
outside the U.S., subject to rights availability)
ISBN 978-1-4668-7156-4 (e-book)

Our books may be purchased in bulk for promotional, educational,
or business use. Please contact your local bookseller or the Macmillan Corporate
and Premium Sales Department at 1-800-221-7945, extension 5442, or by
e-mail at MacmillanSpecialMarkets@macmillan.com.

First Edition: April 2017

10 9 8 7 6 5 4 3 2 1

To qualify as a global citizen and not just pretend, a wise man once told me, you must live in other countries and love the people there more than your own. At least three if you can. The more different, the bigger the challenge. I can claim to have made it with the Koreans, which is a good start. I know, because I root for the Koreans in the FIFA World Cup. And so, this book is for them. I dedicate it to my wife, Arem, who, for me, is their representative.

CONTENTS

ROOTS

WEALTH

POWER

NEXT

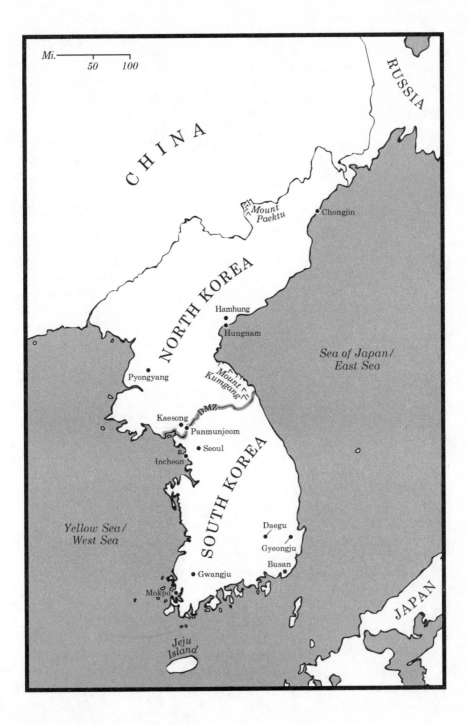

TIME LINE

1945   World War Two ends; American Military Government rules South Korea; Soviets control the North.

1948   Jeju Uprising; Republic of Korea and Democratic People's Republic of Korea established as separate states.

1950   North Korea invades.

1953   Cease-fire.

1960   Student protests topple Syngman Rhee; cabinet system established under Prime Minister Chang Myun.

1961   Military coup by Park Chung-hee; country returns to an American-type presidential system.

1967   Annual exports reach 300 million dollars, per capita GDP 150 dollars.

1970   Annual exports reach 1 billion dollars, per capita GDP 250 dollars.

1971   Park is reelected.

1972   First North-South talks; Park establishes Yushin constitution.

1974   First Lady Yuk Young-soo is assassinated.

1977   Annual exports 10 billion dollars, per capita GDP 1,000 dollars.

1979   Park Chung-hee is assassinated; Chun Doo-hwan takes control of army.

1980   Chun introduces martial law; uprising in Gwangju.

1981   Chun becomes president.

1987   Protests lead to democratic election.

1988   Roh Tae-woo is inaugurated; Summer Olympics staged in Seoul.

1993   Kim Young-sam is inaugurated.

1994   North Korean leader Kim Il-sung dies; his son Kim Jong-il takes over.

1996   South Korea joins Organization for Economic Co-operation and Development.

1997   Asian financial crisis.

1998   Kim Dae-jung is inaugurated.

1999   *Shiri*, first of a new generation of blockbuster movies, is released.

2000   Boy band H.O.T. performs in Beijing; first North-South summit; Kim Dae-jung wins Nobel Peace Prize.

2002   FIFA World Cup held in Korea and Japan; TV drama *Winter Sonata* gets cult following in Japan; singer BoA becomes a star in Japan.

2003   Roh Moo-hyun is inaugurated.

2004   Park Chan-wook's *Oldboy* wins the Grand Prix at Cannes.

2007   Foreign minister Ban Ki-moon becomes UN Secretary-General; Roh Moo-hyun and Kim Jong-il hold summit in Pyongyang.

2008   Lee Myung-bak is inaugurated.

2011   North Korean leader Kim Jong-il dies; his son Kim Jong-un takes over.

2012   PSY's "Gangnam Style"; Kim Ki-duk wins the Golden Lion award at Venice for *Pietà*.

2013   Park Geun-hye is inaugurated.

2016   *The Vegetarian* by Han Kang wins Man Booker International Prize; influence-peddling scandal rocks Park administration.

A NOTE ABOUT ENGLISH SPELLING OF KOREAN WORDS

There are a number of schemes for rendering Korean words in the Latin alphabet. I mainly use the Revised Romanization introduced in 2000 by the South Korean government. With North Korean place names, courtesy demands that we use North Korean spelling. This comes from a slightly revised version of the McCune-Reischauer system, which was developed in the 1930s by two American academics, George McCune and Edwin Reischauer, and is still in use among scholars outside of Korea. The other exception is with personal names. In those cases, I use whatever the owner prefers. If I'm deciding for them, I use the South Korean system, with a nod to familiarity in that I don't call any Kims Gim or Parks Bark.

PREFACE

This book began as an update to an earlier one, *The Koreans*, but so much has changed that it turned into something new.

In that first book, which was written in the late 1990s, I suggested that the miracle on the River Han, as South Korean economic development was commonly described, had given rise to a second miracle of democratic development, and would lead to a third: reunification with North Korea, but on South Korean terms. These three remarkable and unanticipated changes would, I thought, complete the reinvention and healing of a once-backward country whose spirit had been broken by Japanese colonial occupation and by its division into North and South by outside powers. I anticipated the sequel by this time to be *The Unified Koreans*.

Besides being wrong on timing, I have refined my view of this emergence and of what it means. First, while it is true that foreign occupation and national division left both North and South Koreans with a shattered identity after World War Two, I fear that I missed something that now strikes me as obvious about the modern development of the South Koreans: that the source energy driving it was defiance, not of the Japanese who colonized them, but of an entire history that had delivered them to a broken present. They refused to accept the place the world thought they occupied. Their defiance was set alight by anger against their brothers and sisters in the North and drove them to find the right way to compete.

This posture seems petty now. At the start the North was stronger economically and in terms of morale and confidence, but it has become an isolated and sad state whose leadership is mocked around the world.

It is ironic that the North Koreans are now seen as defiant—waving around nuclear weapons, celebrating their racial purity, congratulating themselves for their independence from foreign influence, and flouting international rules and diplomatic courtesies, while all the time looking for handouts from their enemies.

But the North Koreans are blowhards. Their defiance never took them anywhere. They are posers, a flag in one hand and a begging bowl in the other. It is the South Koreans who harnessed defiance and made something of it. It is their habit now, as they set about achieving something, to plug into this source energy as it carries them along, achieving if not everything, at least more than outsiders like me imagined they would.

This energy grew from the horror of civil war, from horror at the cruelty that came out of them as much as it did out of the North Koreans, and from their furious outrage at the arrogance of the aggressor, an arrogance the northerners continue to exhibit to this day.

The first president, Syngman Rhee, felt that defiance and he expressed it in empty threats of "marching north" that annoyed his American mentors so much they considered replacing him. However, it was President Park Chung-hee, who took over in 1961, who tamed defiance, put a hard hat on it, and set it to work to build a nation that would never be wrecked again.[1]

The second change in my view of Korean development concerns its significance to the world. It now occurs to me that the real importance of the Korean story is the way it demonstrates not only that, if one of the poorest and least developed people in the world can do it in two generations, then any country can give a good standard of living to its people, become democratic, and take its place with the great advanced nations of the world, and do so in a relatively short time. There are plenty of reasons why this doesn't happen, but there is now no longer a lasting excuse.

The Koreans give us the confidence that eventually every nation will. I suspect that, when that time comes, the concept of the nation-state will have done its duty and may be retired, but that is another theme.

I have stuck to the familiar notion of "miracles" to characterize the unexpected nature of each step. In the previous book I suggested that reunification with North Korea would be the third miracle. I may be overly influenced by the lack of interest we who live in South Korea have for North Korea, but I no longer see reunification as so crucial in terms of global significance. The South Koreans have become advanced and internationally accepted and the northerners may graft onto that achievement sooner or later, but the timing and importance, while it will change things, is the Koreans' business.

Instead, I would suggest the third miracle that completes the Korean arrival is something more nebulous: the cultural emergence and in particular the international awareness and acceptance of South Korean expression to a point of familiarity. That is, acceptance of its culture as part of the global culture. While many countries have globally famous novelists, athletes, or politicians, such figures tend to stand out as exceptions. With truly advanced countries, like France, Australia, and of course, the United States, the culture itself assumes a familiarity. Such familiarity in Korea's case has been taking place since the turn of the century. It was so unexpected that it has astonished everyone, particularly the Koreans themselves. That's what makes it a miracle.

PORTRAITS

1

THE BROKEN SHIP

"What's the captain doing?"

In the last minute of consciousness a drowning person, it is said, will have a clear thought that is a mix of acceptance and disbelief. *This is how I die. . . . But this is ridiculous, I can't leave like this.*

So it must have been as the *Sewol* ferry sank. In the flailing panic, *I am drowning. . . . But I was supposed to have been on yesterday's ferry.*

Most of the dead were teenagers. They had been trusting even as the foul water moved over their cabin floors. *But I waited like the man said. . . . I have exams. . . . Daddy.*

Over three hundred died that spring morning in 2014. The last minutes were staggered over two hours, from the moment the over-loaded ship tilted to when it rolled over and sank with cruel grace.

Most people were in the cafeteria when that accident happened. Some were on deck, smoking.

Senior crew rushed to the bridge where Third Mate Park had been directing helmsman Cho. She was crying. They called the vessel traffic service and, several times, the ship's owners. For reasons of culture and character nobody knew to take charge. The vessel-traffic serviceman in nearby Jindo Island instructed that passengers be told to put on life jackets and extra clothing. Communications Officer Kang went on the intercom and announced that everyone should remain in their cabins. It would be dangerous to move along the listing bulkheads. If people jumped into the sea the cold and currents would take them.

"Nonsense!" a student shouts when he hears this.[2]

"I want to get off. I mean it," says another. A minute later, the same message. Don't move.

"What? Hurry! Save us!"

"Are we going to die?"

"We're going to make news with this," says a boy, being brave.

"This is going to be a lot of fun if we get it onto our Facebook."

The stay-put announcement comes again.

"Should I call Mom? Mom, this looks like the end of me."

The children, all from the same school, put on life jackets. One gives his to a classmate.

"What about you?"

A boy shouts he doesn't want to die. "I still have lots of animation movies I haven't watched yet."

"What's the captain doing?"

Captain Lee, who has rushed to the bridge in his underpants, asks when the rescue will arrive. The man in Jindo says he has to decide whether they should abandon ship, that a rescue crew will be there in ten minutes. Two crew members drink beer to calm themselves.

The heroes that day are not on the bridge. Passenger Kim Hong-gyeong leads a group of passengers who hoist twenty trapped students to safety with curtains and fire hoses. Cho Dae-seob hands out life jackets to fellow students and helps the girls out first. Five-year-old Kwon Hyeok-gyu puts his life vest on his little sister Ji-yeon and goes to find their parents. A student, Park Ho-jin, sees her crying alone and carries her out of the ship.

English teacher Nam Yun-cheol and some crew stay aboard to help. Their bodies are recovered later by divers. Park Ji-young, twenty-one, says she'll leave when the other passengers are all out; so do Kim

Ki-woong and his fiancée, Jung Hyun-sun. Cashier Yang Dae-hong texts his wife, "The ship has tilted too much. There is money saved in the Suhyup bank account. Use that for our older kid's college tuition. I have to go save the kids. I can't talk anymore. Bye."

Forty minutes after the accident, Captain Lee issues the order to abandon ship. He is one of the first off. He doesn't tell his rescuers who he is.

Of all the images, one of the most searing is of the water lapping at the windows of the last cabins still above the surface. At one in the afternoon, there are two or three flashes of light, reflecting movement behind one of the windows: someone, probably a schoolboy, is attacking it with a chair. But it doesn't break. Such is the impact of the constant coverage of the disaster that millions of Koreans go to bed trying to smash that window, then turn to face the oncoming water, unable to bear what follows.

For the Koreans, this tragedy is a metaphor: Throughout history they had ignored the sea around their peninsula and chose instead to crouch in valleys away from the world. Then the South Koreans defied history and took to the sea as traders and in their rush to make money, cut corners and trampled over one another. *The broken ship is our greedy country. It has cost us our innocents.*

"As an adult in this society I feel great remorse and responsibility for this accident," the actor Choi Min-soo told an interviewer.

For Kang Min-kyu, the deputy head of the school most of the victims attended, the agony was overwhelming. "Surviving alone is too painful when two hundred lives are unaccounted for," he wrote after being rescued. "I take full responsibility." His body was later found hanging from a tree near the gymnasium on Jindo Island where the families were camped out waiting for news.

Such was the disgust at the familiar corruption and incompetence that oozed out when the surface was scratched—illegal overloading, embezzlement by the family who owned the vessel, failure of regulators, absence of safety training, lack of leadership, cowardice, the botched rescue—that public anger boiled over. Like a matador turning a bull, the presidential office tried to direct it at the crew and criminalize their incompetence. The court obliged and found Captain Lee guilty of gross negligence, equated it with murder, and gave him thirty-six years. Chief Engineer Park Gi-ho was found guilty of murder for leaving an injured mate and given thirty years. Thirteen other crew members were given sentences of between five and twenty years.

The tragedy froze the nation. As they did in old Korea when a king died, artists cancelled performances, officials postponed festivals, and people stopped shopping and eating out. Those in the public eye who wanted to carry on with their lives had to do so carefully. When the teenage son of a candidate in the Seoul mayoral race criticized victims' families for throwing bottles of water at the prime minister—"This nation is uncivilized because the people are uncivilized," he wrote—his father had to come out and apologize.

In early May, Children's Day came and went, followed two days later by Parents' Day, when children typically give their moms and dads red carnations. On the seawall at Jindo's Paengmok Port, which had become a mass of yellow ribbons, two signs read: "Come home, Kang-min. Dad needs you to pin a carnation on his chest" and "I miss you, my son. Your Mom also needs you to pin a carnation on her chest."

Parents came to the lapping shore and tossed flowers into the sea. At that time every teenager in Korea would have queued to give a red carnation to those bereaved parents.

After the tragedy, the Koreans turned on themselves with disdain. The story of their development is not that of a bucolic people who just became hairdressers and bankers. The life left behind was harsh. The old Confucian culture was oppressive and, as it changed, rapid development created its own rough edges. The Koreans are an impatient people and yearn to be as good as they imagine advanced peoples to be. But they are too hard on themselves when their country falls short in their own eyes.

For Korea is a work in progress and her story is not about falling short.

2

OUT OF GANGNAM

The Koreans began with nothing.

With the opening riff of "Gangnam Style" the club burst into life and the students, still in their first week and getting to know one another, piled into a mass horse dance.

My daughter joined in. A man galloping alongside noticed her mouthing the lyrics.

"You know the words?" he yelled over the noise.

"Yes, I speak some Korean," she yelled back.

"Really?"

"I used to live in Korea."

"Oh, my God! That's amazing!" He passed on this discovery to his friends.

"Actually, I was born in Gangnam."

"No way!"

"Way!"

And for a few minutes she was a celebrity, connecting clubbers in Salisbury—officially a city because it has a cathedral, but really just a humble English town—to the global phenomenon of PSY. He, of course, is the Korean rapper who in the summer of 2012 turned the world on to a new idea: that South Koreans were not the workaholics and swots we had thought them to be. No, they were creative, they were stylish, they were sexy. And they were confident enough to make fun of themselves. Korean was the new cool.

That was a far cry from my reception twenty-five years earlier on a trip home from South Korea to the UK. I don't recall it exactly but the dialog went something like this:

"Korea? That's part of Vietnam, isn't it?" a relative asked.

"No, you plonker," an uncle said in that put-down bantering way of the British family. "It's a fucking country."

"Two," another said. "North and South."

They turned to me for confirmation. We had been banished by the women before an extended family reunion lunch and were standing in an awkward circle in a pub, clutching our first pints.

"Yes. The North is communist. The South should be a democracy. But it's not. I guess it's a dictatorship. But it's an ally." They paused to sip their beer. This was a lot of information.

"You're in Seoul, aren't you?"

"Yes."

"Where's that then?" said the cousin who'd started the conversation.

"It's the capital, you twat," the uncle said. "I knew some blokes who were there in the war."

"What war was that then?" said the cousin.

"What war do you think it was? The Korean War!"

"Oh, that's why I thought it was Vietnam. I got mixed up."

"You can say that again."

The level of awareness of my chosen home among the participants in this geopolitical discussion was sobering therapy. I didn't say it out loud but back then I believed the Koreans were already soaring to global center stage. My relatives' ignorance made me wonder whether I was not going over the top and justifying my own flight from a Britain that seemed bound by self-deprecation and moaning. Just because living among Koreans made me feel purposeful—I found myself walking faster in Seoul than I had in London—didn't mean I had happened by chance upon a special providence.

Back in Korea any doubts about my decision to have moved there wore off with the jet lag. The country felt so dynamic and important. It seemed to me as if the people had been stretched back by a giant historical catapult and released. They were hurtling into the future.

Actually, there was nothing fanciful about this perception. When I arrived in Seoul in 1982, the Miracle on the Han, as economic development was termed, had been going for fifteen or so years and was very visible. Foreign visitors who had known the poverty of the recent past or who, as first-timers, had come expecting something bombed out, marveled at the jammed markets and stores, the speed with which orders were met, the fourteen-hour days and six-day workweeks, and the cityscapes filled with cranes. Seoul rattled with jackhammers. Just a few years earlier, people would pray for rain before they traveled out of the capital to avoid a journey wrapped in their own dust devil. Now the roads were being surfaced and the dust brushed off cars every morning was from construction.

That the Koreans were on the move and escaping poverty was undeniable. The odd thing, though, was that few outsiders saw them going any further.

Foreign specialists I called on as a journalist for perspective—diplomats, academics, bankers, security officials, as well as longtimers like missionaries and former Peace Corps volunteers—said growth had maxed. Whatever the planners were embarking on next struck these experts as foolhardy. Economic plans wouldn't work and any idea of democracy was doomed. The more articulate the expert, the more convincing his pessimistic thesis.

I would have liked to argue but lacked the mental infrastructure. With economics especially, my roads were still unsurfaced. Visibility on a lot of issues was zero. Like most journalists I had a slim grip on anything to do with money. Fortunately, though, my fine British schooling included six years of Latin, and that helped me see the bigger picture. "Export," I could confirm, meant carrying out, and Korea had a carrying-out economy. Carrying out was done mainly by ships, which Korean companies had taken to making; small carrying-out stuff was put in containers, which Korean companies were also making. You get the picture? Koreans started by carrying out and then followed it up by making everything that went along with it. They still do. They might not have invented anything, but they quickly took to making parts of things and assembling them on such a scale that they cornered global markets. Carrying in was okay as long as the goods being carried in were useful for the people making stuff to carry out. Of course, no amount of carrying out would work if the merchants couldn't vend—from the Latin *vendere*—in overseas markets. Success abroad was the key to success at home. If a company was good at vending in alien forums, the centurions in government cleared the home battlefield for them—ordering banks to lend, keeping out pesky competitors, and letting them foist whatever they made onto the populus.

Beyond that understanding, I found myself in largely unexplored territory.

Not that this prevented me from writing about the economy and criticizing government policy. No great mystery there. Reporting is a daily journey into ignorance. The skill lies in the ability to identify people in the know, ask the right questions, and go with the ones whose responses you trust.

Which brings me back to my foreign experts. I also relied on them to make sense of the politics. The prevailing view here was that Korea would always be a dictatorship. That's what the Koreans I relied on also felt. I disagreed with all of them. My instincts told me that change was coming. I just wasn't any good at figuring out why, or expressing it.

"I don't know what you've been smoking," a senior Western diplomat (correspondent-code for the American ambassador) said at a lunch with a foreign press group after I'd said I felt democracy was around the corner. He had a point. That weekend, police had put opposition leaders under house arrest and tear-gassed a mass democracy protest. My traitorous colleagues around the table agreed with him. Dictators had been here for five thousand years and weren't going away.

But, I wondered, how come the policemen and students in democracy protests are so similar? They were brothers. So were the politicians. Opposition activists and government people came from the same schools and held the same values. The government folk shared a sense of national embarrassment about the then–military dictator, Chun Doo-hwan. He was there, so you simply did your best to get on with life, and for some who hated the previous dictators that meant joining his party, or joining the tame opposition—the ones we called opposition-by-day-ruling-party-by-night. They'd argue for their own interest but no one believed he should be there. Even religious people thought God must have been watching a baseball game and hadn't seen him sneak in. The Koreans had no serious ideological, religious, or racial differences. Being human they chose some issues to bicker over but these didn't run deep. That was because they weren't even a generation out of the rice paddy, certainly not long enough to build differences the disadvantaged could accept. Everyone's life was improving each year. A few people were getting very rich but their fingers had not yet fastened around the neck of opportunity. The dictator was scheduled to step down. Would he do it? Yes. He'd promised the American president. Seoul was hosting the Summer Olympics a few months after the end of his term. It would not be wrecked. That's how I saw things.

Not that this mattered. For reporters, future forecasts are part of reporting on the present. By the time the future arrives, they're past. No one gets called out on it. But the pessimism about Korea did represent a collective failure of imagination. The explanation is that journalists, diplomats, and businesspeople worked in short time frames and found safe refuge in criticism. The critics around us, Koreans and foreigners, were of two sorts. Strategic critics disapproved of the government in power and therefore everything it did got them going. Others were tactical. As the process of growth was one of responding to problems, backers of the solutions not taken were always handy for a critical quote. When, for example, the government announced another five-year plan or decided that, say, electronics was now a strategic industry, the press, in the name of objectivity, would turn to people who would pooh-pooh the whole thing and throw in human rights, labor rights, corruption, and the rest to prove the point.

It was nigh on impossible to avoid this intellectual trap because the Korean leadership was challenging the accepted wisdom about what was needed for a country to grow.

"Outsiders were condescending because the Koreans had chosen an unfamiliar route for development," says John Burton, who was the *Financial Times* correspondent in Seoul through the 1990s. "Their way involved central planning and authoritarian state power, which went against the accepted model of democracy and free markets. There was a reluctance to admit that this way might work."

Even today, some older scholars still wriggle away from the idea of South Korean democracy because it was the political right that delivered it. They will instead highlight the "impurity" of South Korea's post–World War Two origins and argue in the next breath that the world always gets North Korea wrong. In their day, before communism tripped over its own shoes and fell on its face, there was moral and intellectual appeal in the idea that capitalism caused underdevelopment and that socialism was more authentic. The murderousness of communism was never quite as real as the nastiness of free world allies like Park Chung-hee. That much is understandable. But when the evidence proved them wrong, it was hard for many to admit it. One who did was Aidan Foster-Carter, a Marxist who first approached the Korean case as a pro–North Korean antifascist.

"Our twisted template really didn't fit, but like Procrustes we jammed it on anyway," he wrote. "Park Chung-hee never stood a chance. He had served imperial Japan, made a military coup, tortured or killed opponents, and not only hosted U.S. troops but sent his own to Vietnam—on the wrong side. A few of us went further. North Korea had no foreign troops, and its economy at first outgrew the South's. Kim Il-sung's system was hard to like, but this was the steep climb to the future and the 'true' Korea. Stuffing our head with this nonsense blinded us to what South Korea was achieving. My first visit in 1982 was a shock. I found myself in a dynamic developing country, not the wretched comprador neo-colony of my *a priori* fantasies. The self-imposed scales fell from my eyes."[3]

Besides the big-picture matters, there were smaller flaws undermining confidence in South Korea. Development is not simply about a nation's accounts. A country that is developing is getting richer and becoming better and more wholesome morally, practically, physically. Given this, at what point does a flaw represent a critical obstacle to continued growth? That depends on who you're asking. For example, how, expats wondered, could a country whose legal system was based on confession, and thus rife with torture, and whose politicians operated on illegally raised funds, become a democracy? Good point. This was one on a long list of ills: authoritarianism, corruption, male chauvinism, military-style corporate cultures, racism, status obsession, and classism. Actually, not such small matters.

Putting these issues in their context and allowing that they, too, could change at some time, was not easy because they manifested in the people you expected to carry the country forward. As such they seemed immutable fixtures.

Here's an example of what I mean. Shortly after arriving in Korea, I was invited to the home of a young Korean couple for dinner and the subject of the children of mixed-race marriage came up.

"You know, we hate them," the husband said quite unashamedly and, for some reason, with a smile. By "we" he meant not just he and his wife. He meant all Koreans. All felt this way. And feelings, I'd already noticed among my Korean friends, were not something to be kept in check by reason. They were justification for whatever came out of your mouth or made you swing your fist. This gentleman was justifying the marginalizing of the children of Korean women and American soldiers. "We hate them." No more explanation required.

This fellow was not leaning on his hoe with a piece of grass between his teeth. The house was in Gangnam. Thirty years before PSY's song came out, this part of Seoul—Gangnam means the southern side of the river—was under construction. Cranes moved over the sections of land where rice paddies and melon groves had been cleared. I got lost on the way to his house and had to do a few U-turns on some unnecessarily wide eight-lane boulevards laid out through empty land. Within a few years the city had sprawled south and the river that had once marked its southern edge sliced it in two. Gangnam became the swankiest of places. Those roads were crammed.

My antimiscegenetic friend was in a property that ten years later would make him a multimillionaire. He was a typical young, upwardly mobile Korean man of the new generation who aspired to be like people from an advanced nation. You can see why the foreigners who knew them best might assume they would not make it.

The reader may wonder if I did not rely too much on foreign experts for my analysis of Korea. The answer is yes, but only at first. Turning to people who are similar to you is normal in the expatosphere because you have to be able to understand your informants. Once on more solid ground, you naturally turn to local experts. And that brings me to the biggest reason of all to have doubted continued development in Korea. Local sources were the most pessimistic. Their worry that it would all go wrong was the greatest influence on foreign observers. So many of the Koreans we worked with and socialized with were convinced, even in the days of 8 percent annual growth, that the government was fiddling the figures and that the country was actually in recession or, if not, that disaster lurked in the next quarter. They had opportunity and cash in their pockets but they were shackled by uncertainty. That was because they tended to see the levers of society—the companies, the policy making, the banks, the courts—as being manipulated, not by rational and ever-improving systems, but by people. And they were even less generous about the competence, the virtue, and the motives of their fellow citizens than we foreigners ever were. Any moment, people thought, someone with power will take everything from me.

Thanks to this pessimism the Koreans were the last to wake up to their own arrival in the world. I would say that only now, well over a decade into the twenty-first century, are they getting it. Before this, they didn't believe their own propaganda.

Amid the transformation in living standards, in governance, and in ways of thinking, the assessment on the ground is mixed. Nostalgia for what has been lost is heightened as some change has been harsh and led to new levels of unfairness and want. Still, broadly, national development is accepted as an emergence from darkness—from material hardship, from vulnerability and disaster and infection, from brutishness and unfairness. It marks the emergence from a dark outlook, from fear of life, fear of nature and neighbor, to a place where life and love of others are celebrated. I mean this in the sense that celebration of life and love underlie the best modern systems. For example, the social agreement that each adult has an equal vote is an expression of love of others, of their equal value; a health-care system dedicated to the physical and mental well-being of all and an education system dedicated to helping all citizens reach their potential is a celebration of life. For most of history, rulers have seen their neighbors as subjects unworthy of such rights to life and happiness. The first steps to this modern world came with technological change that led to greater wealth, new rules that allowed the wealth to spread, and ideas that sustained the changes and created societies in which all could be free from want. The process was ugly and the first countries to emerge from darkness went on to suppress other parts of the world. Europeans did not take control of foreign soil to liberate native peoples. Similarly, Japan as the first modernizing Asian state did not annex Korea and parts of China out of charity. The emergence of the Koreans, then, is a case of post-colonial emergence not only from their own backwardness but also from foreign suppression.

The achievements of the Korean generation born between 1920 and 1955 is a truly remarkable tale. Leadership was of course a key factor in the country's development but national growth was something the entire generation embraced and contributed to. Their children and grandchildren now look at them as old-fashioned—in the way the men still let the women do all the work at home, in their preference for sentimental music, in how they maintain silences and imagine conspiracies, in how the ghosts from childhoods in what is now North Korea and the war haunt them, in their poor fashion sense, their deference to former bosses, their lack of education, their unwillingness to be challenged, and in their willingness to always, it seems, get drunk. But the young owe their elders. They owe them for what they have been through: the war when families were torn apart, the dictatorships when there was no way to avoid abuse, and the poverty when there were no trips to the beach to punctuate the years of hard work. They are, it may be said, the greatest generation in Korean history. They deserve statues for they are heroic. But no one has told them this and they do not conceive of themselves as such.

Their achievement has immense significance beyond the borders of Korea. If we picture a future in which all nations have made the transition from poverty and fear to material and political comfort, some will have contributed more than others in ways crucial to the benefit of the whole. Some will have given us values and ideas; some will have come up with the best systems and technologies; and some will give us the best cuisine, music, literature, and beloved personalities. At such a time, ironically, it may be natural for national boundaries to melt and for the rules we live by to be set at one end by regional and global government and at the other by local government. Nations may remain for purposes of identity and selecting World Cup teams, but they will no longer need weapons. You don't hear this often said, because the current issues seem so intractable. But it is obvious to me that such a world will come. Wealth and comfort are not for the few. All nations will catch up. I didn't believe this until the Koreans showed the way.

This to me is the significance of their story.

It is a story of miracle-making, for the Koreans began with nothing. There is nothing special about them. No secret formula for the sociologists or economists to reveal how they could move in one generation from the paddy fields into Silicon Valley. The Koreans were not exactly a blank sheet—no people are. But their pockets were empty, they had little usable space and no resources.[4] Their natural recourse would have been the sea but the inclination was isolation, not adventure. Countries are different, but people are people, and the Koreans are the same as anyone else. Their rise out of poverty in the face of such circumstances to democratic capitalism underlines the theme of our age.

The Korean story is all the more remarkable given the geopolitics. Were it nestled between Germany and France, postwar Korea would have surely grown. But it was hanging out of the Asian massif, a little white anticommunist spot on a huge red communist landmass. The whole peninsula, the North included, is the same size as the United Kingdom. The two Koreas have a combined population just short of 75 million, which means that were they to unify, the nation would be almost as big as Germany. South Korea on its own would be the fifth largest were it a member of the European Union. The Koreans, however, have long felt small. This explains why they have yet to fully accept their newfound importance in the world.

They are inhibited by a history of strategic deference to great power. That and their tendency to label themselves, and everyone else, in terms of nationality means that in an international setting the Korean will typically feel he is the person in the room from a small county rather than his individual self.

But that way of thinking, like everything else about Korea, is up for change. The acceptance of their culture overseas in turns gives confidence to the Korean people.

That said, for the Koreans themselves, there is something in their collective national achievement that rings hollow. There is a gaping emptiness at the heart of success. So many Koreans, I would even say a majority, feel themselves to be losers. The waters of the country's remarkable transformation are not holy and offer no baptism. The citizen may occasionally lean on the achievements of the country and feel a little better about herself, like when she's overseas and sees everyone with Samsung phones, but it's not something that sustains her. For that, there needs to be a change in the national ethic.

A few years ago the government in Seoul completed an elaborate project to uncover a stream that had disappeared under concrete and tarmac decades earlier. The undertaking was controversial because there was no perceived economic objective to justify the disruption and the loss. The benefit was hard for residents of Seoul to grasp at first, but I finally got it when I joined the crowds who flocked downtown on the opening day. Here, fittingly in the heart of the capital and fittingly grand—the restored section runs for eleven kilometers—was a nine-hundred-million-dollar government endeavor whose purpose was not to generate income or impress foreigners, but simply to make the lives of the citizens a little nicer. Koreans were not used to that. You could sense the wonderment. My first reaction was criticism: The banks of the river were vertical not sloping, and made of concrete not grass; you had to go right up to the railing to see the water. But the people all around me were mesmerized. The Koreans are a people used to obeying authority, but they do not do so happily. As they bow before power, they're casting around figuratively for a weapon. But here was benevolent leadership. The project helped propel its author, city mayor Lee Myung-bak, into the presidency and prompted similar beautification schemes around the country.

Despite this, leadership has still not found a way to articulate the idea that it is good to make life better for the individual. The idea of sacrifice for the group is too profound.

The challenge for the Koreans is to establish the vision of the happiness of the individual and shake off the old values and habits that stand in the way. That would seal their miracles.

THE DEFIANT LAND

"From the air, it must have looked like a thumbprint."

In the nighttime shots of the Korean Peninsula taken from space, where the blackness between Manchuria and South Korea is so deep it could be ocean, the bottom shore of darkness explodes with light, as if a giant lighthouse sweeping the sky had, at that moment, blinded the satellite.

Twenty-five million live down there in the lighthouse. They make up greater Seoul and are the most precariously quartered mass of people in the world. Seventy percent of North Korean military power is aimed at their homes; 60 percent of South Korean military power is committed to their defense. One scenario for their future has the North bombing them helpless, moving into their section of the country, and suing for peace before their own military and the American allies can react.

Not that you sense any of this on the ground. The bustle and noise crowd out thoughts of war. After the last war, South Koreans got on with life. But they did so angrily. The North had invaded as if entitled to their lives, and the regime has continued ever since to pose as more pure, more legitimate, more Korean. The North Koreans purged their ranks of people who collaborated with Japanese colonial rulers, pretend they did not take orders from the Soviets or rely for aid on the Chinese, and refuse to let their citizens marry foreigners. All this allows them to claim to be racially and spiritually unsullied. The claim, it must be said, has a certain nationalistic logic that tugs at the South Koreans, but anger and pragmatism pull them in another direction.

And that's what the land tells you: Look at us, we are now better, your standards for purity are a delusion, we are the real Korea.

Far from being settled, this bright part of Korea screams defiance. And that blast of light, just a short drive from the demilitarized zone, is its defiant capital.

That pose began unsurely. During the war, many towns were turned to charcoal and ash. "From the air, it must have looked like a thumbprint," the war reporter James Cameron wrote of Pohang.[5] South Korea has since rebuilt, two, three, or four times, each time with more confidence. First was with low buildings, rising ramshackle out of the ground, then with larger and more resilient blocks. Pohang became a great steel center. Greater Seoul is one of the largest agglomerations on the planet. Its high-rise apartment complexes and office towers push upwards like clenched fists.

The whole country is new, even the tatty bits. Nobody lives in the Korean equivalent of Victorian or Edwardian houses. There is of course some history, but not much. The best of what remains are the Buddhist temples, propitiously hidden out of sight in glens and on forest slopes, centuries after the monks were driven from the centers by the Confucians. Besides Gyeongju, the ancient Silla capital, there's little else from the past: some parts of the old Seoul wall, fortresses, early twentieth-century cathedrals, a scattering of old banks and public buildings. Much of what passes for history is modern restoration. The Namdaemun south gate of the old city wall in Seoul, officially national treasure number one, dates back to 1398. But what you see was built in 2013, five years after a man who claimed developers had shortchanged him in a real-estate deal angrily set fire to the previous renovated version.

Traveling around this new country you get the sense you're looping back to where you were yesterday. The same Hyundais shooting the same red lights on the same streets. Once the cars were all black. Most now are white or gray, although the recent arrival of BMW's Mini is making other colors fashionable. Then there's the signage. Above shops, slapped over windows, on panels outside buildings, sticking out from buildings and stuck all over them, the *Hangul* script is a regimented thing—a box of characters equals one syllable. Decorative fonts and designs are available, but few shop and building owners bother to use them. The result is a cascade of familiar options within a kind of uniformity experienced as a chaotic visual assault.

There's a lot of English about now, too. Many road signs, street signs, shop names, menus, ads, notices, T-shirts, and the like are in English. On the roads, it began so the American military could more easily travel and navigate day-to-day life in Korea. Now the use of English is really a reflection of chicness. Meaning is not always important. Take this, for example, on a coffee-cup sleeve from a café called *gout de ciel*:

> *Here's an example from a butterfly an example*
> *That it can lie happy on a hard rock*
> *An example that it can lie on this unsweetened*
> *stone friendlessly and all alone now let my bed*
> *I do not care*[6]

All around, too, of course, are the sounds of the Korean language. After a few days in the country, I took my first taxi on my own, ready to unleash a Korean word—*yeogi* (here)—because I knew where to get off. The driver was listening to what could have been the news on the radio. I tried to identify a word—any word—like you can in a language you don't know: *ba-doong ba-ding Rolling-Stones bee-doo Mick-er Jagger-ga*. But I couldn't. It was as if each word lasted as long as the announcer's breath. I understood later that Koreans give each syllable equal emphasis, throw in suffixes denoting status and grammatical position, and drop verbs in at the end of sentences. Half of those verbs end in *eyo* or *hamnida* which make for a recurring sound. The effect was *ba-ba-ba-ba-ba-ba-bamnida*. It was hard to believe these strings of sound actually contained information.

English is now splattered and transliterated throughout the language. If the poetry on the coffee cup moves you to ask for a refill, that's what you ask for, except there's no "f" in Korean, so it's a *re-pill*. Such wholesale adoption shifts meaning. So the English word *meeting* has become the Korean word for a date. Like the British adoption of French words for underwear and other embarrassing things, English may be used to soften a blow or give a sense of sophistication in a way a native speaker would miss. One notice in local government offices that made me flinch but didn't seem to bother native Konglish speakers was for a "Well-dying Program" for the elderly.[7]

Travel around Korea and you'll find some nice buildings, but you'd be hard-pressed to find a nice-looking town. Apartment blocks are the predominant feature. In most places, there are older blocks stained by rain, and newer ones prettified with colors and patterns; buildings once fashionable in their time are patched with the kind of tiles used for toilet floors; two-story homes have quickly grown old and ramshackle, something added on the roof here, a concrete and corrugated iron bit there, a plastic sheet over tiles, dusty mosquito netting on the windows. Such is the poor esthetic and poor quality of building that twenty-year-old houses look ancient.

Take a coach or train—the longest Korean journey takes a half day—and even in between towns, in parts of the country that might once have been distinct villages, it looks as if planning permission is given on the strength of how buildings look in the catalog, set against a white background.

"So why do you want to build this twenty-story apartment block in the middle of these fields?"

"Er, so the tenants get a better view of the mountain?"

"Oh, okay."

The passing motorists moan for thirty seconds and are gone, headed for the other rural eyesore, the love motel, with a name like Eden or Yes, and a zany facade.

That's not to say there aren't artists and designers in Korea. It's just that this is a country for the producer, not the consumer. In time, the eyesores get knocked down and something bigger and better takes their place (when a developer sees an opportunity); thus, progress comes when, in good capitalist style, someone can make money by providing something better, then better again.

One look at this country is enough to know that, truly, the North Koreans have lost the battle for the better life, for that is what it is about. That result has been in since the 1980s.

An agent dispatched from the North, snuck in by submarine and hiding in the hills and who never sees a soul, will find even the forest conspiring to convert him. It will be richer and more abundant than any he has ever seen. If you look at old photographs from the 1880s, much of the land was bare. It was that way for a long time. The culprit was the man walking through the market with a stack of wood on his back to sell for the underfloor *ondol* (hot stone) system for heating homes. In the twentieth century the Japanese introduced industrial logging, further ravaging the forest stock. By the end of the Korean War in 1953 the peninsula was almost totally deforested. The South in the 1960s decided to reforest. The government created the organizational and technical expertise to achieve this and helped private owners who owned 70 percent of what should have been forested land. Between 1961 and 1995 the stock grew from 4 million to 6.3 million hectares. In the late 1990s the lessons of the land were taken to the towns and cities, which launched urban greening programs. By 2008, eleven billion trees had been planted. About two-thirds of South Korea is now clothed with forest. Conifers account for almost half this area with the predominant species Japanese larch, pitch pine, and Korean pine. Broad-leaved, deciduous trees such as oak fill 28 percent, with the rest of the land mixed.

This covering sings with the seasons. In winter, between snowfalls, brown trees poke out of the lower hills like the stiff fur of a boar's hide. Spring breaks in the south, in Jeju Island, and rolls up the peninsula in a wave of blossoms of magnolia, forsythia, and azaleas, and full green vegetation breaks out of the glens and crawls high up the slopes where it collapses in glorious Canadian colors.

Twenty areas are now preserved as national parks. The demilitarized border zone is the unintended twenty-first. The belt of land that separates the armies of the two Koreas stretches across the center of the peninsula. It has remained untouched since 1953, except by the boots of patrolling soldiers and the occasional defector, and has become so noted as a wildlife sanctuary that some quite serious people think that if we ask nicely the North Koreans might agree to turn it into a nature reserve even before peace breaks out.[8]

Rogue North Korean agents aside, the South Korean countryside is safe. Tigers used to roam the steep mountain slopes but have not been sighted since the 1920s. Wildcats and bears still inhabit the more remote areas such as the Jiri and Seorak mountains, but you never hear of attacks. In fact, it's the bears which should be protected. Some are, at a center in Jirisan National Park. But hundreds more are in cages on farms, milked for their bile and later slaughtered to fuel the demands of traditional medicine.[9] The wild boar is making a return thanks to reduced hunting, and there are several indigenous species of deer. Korea is also a great place for the bird-watcher. The sunset flight of tens of thousands of Baikal teals over Cheonsuman Bay is the greatest of free performances. Saemangeum is reckoned to be the best place in the world to see the increasingly rare spoon-billed sandpiper, nordmann's greenshank, and other endangered east Asian birds such as the black-faced spoonbill, the Chinese egret, and Saunders's gulls. Of all birds, though, the crane is historically the most emblematic of the country.

The grass in Korea is very coarse and not suited for hill walking off the trail. A stunning exception is a part of Jeju Island where an Irish Catholic priest introduced sheep and, after some bureaucratic battles, was allowed to import soft grass from New Zealand for them to graze on.

You don't have to go far to find green. One remarkable feature of Korean cities, and of Seoul in particular, is their mountains. Hiking courses, although undersold to foreign tourists, are popular with middle-aged residents and people who don't go to gyms.

But here's an interesting thing: For most city folk, the mountains they see every day recede into irrelevance. I'm not making this up. Ask any resident of Seoul, foreign or Korean, to name the mountain downtown that looms right behind the Blue House, the official residence of the president, and you'll find most don't know. They might pass by it every day but never think about it or talk about it. North

Korean assassins reached its slopes on a mission to kill the president in 1968 and it was closed to the public for the next forty years. You'd think it would exert some mysterious appeal or at least be a point of reference. But no. It's not known. (It's actually called Bugaksan, *san* being the Korean word for mountain). You can expand this test. Ask any Seoulite to name more than five or six of the forty or so mountains in the city and I'll bet only the hikers will manage it. The only exception is Namsan (South Mountain) in the city center. It has a cable car and the park on top includes an iconic tower complete with revolving restaurant. For good measure, the Korean CIA used to have its domestic spying offices there and "being taken to Namsan" meant a midnight knock on the door, a blindfold and, once you got there, a beating or worse. But the rest of Korea's mountains are unappreciated. I don't know why I have wondered so long about this but I have, ever since I realized that I was looking out of my office window at Inwang Mountain for five years before I thought to ask someone what it was called. I think I had whatever it is that Koreans suffer from.

The approach to leisure makes me wonder if people really enjoy their surroundings. Despite some changes, such as a recent fad for camping, the country is still not well arranged for choice. The city folk pile into the same places. Summer, for example, is announced on time each year with front-page photos of half a million sunbathers sweltering on the sandy crescent of Haeundae Beach, on the edge of the city of Busan. The evening's entertainment there, or at the handful of other popular beaches, involves dinner at one of a line of identical restaurants that sell only seafood and don't have a view of the sea, lots of drink and noise, a lurch to the beach to set off fireworks, the karaoke, more noise, and then the motel. Next day, you drive home to rest.

The reason for the lack of options for leisure is that government still sees tourism as a means to extract money from foreigners rather than as an integral part of the domestic economy and a way for people to recharge their batteries.[10] Political leaders are still from the generation raised on one-day vacations dotted throughout the year. That generation's exemplary figures were in such flight from poverty that they saw no value in even taking those days off.

Once, when I was on a weekend break with my family near the

DMZ, I dropped in to a few real-estate agents to find out who owns it. Actually, this was work, preparation for a seminar about what to do with the zone once peace has broken out. The question of ownership, which I had never heard asked, grew out of an assumption in the seminar topic that experts could decide what to do with the DMZ without consulting the people who owned it. I checked with the government and was told there is no private ownership in the DMZ and therefore no ownership or compensation obstacles to a future grand plan for its use. In fact, I found, that only applies to the North Korean part of the DMZ. My real-estate agents in the towns of Shin Cheorwon in Gyeonggi Province and Haean in Gangwon Province told me a different story about the southern part. One said that in his rough estimate, only 30 to 40 percent of the southern sector is publicly owned, while 50 to 60 percent is privately held, and 10 percent of undetermined ownership. Some ownership dates back to prewar times. Moreover, the land, although it couldn't be used for anything now, was being traded. For example, in November 2007, a Mr. Shin Joong-hyun donated 39,300 square meters of DMZ land he had bought in 1975 to the National Trust. If you want to buy some, here's what I found you can expect to pay: Rough land and hills, 2,000–3000 Korean Won (KRW) per 3.3 square meters; potential farmland, KRW 10,000. (That's an average of US $2 for 36 square feet of rough land and US $9 for farmland).

As for the rest of the country, at the end of World War Two only 10 percent of farmers owned their land. Millions toiled on rented land, some 20 percent of which was owned by Japanese. A land-reform program that the president of the day, Syngman Rhee, tried but failed to resist, redressed this balance so that by the time of Park Chung-hee's coup in 1961, 70 percent of farmers worked their own, albeit small, plots.

It is a measure of just how poor the country was that as the government started nation-building it also had to intervene in a big way simply to ensure everyone had enough to eat. Although they were a rural people, the land could not sustain them. This overlooked part of the economic miracle story lay behind the considerable resistance to what now seem like commonsense ideas about building roads and entering new industries. How can we focus on long-term national development, people—including bureaucrats—wondered, when we don't know where the next meal is coming from?

This was a question that Park Chung-hee, as a poor boy, knew very well. The toughest time was late spring when the previous year's rice was gone and the new barley crop was still ripening. Some people even starved to death during this period. To address this, Park employed the kind of discipline he and his generation absorbed during their Japanese-style education in the prewar colonial period. To young Koreans today, the resulting policies—for example, the designation of "no-rice days" when rice was not to be sold anywhere or eaten at home—seem so North Korean. In 1963 merchants were ordered to mix rice with 20 percent of other grains. Restaurants were supposed to do the same when serving rice to customers. Women were mobilized in public events to encourage and educate housewives in making flour-based meals. White rice, the basis for breakfast, lunch, and dinner in Korean households, was labeled luxurious. Women could do their part for the nation by learning how to make bread and noodles out of other grains and starches. The media did their bit, too, with articles claiming Westerners were smarter and more successful than Asians because they ate bread. I guess all those Koreans, Chinese, and Indians at Harvard are testimony to the power of sandwiches.

Government experts at the Rural Development Administration came up with a high-yield strain of rice they dubbed *tongil* (unification) rice. In 1971 Park participated in a tasting event where senior officials were asked to rate the new rice in terms of color, stickiness, and taste, and to keep their assessments anonymous. Most ticked the "moderate" box. Park, however, wrote "good" for color and taste and "moderate" for stickiness, and then pointedly wrote his name on the sheet to show his support.

Bureaucrats, solders, and students joined in the rice-planting effort to underscore the national significance of the endeavor. In 1975 four million people participated. In 1979, five million. By 1976, some three-quarters of rice-producing land was *tongil* and the country, as Park had hoped, became self-sufficient in rice. Spring hunger went into the history books.[11]

The farming villages are now sleepy versions of what they used to be before industrialization. Once upon a time, everyone, the saying went, knew how many spoons their neighbors had. Now villagers are online like everyone else, following celebrity gossip. Local newspapers continue, sustained by ads, but such is the loss of the sense of community that in the countryside everyone follows the same stories as the people in the city. Perhaps the most noticeable feature of so many villages now is the silence, not just that absence of traffic that can be unsettling for city folk, but the absence of children, or anyone under forty for that matter.

The other change is the influx of foreigners as farmers marry women from China and Southeast Asia. One effect of this is familiarity with the outsider. Not so long ago, even in downtown Seoul, people would stare at Westerners and kids would shout out "Hello!" You still get the stares sometimes but, surprisingly, not from villagers. They are more accustomed to foreigners than city people are.

When Isa Kusumawati arrived from Indonesia to marry her husband, Kim Chang-rae, and live in his home village near the south coast, she became a part of their part of divided Korea. An uncle on her mother-in-law's side of the family was one of the presidential bodyguards killed when Park Chung-hee was assassinated. Her father-in-law was the youngest of seven boys. "His older brothers were all taken during the war by the North Koreans," she said. "He missed them all his life." The family performed ancestral rites for them. Then, in 2003, after paying a broker around twenty-five thousand dollars, they learned that some of them were still alive. "My husband met a cousin in China. We tried to bring them to South Korea. But something happened." She doesn't want to say what.

The best buildings in her village are new shrines paid for by relatives who have moved out in a kind of keeping-up-with-the-Joneses competitive flurry between clans. The average age of village inhabitants is seventy and villagers have elected Kim Chang-rae the village chief and Isa as the leader of the women's organization.

But they see no future.

"I want to go to Indonesia. Life is so hard here," Kim says. "Our children want to go, too. They're in fifth and sixth grade and every day is study, study, and no play." Isa says it's the same story with her Indonesian friends who have married Korean men. The result is a growing community of Koreans in Jakarta, who live relatively well off their savings and by selling clothes and fabrics imported from Seoul's East Gate market.

You would think that with its high-tech infrastructure Korea would be at the cutting edge of modern farming, but farmers are more inclined to protest change. Despite some pockets of activity such as greenhouse-grown bell peppers, agriculture is depressed. One problem is the size of farms, which were restricted by law from the start to ensure that each farming family could own their own land. As people moved into the cities, these laws remained in place, preventing entrepreneurial farmers from creating large-scale production.

But, as some go, others move in. Young people from the city are joining local farmers and trying their hand at organic farming. Another initiative involves cooperatives through which consumers commit to farmers. The largest, called Hansalim, involves two thousand farmers who produce local, largely organically grown products that are distributed to over four hundred thousand households via cooperatives, health-food stores, and home delivery. It even has an emergency fund to help farmers when there are crop failures and unexpected price rises.

In the turmoil of the past century villages not only lost most of their young people, they also lost an old community ethic to modern materialism. That ethic, known as *hongik ingan* (live and work for the benefit of all) went back to the founding myth of the country and underscored the relative harmony within close-knit communities. One component was that everyone was disposed to contribute to the wellness of the village. Another was collective work.

"This is the bellwether culture of Korea. It's one that Koreans need to rediscover," said Lee Charm, the former head of the governmental Korea tourism organization. Lee, who was born in Germany, and took on a Korean name when he naturalized, brings a European perspective to this issue: In Europe, millions of people take vacations or go for weekends to the countryside. Relaxing in these traditional settings reminds them how their ancestors lived and it gives them a connection and a feeling of pride in their national culture. There's an economic point here because if people are confident in their own culture, that confidence can be projected outward in a way that attracts others. The majority of Koreans do not feel that way about their culture. They go to the old palaces on school trips but all they see are external structures. There's no experience. According to the statistics, very few Koreans take vacations in the countryside. Maybe they visit for one day. They need to stay for a few days, relax, and wander around. But that doesn't happen. These days we see TV stars going to the countryside to live. These programs are hugely popular because there is a craving for that. So maybe this will start to change.

Lee cited one initiative, the Beautiful Village Project, which he said aims to direct villages along the French and German models. The former is to market them for tourism and the latter to make them sustainable, he said.

Interestingly, among the villages now being promoted as beautiful are the handful that resisted government pressure to modernize in the 1970s. One of these, Yaedam Village in the southeast of the country, rejected the government's money and tried to keep the old ways of doing things. The symbols of this struggle were the preservation of the sacred tree and the thatched roof, which did begin to disappear over time. Now the resisters are receiving official funding to keep things the old way.

For some years, my father-in-law was the village chief of Gume Nongsan Maul, a small community of forty-three homes. At that time there was a nationwide program to pair up villages with companies and government departments. When he arranged a two-day festival to showcase the community, around one thousand visitors turned up, including school groups and thirty officials from the ministry of justice, the village's partner in the program. Villagers taught the visitors to make bamboo rice strainers, a specialty of the village, and candles from hollowed-out vegetables and mud. They ate roasted sweet potatoes and drank *makgeolli* rice wine.

In contrast to similar events elsewhere, there was no attempt to empty the visitors' pockets. Not only did the organizers pay the four-thousand-dollar bill, they also prepared and served the food and drink. "We want to demonstrate that we can do anything if given the chance," my father-in-law said. He believed this attitude to be the key to the long-term future of the Korean village. He had traveled to Austria and Switzerland to study how farm-stay programs operate, and he reckoned Korean villages had to similarly develop new products—relating to tourism, crafts, and agriculture—in order to remain competitive.

His approach brought a lot of outside support. "Gume is a model for other villages," said Deputy Minister of Justice Kim Ki-hwan, as he munched on a sweet potato.

Village ladies handed out kettles which visitors could fill with *makgeolli*, kept cool in two urns buried in the ground. I had been keeping notes until this point, but after the *makgeolli* started flowing my handwriting deteriorated. I do remember the singing and dancing, though. An improvised open-air stage had been set up and a professional singer entertained the modest-size crowd. It was at this point that the village party spirit kicked in. People of all ages were dancing in front of the stage. Being British, I had hoped to avoid this and stayed with a group of men around a tub of *makgeolli*. But one of the ladies came and dragged me to the dancing spot. My wife and her sister seemed to think this was hilarious. The next thing I knew I was on the stage, entered by my wife as the final contestant in the karaoke contest. My performance won me a sympathy prize of rice and some bags of lotus-leaf tea, another specialty.

If you don't count city-states and other tiny places, Korea is the third most densely populated country in the world.[12] The rough land has shoved people into valleys where historically they huddled in villages. Now they do the same in apartment complexes, which house 60 percent of the population.[13] Statistically, there are 503 people per square kilometer (1.303 per square mile). In real-life terms, though, multiply those numbers by twenty. That's because 70 percent of the land is uninhabitable and no one wants to live on the farm anymore. So, in your average square kilometer in Seoul, for example, you're squeezed in with 10,400 neighbors (27,000 per square mile). The visa form should say: "Only people persons need apply."

In the cities, the numbers become apparent at noon when armies of workers spew forth from buildings in groups and head for restaurants. You can't help brushing by and occasionally bumping into people. They don't care, but might apologize in English when they see you're a foreigner. The shopping and market areas are permanently crowded and, until quite recently, the human decibel level there was very high—market ladies bantered and cackled, drivers yelled at each other, schoolgirls shrieked over secrets and boys taekwondo-kicked one another before racing off down the sidewalks. Now, the mobile phone has shut people up. It's not unusual to see half a dozen colleagues at a table, eating in silence, each preoccupied by their cell phone.

These crammed cities are modern, organized, and clean, but at the same time they are jumbled and messy. Million-dollar apartments are stuffed with junk: too many clothes in the cupboards, too much crockery in the kitchen, *kimchee* jars and exercise bikes on the veranda. Garbage is bagged up and dumped in the street where the cats often get to it before the garbageman comes along with his handcart. City officials know proper bins would be better, but they let things be to avoid putting thousands of elderly collectors out of work. Kitchens and storerooms spill out into the dining areas of restaurants. Workshops and garages tumble across the sidewalks into the streets. Shopkeepers pile box upon box of produce onto the shelves without regard for merchandising, and restaurants stack their empty crates in front of their windows on the sidewalks. Old, new, and out-of-place are side by side: an auto-repair shop beside an old beauty parlor beside an upscale chocolate shop. Elsewhere entire streets are lined with shops selling exactly the same thing; a row of pet shops merges into a line of motorcycle outlets. It's as if the government had declared a zone for each item, then stood back as everyone piled into the competitive chaos. For anyone who has visited North Korea and marveled at the comparable absence of commerce, this jumble of plenty shouts defiance. One European visitor I met way back in the early 1980s walked up to the street from the underground hive of shops beneath the Lotte Department Store in downtown Seoul and declared South Korea had already "won."

Without knowing the politics or even speaking the language, the keen analyst can soon catch how government manages this chaos. The clue lies in the street names. When they took over Korea in the early part of the last century, the Japanese introduced a system that identified property by the number given to the parcel of land it stood on within each neighborhood (*dong*). Streets did not need to be named. As cities developed, parcels were sub-divided and new parcels added and each given a new number unrelated to those of neighboring plots. When I arrived in Seoul, it had zillions of such lots in four hundred and twenty-three *dongs*. Getting from A to somewhere near B was not a problem thanks to efficient public transport, but precisely locating B was painful. The address would be, say, 76-5 Guui-dong (pronounced gooey. Yes, it exists) but only the postman and the local real estate agent would know where it actually was. Before satnavs, you needed directions based on landmarks—like, turn right at the church and left at the barber shop—or a faxed map. When all else failed, someone would come out to the main road to meet you. At the end of the century, the government decided to liberate us from this zaniness and give every street a name and every house a number that made sense. The mammoth naming project could have inspired the nation had we been invited to participate. Seoul alone had around fourteen thousand streets to name and hundreds of thousands of blue plates to nail up outside each building and every house. You can imagine local communities opting to name this street after a famous local person or that one after the temple at the end of it. But, no. That would have annoyed bureaucrats no end. They decided to do it stealthily in-house. The result was predictable. Five hundred large roads got names while the streets and lanes that run off them just got a number. For example, Jahamun-ro 28-gil (ro is road and gil means street). Some long roads have well over one hundred side streets. The numbering is logical but boring. A couple of officials could have done the whole thing in a week. Instead of citizen participation, tradition, creativity, and storytelling, we get efficiency. Nobody was inspired when we were informed in January 2014 that the new address system was to go into effect. The consequence—I still don't know my new address. That's pretty standard for a Seoulite.

In the 1980s, some of the best schools in Seoul moved over the river to Gangnam and the upper middle class followed them, sending apartment prices sky-high. The average modest apartment in the capital now costs half a million dollars. A generation ago, when developers moved in, they struck deals so that some of the new apartments would go to owners of the houses being replaced. Tenants of course had no rights. As a consequence, each wave of development involved unpleasantness. Builders hired gangsters to deal with residents who resisted. City officials and police stood by. Five protesters and a policeman died during a heavy-handed police action against tenants resisting a large-scale redevelopment in 2009 in the Yongsan district of Seoul.[14] Now gentrification is in fashion. Many areas today have little markets, shops that sell cute things, and tastefully presented cafés and eateries featuring diverse cuisines, wine, and craft beer, that are owned and run by expatriates as well as local entrepreneurs. On the demand side, this is driven more by women than by men. The downside is that tenants are being driven out more quietly by rising rents. As this happens, history leaves with the moving van.

"When you walk down these nice areas now, there is no sense of the past," said Suh Joon, a designer who on her own initiative is trying to catch some local history and keep it alive. Her first target was a lane of small craft, accessory, and dining outlets in the downtown district of Gye-dong. It is now crowded on weekends with local tourists. She has made a One Hundred Year Map of the area and has compiled an oral history book with the help of high school students and local residents.[15]

For now, these nice parts are rare. Most areas of cities are drab and look the same. But, if you slow down and stay a while, a different beauty emerges. It comes from the engagement, the community in each place and in each subsection. Korean nationalism lends itself to a love of the people as a concept, but the hierarchical system makes individuals rather indifferent to others who lie outside their circles. For this reason, their default way of empathizing with their fellows is to locate their suffering. They can feel very sorry for the less fortunate and for those who work hard for inadequate reward. What they are not so good at seeing is the beauty in the passion of people and the color in their differences. But if there's a characteristic shared by the cast in the daily street drama of the Korean city it is the raw beauty that comes from the energy and intense involvement with whatever it is they are doing.

Take the line of shoe shops just north of Seoul Railroad Station by Yeomcheon-gyo, the bridge over the tracks. There are sixty businesses making, repairing, or selling shoes in what looks likes one four-story building that stretches for one hundred meters down the road and around the corner, but which is actually a lot of buildings stuck together. The row is dilapidated. From behind, it looks downright derelict. In the dark stairwells between shops you get the feeling that whatever is behind them and upstairs out of sight on other floors is covered with cobwebs. The park across the way was an execution ground. Victims included forty-four of Korea's Roman Catholic saints. The only non-shoe enterprise in the whole complex is my wife's café which opened in 2015. I have driven over this bridge for years, but, after making this investment, I have been able to slow down enough to get to know it. I learned to my surprise that the building itself was once a source of pride. In the 1950s, when it was built, President Syngman Rhee used to point it out to foreign visitors arriving at the station as an example of how Korea was developing. The shoemakers got their start fashioning footwear from the leather of discarded U.S. army boots. In those days, young people coming north to Seoul for job interviews would invest in a pair of new shoes to give a good impression. In the 1970s there was a hostel and a coffee shop which was a hangout for gangsters. One of the shoemakers is known to be the best craftsman. If he displays his new creations in the window, they get copied in no time. Some others relocated in the 2010s to Seongsu-dong, a hipper part of the city. One shoemaker plays the sax; another, now gray-haired, wanted to be a mechanic but changed plans because the relative who owned the shop let him sleep on the pull-down cot at the back; another loves poetry and sits and reads in between customers. His neighbor bubbles with friendliness but is held back by shyness. One small shop is run by a couple who say they've never had a serious argument. She was a nurse, but gave it up when they had children because her husband asked her to. When the children were grown he asked her to join him, so she did and she now runs the business. They commute on a scooter, her arms wrapped around his waist.

Such people are the heroes of their country's astonishing rise, for they are all it had to go on. They had no industrial history or experience of freedom to revive, no oil, nothing natural they could dig out or grow and trade in. Almost every one of them came years ago from a village at that time after the war when, instead of shrinking from the cease-fire line, they and millions of others piled into Seoul and the satellite towns, their confidence derived from American patronage, their pursuit of life forming a collective defiance.

They have been their country's only resource. You don't have to play up their suffering or hard work or abuse or how they're pushed down the social ladder to find there is something magnificent about them. These are the people who have won.

4

THE CASE FOR HANGUK

*"This place is fantastic. I came here expecting
the Third World and I just can't get over it."*

Until recently, Koreans referred to their country as a shrimp, historically bruised as its whalelike neighbors clashed. During the economic
catch-up period in the last quarter of the twentieth century, the image changed. Korea became a tiger, sometimes a little dragon, in a
club with Taiwan, Singapore, and Hong Kong. One writer described
Korea as fashioned by pain and hard work into a rough "diamond" of
a country and gave his prescription for what was needed to make it
truly shine; Gregory Henderson, writing in the 1960s, came up with
the concept of the vortex to capture the political environment in
which power politics and an absence of way-stops—such as parties,
guilds, unions, and other means to park loyalties—swept people
toward the top and created a system that relied not on institutions
and organizations but on personalities and relationships.[16]

The miracle is neither an original nor necessarily more fitting
metaphor than the others. Each makes its point. But I've gone for it

because it does neatly reflect the way Koreans and outsiders have perceived the changes that have taken place in the country in recent years—as unexpected, astonishing, inspirational.

But let's not mislead ourselves into believing that outsiders have always been impressed by our diamond-polishing, sharp-clawed miracle makers. The truth is that until relatively recently, most visitors were quite ill-disposed toward anything Korean. This is worth examining, for it illustrates the extent of the transformation.

In considering foreign perceptions of Korea, we can fix the lens at three settings: the distant view, first impressions, and the close-up perspective of the foreign resident.

First, how have people who have never been to Korea or dealt with Koreans viewed the country in the modern period and how have those perceptions changed? This question matters. When it comes to countries, a little bit of knowledge can be good or bad for business. In tourism, for example, a couple of associations—true or false—are all that's needed to keep people away from a place. Twenty years ago, a survey commissioned by the Korea International Trade Association (KITA) found that only 1 percent of Europeans, 3 percent of Americans, and 23 percent of Japanese believed they knew much about Korea. A few years later I ran a survey through the American and European offices of the company where I worked and found some progress: collectively 8 percent said they were "very familiar" and 38 percent "somewhat familiar" with Korea. (Whatever "somewhat" meant, it wasn't enough to identify the president. Even though Kim Dae-jung had been the best-known South Korean politician for well over two decades, only 22 percent were able to identify him from a list. Fifty-two percent didn't know who he was and 24 percent misidentified him.)

But, as I say, lack of knowledge does not hinder the formation of perceptions. Twenty years ago, if you asked anyone in America or Europe what they associated "Korea" with they would have said: war, dictatorship, tear gas, riot police in Darth Vader outfits, *M.A.S.H.*, dog eating, the Olympics. Businesspeople would have said: development, corruption, tariffs, ships, chips, fakes. And so, if a company executive told his friends he was being posted to Seoul, they commiserated, and his parents prayed for him at church.

That long-lens view of Korea has changed in this century. A 2013 survey commissioned by the Ministry of Foreign Affairs found outsiders primarily identify Korea with cutting-edge technology, Samsung, and PSY.[17] The Samsung connection—and we could add LG and Hyundai Motor to the list—is not due to the sudden recognition of these companies, but rather the growing awareness that they are Korean. They were once thought to be Japanese and did not make a great effort to correct the impression for the simple reason that they did not wish their brands to be dragged down by association with the motherland.[18]

South Korea is not in the clear yet, though. This same survey found the North Korean bat defecating in the South Korean belfry. One in three people were unable to clearly distinguish between the two countries. It's not just that people get mixed up about which one is cool and which is ghastly. It is that the values and behaviors associated with North Korea rub off onto South Koreans. The merciless treatment of its citizens, the militaristic pomp and mental rhetoric of the northern state are seen as somehow being Korean.

That is unfortunate because South Korea and North Korea are totally different. The problem lies with their similar names.

The two sides hardly agree on anything and that includes what they call themselves. The southerners name their country *Hanguk*, short for *Daehan Minguk*, meaning Country of the Great Han People (unrelated to the Han Chinese, the "han" being two different words, with two distinct characters and tone). The northern Korea is named *Chosun*, an abbreviation of *Chosun Minjujuui Inmin Konghwaguk* (Democratic People's Republic of Korea).[19] Each refers to the rival country as if it were a region of its own. Hence, South Koreans call the North *Bukhan* (i.e., North *Hanguk*) and the North Koreans call their rival *Nam* (South) *Chosun*.

But the one thing they do agree on is what outsiders should call them: Korea. Well, actually, there's no agreement as such. It's a tug-of-war. For decades the diplomatic energies of both governments were spent getting as many countries as possible to back their respective claims to be the real Korea. This foreign policy posture would have been confusing if the countries had used their real Korean names. I mean, the English can't really say, "Scotland is ours," but they could if their parts of the U.K. were called "South Britain" and "North Britain."

The word *Korea*, therefore, is an exonym: for foreign consumption only. It is believed to have evolved from "Cauli" which was how the Italian traveler Marco Polo heard other foreigners refer to the Goryeo Dynasty, which ruled the peninsula from 935 to 1392. This became "Corea" and then "Korea."

Here are some versions in use today: Corea (Italian, Romanian, Spanish, Welsh), Corée (French), Coreia (Portuguese), Kaoli (Thai), Korea (Czech, Danish, Dutch, English, Estonian, Faroese, Finnish, German, Greek, Indonesian, Malay, Maltese, Norwegian, Swedish, Tagalog), Koreio (Esperanto), Koreja (Bulgarian, Latvian, Lithuanian, Russian, Serbian, Slovene), Kuria (Inuktitut). To distinguish, people add North or South in their own language. Thus, for example, the Maltese say "Korea ta' Fuq" for North Korea. (Even though it sounds like something you shouldn't say to people who have nuclear weapons.)[20]

So, here's a suggestion for South Koreans: How about a name change? South Korea's rating would soar if it could cut itself from the association with North Korea. So why not let the North have Korea and let the world refer to the South by its real name, *Hanguk*? (To avoid a mispronounced "Hang-ook," they should spell it *Hankook*). Some countries in East Asia, which know the Koreas better, do this already, and use local versions of *Hanguk* and *Chosun*, so why not extend this usage to the rest of the world?[21]

Aside from altering perception, this strategy would also offer some nationalistic satisfaction. Were they to make this change, Hangukians would be following the norm. Most countries go by the same name at home and abroad, albeit with differences in pronunciation. Greece is another rare country that calls itself something totally different. At home, it's Ellada. Greenland is known locally as Kalaallit Nunaat. Another exception is Deutschland, which foreigners called by many names, including Germany, Allemagne, Dogil, Jarmal, Nemecko, Saksa, Tyskland, and Vokietija. That's what you get for starting two world wars.

If distant impressions of Korea were negative until recently, then those of people who actually visited and saw the place were even worse.

Back in the 1980s, I came across a book of quotes by writers and other travelers waxing lyrical about foreign lands in which the Korea section was notable for being a) short and b) bitchy.[22] Beatrice Webb, the socialist, was quoted saying the Koreans were "horrid."[23] The writer James Kirkup didn't seem to regard them very highly either. Western missionaries had dubbed the Koreans the Irish of the East, but he considered this an "insult to the Irish." One winter in the 1960s he had this epiphany:

> Lying between chill sheets that night in my icy room, I tried to organize my first impressions of Seoul. In the back of my mind I felt that the place reminded me of somewhere I had been before. The impression of gloom and darkness and wildness could not be dispelled . . . and everywhere there was the curiously clanging, grumbling tone of Korean speech. From time to time I was reminded of northern Japanese towns in wintertime—Akita, Aomori, Niigata, or Sapporo. But then it flashed into my mind that what Seoul really reminded me of was the Arctic: the bare, freezing desolations on the outskirts of Kiruna and Narvik.[24]

As tempting as it might be to dismiss such writing as biased rather than informed, it is apparent from even the most charitable of foreign observers that until recently Korea presented an unhappy and depressing picture. Here is the diary entry of a gentleman who, sixty years before Kirkup, had come to study the work of the Roman Catholic Church. It was his first night:

> It is scarcely seven o'clock, and yet over all broods a death-like silence, a peaceful calm, as complete as one can imagine. The broad streets seem an immense cemetery, and the mean little flat-roofed houses graves. One might think it is All Saints' Day, for on each grave a little lamp is burning . . . the people themselves are returning like ghosts to their homes,

each robed in white—each and all mute. Without a sound they flit over the roads of the endless graveyard, until they disappear into the depths of some one of the illuminated tombs.[25]

Modern tourists and business visitors would not recognize the country portrayed in such passages. Such is the familiarity with Korea now that visitors come prepared to like it. This transformation has been dramatic and unexpected.

It began in the late 1990s, but I think 2002 was the watershed moment. That was when the Korean TV drama *Winter Sonata* became a sensation in Japan and the singer BoA broke into the charts there. It was also the year of the FIFA World Cup, hosted jointly in Japan and Korea. I first encountered the new view on the subway back from the Ireland-Spain match when I fell into conversation with an Irish fan.

"This place is fantastic," he said. "I came here expecting the Third World and I just can't get over it."

I told him about the Koreans having once been described by missionaries as the Irish of the East.

"Brilliant," he said. "Fokin' brilliant." Then he started moaning about Ireland being backward.

The interesting, and very touching, point about this transformation of the Korean image is that, Japanese fans of beautiful Koreans notwithstanding, it came about through encounters with Koreans themselves. No celebrity tipped global perception into positive territory. Nor did economic prowess, technology, or military might. It was the people. During the World Cup, when every Korean became a Red Devil supporter of team Korea, they made such an extraordinary impression that foreign fans longed to be part of whatever it was they were part of. One of the attractions was the wholesome vigor that escalated as the team went from win to win all the way to the semifinals. One of my old journalist friends who had come over from England to cover the events told me the Korea-Italy second-round encounter in Daejeon was the most exciting soccer match he had witnessed in his life. The game itself, the significance—the South Koreans upset the world-class Italians, just as the North Koreans had in the World Cup in 1966—and the atmosphere generated by the

Korean fans put the experience, he said, in a category of its own. The other notable characteristic of the fans was their sweetness, especially the crowds who gathered in the millions in front of the huge screens erected in city squares. Most were schoolchildren and students. They didn't know much about soccer—the offside rule seemed to cause confusion—and they even booed the referee nicely. They supported their own country with a passion, but that didn't make them oppose the fans of other teams. Far from it. They embraced them. They sat down in the streets on newspapers to watch the matches and cleaned up after them to save the street sweepers the extra work. That's the new Koreans for you. They are people who feel sorry for street sweepers because they see their parents and aunts and uncles in them.

Feature stories about these fans by foreign reporters gave readers around the world their first glimpse of the new Koreans and they liked what they saw. Even the British tabloids discovered that stories about Koreans did not have to be about dog eating or the North's wacko leader.

While it is true that since the opening of Korea in the 1880s visitors' first impressions were overwhelmingly negative, it is also true that outsiders who came to really know the Koreans invariably fell in love with them. When Isabella Bird Bishop arrived in Busan in 1897, for example, she found it to be "a decayed and miserable town" full of "mangy dogs and blear-eyed children."[26] The people lived in "low hovels built of mud-smeared wattle," their refuse carried off in "reeking ditches" that lined the streets. But then this: "The distaste I felt for the country at first passed into an interest which is almost affection, and on no previous journey have I made dearer and kinder friends, or those from whom I parted more regretfully."[27]

When the Catholic traveler Peter Vay, who had likened Seoul to a graveyard, visited a missionary school, he noted:

> Of all my surprising experiences in Korea—a country rich in surprises—nothing equaled my impressions of the new college and seminary at Yong-Sang. There young people of twelve to fifteen gave as precise answers to questions put to them as one

could hear in the best European high schools. And there Korea's primitive children can express themselves fluently in classical Latin. It was interesting for me to get an insight into their capabilities and observe their industry. For hours they would pore over their books if the teacher would not call them away for recreation. . . . I saw young Korea in a new light.[28]

Twenty-first-century Korea, like anywhere else, has its fans and critics among the resident expatriate population. Two characteristics stand out. One is the sheer extent of criticism and the other is the deep affection. You don't need a PhD in human relationships to appreciate that these conflicting attitudes are not unconnected.

The criticism can be looked at from two perspectives. One is the preponderance of things that are annoying. For example, since Koreans are not accustomed to having doors held open for them, when it's done by the keen-to-please foreigner there's often no acknowledgement, let alone reciprocation. The chain of people holding the door for the person behind them quickly gets broken. I attended a speech by an expert at the U.S. Eighth Army library in Seoul once and he was asked why Koreans were so rude. His attempt to explain that Koreans are polite in different ways from Americans failed to impress the audience of military family members. These were people accustomed to wishing that even total strangers "have a nice day."

Spitting is another thing. You'd think in a crowded city, people would gob into tissues. But no. It's as if Jesus once said that human spittle fertilizes concrete. Doing your bit for the sidewalk has gone into the culture. Talking of which, there does seem to be a deep spiritual connection with porcelain that brings out the urge to spit. If you sit there for a while in a public toilet, and listen to other men coming in, you'll soon get the pattern. Footsteps, a moment of shuffling, and then one of two rituals sounds: a quiet slap of spittle on the porcelain, or the sudden hawking, as if a duck is being strangled, followed by the phlegm slap.

While we are in the men's room, there is one issue that doesn't get raised in polite society but which someone needs to whisper in Korea's ear about and that is the habit of disposing of toilet paper in a separate basket, which usually never has a lid, instead of in the commode. This is the practice in most small and medium, and even some large, commercial buildings, and in houses. I've not got any scientific studies to back this up, but I suspect this might be why toilets smell in all but the newest buildings. Not only is the stinky basket everywhere, but defecators who have grown up with the habit never quite shake their reluctance to flush paper away even when they move to posh new apartments. A show of hands revealed that 75 percent of my office staff still opt for the basket. Strangely enough, I had lived in Korea for a few years before becoming aware of this issue. No one actually tells you this stuff. I had noticed the plastic basket and also been aware of a vague unclean smell in the toilet in my office building. But I never gave it much thought until one day I found myself stranded without toilet paper, an experience that is only funny in movies. For the first time, I took an interest in the paper right there beside me in the basket.

Being a reporter, I decided to investigate and made a few calls. The head of the sewage disposal department at my local district office said there was no reason to worry about toilet paper in the bowl because it is designed to disintegrate quickly. A plumber concurred, saying that the only thing to worry about is blocking the U-pipes behind the bowl, which, like shit, happens.

For a historical and more technical perspective, I turned to Peter Bartholomew, an expatriate expert in ancient Korean buildings. He said the issue is connected with the size of septic tanks. They're too small. That's because in the old days human excrement was collected regularly for fertilizer, so you didn't need big ones.

"There is only one compartment in these small tanks," he said. "In more modern tanks there are two or even three compartments separated by baffles which allow staged decomposition along with the toilet paper, thus ensuring the final effluent from the tank is almost totally decomposed liquid, devoid of any solids."

The collection trucks—or "honey dippers," as he called them—prefer this pure "black water," but because local governments require the tanks to be pumped out every six or twelve months, they have to come around before the contents have completely turned to liquid. The solid materials such as toilet paper apparently cause problems with their pumps. As with all things in Korea, the problem ends up being the government's fault.

But back to the theme of lack of consideration for others. This is altogether more dangerous when it comes to driving, where the expat criticism is entirely justified. School, business, and the law bring on a whole new range of annoyances. I could go on. In fact, I will go on in later chapters but, for now, let's consider the other way of looking at the moaning foreigner.

Listening to a moaner, there comes a moment when you find yourself reflecting less on the crime being pointed out than on the three proverbial fingers in the moaner's hand that are pointing back at himself. You wonder why he is disposed to moan. This is an important question to ask of the expatriate in Korea because some really do moan. It's not as bad as it was in the days before you could get Starbucks and good wine, but it's still out of proportion. So much so that a new phenomenon I've noticed is of newly arrived expatriates complaining that the country is not nearly as bad as they had been led to believe reading foreign blogs and following online discussions.

So, why does the foreign moaner in Korea moan to the point that new arrivals moan about his moaning? My pop-psychology theory is that he feels shut out. How does this work? If you lean into conversations between Koreans at coffee shops, on phones, or along the street, you can hear *"uri nara"* (our country") and *"miguk"* (America) and *"waeguk"* (foreign) all the time. For Koreans, of course, nationalism and patriotism are one and the same and their love of their own country and sense of identity they draw from it is quite normal to them. That is because they have been taught from an early age that being Korean is the meaningful glue binding them to their fellow countrymen. Koreans know they are free individuals, of course, but they grow up half-thinking they belong to the state. That's slightly different from being, say, American and, of your own free choice, wanting to do something for your country. This aspect of their identity is set for Koreans, not in the family, but at school. After the national anthem at the commencement ceremony at my daughter's Korean kindergarten, the principal gave a nice address, the subtext of which was, "Now we're going to start turning you into people whose mission in life is to work for the national economy." And though the expatriate lives among Koreans, he also lives outside this super-glued group because Korea Inc. does not expect its foreign residents to serve, even though many of them choose to out of love.

At the same time as being critical, expatriates develop deep bonds of affection for Koreans. Many have told me they didn't realize how strong this feeling was until they left. The expatriate in foreign business centers such as Singapore, Hong Kong, Tokyo, Shanghai, and Dubai doesn't seem to have the same experience. I've never seen a study but anecdotally it seems the case that many expatriate men, both those who remain and those who leave, marry Koreans and thereby extend their connection for their lifetime and indeed through the generations.

In the past, when the expatriate was a soldier, diplomat, or executive with no interest in permanent residence or citizenship, Korea kept him at arm's length by giving him privileged treatment: The police would let foreigners go but prosecute locals. In the days before speed cameras, when traps were set on the expressway, all I had to do to get waved through was lean forward and show my foreign face. A hundred little laws had clauses that allowed the foreigner to evade the restrictions placed on the Korean citizen.[29]

In the last decade or two, though, the expat scene has changed. Large numbers of foreigners have entered the country and become citizens. Most are from the Korean-settled area of China, but many are from Southeast Asia and have come either as brides of Korean farmers and fishermen (one in five of that group now marries a foreigner) or as laborers. Some of these people, however, are in the country illegally. In 2014 over 1.5 million foreigners were living in Korea, and though this makes up only 3.1 percent of the population of 51 million, these foreigners nevertheless represent a challenge to which so far the country is responding well.[30]

Although it translates as multiculturalism, whereby immigrants may integrate while keeping their own traditions, the government's *tamunhwa* policy is actually one of assimilation, albeit softer in that locals are encouraged to learn about immigrants' original cultures. There are multicultural family-support centers and citizens of mixed heritage are now welcomed in the military.[31]

This changing scene is prompting a debate about what it means to be Korean.[32] At an event in 2014 honoring young Korean men and women of mixed heritage, the prime minister referred to them as people the country should consider as "assets."

For as long as foreigners have been associating with Korea, they have been confused by their experiences of it. The reason is that things are not explained. In a society where persuasion is more customarily exercised by the pulling of rank, and sometimes even today by the end of a boot, the need to explain is often overlooked.

This is particularly the case with men in authority. I notice this when I go with my family to the village to help in the fields. One October day we arrived to find other relatives from the city squatting in the furrows attacking the mounds of earth with hand hoes. We were at this point advised that we had come to harvest sweet potatoes. This would have been useful to know in advance; I wouldn't have worn my new shoes.

Some of the sweet potatoes were as big as newborn piglets. It took an hour or two to clear the whole patch and bag them up. After that, we scrambled up beside the family tombs for a picnic. For all I knew we were going to hang out there for the rest of the afternoon. But no. The order came and we piled into the cars and bounced off down a rough dirt track. The convoy came to a halt in a field full of large plants that had been cut and laid uniformly in dry, brown clumps. I figured they were weeds. I picked one up and sniffed it. The aroma was strong and distinctive.

"Perilla," someone said. My vast farming experience stretches to vacation work in the east of England, picking strawberries, planting and harvesting potatoes, driving tractors, and making haystacks. This was a new one.

Someone pointed at a large folded-up tarpaulin. "Get that."

People began unfolding it.

We ended up spending the next two hours laying the plants on the tarp, threshing them so the seeds fell out, chucking the deseeded plants in a pile to one side and ferrying the next bunch over, until the whole field was done. Then we sifted the pile of seeds through a fabric sieve three or four times to clear out the chaff or whatever it's called and folded the tarpaulin over the seeds, placing the large parcel in the back of the jeep. Each step in this process was prefaced with a monosyllabic order. At no point was anything actually explained or described. Nothing like, "We'll have to sift the seeds through this sieve at least two or three times to get rid of all the bits of leaf and stuff." I found myself at times holding the corner of the tarpaulin not knowing which way to go with it. I'd try to look engaged as I awaited the next order. When it came—Here! Stop!—it seemed obvious. I see now how people raised in authoritarian environments can think they are stupid until they're in charge themselves. If Descartes had been Korean, he would have said: "I am in charge, therefore I am."

This is often how things are in Korea. Doctors prescribe your medicine without explaining what's wrong with you; work crews attack roads without putting up helpful signs advising drivers of a diversion ahead. And so it goes.

An interesting corollary to this is that when no one is in charge, everyone takes charge, yelling contradictory orders and creating general confusion, yet the task itself is both completed *and* enjoyed.

In this zone of minimal explanation, the outsider finds himself learning important things by chance and circumstance. Here's an example: In 2013, protesters camped out for months in the Seoul city center, near the entrance of an old palace, thus spoiling this popular tourism site. The protesters had lost their jobs in 2009 when the SsangYong Motor Company went bankrupt and was restructured by government receivers. I found it hard to muster sympathy for these autoworkers, who were acting as if they'd had no part in the company's collapse, and actually had a right to be reinstated. When city officials finally had enough and dismantled the protest tent, I wondered what had taken them so long. I was surprised, then, that all the Koreans around me, including my family and colleagues, were appalled by what the officials had done. (So was the court: The city's action was later ruled illegal.) It was only then, when I asked why, that I learned something that would have changed my perspective from the outset had I known.

"They'll never get another job," one young woman told me. Yes, they could drive a taxi, run a small restaurant, or work for an auto-parts supplier, but they would never get a job in another auto company at their same skill levels. Why? Because big companies don't like to recruit talent from other companies. They employ people who are at the beginning of their careers and mold them as loyal soldiers. Also, the workers in question were in a group that had rejected the choice of voluntary retirement or unpaid leave and had then been dismissed. That made them "troublemakers." No company would take someone so labeled. "Everyone in Korea knows that," she said. I didn't. I'd been reading the papers every day about this issue for ages and this context had never been mentioned.

For the foreign reporter, this represents a challenge. Koreans can be obscure and uncommunicative at the same time as they are being outgoing and forthright.

This apparent contradiction comes from the old authoritarian family culture and the centuries-old view that education involves not discovery, but the imparting of truth by the all-knowing teacher to the ignorant pupil. Even in modern schools, the lack of discourse and the lack of training in the arts of explanation and persuasion means that Koreans are poorly equipped as adults to work smoothly with one another. Every task involving more than two people needs a leader. A committee of folk representing different agencies or constituencies is a formula for chaos unless it is headed by someone accepted by all as senior. The lack of practice in debate also means that people are not accustomed to weeding out bias and emotion from their opinions. This manifests in different ways depending on the level of intimacy. In conversation with people at work or outside the circle of close friends and family, Koreans invariably opt to agree with you. It'll be the foreigner in the class who chirps up with, "I don't know if I agree with that," or "Yes, but . . ." The polite deference of Koreans to your opinions can actually delude you into thinking that you have better ideas than you actually do. Your Korean spouse, on the other hand, will disagree with almost everything you say. The thoughtful partner who loves his wife will soon learn not to try and defend his theses.

But back to our reporter. It is difficult for her to know when her Korean sources are telling her what they think, what they think she wants to hear, or what they want to happen. I found this last one to be especially irksome some years ago when I was trying to find out what South Korean experts thought about eventual reunification. Before the Berlin Wall fell, they would say whatever they thought because the whole issue was a fantasy. No one could visualize it. But after 1989, reunification looked possible. That was when the South Korean government realized the country didn't have the capacity to annex North Korea. The only option was for a process as long and drawn-out as possible.

This view is now so taken for granted that it is hard to convey how revolutionary it was in its day. I first heard it in early 1991 in a discussion with an assistant foreign minister who had become one of my best sources.

"Let me go off the record for a moment," he said.

"OK."

"We don't want it."

"What?"

"Unification."

"Well, it's not really in the cards right now," I said.

"No, I mean it is no longer our objective." He leaned forward over our coffee cups and spoke in slow, clear syllables. "We . . . Do . . . Not . . . Want . . . To . . . Unify . . . With . . . North . . . Korea. Now, if you were to ask me on the record for our position on reunification . . ." he said.

"What is the position on reunification?" I played along.

"We Koreans are a divided people and our goal is to become one again. We want democratic reunification with the North. For this process to be peaceful, we favor a gradual, step-by-step process." He leaned across again. "Off the record?"

"OK."

"The longer the better. And, for me personally, never is fine. I'm from Busan which is almost as far as you can get from North Korea and I don't care. Do you understand what I am saying?"

In case the reader wonders why I am breaking the off-the-record rule by describing this confidential dialog, the gentleman in question has since passed away and the position he was conveying—favoring "gradualism" over collapse-and-absorption of North Korea—has become official policy and accepted by most Koreans as the only way forward.

Another, more practical explanation for lack of clarity is that the people in power who know stuff don't like talking to the press except in the most controlled of situations, and the spokespeople they designate to deal with reporters are too low on the ministry or corporate ladder to know enough.

Thus, in the fall of 2014 when the North Korean leader Kim Jong-un disappeared from view for a few weeks, the government in Seoul declined to come out and tell reporters what it thought—that nothing was out of the ordinary. Without this anchor opinion to allow us all to make sense of Kim's absence, international media started running with rumors of coups and terminal illness from random experts who had zero evidence. The longer Kim was away, the nuttier the conjecture became. In the end, it turned out he'd had ankle surgery.

For the outsider trying to nail down information and make sense of it, these difficulties make Korea one of the harder places to deal with. As one foreign journalist put it to me many years ago: "You need a high-level bullshit indicator to figure out what's going on."

Korea may be hard to read day to day. But viewed over the long term, its issues have been quite simple and definable. In the 1950s the two halves of the country went to war. The question was: Would the southern side—which the West was supporting—win and survive after the slaughter? In the 1960s the weaker South began to develop economically and the question was: Would it succeed? By the 1980s the question was: Would democracy ever come? In the 1990s the question was whether the powerful South could switch, in the interests of further growth, from a centrally directed economy to more of a free-market economy. In the new century, the question is more whether Korea can upgrade its systems, its political culture, its corporate-management style, and its general way of doing things to the level of a truly advanced nation.

For the first time in its history, its international reputation is actually ahead of that curve. The world already sees Korean as advanced and no longer feels the need to call it a dragon, a tiger, or a diamond, or talk about miracles. Korea is now known. The Hanguk version, that is.

5

THE GROUP AS REFUGE

"Korea has great bells. The Japanese stole them because they were so good. Chinese bells go biingg, but Korean bells go BONGGGG!"

At some point a long, long time ago, as the ancestors of modern Koreans gathered food, nursed wounds, and sought refuge, they asked a question: Why do I suffer? Such a question must go back to the shift from compulsion to curiosity and wonder. In fact, given the intensity behind it, the question itself may have caused the shift. When "I suffer" became "Why do I suffer?" the mind opened to other questions—Why does the mother cry? Why must I kill to live? Why does my neighbor's pet woolly mammal leave his droppings outside my cave? Why does the sun burn? Why is there pain? Why does everything change? Where have my elders gone? Why have those I ran with grown old? What lies beneath the soil and in the darkness between the stars and beyond my own end? And, then, the point: If I know, may I remove suffering?

In some sense, each person is his own priest. But, in the tribe, the dreamers and the crazy ones produce the enduring stories: There are gods; they are in everything; they live in the sky and fight among themselves; the dead "live" and their spirits do mischief; bad things happen because I am bad; bad things happen because other people are bad. Such ideas led to behaviors. The monk under the waterfall believed the ill-disciplined pursuit of his body's needs brought on suffering; the inquisitor was cruel because he believed he had a devil strapped to the rack. And so on.

The ancient Koreans came to an interesting conclusion about suffering: We are born with inherent goodness, they thought, but we suffer because our existence as individuals limits us. We struggle and bring on suffering because we are separate and alone and selfish. The solution is to identify with the group.

The group the Koreans have identified with for centuries has not been the nation but the family line. In lineage, they found a solution to loneliness, an incentive to goodness, and a promise even of immortality, for as they revered ancestors and sacrificed for descendants, so, too, did they expect to be remembered. This group orientation makes people prioritize relationships with others over a relationship with an imagined deity and leads to a societal emphasis on ethics over theology.[33]

Korea has had its hermits, ascetics, and mystics, but the group-orientation theme took greater hold in the culture than any of their other ideas. It underpinned the acceptance of foreign religions, which reached their shores over the centuries.

In modern times the most significant change to that underlying culture has been materialism. The Japanese occupation, the civil war and division weakened faith in the culture. Many began to despair of their society, to feel it was useless. When the country fell under the Americans' wing and tens of thousands of U.S. soldiers began to live in Korea, the locals were drawn to this attractive new and foreign culture. Koreans began to value the pursuit of money and the technologies that made life easier and more enjoyable.

"Under the Park dictatorship in the late 1960s and 1970s, the whole country went materialistic and we started to compete more and more intensely," said Park Jin-seng, a therapist in Seoul. A government slogan, *chal sara boseyo* (let's live well), quickly came to define the new way of thinking not only of the secular, but also of the religious Korean.

Today, South Koreans live in a free marketplace when it comes to beliefs. No authority straps them to faith or, as in atheist North Korea, non-faith. From the harshest periods of poverty and repression until now, the South Koreans have enjoyed the freedom to choose their prophets, messiahs, and preachers, new or old, and to sing, study, chant, and pray as they please in the temple, church, and in private homes and, more recently, in the mosque, Hindu temple, and synagogue.

The only antireligious bigotry by the state itself in living memory was an effort to wipe out shamanism in the name of modernization. This was especially intense in the 1970s when village leaders were encouraged to cut down sacred trees. Likewise, totem poles and shrines in many villages were burned. Some villages later restored shrines to mountain gods and put preservation orders on old trees, but this was more to encourage tourism than out of religiosity. The process of acknowledging shamanism as a feature of the Korean spiritual landscape remains slow because Christians in the bureaucracy see its superstitions as a national embarrassment and half suspect that shamans are in league with Beelzebub.

The other shadow over the picture of religious freedom is the jailing of young male Jehovah's Witnesses who reject compulsory military service. Even democratic administrations have made no effort to accommodate the rights of these pacifists. Eighteen thousand have been imprisoned since 1953 and guards beat at least five to death between 1975 and 1985. Currently there are about six hundred Jehovah's Witnesses behind bars, giving South Korea the dubious distinction of being the world's leading jailer of conscientious objectors, at least on the basis of known statistics. Remarkably, this is a nonissue for Koreans. Most are unaware of it. That's because the offenders take their punishment with silent dignity, and nobody else makes any noise on their behalf. However, the courts in 2016 ruled in favor of these conscientious objectors, arguing they should be allowed to do alternative forms of service.[34]

Apart from this, the different faiths coexist. Indeed, they often coexist within the same family. It is common to find a husband who could loosely be called Confucian married to a Buddhist wife and whose children are Christian. Differing religious preferences are not critical challenges to the underlying materialistic culture that also retains some part of the old emphasis on the extended family, and calls for people to accept their place within this hierarchy. An exception may be many Christians' rejection of memorial rituals for ancestors, but as these rituals are more about respect, rather than worship, many just go along with it.

The peace is occasionally broken. Protestant Christians have been known to enter Buddhist temples to order Satan out. Fortunately, South Korean Buddhists are laid-back in the face of such provocation. But they have had their moments. For example, the bloody clashes between rival factions within the Jogye, the largest Buddhist order, resulting from struggles over temple finances and control. This conflict can be traced back several decades. With the military coup of 1961, many hoodlums fled to remote temples and became monks. Some rose up through the ranks and resorted to their old habits when reformist monks threatened to remove them. The image of shaven-headed bonzes, with their gray robes flying, battling riot police with iron pipes doesn't fit, but Korean Buddhism has been undermined by its willingness to give all comers a chance to improve themselves in this life. It'll take anyone as a monk.

A discussion of a country's soul calls for statistics. Those available come from three sources: occasional surveys, the five-year census, and annual forms submitted by registered religious groups to the Ministry of Culture, Sports, and Tourism giving numbers of believers, employees, and properties.

The 2005 census was the last to include religious affiliation in the household, and showed 46.9 percent of Koreans with no religion, 22.8 percent Buddhist, 18.3 percent Protestant, 10.9 percent Catholic, and one percent "other." A Gallup Korea survey of fifteen hundred adults in 2014 found that the figure for nonbelievers had increased to 54 percent, with twenty- and thirty-year-olds accounting for the change.[35]

According to figures supplied by the religious organizations to the government in 2011, there are 265 Buddhist sects, 232 Protestant denominations, and 52 other religions new and old, international and local. One of my friends was for three years the official responsible for providing these stats for the minor religion he had joined. He told me actual membership was forty thousand, a figure I considered a stretch because the group was into numerology and saw meaning in the number forty (days in the wilderness, wandering in the desert and so on). He said that each year he added forty thousand more members.

Why?

"So the government will take us more seriously," he explained.

God must be powerless in the face of such fibbing because others have been at it, too. In terms of actual devotees, from 1985 to 2002, Buddhists claimed to have grown from 8.5 million to over 37.5 million, Protestants from 6.5 million to nearly 19 million; Catholics from around 1.9 to over 4.2 million; Confucians from 483,366 to 6,004,470; and "others" from 305,627 to 15,676,110. The total number of people who claimed affiliation to a religion increased during that seventeen-year period from 17 million to 82.1 million. That means that while only 42 percent of the population was religious in 1985, by 2002 it was 170 percent.

The "others" category includes familiar as well as homegrown faiths: there are, for example, around forty thousand Muslims, mostly South Korean men who converted when working on construction projects in the Middle East in the 1970s and 1980s. Those who are active worship alongside an estimated one hundred thousand foreign-born Muslims at several mosques around the country. There are two Hindu temples. A Chabad House caters to several hundred Jewish expatriates. Some Koreans have converted but none live in Korea.[36] As the Koreans believe the Jews punch above their weight in education and business in the world and want to find their secret, the Talmud is widely taught in popular, accessible form as an educational tool.[37]

The largest group of "others" is the 130,000 followers of *Won-bulgyo*, a distinct South Korean form of Buddhism that, in contrast to mainstream Buddhism with its focus on the cultivation of the monk, focuses instead on the lives of the laity. There are a number of native faiths, including one that worships Dangun, the mythical founder of Korea, and new sects with Christian, Buddhist, or shamanic roots.

Another feature of the Korean religious scene, and another reason to treat the statistics with a pinch of holy salt, is fusion. Christians, Buddhists, and atheists in Korea practice Confucian ancestor rituals and regularly seek advice from shamans and fortune-tellers. Indeed, the notion of exclusive adherence to a religion is relatively new. Notably, the Korean word for religion came from Japan at the end of the nineteenth century. Prior to that, religions were seen as "teachings," which came from texts, folk beliefs, and oral traditions.[38] In 1916, Japanese colonial authorities made the first effort to collect data and found only 3 percent of the population with a specific affiliation. By 1964, the figure was still only around 12 percent.

This lack of insistence on commitment and the consequent fusing of belief systems explains how the values of all the religions that have influenced Korea remain within the Korean mind.

Buddhism was introduced by monks from central Asia and China in the late fourth century and was the predominant faith up to the end of the fourteenth century. The initial promise to rulers was that the religion would ensure their health and authority. Centuries later monks began to delve into the deeper elements of the teaching. One such monk was Wonhyo, who in the seventh century famously discovered one morning that the cup he had drunk from in the night was actually a human skull. This experience of refreshment and revulsion from the same object led him to a profound understanding of the Buddha's lesson that human beings suffer in life because our inherent goodness is overruled by our own attitudes and assumptions.

Zen Buddhism arrived in the ninth century, bringing with it the idea that suffering could not be removed by analyzing the world and our experiences, but that it could be transcended through meditation. The Zen concept of no past or future, just a constantly flowing present, influences the sense of immediacy and impatience common to most Koreans across all faiths. Also, the Buddhist idea that the spiritual and physical worlds flow into one another is more pragmatically appealing to many Christians than the idea of waiting for an afterlife, which is why many Christians ask fortune-tellers to tap into the spiritual world for advice.

Buddhism today offers alternative routes up the mountain: While study and meditation may work for monks, lay believers take the more devotional approach and call on buddhas to heal sickness, and help with salary increases, their children's exams, infertility, and other problems. The acceptability of the various approaches underscores the attitude common to Koreans that results are more important than means and that it therefore makes sense to hedge bets.

Daoism arrived at the same time as Buddhism. It was never formally or significantly adopted but some of its ideas are identifiable in the Korean mental makeup. For example, the Daoist ethos that, "The way that can be discussed is not the way" figures in Korean attitudes and is one reason for the animosity toward discursive argument. Instead of questioning the teacher and elder, the junior should learn through reflection and obedience.

Confucianism also appeared around the same time. It did not function initially in Korea as a religion. Rather, it was the means by which Koreans copied China's approach of managing people via a central government bent on order and harmony. From the late fourteenth century onward neo-Confucian scholar-bureaucrats eclipsed Buddhism. Through education and social regulations, Confucian values and ceremony permeated all levels of society. This faith called on the individual to seek knowledge and to think and act with sincerity. He also had to know his place and behave appropriately in five key relationships: as subject to ruler, as son to father, as husband to wife, as elder to younger brother, as friend to friend. Only in the last was he an equal.

This strict ideological form of Confucianism has its fans in Korea and the legacy is apparent today, but few would endorse a full-scale comeback. It's one thing to study the words of the sages, your smart phone by your side, in a room of books heated at the flick of a switch, in a democratic country fueled by nuclear and other types of power paid for by other people's taxes. But the state that wobbled into the twentieth century might as well have been run by junkies. Confucianism failed the Koreans big time, both as a scheme for cultivating the self and for ordering the family and the wider society. I sometimes fancy that the neo-Confucianists were like fourteenth-century communists, well-meaning, purposeful and all fired up with a framework that explained everything and pointed the way forward. If I'd been there, I'd probably have been one. But, like communism, once they got power their religion never lived up to its promise. Perhaps such systems are too utopian to ever do so. The Confucian revolutionaries dreamed of a state of virtuous men led by the most wise and refined among them and, to this end, set up an education system centered on poetry, calligraphy and ethics and determined that high office could only be reached by passing examinations. Instead, corruption flourished, justice was vicious, the caste system rigid, and the rules petty and spiteful. And when they saw the dream slipping away, they did what all people seem to do when they are unrestrained by democracy: They came up with rival explanations, developed factions around them, and set about one another like savages.

Still, the Confucian influence of this period went deeper into Korea than it ever did in Japan or China and it remains evident today in ancestor rituals and in the emphasis on vertically ordered human relationships. It is also apparent in gender inequality.

I was drawn when I first arrived in Korea to the good manners and sense of propriety which I imagined was Confucian. At the same time, I was struck by people's earthiness. These sages stamped their feet and belched and farted in public. You would think Confucianism would have relegated this kind of behavior to the unwashed masses, but not so. Now, the explanation for the farting may be that until recently, 90 percent of the people were farmers—no offense— but another source of this outgoing behavior is the existence of a deeper sentiment in the Korean psyche. From ancient times beliefs about the nature of existence and the practices that defined the Korean response to it were ordered by shamans. Their role, as with the role of any other religious priest or elder, was to help people cope with what life threw at them, including hardships and the inevitability of death. Shamanism is not easily defined and its history is undocumented. The term loosely covers multi-deity religious practice and superstitions that began in prehistory. In ancient Korea the rulers served as shaman-kings. In theory, shamanist belief was holistic and tolerant. It did not endorse the contradiction and conflict seen in other faiths. There were no divides, such as good-evil, body-spirit, physical-spiritual, perfect God-frail man. Instead, life was a continuum, the individual was seen as a whole and everyone, man and woman alike, was seen as being of equal value. And even within the individual, different attributes were not singled out and given

superior value over others. Whether more courageous or more sensitive, you contained both qualities in equally valid ways: each of
them contributing to who you were. Gas was gas, and whether it
came out the front or the back, so to speak, it had still been part of
you. So why not let it out?

The shamans did not claim to know how and when existence
began. And they ruled out an omnipotent deity. Rather, in their view,
human beings existed as notes in nature's rhythmic tune: We are here
before we are born, and we remain as part of nature after we die.
Thus life should always be lived to the full. To be truly human, you
must act with all your energies.[39]

In shamanist thinking, causing emotional pain is a great moral
crime because it blocks other people from being fully human. In
shamanism there is no objective god setting absolute rules; thus,
moral judgment becomes a matter of relative emotional hurt. Stealing
money is less of a wrong than shaming someone. Unless of course by
stealing from them you really do damage or embarrass them in some
way. If so, your defense would be: "But I didn't mean to hurt them."

The shamans believed that negative emotion needed to be as-
suaged because, unchecked, it could cause remote damage. Venge-
ful women were often blamed for mishaps. The unhappy dead could
influence nature and bring calamities down upon the living. Single
women who died unfulfilled were also seen as especially problematic. Such ideas live on. After a Korean airliner was shot down in
1983 by a Soviet jet the spirits of two single female flight attendants
were married to two single male passengers in ceremonies arranged
by the bereaved parents to ease their imagined frustrations.

The most vicious form of vengeance by spirits would be to attack a
victim's lineage, especially his children. But the worst thing the living
could do to someone they hate would be to commit suicide because
of them. Suicide as a form of protest even today has a terrible emotive
power in South Korean society. Instead of evoking disgust, it tends to
evoke pity and may stir people to take revenge. In the modern development period, several workers and students immolated themselves
or jumped off buildings, or both simultaneously, as acts of protest.
When protesters occupied buildings, police would place mattresses
around them and arm themselves with fire extinguishers before

storming them, in anticipation of suicide attempts. In North Korea, the authorities dissuade citizens from this ultimate form of protest by demoting the family members of a person who has committed suicide down the country's caste system. When Hyeonseo Lee's father committed suicide, her mother used nearly all her savings to bribe hospital authorities to change the cause of death to "heart attack."[40]

There has been a traditional idea that the dead continue to have feelings: They get cold and hungry, so food is put out for them and they are believed to consume its essence. The shamans said the spirit decayed slowly with the body in a natural process. This idea lies behind Korean aversion to organ donation and cremation. Also it was the reason that a body traditionally had to be buried in a propitious place. For this reason, the grassy mounds of family tombs are a familiar sight on the lower slopes of the country's hillsides. Even in the early twentieth century, passersby would come across bodies wrapped in mats, decomposing in the sun while the family searched for a site: The consequences of burying an unsettled spirit were worse than the risk of disease.[41] In the last twenty years, however, with the concern over lack of burial space, the South Korean government has successfully encouraged a preference for cremation.[42] The notion of what actually happens at death may vary from faith to faith, but a common Korean concern is that the children of the deceased show their filial respect and that the spirit not be lonely.

Shamanism is still widely practiced. One place to see it in action is Inwang Temple, a compound of shrines and prayer halls on the southwest slopes of Inwang Mountain, a 338-meter (1,109 feet) peak smack in the middle of Seoul that is popular with hikers and patrolled by security forces protecting the nearby Blue House, the president's residence.

The temple is not easy to find. It is not marked on the nearby subway station neighborhood map and at street level only a small sign can be found pointing in the right direction off the main road. The sign, marked with a Buddhist symbol, is in Korean only, in contrast to street signs that are usually in Korean and English. There is no indication that it is, in fact, a center of shamanism.

This reluctance to promote is a legacy of the old persecution. Until very recently, there was no legal category for registering shamanic sites and buildings. The Buddhists—God bless them—provided refuge during the persecution and allowed shamans to build in their temples' grounds and pretend to be monks. Some of the refugees even shaved their heads and wore gray robes to look the part. The move away from this furtiveness has come about in recent years as the central government has ceded authority to the local governments to register buildings. It has happened quietly to minimize possible protests from Christians, so if you're reading this, don't tell anyone.

I once joined a tour of Inwang Temple with a group of twenty Korean tourism students led by their professor, David Mason, an American.[43] "There's live-action shamanism happening all over the mountain," he promised. The temple, a twenty-minute hike up the hill, consisted of several small prayer rooms, shrines, and other buildings. One appeared to be the main prayer hall of a Buddhist temple complete with all the right trappings but, in fact, Mason explained, it was also was shamanist. He stopped at a large black bell.

"Korea has great bells," he said, digressing. "For fifteen hundred years, Koreans had the best technology. The Japanese stole Korean bells because they were so good. Chinese bells go *biingg*, but Korean bells go *BONGGGG*!" There was method in his humor. Mason was trying to relax the Christians among his students. Beelzebub lurked nearby.

He led us to a small one-story wooden structure, painted brown and green, with a traditional porcelain-tile roof. The *Guksadang*, as it was called, was the shrine for Korea's guardian spirits, housing those of the founder of the Joseon Dynasty (1392–1910) and other generals. Inside were fifteen paintings, some of them three hundred years old, including one believed to be the oldest existing depiction of Dangun, the mythical founder of Korea.

"In the old days people thought that each bump in the land was pushed up by a spirit," Mason said. "They used to worship them and, although it's not widely known, a lot of people still do. This shrine was built across the valley on Namsan Mountain in 1395. It was moved in 1925 by Japanese colonial authorities. The Namsan shrine was for a male mountain spirit while Bugak Mountain to the north had a female shrine. There used to be a ceremony where they'd bring down the spirits and let them mate for five days for the good of the country."

As the students considered this weirdness, all of a sudden the pigeons on the roof took flight en masse and swooped back overhead, beating their wings. Beelzebub. Everyone was spooked.

A little farther along a woman in jeans and T-shirt was performing repeated prostrations in front of three paintings in another shrine. She held a string of beads to count her bows. One of the paintings here depicted an elderly man with a flowing white beard accompanied by a tiger. This was the mountain spirit.

We left the buildings and followed the path up the mountain. A man stood in front of a rock face holding his arms in the air. In one hand he rattled a fistful of bells. In the other, he flapped a fan depicting the mountain spirit. A woman beside him, the shaman, was giving instructions.

Elsewhere, large rock fronts bore the evidence of ceremony. Mason pointed out a formation of two rocks called *Seonbawi* (Zen Rock), so named because they look like two monks meditating. To modern eyes, they look distinctly like Ringwraiths, the unreal horse riders who sought to kill Bilbo Baggins when it was revealed he had the One Ring. Pigeons squatted in the pockmarks of the blackened rock.

"This is probably the most worshipped set of rocks in the world," Mason said. In the fourteenth century, when Seoul was selected as the capital site, the king's two most powerful advisers were divided. One argued for Confucianism and wanted the *Seonbawi* to be outside the city walls. But the monk Muak wanted the rock to be included. He predicted that if it were, Joseon would last for a thousand years. If not, the dynasty would fall after five hundred. He lost. *Seonbawi* lies just outside the old city wall. But his prediction came true. (For the record, Muak also predicted that the next capital would be Gyeryong Mountain in the central part of South Korea.)

Shamans perform rituals of chant and dance to invoke various gods to exorcise evil spirits and to seek their aid. Some summon ancient Korean and Chinese warriors to draw on their strength and protection. Back in the 1980s a shaman called Hyun Myungboon venerated the late American general Douglas MacArthur in this fashion. Mrs. Hyun lived in Incheon, which was the site of Mac-Arthur's counterinvasion against North Korea in 1950. She was once featured in a TV documentary. An observant policeman watching the program spotted a carton of Marlboro cigarettes on the altar. Possessing foreign cigarettes had been a crime since 1952 when the government sought to clamp down on the black markets outside U.S. military bases. Mrs. Hyun and the TV producer were arrested but released after convincing police that the cigarettes were not for her, but for General MacArthur.

Fortune-telling is hugely popular with Koreans, young and old. Businessmen ask fortune-tellers for advice about partners and investments, parents want to know the best time for their daughters' weddings, and politicians may send their wives or secretaries (it wouldn't look good to be open about these things) to get input about the election campaign, and sometimes, even which party to join.[44]

Fortune-telling is about the only form of spirituality that really has continued to exist on both sides of the DMZ. For example, people living near the China border, who are engaged in illegal trade, will ask fortune-tellers for the safest days for smuggling. Despite crackdowns, defectors say, the soothsayers survive because the leadership also uses them.

Faith healers are also popular, and I have visited them myself. Once, it was for a swollen big toe, which was causing an ingrown toenail. I'd already had the toenail yanked out three times in clinics. These mini-operations, and two painful experiences at the hands of doctors earlier in Britain, had made me very open-minded about alternative medicine. The healer was a jolly Christian woman with large hands and an unusual story. Once grossly overweight, she had tried all kinds of diets. But nothing worked until one day she went to the mountains to pray and received a revelation that she should slap herself, continuously and hard. This had worked for her and she wanted to try it on me. "It will bring the bad blood to the surface," she said. She explained that the body is often blocked from healing itself by the collection of bad blood in certain places. The slapping drives this bad blood to the surface in a bruise and it disappears in a few days. I liked this theory because it didn't involve intrusive instruments. But the slapping was something else. She began attacking me with shamanistic gusto, raining stinging, rhythmic blows with the palm of her hand down on the back of my knee, where she reckoned the bad blood was blocking the good, healing blood from reaching my toe. It was excruciatingly painful. *In extremis*, I gripped the mattress and whimpered.

"Ah, we have black blood," she announced, still slapping. We did indeed. It rushed so eagerly to escape that it broke the surface. She stopped after a few minutes and wiped my leg.

Soon I was back at the hospital with another ingrown toenail. This time I went to an international clinic where a French doctor proposed a different remedy. He suggested I roll up a strand of cotton wool and place it under the nail and change it daily, so that as the nail grew, it would be trained upwards and wouldn't go digging into the toe. This simple solution worked. Later, a blood test revealed I had gout, and that the swelling of the toe was caused by excess uric acid in the blood. So, it was in the blood after all.

Speaking of which, do you know your blood type? If you're like me and you don't—I've been told more than once but I forgot—it's best to keep it that way to avoid the fad in Korea to pigeonhole and matchmake people by it. Koreans kind of half-believe in blood type as an indicator of character like they do with star signs. The notion has its origins in Japan in the 1920s. The idea is that people with Type A are conservative and introverted, people with Type B are independent and passionate (this is a bad thing if you're a man, by the way), Types Os are outgoing and optimistic leaders (actually, I think that's me), and ABs are cool and rational. In matching, A and O go well together as do ABs with other ABs. I have a friend in Japan who was once asked quite seriously what his blood type was by a Christian friend of his long-suffering fiancée. She meant well but the question irritated him. "S," he said (as in S for Satan).

In keeping with the shamanist passions, Koreans have hurled themselves into religion. They outdid their Chinese mentor in the application of Confucianism. In the same way, North Koreans outdid Stalin and Mao in their application of the communist personality cult of Kim Il-sung, who ruled as a kind of shaman-king figure.

6

JESUS AND LOCAL MESSIAHS

One missionary said Korea needed a "mighty baptism
of convicting and converting power" and wanted to see
Korean sinners alarmed because of their sins.

Christianity was a rather late arrival, but when it finally appeared, Koreans took to it with typical passion. With it came the idea of the single, all-powerful deity, blowing away all spirits who messed with people's minds. It also brought the idea of an exclusive faith and the practice of communal worship.

Roman Catholicism in Korea dates to 1784, when a Confucian scholar named Yi Seung-hun was baptized by a French priest in Beijing and set about converting his friends and relatives. The winning idea for those first converts was that God would help them be better Confucians. He was an attentive and willing guide who would guide them through the caves of their natural selfishness to the light of sagehood. Had it stopped there, the history might have been different, but the early Catholics also accepted the revolutionary idea that the relationship with God was more important than that with the king. They rejected other forms of worship as disloyalty.

That was a challenge. In 1791 the authorities executed a convert named "Paul" Yun Ji-chung for failing to conduct a proper mourning ceremony for his mother. In four major persecutions over the next eighty years, they put over eight thousand Catholics to death. One hundred and three of them were canonized by Pope John Paul II in 1984, making Korea the country with the fourth largest number of saints. In 2014, Pope Francis beatified the first martyr, Paul Yun Ji-chung, and 123 others, in the third of the four steps to sainthood. Several Irish priests and a U.S. Army chaplain killed during the Korean War are among more candidates for beatification.

The Protestant history is altogether different. The first missionaries arrived in 1884 when Protestant Christianity was being identified by the royal court with America, with protection from other foreign powers, and with modernity. Some missionaries became confidants of the king and queen. They were thus able to open the first Western-type schools and hospitals. They inspired, converted, and educated many of the reformist politicians. At the other end of the social scale they reached out to the lower classes with a love and care that ordinary Koreans had never experienced. There is one extraordinary story of the conversion of an entire village after a foreign lady was observed crying over the dead body of a cholera victim. Faith healing by Christians also accounted for significant conversions, as indeed did the modern healing by missionary doctors, and education by missionary teachers.

Protestant growth in Korea, at a time when the faith was making little headway in Japan and China, was the result of a perfect storm of factors. Besides the important support from the palace and their own embassies, the missionaries, who were mostly American but also British, Canadian, and Australian, were relatively well funded. All agreed to cooperate rather than compete and worked in different parts of the country, with the Presbyterians getting the northwest which became noted for its fervor. They adopted the ideas of John Livingston Nevius, a missionary in China, who called for the education and empowerment of local pastors as soon as was feasible.

Another key factor in the growth of Protestantism was the translation of the Bible into Korean and use of the native language in services. The Catholics by comparison did not switch from Latin until the 1960s. In addition, in Jesus, Koreans found for the first time a god with whom they could unveil their personal anguish and at the same time invest their instinctive filial devotion.

Despite good results in terms of the number of conversions, the early missionaries were frustrated by the lack of personal spirituality. One missionary said Korea needed a "mighty baptism of convicting and converting power" and wanted to see Korean sinners alarmed because of their sins.[45] Such a mighty baptism did come, though under unusual conditions. In the early twentieth century a wave of antiforeign feeling, particularly anti-Americanism, had swept through the Christian community because of America's approval of the Japanese occupation. When Robert Hardie, a Canadian doctor, confessed at a Methodist missionary meeting in the eastern town of Wonsan, in what is now North Korea, to a sense of personal sin as well as depression and frustration in his yearning to connect with God, it led to an outpouring of what believers described as the Holy Spirit. Other foreign missionaries and Korean converts opened their hearts and confessed to mutual hatred, petty grievances and, in some cases, to actual crimes. The phenomenon spread to Pyongyang, where in 1907 it burst out in what is now seen as a great Christian awakening. Through this process, a shadow of guilt and self-loathing appears to have lifted. Many who went through this experience devoted themselves to the development of a modern national identity, and to the resistance to Japan. The revival movement also established Pyongyang as the "Jerusalem of the East," a historical irony given that it is now the capital of atheist North Korea.[46]

Three years later the Protestants claimed to have 140,000 members, fourteen times the number at the turn of the century. By 1930 they were the most popular religion in the country. And that was before the real explosive growth of Protestantism that went hand in hand with the mass urbanization of the 1960s.

Although Christian love and Buddhist compassion are familiar concepts, the emphasis among Korean believers tends to be less on charity and service to others and more on using religion to earn your place in this life. For example, the Full Gospel Church, which claims 750,000 members—the single largest congregation in the history of Christendom—has a very simple appeal: Accept Jesus and guarantee your health and wealth, two items that always appear at the top in polls about what Koreans most worry about. The founder, David Yungi Cho, applied a beautifully simple strategy for growth: Home groups, made up mostly of women, would meet once a week for Bible study, to pray for the sick members of their congregation, and for their husbands' promotions.[47] His congregation burgeoned, with the massive influx of people from the villages into the cities in the 1970s. When the numbers approached twenty, a cell split into two. On Sundays, hundreds of these small groups descend on Yeouido Island in Seoul, where Reverend Cho built a church so big it resembles an indoor stadium.

The minor religious landscape has been similarly intense and colorful. But it is hard to get a clear picture. For some reason, religion doesn't lend itself to good reporting. Accounts of new religions are either propaganda at one end *or* breathless prejudice—as if anything new must be a coven—on the other. There's little in-between.

Some years ago, I was with a group of journalists and curious onlookers outside a church in Seoul waiting for the stroke of midnight, when the faithful within expected the world to end. As the time approached the joking and the general decibel level among us intensified. At one point I took off my shoes and laid my glasses on top of them and, pointing to them in alarm, turned to a Korean TV camera and said, "But he was here just a minute ago" and immediately felt stupid. It occurred to me that for the people in the church, some of whom occasionally looked down at us from a third-floor window, we were feeding the notion of the baying crowd of disbelievers, hell's inmates being left behind, and that the real weirdness was not confined to the church but was in the whole scene—mockers as well as mocked. A while after the appointed hour, the congregation, heads held low, filed out and were met with a torrent of verbal abuse from the crowd. I felt sorry for them. Let he who has never believed the unprovable or been deluded cast the first stone. All religions have notions that are zany to nonbelievers. All begin as cults. The confident inquiry to such phenomena should be to ask whether there is meaning in cultish belief instead of forcing the new through a gauntlet of mindless contempt and prejudice and withholding respect until sufficient payment of suffering has been exacted.

That said, Korea's open-mindedness to religion explains the relatively large number of sects of various persuasions. It's hard to quantify, in part because so many small sects have no desire to be known. I tried hard for a long time to persuade one of these, the Pure Water Church, to let me meet its founder, but they were uninterested in explaining themselves and unconcerned about expansion. At any time, then, congregation numbers are simply guesswork. By one reckoning there were at least seventy messiahs with followers in South Korea in the early 1960s.[48]

From what we do know for sure, there has in the last two centuries been an intense messianism in Korea. One of the best-covered examples is the *Donghak* movement of the second half of the nineteenth century, which developed as an alternative to Catholicism. Its leader, Choe Je-u, said God had asked him to save mankind. This makes him the first known Korean to claim to have spoken to the one God. During a ministry of only three years he spread a doctrine through songs and tracts drawing on the different faiths. As Choe referred to a supreme God and not to spirits in the plural, the government perceived his ministry as a challenge: It regarded itself as the supreme authority. His downfall was also caused by bad timing. At the same time in China, a messianic figure, Hong Xiuquan, was leading a civil war known as the Taiping Rebellion, which resulted in at least twenty million deaths, making it the bloodiest conflict of the nineteenth century. Choe was tried for sedition and executed. Thirty years later, a peasant revolt by his followers prompted the Korean king to call for help from China, which led to a war in Korea between Japan and China. The religion was renamed *Chondogyo*, and its believers joined Christian-organized protests in 1919 against Japanese colonial rule, which were suppressed. The religion continues to this day.

When a gentleman named Gang Il-sun struggled to understand the failure of the *Donghak* movement to achieve change, he became convinced that he had special powers himself. His followers believed him to be God incarnate, to have appeared on Earth to save the world, an echo of the claim of Choe, the founder. Gang preached for seven years and after his death in 1909 his wife claimed she could channel him from the spiritual world and revived the movement under the name of *Sondogyo*. Her own cousin then formed a rival sect and the religion rapidly fragmented into around one hundred factions. The best known today are *Daesun Jinrihoe* and *Jeungsando* (the "Tao of Jeung-san," which was Gang's pen name). *Jeungsando* claims to have three hundred thousand members worldwide, and *Daesun Jinrihoe*, claims six million members in Korea, a figure probably based on something like the number of leaflets handed out than actual believers.

Since the *Donghak* and the arrival of Protestantism, there have been numerous obscure groups that never outlived their founders. A sect in Pyongyang in the 1930s and 1940s, for example, in anticipation of the return of Christ, hand sewed a set of Korean and Western clothes for Jesus for every three days of his life from birth to the age of thirty-three, as an act of devotion. Hundreds of people were engaged in this endeavor. Their leader was a woman, who once made her husband bow to her several thousand times throughout one night as an act of penance for an offense.[49]

The best-known religion to emerge from Korea is Moon Sun-myung's Unification Church. Moon, who died in 2012, taught a view of God that was quintessentially Korean, combining shamanist passion and Confucian family patterns in Christian form. Moon's God was the miserable parent who suffered in lonely agony in a world of children who lacked filial piety toward him, and who acted destructively in relation with one another. Moon said that praying for God's help was selfish and thoughtless because it only added to the cosmic suffering. The spiritually mature person should seek to ease God's suffering and care for the world. Moon said that in his teens he prayed for "wisdom greater than Solomon, for faith greater than the Apostle Paul, and for love greater than the love Jesus had," and developed a Christ-like missionary zeal to heal what he perceived to be the broken heart of God.[50] Although presumptuous and implicitly blasphemous to Korean Christians, this kind of Olympian ambition was characteristic of many Korean men of his generation, and especially manifested in business and politics. Moon claimed that Jesus was murdered before he could marry and have a family, and that his own mission was to continue where Jesus left off. He and his wife were the "True Parents" who would represent God on Earth and unify the world based on unity between religions. It remains to be seen whether his religion will last.

Another messianic figure was Park Tae-sun. A charismatic healer, Park was expelled from the Presbyterian Church in the 1950s for heresy. Eight years later his Olive Tree Movement claimed almost two million followers in over three hundred congregations. The denomination that had expelled him had a membership of only one hundred thousand. Although his numbers claim was obviously exaggerated, Park demonstrated what energetic leadership could achieve in Korea with government approval. Under the 1948–60 government of Syngman Rhee, a Methodist, Park had been jailed several times on charges ranging from murder to being pro-communist. But under Park Chung-hee (no relative) in the 1960s and 1970s, he flourished, building two towns for twenty thousand followers (probably closer to the actual membership figure) and setting up heavy industry. Believers were conservative and didn't smoke or drink alcohol. They also avoided pork because Park said pigs were greedy, and peaches because he claimed it was this fruit, not the apple, that caused the fall of man. Their church services featured vigorous hand clapping, often for hours.[51]

At this same time, a gentleman by the name of Yoo Jae-yul, whose Tent Temple movement gained several thousand members in the 1970s, was claiming that Armageddon would break out when the chosen saints entered a refuge prepared by God just south of Seoul. This fortunately did not happen and Yoo was accused of fraud, after which he handed his movement's assets to the Presbyterian Church and emigrated to the United States. An interesting footnote to this story is that Yoo is the father-in-law of the rapper PSY.

A contemporary group called the Shinchonji Church, founded in 1984 by Lee Man-hee, who had been in the movements of both Park and Yoo, claims to have 150,000 members. Its churches are arranged in twelve tribes named after the apostles. It also has several thousand members overseas.

Similar to the True Parents of the Unification Church, a messianic couple called the Two Incarnations taught that Korea has a providential mission to heal mankind's spirit and revive its original vitality or *ki*. They claimed Korea was chosen for this mission because the country is located "in the best place on earth" from the point of view of global geomancy. They said the shape of Korea is also extremely significant. It is like a rabbit with large ears—"to listen to the voice of the creator"—and also like a penis hanging out of Asia. Its female equivalent is rabbit-shaped Paraguay, which lies snuggled between its Latin neighbors "like the pubic region of a woman." The couple visited Paraguay and held healing sessions. They taught that the Korean people have kept their blood pure by not marrying foreigners. Traditional forms of working, such as carrying water jars on their head, and recreation such as using a seesaw, have been heaven's "secret methods" to keep the people's *ki* strong. With such insights, ambitious healers tap the Koreans' traditional sense of their own uniqueness.

Another character on the Korean religion scene is Jung Myung-seok. A former Unification Church member, Jung founded a church that has gone by several names, but is officially known as the Christian Gospel Mission. Jung is currently serving a ten-year jail sentence for rape. He denies the charge. I have sufficient mistrust of the Korean legal system to be willing to hear his side. But it does appear that he taught that women could be saved from sin by having sex with him. This does seem to be a common temptation for men of the cloth and it makes you wonder why religious leaders don't hedge a little and tell their female followers that this should save them from sin but if it doesn't they should do it again.

I saw Jung once at an event held at a Unification Church–owned theater, where one of his followers on the staff had arranged for his group to rent the facility. At one point, Jung went up to the stage and prayed, standing with his arms out horizontally, each held up by a female aide. I didn't know about the sex stuff at that point. His method of prayer was different from the weepy oration of most Korean Protestants. He was chatting with God as if they were friends. The audience was moved by the intimacy of this and many started to mumble hallelujahs under their breath. At this, a ripple of contempt ran through the back rows of Unification Church members staffing the theater. They looked at one another and rolled their eyes. If there's one thing a cultist can't stand, it's a cult. It was a telling moment.

Once the dust has settled on a new religion and the claims of its founder no longer seem so breathtakingly arrogant or downright mental, and the controversies engendered no longer so important, it is possible to see context in their emergence. Now, for example, we have no interest in the offense caused to the establishment by the *Donghak* peasants. But we can appreciate the bold new idea they espoused that challenged the mind-set that had kept Koreans in shackles for centuries: Choe reinvented God in a way that appealed to the ordinary and oppressed. God existed, not in a distant heaven, he said, but within the mind of man. Man was not a sinner, but a manifestation of God, even for you, the peasant.

The new religions that claim that Korea is special may appear flaky or even offensive and, considering where Korea was at when the republic started in 1948, downright deluded. But they articulated something that was in the air in Korea in those days, a kind of manifest destiny, an earnest nationalism that sought to benefit mankind.

In this way, new religious figures play a similar role to artists in a society in that the geniuses among them somehow tap the soul of their people, the heart of their age. While the artists may seek simply to articulate what they find there, the religious leader seeks to redirect it or harness it and inject society with new life.

If that is the case, then the mission for today's religions in Korea or for the next new one is to address the question of happiness.

7

SUFFERING IN THE REPUBLIC OF OTHERS

"Too many have unrealistic expectations.
They don't have to feel like losers. But they do.
It's the result of twenty years of brainwashing."

Koreans have the blues and can't get out of it.

It was not easy to for me accept at first that such warm and outgoing people are actually in a black pit of depression but surveys show this is clearly the case.

Here's the Korea we foreigners see first: A chilly October day in 2011, and a German businessman is walking through a market in the city of Daegu. He stops at a stall and gestures at a piece of fruit.

"How much?" he asks the stallholder, holding out his hand and moving thumb and finger together.

The lady looks at his hand and, ignoring his question, walks around from behind her counter and takes his fingers in hers and rubs them to warm them up, talking to him in Korean. He doesn't understand a word, but figures it is about his freezing fingers, not the price of fruit. The man is astonished, a little embarrassed, and at the same time very moved.

When he reported his experience that night, colleagues told of similar encounters. One group had taken the train to Busan and got lost. No sooner had they opened up their map to try to figure where they were than a man on a motorbike stopped and offered to help. He parked his bike and walked them to the station.

The Germans were tourism experts attending their association's annual conference and were in Korea for the first time. The event itself was being executed with flawless efficiency. Local staff members were hardworking and obliging, always on hand to help, but their deference made them distant. But in their free time the visitors encountered this other side of Korea—the spontaneity, friendliness, and warmheartedness of her people.

But stay awhile and you sink a little into the pit. You see the anger, the irritation, the moodiness, the resignation, and sense of failure.

Birth and suicide rates of a country are a good sounding of this. On average, a South Korean woman will have 1.21 babies. This puts her almost at the bottom of the world's childhood charts.[52] It means some will have two, many stop at one, and many will have none at all.

In 2012, 29.1 per 100,000 people killed themselves, compared to the average among Organization for Economic Co-operation and Development (OECD) member states of 12.1.[53] This is the highest rate in the industrialized world. What's surprising when you consider that Koreans pulled off such a miracle of national growth is that the main reason for suicide is money. That's the view of Park Jong-ik, a psychiatrist and adviser to the Korea Suicide Prevention Center:

For adults, the most significant factor pushing them to commit suicide is economic. With over-sixty-fives, where the rate is extremely high compared to other countries, the main factor is health problems, but even this issue is really economic. To encourage use of smaller clinics, the government will pay up to 80 percent of the bill for some treatments in a clinic but only 40 percent at a hospital. Despite this, people trust the hospitals and use them more. Who pays? Their children. This is where we see the remnants of Confucianism. I am old, I'm sick, I've been given two years to live and it's expensive. So I

kill myself to save my children the cost. Actually, the real suicide rate is even higher than the statistics. Many people just
give up on their treatment. Or, if they're told to stop drinking, they just carry on and drink more. The suicide is indirect
to avoid bringing shame to the family.

The turning point in the misery index was the financial crisis that
struck Korea and other Asian countries in 1997–8. "That was when
the suicide rate drastically increased," said Park Jong-ik. "You could
say the factors were economic in that many people lost their jobs.
But more important was the change in atmosphere. Before the
crisis, Koreans were competitive, but the sense was of people co-
operating and surviving together. But after the crisis, we needed to
beat other people in order to survive. The direct impact of this was
on the working man in particular but it led to a big change in the
overall social atmosphere."

A survey in 2013 found that 11.2 percent of teens, 17.9 percent
of people over seventy, and 13 percent overall said they had suffered
from depression in the previous twelve months. The figure was higher
for girls (16 percent) than boys (6.7 percent) and higher overall for
women (16.5 percent) than men (9.7 percent).[54] (We should note,
however, that, despite stories about how stressed they are because of
parental pressure and the competitive atmosphere at school, the suicide rate for children is no higher than in other countries).

The low rate of people seeking professional help is attributed to a
stigma associated with psychiatric support. Another unacknowledged
explanation is lack of trust in the government's promise of confidenti-
ality. There's good reason for this. A chief of police recently admitted
that police recruiters check the medical records of applicants. One
psychologist told me that a patient he had treated for stress called to
ask his advice about a job application: The form asked whether the
applicant had ever had psychological treatment. The patient had in
fact been a judge but had stepped down to work at a law firm, got
bored, and was reapplying to the bench. "I recommended that he lie,"
the therapist said. "He followed this advice and got the job."

The question of happiness can be approached generationally. The
older generation carries the wounds of war and poverty. Ask anyone

over sixty for their life story and you will uncover agonies that you cannot imagine yourself going through. During the Korean War, peasants who stayed in their villages risked kangaroo courts when the North Koreans came in, or murderous retribution by South Korean troops after the communists had been routed. The safer bet was to flee. On the chaotic refugee trail, millions lost touch with close family members; kids found wandering ended up in orphanages, some too young to know who they were; in the winter, women were sometimes seen kicking a hole in the ice on the edge of the river and pushing a bundle down into the water—the baby they could no longer feed.

In the past there was no choice but to suppress feelings and get on with life. This led psychiatrists, political theorists, and artists to refer to a specific psychological condition, which they attribute to this collective experience. Called *han*, it is a kind of rage and helplessness that is sublimated and lingers like an inactive resentment. *Han* first emerged as a topic of literary criticism in the 1940–50s. Its expression was seen in songs and tales of unrequited love in old Korean literature, as well as from colonial-period writers such as the poet Kim Sowol. A more explosive version entered the popular, political realm in the 1970s, when it became a key component of modern novels and of *minjung* (masses) theology, which could be loosely described as the Korean version of neo-Marxist Liberation Theology.

In addition to the specific agonies caused by political circumstances there is a cultural backdrop that for centuries has predisposed Koreans to suffer. "Western history, you could say, is a history of disobedience," said psychiatrist Paek Sang-chang. "It tells of the struggle for individual freedom. But our history is one of the struggle to obey." Korean heroes are the loyal subject and the filial son, whose exemplary virtue is their suppression of self in the course of obedience. "Psychoanalytically speaking, this means prohibition of one's own instinctive urges." If a man loved a woman, for example, but his parents ordered him to marry another, he would obey, and live with *han*. This is a typical Korean experience. "*Han* has hung like a tranquil mist in the valley of our hearts."[55]

For the new generation in Korea, though, poverty and war are remote, and filial piety is no longer a cultural lynchpin. Most have grown up middle class in a peaceful democracy. But still, they are unhappy. That lingering misery is no longer tranquil and no longer hangs like mist. It is altogether more intense.

Of course, people busy themselves in gyms, and with work, and going out. Some connect with nature to detox from city life. But not many. I don't believe the hikers in Seoul, all properly kitted out and wielding ski poles—"important to protect your knees," people stop and tell me in English when they see I don't have any—are communing with nature so much as communing with one another. And therein lies a clue. They are almost all in groups: extended families, workmates, alumni. Some are dating groups, mountain-hiking clubs for available forty-year-olds and others for available fifty-year-olds and so on. Of course, they can enjoy a view, but their mind is on the group dynamic.

This fits the idea inherent in the culture that predisposes people to find meaning by identifying with groups. They are drawn to undertake what people from other countries might see as solitary, or family, events, in groups. Those who don't, stand out. I knew a manager in Seoul's downtown Lotte Hotel who at weekends would go around the country on long solitary mountain hikes. I could perfectly understand the impulse. I did the same at a boarding school in a village at the foot of the Ochil Hills in Scotland from when I was eleven. I kept a record of the height of each peak, the date I climbed it, and how long it took. But when this Korean man told me he did it, too, I felt there was something wrong with him. It didn't seem right. Koreans are supposed to do stuff in groups.

This group orientation is the starting point of what makes Korea foreign for the Westerner. It is, it seems to me, also the key to the cell door of their unhappiness.

The problem with the group, at least as it tends to work in Korea, is that it leads people to be overly concerned with the views of others. Of course, for social beings, the views of others are important. But they can also represent a form of tyranny. If a young man's parents want him to be a doctor but he feels called to be a chef, he should put Mom and Dad in their place and rustle them up a ratatouille. Likewise, if two people are in love and want to marry, but her relatives don't think he is good enough, she should put them in their place. Some, of course, go against their parents and hope to win them over in time. I've known people, though, who have caved years after such a move and divorced. Either way, they feel wretched. In the culture it is not ethically correct to go against your parents. That road less traveled is not celebrated. Group-oriented ethics require the individual to give up her dreams and follow others. Not just because others have authority, but because it is more virtuous to sacrifice. She should feel a better person for doing so.

Thus, for Koreans, when the priority is very much on what others think, the struggle is not to accept themselves—as it may be for Westerners—so much as to align themselves with the idea that others have of them.

"With their cultural emphasis on face, on what others think, Asian people in general have a high concern about what they think other people think of them. In Korea, this is more intense than in, say, Japan or China," said Kim Young-hoon, a social psychologist at Yonsei University. "Koreans will choose their school, their house, their car on this basis."

They'll also decide a lot of other things because of what they think others think. Like, a two-year age gap between husband and wife is okay (in fact, common, because when young male students return to college after military service, the girls in their class are two years younger) but ten years is something to be permanently embarrassed about. The concern about others is there in every waking moment.

If that extreme sensitivity to the views of others forms the foundation, then the first floor in our model building of the Korean psyche, is the sense of hierarchy. In modern democratic Korea, people know that in theory they are equal, but that in reality they are identified and valued according to their jobs. The higher the position, the better they think they appear in the eyes of others.

"To rise higher, though, you must compete," Professor Kim Young-hoon said. "This is the most important driver for Koreans. It explains why we are so fiercely competitive. The reason for the drive for education is that school credentials are the key to the top positions." As fierce as it is, this competition is handled with subtlety. That is because of the fundamental obsession with what others think.

When a person is successful, he must behave with modesty to avoid being negatively thought of by others.

The reason so many Koreans today tell pollsters they are unhappy is because they are not doing well in that competition. The path to success requires educational qualifications and it is narrow: via a handful of top universities.

A challenge for Korea now is to vary the paths to success and to separate social ranking from the sense of worth. This is easily said, but the concept is so deeply ingrained that it seems impossible.

It never ceases to astonish me how people change according to how they think they are viewed by others on the social ladder. Many years ago, when Korea was a dictatorship, the staff members of opposition leaders Kim Dae-jung and Kim Young-sam used to regularly drop by my office. The foreign press in those days was a lifeline because the government restricted coverage of their bosses by the local press. These gentlemen were humble and not well off. Some lived off their wife's salary. Sometimes they lost hope. It was widely felt in the days before democracy that Korea had always been ruled by authoritarians and that democracy was a pipe dream. Would-be politicians would go to fortune-tellers to ask whether there was any point in joining the opposition. These guys were committed but I am sure they wondered if they had made a lifelong mistake. Their speech, the quality of their dress, their posture and whole demeanor reflected this sense of aide-to-a-possible-lost-cause. Two men in particular stand out in my memory. Fast-forward a decade and both had become elected lawmakers. One went on to become the mayor of the city of Incheon and the other the chairman of the ruling party. When I met them again after several years, everything about them had changed—quality of suits, manner of speech, posture and, to my disappointment, attitude to me. "Oh, yes, Mr. Breen, I remember you," one of them said distantly, for the benefit of his aides in the room. Remember me? You were in my office every day. We were mates. Once you broke down lamenting the hopelessness of it all and I had to comfort you and convince you that democracy would come to Korea and that you were holding the torch for it. The transformation at the top of the ladder was nothing short of astonishing. What lay behind it, I realized, was not that my former buddies now had the cash to buy expensive suits so much as the change in how they thought people—me excluded—perceived them. Now the cringing masses were lining up outside their offices for favors.

When you picture yourself in hierarchical relationships with all those around you, you are never alone. If there were a way to measure it I am sure we would find that Koreans spend far more time thinking about people than, say, about ideas. In his eureka moment, your Korean Einstein would think, "$E=mc^2$. Bingo! OMG, wait till Professor Lee sees this. He'll freak. This is going to be so sweet. But I'll have to maintain my humility. His secretary will love me for this. Maybe I can ask her out. Oh, but that could get complicated."

In the world of hierarchy, it is hard to be spontaneous and innocent. You learn early on to be sensitive, to gather intelligence, and to plot. There is no joy in conversation. There is meaning in the level of the people you are conversing with and what they can give you, but there is no joy in conversation itself.

And that leads us to one characteristic of Koreans that puzzles the Westerner: their comfort with silence. One American reporter in Seoul who had written a well-received book on Korea told me after he moved to Hong Kong: "I come across a lot of Koreans here. But, you know, there's one way in which they're different from everyone else here. Some guy will come up to you at a reception with a drink in his hand and say, 'Hello, my name is Kim.' And then he'll just stand there. I don't know what to say. And it's not like he's got nothing to talk about. He's probably with Goldman Sachs."

This disquieting refuge in silence can again be understood in terms of that obsession with what other people are thinking. "We are always worried about the reaction of others to what we do or say," said Kim Young-hoon, the social psychologist. "For that reason people often prefer to keep quiet. It's better not to speak than to say something that people might think is stupid." It is quite common, for example, to have a business lunch with three or more people in which the junior people actually say nothing throughout the entire meal. While the Westerner, who is especially averse to silence, struggles to include everyone, or just gives up and is left feeling rude that he is only talking to one person, the young Korean is safe and protected in his shell. Koreans are hardly unique in being sensitive about saying something stupid. But the withholding is such an ingrained habit that it can of itself lead to stress and depression.

I would also note in this "face culture" a tendency to moral corruption. When a person whose overriding concern is for what others think of him finds himself alone, there's a risk that his ethical compass switches off. Similarly, when he finds everyone else at the trough, he sees no wrong in dipping his own snout in. Judging by the daily stories in the newspapers, corruption is endemic in Korea. It is far less visible but, judging from anecdotal experience, widespread among families. One of my American friends developed a personal yardstick for honesty after witnessing relatives of his Korean wife refuse to repay loans. "I consider a person honest," he said, "if they are presented with an opportunity to steal one hundred thousand dollars from another person without any repercussions but turn it down."

One notable effect of the central presence of hierarchy is on humor. There are, for example, no situational comedy shows around characters who are vicars, doctors, or judges.[56] Not because people won't laugh but because the professional associations will complain. With people taking their social position so seriously, the comic faces many such no-go areas. Things did lighten up in the 1990s with politicians as the butt of jokes, but in 2008 after the former Hyundai CEO, Lee Myung-bak, became president, that door shut. Chung Bong-ju, a former politician and one of the hosts of a satirical podcast, "I am a Petty-Minded Creep," which lambasted President Lee, was sentenced to a one-year jail term in 2011 for "spreading false rumors." The case went all the way to the Supreme Court.[57]

If we take the elevator to the second floor in our Korean psyche model house, we find emotionalism. I have run this idea past some Korean specialists but they don't see it as a noteworthy characteristic. But outsiders tend to agree that, in contrast to the inhibited Japanese, the Koreans are loud and free. Parents do not typically raise their children to temper their emotions with reason or to hold back in expressing them. While an airplane full of Europeans will bristle when a child starts yelling, the Koreans are as comfortable with noise, as they are with silence when the occasion demands. (This is beginning to change, though, with some restaurants now banning children to the delight of many younger Koreans.)

Koreans have a lot to be emotional about. Life on the hierarchical ladder is a never-ending source of frustration and anger on the one hand and fulfillment and joy on the other. The perceived slights from others and the critical comments of the unrestrained are like the feet of people on the ladder on your hands and in your face. At the same time, though, the presence of those above willing to care for you and help you out is an enormous source of warmth and confidence. When there are older people looking out for you and youngsters relying on you, you cannot be alone.

Because they are comfortable with emotion, Koreans can be very forgiving of emotional outbursts. Indeed, they can be remarkably tolerant when confronted by someone behaving unreasonably because that person is drunk or in an emotional state.

In some regards Koreans used to be far more restrained than they are today. The great-grandparents of modern Koreans were taught to hide their affections, for example, and didn't even hold their children in front of others. But that changed with the arrival of American culture and the idea that if you didn't let your emotions out you could get physically ill.

While the instinct for harmony is there, with the jostling for place on the social ladder and their willingness to let their emotions out, Koreans can be exceedingly fractious and argumentative. But there can be subtleties at play. Letting rip with strangers is one thing. But when there is a relationship, there are certain and complex considerations to follow.

It is astonishing how nasty Koreans can be to people they perceive to be both beneath themselves and unable to fight back (usually because they'd lose their job if they did). Take apartment guards, for example. A survey in 2014 found that four in ten suffered verbal abuse from tenants in the block. Six percent said they were abused on a daily basis.[58]

An even darker story concerns the apparent abuse of mentally disabled people. In 2014, authorities found that a number of salt farms on remote islands in the southwest had been keeping mentally disabled workers in virtual slave conditions. The story came to light after one victim wrote to his mother about his plight. There was public outrage over the uncomfortable fact that he had chosen to write his family rather than seek help from the police lest they report him to his "owner."[59]

But sometimes the rules appear to change. For example, managers take all kinds of abuse during strikes and in negotiations with unionists and are supposed to just sit and take it, like a wise parent absorbing the tantrum of a child. Woe betide anyone who rants back. That would be breaking the rules and, when done by a foreigner, can easily be taken as an insult to the Korean people.

Koreans now have recourse to the law and democratic institutions to resolve conflict. But the old ways, when problems were solved by power, still work. Try calling your phone company and politely explaining there's a problem with your bill and you'll get the runaround; throw a tantrum, and they'll put the supervisor on the line and he will solve it for you. Freaking out is logical.

If the Koreans are explosive, they are also exquisitely sensitive. In fact, they tend to dwell too much for our liking on their delicate feelings. The *kibun* (feelings, or state of mind) is of prime importance. Not only does feeling good make you feel good, but also it's better for your health. When you feel bad you are justified in behaving badly, rejecting business proposals, barking at your wife and secretary. The *kibun* is translated as mood, but is accorded higher importance than we would accord that word. It is perhaps best described as that part of you that extends beyond the physical body, your inner atmosphere or, perhaps, your continental shelf. This invisible part of you can be damaged by loss of face, disrespect, bad news, or unhappiness. Or by the appearance of someone who threatens you, or who damaged your *kibun* before.

The best advice to the foreigner is to live by the courtesies of his own culture in dealing with Koreans. Even so, it is possible to slip on this cultural cowpat. Take business cards, for example. To an American, they're a reminder of who he is; to a Korean, they represent who he is. Stick pins in it and you're sticking a pin in him. I notice most foreign business visitors these days accept cards and offer their own with two hands, then place them reverently on the table for the duration of the meeting—they've read the book. But some haven't. Jeffrey Jones, a lawyer with over three decades experience in Korea, once took a foreign client for a meeting to discuss a possible joint venture with the president of a Korean company: "After half an hour, we switched the discussion into Korean. My mistake was to not keep my client updated as to what we were talking about. After a few minutes he got bored and started innocently playing with the business cards that, like everyone else, he had put in front of him. He absentmindedly folded one and put it in his pocket. It was the Korean company president's card. This ended the meeting."

With their awareness of the "inner man" and the appreciation of harmony to avoid *kibun*-damaging, Koreans are very adept at sensing people's character and mood and at helping you out of foul temper, be it by giving you space, silence, or gifts. I once had an argument over something with my office manager. Afterward, I carried on working in seething silence. He went off. Ten minutes later he came back. He'd been out and bought some apples. He quietly cut them up and came over and sat down beside me and offered me a small fork to dig at them. This wordless gesture washed away all my irritation and impressed me very deeply. My priority had been with proving the correctness of my opinion, whereas his was with the relationship and office harmony.

Here lies a cultural difference that invites great misunderstanding, for it is not easy for one side to see the virtue of the other. When is one individual being correct more important than a group being happy? Obviously sometimes, but much less often for the Korean who places his emphasis on ethics in relationships, and less on the individual and his or her conscience. The Korean naturally seeks harmony in relationships over objective truth and goodness.

With *kibun* being an important factor, there is a lot of talk about "timing" and "feeling right" by Koreans when they are making decisions. We should not assume that *kibunists* are irrational. In fact, Koreans can be remarkably rational and calculating on issues which we Westerners tend to consider as emotional. Take choosing a life partner, for example. A significant number of spouses still meet through matchmakers, professional or amateur. They may factor in all considerations, as well as attractiveness and character, and mix it up with their intuition and make a decision that we tend not to be able to make because we may not think of marriage until we've fallen in love, by which time it's too late to retrieve ourselves.

On the positive side, when you put the hierarchical outlook and emotionalism together, a meaningful quality emerges: the ability to strive vigorously to be better. The obsession with hierarchy creates ambition in that, if you see people as ranked, it is natural to want to climb; the acceptance of emotional expressiveness, meanwhile, allows people to articulate their dreams and helps temper the fears that might otherwise hold them back. Thus the individual Korean is unleashed on society to rise and be well-thought-of in the process. This dynamic lies behind South Korea's national growth. The challenge now for Koreans is to find happiness within this dynamic. They are looking to achieve this with social programs, increased attention to mental health and issues like bullying and work stress. But part of the answer calls for a change in attitude or, as one Buddhist monk put it to me, "We must tell ourselves we are already happy. Because we are."

NATIONALISM AND OTHER THINGS

*"Nationalism needs a military so that young men doing their
service develop the willingness to die for the country."*

One of the best-known things about the Koreans is that they are nationalistic. There's nothing new there. The world is nationalistic in the sense that it is organized in nation-states. Few people oppose that. The Koreans aren't the kind of nationalists who think their country is best. Quite the contrary, they have a low opinion of their country's past and aspire to be like those they consider better. To achieve this, they have modeled their systems on those of other countries, particularly the United States and, less admitted, Japan. The Koreans are nationalists in that they tend to consider their country's perceived interests, especially economic interests, to be more important than those of other countries. They have been raised in recent decades under the flag of sacrifice for the national interest. If they oppose something for, say, environmental reasons, such as the hosting of the 2018 Winter Olympics, they would have to argue that the games are not in the national interest in order to get broad buy-in.

This form of nationalism requires obedience. In reality, a citizen does not need to support his country's interest. I mean, if a British company were participating in an international bid for something, British citizens would laugh if their government suggested they should support the company's efforts just because it was British. In fact, the arguing for national interest is the job of the government official who is paid to represent the country. The Korean citizen has been persuaded to obediently align himself with this effort.

As deeply rooted as it appears, this nationalism is actually quite new for Koreans. "It started after independence from Japan in 1945," said historian Lim Jie-hyun. "Before that, there was what I call emerging nationalism." The nationalistic ideology does not develop spontaneously: "It needs an education system. If kids don't go to elementary school—which they didn't in Korea in the old days—they will not get educated in nationalism." The nationalistic education began in 1961 after the takeover of the army general, Park Chung-hee. "Previously, our system had been influenced by pragmatism and was intended to raise citizens with critical views. Suddenly all was changed into national subjectivity. Similarly, nationalism needs a military. There, young men doing their military service develop the willingness to die for the country. The voting system also helped make people nationalistic. The message was: 'Now you have a vote to decide on the destiny of the nation.' And all of this contributed to the development of democracy."

There are three standout characteristics of South Korean nationalism. The first is ethnicity. While other countries have their own distinguishing features—freedom in America, culture in France, and so on—what sets Koreans apart is the belief in a unique bloodline. This myth (for there is no such thing as national blood) is shared by North and South. Once at a military meeting in Panmunjeom in the DMZ, a North Korean general expressed his concern that the marriages of South Korean farmers to ladies from Mongolia, Vietnam, and the Philippines would pollute the national bloodline. The sophisticated South Korean delegate could have made a point about the global village. Instead, he said not to worry: "It's just a drop of ink in the Han River."[60]

The idea of being distinct by virtue of a unique bloodline is conveyed by an image Koreans have long had of themselves of being a "frog in the well," alone and with no sense of what lies outside of the dank walls. Sometimes, a little incident reminds you of this. Some years ago, the head of a government agency hosted around twenty foreign diplomats at a Korean-style dinner where they were seated on the floor on two sides of a long table. During the meal, he conducted toasts, Korean-style: He would call someone's name, make sure their glass was full, and raise his own and, in good humor, say something relevant like, "Mr. Smith! God Bless America!" (I'm making up the names.) Every few minutes, he'd make eye contact and do another one. "Mr. Jones, God Save the Queen!" "Monsieur Thiebault, Vive la France!" After an hour of this, he arrived at the representative from the German embassy. "Herr Schmidt!" he called. The conversation lulled as the German diplomat raised his glass. The official paused to think of something. "Heil Hitler!" he shouted.

When Kim Moo-sung, the chairman of the ruling party, in December 2015 found himself standing beside an African student in a line of volunteers delivering coal briquettes used for heating in poorer neighborhoods, and told him his face was the same color as the coal, such was the outrage that he was forced to apologize.[61]

It would be wrong, however, to suggest that insensitivity of this sort is common to all Koreans. Although race as the distinctive feature for a nation appears inherently problematic, the Koreans' nationalism is not aggressive. In its North Korean form, the victims of its Nazi-like excesses are its own people, not outsiders; South Koreans see their version as benevolent and, in their best moments, as benefitting the world. In his biography, Kim Koo, an independence leader and the figure many South Koreans wish had been their first president (his face was chosen in 2009 for the 100,000-*won* note, but the plan to issue the new note was dropped), articulated it thus:

> (All) ideologies and religions change. Only the people of the same blood lineage exist on this Earth as a body and a community bound eternally by the same shared destiny of collective rise and decline. . . . It is only good and imperative that people all over the world strive for improvement and progress

leading toward (the) grand and beautiful goal of the universal brotherhood of mankind. But, even in striving for this, one should not depart from reality. The truth of the present reality is that each people form the best possible nation of their own and give birth to and nurture the highest possible culture of their own. After this, nations can exchange what they have with one another and so live in mutual cooperation with one another. This is the democracy in which I believe, and this is the most certain and valid truth in the present stage of human history. . . . I believe it is a mandate given to our people by Heaven that we should help humanity find its way along this path. . . . The enterprise of our people which I desire is certainly not that of conquering the world by force or by economic power. What I am proposing is that we do that which will lead to a world in which we ourselves live abundantly and in which humanity as a whole lives in abundance, peace, and happiness. This world will come true only by establishing a culture of love and peace. Do not say that this is a pipe dream because no people in history has ever done something like this in the past. My point is that we should do this precisely because nobody has ever done this in the past. Only when we realize that this great enterprise has been left undone by Heaven for us to fulfill can our people recognize their true path and their true tasks.[62]

The second feature of nationalism is victimhood. Victimhood is sweet temptation because it confers righteousness. Even the bad things about you are some other bullying country's fault. This was the sentiment at the end of World War Two, after thirty-five years of rule by Japan, and it has now been extended all the way back in history. Young Koreans are taught they've been invaded nine hundred times but have never themselves attacked another country. (Far from being exceptions, participation in the Vietnam and Gulf wars are seen through victim lenses as examples of American pressure.)

The third characteristic of South Korean nationalism is lack of confidence. Koreans take little genuine pride in what is in fact a very long and remarkably well-documented history. That is because the way they live today does not come from that history. It was adopted from the outside after World War Two.

"Our thinking and way of life were borrowed," said one Korean official who asked not to be named to avoid being seen as criticizing his country. "It's like we're wearing shirts and pants that don't fit. Take education. Most majors we study were not created by us. Nor are the sports we play, the music we listen to, the movies we watch, or even the food we eat. Most specialists and experts study abroad. In their minds, the ideal destination is not here. They always refer to some other place, like the United States, where things are done better. When I meet a foreigner, I presume you know things better than me and that you have more experience than me." One result of this lack of confidence is that outsiders of modest achievement like me get better access to and treatment by top-ranking Koreans than the local genius does.

There is an assumption, instilled by nationalistic education, that people are linked to their country's history, proud of the good and ashamed of the bad. This is a simple point but it is hard to really get it. It means I should be embarrassed that Jack the Ripper tours are so popular with foreign tourists in London and that the beefeaters at the Tower tell these foreigners all the gory stuff that happened there. But that's how it is with Koreans. As much as they may love it abroad, Korea's own tourism avoids dark history. With the significant exception of Japanese rule—where museums are gory to the point of being offensive—the penchant is for offerings which are bright and where visitors skip off gaily as if Mom had just laundered their white shirts in Tide.[63]

This idea rubs up against awareness that foreign tourists are fascinated by the Korean War and by the menace of North Korea. One inventive solution: On the Korea tourism organization site, the DMZ has been rebranded as the Peace and Life Zone.[64]

It's the same with the way history is taught. It's no wonder then that Koreans don't have much time for theirs. As one whose eyes also glaze over in castles and temples, it took me a while to see this. The revelation came one dark evening in the bar of the Seoul Foreign Correspondents' Club in the city center. We were talking about tourism.

"What do you see out there?" said a Korean friend, a tourism expert. He was pointing down to the grounds of the historic Doksu Palace. It was pitch-black.

"Where?"

"Down there." He pointed again.

"Well, it's the Doksu Palace, but you can't really make it out," I said.

"Exactly," he said.

"What?" I wasn't quite following this Socratic method.

"Can you imagine any other major capital city in the world which hides its most historic sites like this? All our other palaces are the same. You can't see them at night. They should be floodlit for everyone to see."

This piece of common sense had never occurred to me and I had never heard it mentioned before. You get so used to things. In the center of this modern city, amid the lights from offices where people were working late, the streetlights and cars, were patches of blackness that concealed its most fascinating monuments.

"Is it because they don't know what tourists like to see?" I ventured, instinctively proposing that we criticize the government.

"It's because we Koreans hate our history," he said. "We don't want to think about it and we don't want to show it."

Koreans are not sure how to consider their history. This is a complex issue that starts with the way people are educated. The academic approach to information gathering and learning is not based on the analytical, empirical approach, which we use in the Western system, whereby we tend to start with a theory. Upon this foundation, we pile bricks of information. The theories are modified, the significance of the information adjusted. But essentially this is how we analyze, understand, and remember things. To give an unrelated example, almost every wildlife documentary is based on an evolutionary theory of the survival of the fittest. It is simple. Animals live to survive and reproduce. Every piece of information is explained and becomes interesting and relevant because it shows the million ways animals defend themselves against predators, find their mates, protect their young. You could look at history in a similar way. How did this society begin? How did it develop? Why did it collapse? We tend to look at human society age by age and by gleaning what information we can from artifacts, music, and other evidence of the flowering and changing of culture. But Koreans are not taught political theory, as such. They learn facts.

Historical facts are important from the point of view of a nationalistic, semipolitical pride. Questioning and analyzing them is not seen as valid. In fact, raising a question in class, even at university, is seen as a challenge and an insult to the teacher. In our own history, painful memories and victories are classified, categorized, prioritized, discussed, and used as supporting evidence, and in this way remembered. In Korea, details disappear, and memories are only triggered by anecdotes.

As a young American Peace Corps volunteer in the late 1960s, Peter Bartholomew taught at a school near the eastern end of the DMZ.

In those days, the North Koreans were trying to create a Vietnamese-type uprising. They sent spies and saboteurs. At dusk every day you could hear rifle fire and a couple of times a week South Korean paratroopers were dropped and shore batteries would start up. Bodies of infiltrators would be displayed out in front of local police stations to show what happened to North Koreans and collaborators in the villages. If they caught one alive, they'd make the same point by hanging him from a chopper and flying over the villages. But you don't hear these stories. You only hear about the big ones, the few occasions when there was a large group of guerrillas. But these incidents were constant. There was a state of semi-war for years, but it's never mentioned. I don't mean officially. I mean in conversation with the people who experienced it. Why? Because there's nothing to trigger the memory.

The point is that in the Western mind, such memories would be classified in a way to give them relevance, and accessibility, so that they would be recalled more readily.

Bartholomew, now a businessman based in Seoul, is an amateur expert in Korean architecture. He was once invited to give a lecture on the architecture and landscaping of the royal palaces to an audience of academics and government officials. "They knew more about the subject than I did, so I was a bit nervous. I gave a presentation on how the palaces were organized, the economics involved, why they were expanded, abandoned, how aesthetics, royal affairs, and politics affected them, and how you could see all this by looking at them. When I'd finished there was silence and then they applauded. People came up and said that they knew all the facts I had mentioned and more, but that they had never thought of drawing parallels and linking them up in this way."

The Korean way is not to categorize, not to create in the listener's mind an overall picture of the buildings and why they were built in a way that visitors to the palaces could relate to. Similarly, there is no ability to convince people why they should visit, say, Doksu Palace. Until I met Bartholomew, it always struck me as a boring collection of buildings with sloping roofs. Why bother to floodlight them? Why, indeed, even Koreans would ask. They are unaware of the fascinating tales of intrigue and gore that went on in these buildings, which could be brought alive for the visitor.

The way people think affects their ability to explain themselves and persuade others. A case in point concerns a tiny islet between Korea and Japan called Dokdo by the Koreans and Takeshima by the Japanese. Centuries of mutual dislike seem to have coagulated around this dispute. The Koreans have by far the better case, not the least because they occupy the place. Japan gave up rights to sovereignty over Korea at the end of World War Two, but claims the islet became Japanese just before formal annexation in 1910. This is a piece of legal trickery because Japanese domination of Korean affairs, through "advisers" in government offices, began in 1905. With a bit of research the Koreans could have found out the name of the Japanese adviser who arranged the transfer of the rock and made a perfectly reasoned case that it fell into the category of claims that Japan abandoned in 1945. They could even do so with some humor. Instead, they sabotage their case by refusing to address it except with table thumping and nationalistic bluster.

To put nationalistic victim mentality in its place, this Dokdo issue is more important for South Koreans than the suffering of tens of thousands of people nearby in the North Korean gulag.

It's when that consequence of nationalism manifests that foreign residents of Korea throw up their hands and declare that they don't get the place. Everything seems so normal and impressive, and then suddenly everyone goes nuts. It's like catching a professor whose intellect you admire prostrating himself and weeping in front of a painting of the mountain god.

Another consequence is that Koreans tend to assess people first and foremost by their nationality. This superficial habit of labeling people is of course not exclusive to Korea, but it is divisive and lies at the root of racism, tribalism, class-consciousness, and social engineering.

I'm reminded of an episode from the 1988 Olympic Games in Seoul. A month or so before the games, I received a phone call from an American sports reporter working on the daily *Korea Herald*. He had been asked to proofread the English translation of the parade of nations commentary for the opening ceremony. This was to be the version aired on the translation channel that English speakers in the stadium would tune in to. It would then be translated into eight other languages. The author, a Korean scholar, had written up a few lines about each participating nation. Some were diplomatic time bombs. Hondurans, for example, might have paused in mid-applause when their team entered the stadium had they heard themselves described as citizens of a "well-known Banana Empire." Zambia was the "home of the pygmies, people that do not reach a height of higher than forty centimeters." My favorite was "Ireland, also known as Guinnessville, because it is the home of the Guinness Book of Records."

My giggling friend had been asked only to check the spelling, not to comment on the text, and was being deviously tempted.

"Should I tell them?" he asked.

He did and the controversial commentary was axed by the chairman of the Olympic organizing committee.

Labeling is not altogether a bad habit. So many features of Korea that we can identify are strengths as much as they are weaknesses. Changing labels, such as your job title or rank, can help you reinvent yourself. Ceremony works in a similar way, and Koreans love ceremony. As one who abhors ceremony to the extent that I avoided my own graduation, it took me a while to appreciate the deep purpose behind the formality, of dressing up in funny clothes and doing things you don't normally do. Ceremony is the means by which you update your software. At a wedding, for example, two people go into a building, go through a ritual, and come out twenty minutes later having forever transformed in some magical way the way they conceive of themselves. Why? Who knows? People don't care, as long as it works. My failure to attend my graduation ceremony when I was twenty-two might explain why I was still thinking and behaving like a student at age thirty-two. In some ways, I still am. But Koreans are able to find closure, reinvent themselves, and move forward using ceremony.

As I reject any labels put on me by Koreans, the hypocrisy of lumping them as one group, and claiming they think and behave like this or like that, does not escape me. As intellectually attractive as it is, I fear it only makes limited sense to talk about a national character.

Nevertheless, I can confidently assert that Koreans are far more gregarious than, say, the British. At least, I will say this about Koreans over thirty. I am not sure yet about younger Koreans. It is possible that the cell phone and the PC are turning them in on themselves. But older Koreans are so into people. You don't find them wanting to get away from it all, and they don't make a national habit out of rolling their eyes at the prospect of being with their parents. They work hard at their relationships. They don't have fixed bedtimes and will stay up half the night talking with you, flop asleep on the floor, and get up early and go to work the next day.

Although we consider East Asians generally to be conservative and Westerners to be liberal, it is my subjective experience that Koreans are much more accepting and embracing of differences. I imagine that, as Confucians, the Koreans have an instinct for harmonious relationships with people, whereas the Christian and law-based culture of the West makes Westerners more concerned with issues of right and wrong and good and evil. The Koreans are less critical.

9

LOVE AND LEARNING
WHEN YOUR DNA ISN'T YOURS

"Hmm, I don't see a penis."

Training in life for a Korean begins in a nuclear family in, most likely, a city apartment, where, in contrast to her grandparents who grew up in large families with relatives in the village, she may be the lone child.

The glue that has held her extended family together forever is lineage, an attitude to family that is best understood as a line of code, "Your DNA is ours." Human beings move in their own streams, my parents flowing into me as I will flow into my children. From this code comes purpose. A man's single most important duty is to father a son, a woman's to join that man's family and bear its children.

Until recently, it was illegal for people from the same family clan, such as the Andong Kims, for example, to marry, even though the common ancestor may have been ten or twenty generations distant. There was nothing natural about this stricture. It applied only along patrilineal lines. There was very noisy opposition from a substantial, conservative segment of society to abolishing that ban. Confucianists in white robes demonstrated outside the National Assembly when the bill was being considered.

The old bonds of lineage have long shaped convictions about where ego and rights start and stop, about the extent to which family members can pry and control, that clash with those of the modern citizen. Traditionally, Korean family members merged into one another, interfering and clinging and interdepending to an extent that would drive the modern descendant, and in fact does, to the therapy group. Close physical contact is the norm. As infants, today's middle-aged Koreans spent half the day strapped to their mother's or grandmother's back. Carriages and playpens were rare because they separated parent and child. Children had the same bedtime as their parents and slept in the same bed until they entered elementary school at age seven.

Traditionally, the father was not so involved in family life. In many ways, he was a peripheral figure, making his appearance when the child, especially a son, needed direction and was old enough to listen and follow instructions. Thus older Koreans have deep attachment to their mothers and can be reduced to tears recalling their devotion. A father is often more fondly remembered for the guidance he gave and the sacrifice he showed toward a noble cause, like Korean independence or democracy, than to what he invested in the family.

These patterns have changed, although the old echoes still bounce off the bedroom walls. The extended family no longer lives together. Wives no longer quit work when they marry—a company must pay three months' maternity leave and hold the job open, unpaid, for an additional two if so requested—and have only one baby, maybe two, if at all, and certainly not five or ten like their mothers did. And it is more common now to see a baby strapped in a harness to the young father than to the mother. The exception is at home at night when the infant is restless. That's when granny deftly scoops him onto her back, a one-arm move the parents avoid for fear of dropping him, and ties him in a purpose-made blanket and walks up and down the living room until he's asleep.

Korean infants are more indulged than ordered about. You can tell the boys who were not taught to defer pleasure. As adults, they still want everything right now. They are impulsive and focused on the short term, and they throw tantrums when they don't get their way. A Western observer seeing the generalized patterns will consider Korean parents overtolerant of their children. They don't lecture them. In fact, they don't even explain much. As a result children learn by imitation and by knowing what makes grown-ups mad. Instead of being taught abstract principles—like, no you can't have that, because it's wrong to eat between meals—the tendency is to learn that some things are wrong in certain situations. You can't have it, because Dad's in a bad mood right now. The presence of older and younger brothers and sisters, and grandparents, all in the same house, used to provide a natural form of discipline. But this is often lacking in modern one- or two-child families, with the result that many adults complain the nation is raising a lot of spoiled, flabby-assed game addicts.

Another problem that goes back a long way but which manifests more starkly in the nuclear family is lack of communication. It is not done for Korean children to bring their problems to their parents. When families were large and extended, it was bad form for parents to demonstrate affection. Father may have been an austere figure and mother a saint, but physical affection and joy was experienced with siblings. Thus Koreans are not accustomed to seeing their parents as human beings with the same needs for love and fulfilment as they.

The emphasis in the parent-child relationship is on duties. Before urbanization shattered the extended family system, parents were required to work like slaves to provide for their children, correct them when they did wrong, and set a good example. In return, they got loyalty. Children, and particularly the eldest son, took care of them in their old age. Many Koreans are most deeply motivated to succeed in life or do what they do out of a sense of repaying the suffering and sacrifice of their parents. When parents are seen as victims, of the Japanese, of the military dictators, of poverty, this repaying becomes the motivating source of great filial energy. In the modern era Koreans have had opportunities to achieve greatness that were denied their impoverished parents.

The pattern of these ties is applied to close friends, alumni, and hometown. I found a lot of these attitudes rubbing off on me after a few years in Korea. You start looking for common ground and expecting obligations and favors when you find it. Many years ago, I strategically introduced myself at a reception to Yun Po-sun, who had been the president at the time of Park Chung-hee's coup, knowing he had graduated from the University of Edinburgh about fifty years earlier than I did. He responded with great warmth and invited me to his home a couple of times simply on the basis of this common connection.

Despite the projection of familial terms onto colleagues and even strangers—it's normal to call people older brother, older sister, grandmother, or grandfather—Koreans actually find it hard to extend the close trust learned in family and with childhood friends to strangers. If the individual is an island, connected under the water to family, there be monsters in the trench between them and the rest of society. People out there are "nonpersons" and there is no sense of obligation to them. There is no guilt about behaving unfairly or rudely toward someone who is "outside." Modern society outlaws overt bias, but you can't force people to bond with strangers. This unwillingness to connect manifests more subtly in the avoidance of eye contact and in body language that sends a certain keep-your-distance message.

I notice this coldness to other people when I slow down at a crosswalk. There are so many people in Seoul that cars don't normally do this. But when you do stop, it is very rare for someone to acknowledge you for it. In fact, once they know you've seen them, they often saunter more slowly across. Students are the worst.

As this suggests, Koreans are not big on civic-mindedness. At this writing, there is a campaign to remind people that it's an offense not to let emergency vehicles through. Most drivers think in power-abuse terms and assume the bastard has switched on the flashing light so he can get through quicker. Such attitudes give a sense of how Koreans view their country. There is, if the truth be told, a distinct lack of patriotism in Koreans. There may be nationalism, a fierce adherence to an identity, but there is not love of country.

Extended families usually get together for lunar new year and harvest thanksgiving holidays. In families where there are many siblings and cousins, gatherings are often great sprawling events that may begin with rituals in front of ancestral tablets, a visit to ancestral tombs and progress into gargantuan meals with, for the men especially, gallons of alcohol. The unusual feature of these affairs is that it's the older generation which misbehaves. The twenty-year-olds may not touch a drop and end up helping Dad, and sometimes Mom, shitfaced, into the car. If relatives have traveled a long way, the men may all crash on the floor of one room and the women in another. But this heaving—and often there is heaving—jollity among blood relatives does not mean that there are not conflicts and resentments.

Relationships between mothers and daughters-in-law are traditionally fraught with unexpressed disapproval and annoyance. Many first sons fail under the pressure of expectation. Other siblings may resent the love and favors bestowed on the eldest. A marriage can be a pain for the remaining singles in their twenties and thirties who get interrogated by uncles about their life plans. It is common for family members to cheat each other, especially when there's lots of money around. If a relative or a close friend has no collateral for a loan, he may ask you to help out. It may be difficult to refuse without damaging the relationship and, anyway, the borrower may present it in a way that makes it appear like just another example of meaningless bureaucracy, a signature on a bit of paper. When he defaults, the bank takes whatever you put down as collateral. I know of one couple who lost their house in this way.

When you are your DNA, you don't belong to yourself. That was clear in the past when it came to marriage. Which was, until recently, alarmingly young. One elderly acquaintance from North Korea was only thirty-five when he fled south but had already been married for twenty-three years. His wife was forty-two. In the early years, she would come and meet him from school and carry his satchel. This was not a rare story for the tabloids ("Korean lad pulls teaching assistant"), but a normal family arrangement and one which—yes, I had to ask—went unconsummated for some time. He left her behind to avoid the communists, thinking he'd be back soon but never saw her or his children again.

Even today, while outright arranged marriages are quite rare, the influence of the family in the choice of spouse is still enormous. This makes the process very calculating once a person decides it is time to marry.

"The shift to romantic relationships may be less than popular culture suggests," said James Turnbull, whose blog, The Grand Narrative, covers Korean sexuality and culture. "Specs such as income, family background, height, and even blood type become very important. The mentality and family influence of arranged marriage still exist in these factors."

It is very common for people in their twenties to be in long relationships, often with someone they met at college, and even secretly live together, then break up and marry other people in a matter of months. Young people can be remarkably shy about asking one another out, which makes it difficult to find partners. A lot of women rarely go on dates because they're not asked. Then they go overseas on vacation and find foreign men hitting on them before they're through immigration. As a result, there are all kinds of enterprising methods in Korea for bringing Adam and Eve together: hiking clubs, speed dating events, large dating events for the twenty-to-thirty-five set in restaurants, where, if you don't hit it off with someone, you can move to another restaurant that's taking part in the project.

All this effort means that fewer people marry as virgins. For men, this number is very low. Many have their first, and a lot of subsequent experiences, with prostitutes. Far from being furtive, they often do this in groups of friends or colleagues.

"I caught a seventh grader coming out of a brothel once," said Kim Kang-ja, a retired policewoman and former district police chief in Seoul. "He told me he didn't want to be a virgin."

Although it's illegal, attitudes that equate manliness with such behavior make the policing of prostitution difficult. A prostitute in Incheon in 2012 filed a complaint with police after a dispute over money with the brothel owner. As the customers had used credit cards, the police were able to identify them and make arrests. It turned out they were officers from another police station in the city who'd been out celebrating their promotions.

"One colleague told me our male colleagues all went to brothels and competed with each other for how long they could do it," Kim said. "High-ranking officials in the police, the tax offices, and elsewhere buy sex, regardless of their age, profession, or region. It's everywhere. This sex culture where men think money can buy anything distorts their view of women."

Supply meets demand, she added, because of the "materialism of women." The consequence is a twenty-billion-dollar industry involving two to three hundred thousand women.

When her jurisdiction included the Miari Texas red-light district of Seoul, Kim found two types of prostitute: "I figured around seven out of ten of the women could live without engaging in prostitution. They lived with their parents or were married and did it to earn money to pay for plastic surgery or things they wanted. The others needed the income. It was their only way to survive."

After a law allowing for crackdowns on prostitution passed in 2004 without consideration of these differences, she found that women in the thirty percent group were the more visible target and therefore more likely to be caught. That was because they worked in brothels in red-light areas near railroad stations and military bases, while the seventy percent tended to work more discreetly in high-class drinking establishments or could be summoned through Web sites. This led to demonstrations by prostitutes, hidden behind face masks, demanding the right as citizens in a free country to sell sex.

The seventy percent, meanwhile, quietly carried on or developed new ways to connect with potential customers that remain difficult to detect. For example, they signed up with karaoke bars, many of which have secret entrances that allow them to slip in when called by bar owners to entertain customers. In Ulsan a few years ago, when a team from a conglomerate went out to a karaoke bar and the executive in charge asked the owner to arrange for some women, one of the women who arrived turned out to be the wife of one of the men in the room.

Kim now favors legalizing prostitution for the thirty percent group—those women who more desperately need the work—and having government regulate it. She admits this is a pragmatic compromise, and that she still hopes society will outlaw the profession: "I find myself asking whether Koreans will always be this way. Materialism will always be there. But there is now a change in the attitude of men toward their families. In the past, men preferred drinking with colleagues. Now more and more want to go home to be with their family. This is very positive."

With modernization, women's rights have improved but Korea remains very low on the list of nations with a good track record on gender equality. Despite the inauguration of the first female president in 2013, there has even been a backlash of sorts in the workplace. Men now find themselves competing with women for jobs and are not amused at the lack of affirmative action in their favor. Many of them feel that men are primary breadwinners, while women work to make extra money or for something to do in their spare time.

This competition has led to denigrating terms such as *doenjang yeoja*—young women who skimp on essentials and live on bean paste (*doenjang*), spend their money instead on luxury items and hang out in Starbucks in rich neighborhoods waiting to be picked up by rich men.

A good measure of the modern woman's lot is the extent to which the fleeting male view of a woman—how she looks as she passes by—is enshrined in modern society. The obsession with physical beauty, shared by women, is embarrassingly superficial. Women applying for jobs must attach their photos (men, too, but they're not nearly as judged).

At the kindergarten and elementary school now, some fathers pick up their children. I know some couples where the wife is the breadwinner or at least earns more. Among these, though, some wives say they also do all the housework. I've learned to be skeptical when people moan about their spouse, but this one rings true. I'd bet a random thousand secret cameras would show ninety percent of men doing not much more than ten seconds of household chores a day if you don't count taking out the garbage on the way to work.

If women's rights are on the slow train in Korea, those of sexual minorities go by horse and cart. Despite the appearance of conservatism, South Korea, as we have seen, changes at an astonishing pace. Of course, when it comes to rights, legal changes take pressure and time and there's always someone who disagrees. But social change meets less resistance. It happens through demand, not debate. Consider, for example, in the streets of Seoul, you occasionally see a man, a placard preaching damnation strapped to his back, warning mankind through a portable loudspeaker that is high on volume but low on quality. If this were New York or London, he'd be met with such disdain that he'd give up. But in Seoul, nobody says anything. If you ask, they will say it's irritating or, if they're Christian, embarrassing. But I get the feeling that, unasked, people actually aren't thinking anything. The inner monk is running the show. They're just letting it be. And so it is when someone says they want this or that equal right. The problem comes when there is opposition, not because opposition has a point that we must now discuss, but because opposition, too, exists. It wants something contradictory.

Thus it is with sexual minorities. In 2014, Park Won-soon, a former human rights lawyer and then the mayor of Seoul, told *The San Francisco Examiner* that he hoped Korea would become the first Asian country to legalize same-sex marriage.[65] The mayor was proposing a Seoul City Charter of Human Rights that would include this. Christians, however, reacted with such force that the mayor backed away, saying the charter was "not worth pursuing if it causes social division." As politicians consider it political suicide to take on Christians, and other groups with votes, like taxi drivers and farmers, this will be a hard-fought battle, especially as there is a more committed opponent than the stereotypical conservative: the Full Gospel Church includes many former sex industry workers and believers who say Jesus has helped them turn away from homosexuality.[66]

Given their concern for lineage, Koreans are not big on adoption. Even modern Koreans exhibit an unconscionable disregard for discarded babies. It's been foreigners, Christian missionaries and American soldiers, who have stepped in. Since the Korean War, only four percent of abandoned babies have found homes in South Korea. Around two hundred thousand have been adopted overseas, over seventy percent of them by Americans, and over two million raised in orphanages. The government came up with a plan to completely phase out foreign adoptions out of nationalistic shame after newspaper articles accused the country of "selling its babies." The plan was dropped in 1994 due to the continuing low rate of adoptions by locals. In 2007, the government restricted the portion of overseas adoptions to ten percent of the annual total.[67]

That said, figures for local adoptions are misleading for they do not include the childless couples who adopt from family members. Also, there is no way to measure the numbers of adoptions where documents are falsified from birth. Small clinics are quite willing to do this discreetly and save families exposure and the hassle of legal adoption. Often only the husband, wife, and the doctor know. The woman will fake pregnancy, complaining to her friends and in-laws about morning sickness. In some cases, clinics act as matchmakers. When the time comes, the woman will check into a clinic where an unmarried woman is having a baby and has agreed to give it up. The two mothers may not actually meet. The clinic will write out the birth certificate in the adopting parents' names and hand the baby to them.

Such secrecy is extended to the child. He or she may never be told they are adopted because parents feel awareness of the lack of blood connection may make a child break the relationship. Not surprisingly, in vitro fertilization is big in Korea.

The traditional preference for sons manifested strongly until the 1990s in the form of pressure from mothers-in-law. Many would pressure their sons to dump a wife who could not produce a boy. Modern science provided the victims of this pressure with a way to gender-cleanse the unborn in the form of selective abortion. This problem first showed up when today's thirty-year-olds started elementary school. Teachers wondered why there were more boys in every class. The trend was traced back to the arrival of the ultrasound. Females were being aborted on a massive scale. In response, the government made it illegal for a doctor to reveal the sex of a fetus. This helped restore some balance but doctors were still letting on to patents who were insistent.

"I've got two boys. I hope this one's a girl," an expectant mother would fib.

"Hmm, I don't see a penis," the nurse might say. That's all the pregnant lady would need to hear. Armed with this intelligence, the expectant mother would go to another clinic and request an abortion.

The historical DNA outlook on life required a young upper-class man in old Korea to be somebody. Now that the lid has been lifted off the old kimchi pots of class, all young people, including women, may aspire to anything. Although for modern Koreans such aspiration is individual, the old echo is there. You must be somebody for your lineage. Such attitudes lie behind the obsession with education.

Koreans have had a lot of practice with formal schooling. The earliest reference is to a *Daehak* ("great school," now the word for "university") in the year 372 and a *Kukhak* ("national college") in 682. In the year 992, an institution called *Kugjagam* was set up to replace the earlier schools and education changed its focus to help prepare upper-class youngsters for civil service careers. In 1398, the new Confucian regime replaced it with *Sungkyunkwan*, now Korea's oldest surviving university. Traditionally, an ambitious boy could rise to the top—which meant becoming a government official—by memorizing the Chinese classics and passing the civil service exam. It took the arrival of Protestant missionaries in the 1880s to begin the process of change. Within a few years, they had established Yonhui (later renamed Yonsei) and Ewha University in Seoul, and Soongshil College in Pyongyang. A few years later Korea University was established by a private citizen and Buddhists founded Dongguk University. Future leaders of Korea emerged from this handful of campuses.

Although the Japanese colonial government in the first half of the twentieth century introduced a modern system with both private and state-run elementary, middle, and high schools, most families could only afford a few years of the old-style, village Confucian tutoring for their children. By 1945, only twenty percent of Koreans were literate.

After independence, resources were severely limited and, during the Korean War, these were further depleted when many teachers joined the North Korean cause or were forcibly taken north. Some who remained fled to Busan, where they taught classes in refugee camps. The government set up a Wartime Union College and opened state-funded universities in provincial capitals freed from North Korean forces. Teachers and children huddled in overcoats, often in war-damaged buildings. They were short of textbooks, paper, and pencils. The 1950s were a time of sheer struggle to survive, and the kind of opportunities in business and politics that arose were often taken by the forceful and the enterprising, not the educated. But these people went on to surround themselves with better-educated assistants, the boys who had broken the ice in their inkwells on winter mornings and shivered through their lessons, and then gone on to get their PhDs from Harvard and Yale.

By the late 1970s, Korea had the highest level of education vis-à-vis wages in the world. Today, literacy is one hundred percent, thanks to the *Hangul* spelling system which is so uniform that a young person does not need to spend years learning how to read and write in it. Ninety-five percent of all Koreans graduate high school and, of these, four in five enroll in college. These figures make the Koreans the most highly educated in the world.

There is one unfortunate feature to this, not a rule applied to all, but a direction at the outset. Children are more driven to achieve credentials than to be good. While in kindergartens today there is a great deal of professionalism and concern among teachers to raise moral, caring children, parents at the school fence push teachers for results. They anxiously enroll kids in piano, ballet, taekwondo, English.

Studies show that with children in the early grades, praising character rather than behavior is more conducive to confidence and learning. In other words, telling a child she is good at languages after a good result in her English has a deeper impact than praising her for the exam result, which risks the interpretation, "Mom only cares about the good results, not me." Criticism over results follows a similar pattern. Mothers especially can be so anxious that they respond to bad test results with anger or threats, or by withdrawing affection or being moody. The net effect of such behavior is that children feel useless instead of feeling that they didn't work hard enough, which in turn might motivate them to do better the next time. It is little wonder that school violence and bullying is at its worst in middle school.

Oh Kyung-ja, a retired professor of psychology believes it is natural for young people to be unsure of themselves but that the Korean system seems to sustain such insecurity:

Everyone has deeply ingrained insecurities. We are thrown helpless into the world, grow up, and run into frustrations.

Some societies impose more pressures than others to be good and avoid being sidelined. Korea has really enhanced academic achievement which inevitably gives a sense of inferiority to the majority of children because only one can be number one. When I was at school, our weekly score was posted on the wall. In fifth grade, we would have to change our seats in the classroom according to these marks. To get to the best middle school, there was an exam. If four hundred got through, hundreds more didn't. It was the same at high school and university. Even within Seoul National University, which is considered the top, the law and economic departments are considered superior to others. Some select just twenty out of hundreds of applicants. Then even the twenty are competing. Few people go through life without failing. I went to the United States so I could forget all about this.

Now those intermediary exams have been stopped and children go to the neighborhood schools (although they may go to private schools at the elementary and high school levels) and competition is focused on the university entrance exam. "This makes the experience of education now like running a marathon without prescreening. Too many young people have unrealistic expectations," she said. "They don't have to feel like losers. But they do. It's the result of twenty years of brainwashing."

The rank order is so deeply ingrained that parents are resisting efforts now by schools to deemphasize it.

"I didn't group my kids into classes according to ability like most kindergartens," said Rob Ouwehand, when he was the director of a private English kindergarten in Seoul, "Parents would ask me if their kid was in the brightest class. I'd tell them that we've stopped doing classes by ranking. 'We're aiming for a personality mix that allows for more social development,' I'd say. Then they'd go, 'I see . . . but is my kid at the top of his class, at least?'"

The great irony is that the quality of the education they are torturing themselves to receive is questionable. In school, young Koreans are taught a number of things about life that we would find objectionable. For example, that in the world there is one way to success.

This is not a culture in which diversity is seen as a value or an ideal. Koreans see virtue in unity: one mind, one people, one system, one race, one path. The education system reinforces this idea. The artistic but ill-disciplined student, or the creative thinker who wants to challenge established thinking, may have nowhere to go. Education in Korea is all about what appears in the textbook and in the exam; life experience, critical thinking, and creativity receive little attention.

I was once asked by the head of a global company if I could write a report he could send to the head office explaining why the people he was hiring were so unprepared for the workforce. "They're well educated but they can't problem solve," he said. "They're nice people but they just sit there and agree with everything I say." He couldn't believe they had actually attended the nation's most prestigious universities. As a result of the report, in which I suggested that graduates from second-tier colleges who had a chip on their shoulders could prove to be bigger risk-takers at work, he introduced a ban on hiring from Seoul National, Yonsei, and Korea universities for the duration of his five-year posting. I felt a little guilty about that.

A symptom of both the frustration with the school system that wrecks the teenage years with pressure, and at the same time an indicator of the lengths families will go to for any advantage is that, given the chance, every mother would turn her back on a Korean education and enroll her child in a foreign school if she could afford it.

The government by law prevents Korean parents from sending their children to the foreign schools in Korea unless they have previously lived and studied overseas for three years. For this reason, around the turn of the century, middle-class parents started sending children to elementary, middle, and high schools abroad. The cost, I was told by friends who were "goose" fathers—who lived alone in Seoul and flew to the U.S., Canada, Australia, and New Zealand, where their wives had taken the children—was about the same if the cost of extra tuition from cramming institutes was factored in. The numbers peaked in 2006 at around thirty thousand and have since dropped by 2014 to eleven thousand. One reason is that the government has created an "education-free zone" on Jeju Island and permitted three foreign schools to operate there for tuition-paying

Korean students. Similarly, around a quarter of a million Koreans opt each year to study at universities overseas.[68]

Such figures reflect the desire for Koreans to excel now that the opportunity is available. It is an opportunity that, as they are well aware, generations of ancestors never enjoyed.

ROOTS

10

BEGINNINGS

*There is no reason to strain ourselves
unreasonably to copy the Chinese way.*

Through a great sweep of history, much longer and better chronicled than the European story, the Koreans have remained a distinct people. They have a tradition, language, and identity of their own, preserved thanks to relative geographic isolation, and through warfare, strategic subservience, and sullen resistance.

To understand modern Koreans, this national biography is best read in three broad periods: the long era from prehistory until the arrival of the neo-Confucian state in 1392; the five-hundred-year experience under China's influence; and the twentieth-century colonial rule under Japan. This brings us up to the split into two countries and the big question of how it will play out.

Scholars believe that today's Koreans are descended from the Neolithic families that came into the peninsula in what were probably three successive migrations between 5500 BC and 2000 BC. There is evidence that Paleolithic man lived thirty to forty thousand years ago on the peninsula, but there is none that links them to present-day Koreans. The first Neolithic Koreans grouped in clans that identified themselves by totems taken from nature, and worshipped gods of the wind, rain, and cloud. They lived in pits and caves and relied mostly on the coastal areas for food. They were eating rice by 4400 BC and millet by 3600 BC but full-scale farming came late, after the appearance of bronze around 1500 BC.[69]

Bronze Age clans appear to have lived side by side with the older Neolithic inhabitants, but to have been ethnically different. They may have been tribes of the Altaic language group of central Asia. The newcomers were not as artistic as the Neolithic natives, judging by fragments of their pottery, but they had better weapons and prevailed. This story is not completely understood and the details are still contested. But we do know that the Altaic tribes that came into Korea saw themselves as "sons of heaven" and that they built dolmens at burial sites, some of which still exist. Two points from this period are apparent: First, there's been no ethnic mixing since that time on any significant scale with the possible exception of the Mongol invaders of the thirteenth century, which makes Koreans among the most genetically homogeneous on earth; and, second, the original Koreans were ethnically and linguistically different from the Chinese tribes.

There is a theory that the Altaic tribes scattered eastward to Mongolia, Manchuria, and Korea, and westward where they ended up in places like Hungary and Finland. But this is based on some flimsy similarities in language. Archaeological evidence would offer better proof but there is, of course, only so much you can deduce from jugs—and they don't offer much of a story to tell your children. As you would expect, there are other explanations for Korean origins that better suit the human need for meaning and which are better preserved by the anecdotal mind. My favorite comes from old texts recording a history that allegedly began nine thousand years ago with a couple called Na-ban and A-man, the parents of the original five races of mankind. These two met at an Eden-like place where four rivers rose, which is taken to be either Lake Baikal in Russia or Lake Chonji on the present-day border of North Korea and China. We're talking here about Adam and Eve, who were, according to this theory, Koreans.

The standard account of Korean origins is contained in the myth of the first great ruler, Dangun.[70] His story is worth outlining because the governments of both North and South Korea make significant use of it.

According to ancient records, Hwanung, the son of the celestial being, Hwanin, descended from heaven and lived as a king among the humans. He came with three thousand followers. A bear and a tiger living in the same cave asked Hwanung to transform them into human beings. The king gave them a bundle of sacred mugworts and twenty cloves of garlic and said: "If you eat these and shun the sunlight for one hundred days you will assume human form." The bear succeeded and after twenty-one days turned into a woman. The bear-woman prayed for a child. Hwanung turned himself into a tiger-man, swapped pajamas with her, and they had little Dangun. In the fiftieth year of the reign of Emperor Yao of China, Dangun made the walled city of Pyongyang the capital, called his country Joseon, and ruled for fifteen hundred years.[71]

So much information peeps through this tale. In particular, the year is precisely identified as 2333 BC, which lays the foundation for the often-heard claim in modern Korea that the country has five thousand years of history. This was when the Great Pyramid was built in Egypt. We can presume that "heaven" was up north, and that the bear and the tiger were the totems of resident Neolithic tribes being usurped. It has been suggested that Dangun was the son of a Bronze Age chieftain and a Neolithic woman of the bear tribe. Korea's political culture dates back to the walled-town states of this period. Their leaders were called *Dangun Wang-geom*, which suggests that Dangun could have been several people, especially if we take the fifteen-hundred-year reign seriously.

Dangun is said to have worshipped on the top of Mount Mani, a peak near the coast west of Seoul. I climbed it once on a lone search, hoping to learn something about the father of the Korean people. It was a wet and murky day in early spring. I parked the car at the foot of the mountain and walked up along the well-trodden tourist trail. As I made it up the steep path, I got into thick cloud—appropriate, I thought, for this climb to prehistory. The wind blew in unnaturally loud flurries, which I fancied were evil spirits trying to frighten me off. I wondered why the wind wasn't blowing away the mist. It hung there trying to spook me. By the time I got to the top I was in a really shamanistic frame of mind. Then, there it was—a large stone altar looming ahead in the mist. When I clambered up on it, I was in for a real shock. I don't know what I had expected but it was certainly not something this new. Even accounting for some recent restoration, this construction was not forty-three-hundred years old. In fact, the altar looked distinctly modern. Something was fishy.

The source of the Dangun story was a patriotic Buddhist monk named Ilyeon who was writing in the 1280s, when Mongol hordes swept into Korea. He relied on written sources from several hundred years earlier that no longer survive.[72] But even those chroniclers were writing about events that had allegedly happened a good twenty-seven hundred years earlier, unless of course the dates then were calculated differently. Shrines to Dangun are believed to have been built around the fifteenth and sixteenth centuries. However, the idea of him as a common ancestor with heavenly connections is embarrassingly modern, twentieth century in fact. The religion *Daejong-gyo*, which kicked off Dangun worship, began in 1909. Nationalist historians in the 1930s, when Korea was ruled by Japan, reworked the myth into its present shape as a counter to Japanese efforts to work Koreans—as "adopted" citizens—into their own fictional sun-god genealogy. Previous Korean rulers had sought to trace their lineage back to different figures. For example, the Yi clan, which ruled when those first known shrines to Dangun were built, considered Chi Tzu a more important ancestor. He was a Chinese sage whom legend credits with settling in Korea and calling the state *Joseon* in the twelfth century BC. In 1948, the government declared that the people's history had begun in 2333 BC and made Dangun's birthday a national holiday.[73] The cement on the altar would not even have been dry. I expected to find something four millennia old; instead I learned something more relevant—the rewriting of history.

Some Christians have proposed Hwanin, Hwanung, and Dangun as a kind of holy trinity with the bear as a Mother Mary figure. A cheekier attempt to hijack the myth to fit modern purpose has been made by North Korean authorities. In the 1990s they excavated a tomb they claimed to be Dangun's, and put his eight-foot-long bones and those of his wife on display. The none-too-subtle message being that the Kim dictatorship is the continuation of the line stretching back into the collective memory and therefore the legitimate authority on the peninsula.[74]

Before we leave Dangun, we should note that, according to ancient Chinese historians, it was he who named his state *Joseon*. This word is usually translated to mean "Land of Morning Calm." *Gojoseon* (Old Joseon) as it is now referred to, was a territory covering roughly the Pyongan provinces of modern North Korea. This name lasted, if our chronology is accurate, from 2333 BC to 108 BC. A new regime in 1392 revived the name, which lasted into the twentieth century. When the Japanese ruled Korea they called it, in English spelling, Chosen. North Korea retains this word in its name, *Choson Minju-jui Inmin Gonghwa-guk* (Democratic People's Republic of Korea).

While Koreans have been willing throughout their history to absorb Chinese cultural influences, they have strongly resisted political control by China. In the first century BC when the Goguryeo state was being founded, China's Han Dynasty established four commanderies, or colonies, in the northwestern part of the peninsula. When the dynasty collapsed and China was fragmenting into local states, Goguryeo conquered these colonies and expanded deep into what today is the Manchurian part of China. This historical legacy and the fact that there are almost two million Korean-speaking Chinese in an autonomous area next to North Korea today has laid a foundation for irredentism. This albeit dormant desire to recover lost territory was one factor on the minds of the Chinese in 1950 when they entered the Korean War on the North Korean side. An adviser to the South Korean joint chiefs of staff in the early 1990s told me how shocked he was to have some young officers come up to him after a lecture asking whether he agreed that an eventual unified Korea should reclaim this lost territory. China has been sufficiently upset by South Korean visitors stirring up nationalistic sentiment to have complained about it to Seoul.

By the fourth century BC, the peninsular tribes had consolidated into three kingdoms—Goguryeo, Baekje, and Silla.

The founding of China's Sui Dynasty in 581 was bad news for Goguryeo. China's neighbors had always suffered when she was unified. It took seventeen years but the first invasion came with Sui China seeking to pacify those it called "Eastern Barbarians." This one was repulsed and, after another few years' building up to it, the Chinese invaded with a force of more than one million troops.

This time they were up against a foe of cunning genius. Goguryeo Army Commander Eulji Mundeok mixed head-on attack with guerrilla tactics, when it suited him, and strategic retreat and deception, when the odds were harsh. We don't know what Eulji looked like, but one classic portrait suggests a refined kind of killer. It shows him in armadillo armor, his head sticking out as if it were separately connected and could slide back into the shell. The retractable head is swathed in more armor and topped with a two-horned crown, leaving just the face showing, for communication. An inverted black pyramid of a beard points down perfectly from the chin and an RAF fighter-pilot moustache swoops symmetrically across the cheeks. Between these is a thin, mean mouth and, above it, mean, dead eyes. If there were audio the face would say "I will now eat your liver." In reality, he may actually have looked like a vicar, because when three hundred thousand Sui soldiers besieged the capital of Pyongyang and Eulji entered their camp to say he wanted to surrender, they believed him. History hasn't recorded exactly what happened. Perhaps there was a handshake and a ceremony. All we know is that Eulji was allowed to depart, intelligence-gathering mission accomplished.

Back at base, he passed on the observation that the Chinese troops were weak with hunger and in no shape to fight. As the Sui force turned back to China, he pursued them mercilessly. Only twenty-seven hundred survived, according to Korean records. It was one of the most calamitous defeats in Chinese military history. Enfeebled, the Sui Dynasty collapsed shortly after.

The repulse of this threat to Korean civilization is still celebrated. In addition to the name of the road by the Lotte Hotel in downtown Seoul, Eulji is also the name for annual U.S.-South Korean military exercises.

Goguryeo itself, however, would only last another fifty years. After its victory over the Chinese it swiveled its sights south and took on Silla and Baekje. This rivalry echoes in present-day regional loyalties. In postwar South Korea, the southwestern Jeolla region, roughly the same area as Baekje, has contended for political power against the conservative southeastern Gyeongsang region, the Silla homeland, while communist North Korea has assumed the mantle of Goguryeo.

The ultimate victor of this three-corner contest would be Silla. Historians in different eras have always found this a surprising outcome, not only because Goguryeo was battle tested, but also because Silla was handicapped: It had a female ruler. Queen Seondeok had strengthened her position within Silla after coming to the throne in 632 by sponsoring the growth of Buddhism as a way to gain popular acceptance. This development also reflected the influence of China's Tang Dynasty, the successors to the Sui. Korean monks went to study Buddhism in China and enormous, exotic temples were built.

Differing Buddhist sects placed varying emphasis on scriptural study, prayer, and Zen meditation. The monk Wonhyo appealed for harmony between the sects and, as penance for breaking his celibacy vows and fathering a son with a princess, spread a simple form of the faith—Pure Land Buddhism—based on a single chant. He converted over 80 percent of the common people.

At this time Silla was being attacked by its western neighbor, Baekje, a kingdom with a rich artistic culture and which traded with China and Japan. Baekje scholars were sent to Japan to teach Chinese classics, which had a significant impact on the development of the then-emerging Japanese nation. Its royals married into what would become Japan's imperial family, a fact that Japanese nationalists tried to keep hidden until Emperor Akihito acknowledged it in 2001.

When Queen Seondeok sent her nephew and top diplomat, Kim Chunchu, to Goguryeo to ask for help in fighting Baekje, the northerners incarcerated him, releasing him only after Silla threatened war. Silla then turned to Tang China. When Kim succeeded his aunt and became King Muyeol he and his new Chinese allies attacked both Goguryeo and Baekje.

The military hero of these wars was Kim Yusin, the king's brother-in-law. While Eulji is remembered for repelling a Chinese

invasion, Kim is credited with unifying the three peninsular kingdoms. Kim was a product of the Silla's elite *Hwarang* (Flower of
Youth) Corps, which some argue served as the model for the Japanese
samurai and their bushido code. Members were trained in warfare,
poetry, music, patriotism, and communal life. The core principles of
Hwarang training were loyalty to the king, filial piety, comradeship,
bravery in battle, and discrimination in the taking of life.

According to ancient records, the gods looked out for him. Once,
the young Kim was on a spying expedition unaware that his com-
panion was luring him into a trap. In one village for the night, three
girls served him some tasty cakes and, as teenagers do, Kim fell in
love with all three of them on the spot.

> "My beautiful ladies," he said, "You are three laughing flowers
> and I am a humming bee. Will you suffer me to suck honey
> from your golden hearts the whole night?"
>
> "Yes," they replied coyly, "we understand. Come to the for-
> est with us and there we shall have our pleasure in beds of
> fragrant flowers, unseen and unheard by the other boy."
>
> So Kim Yusin went into the forest with the three girls, but
> as soon as they arrived the girls changed into noble goddesses.
> "We are no laughing flowers or nymphs," they told Kim Yusin,
> "but three goddesses who guard the three sacred mountains.
> We have come to warn you that you are being lured by an
> enemy spy. Be on your guard! Farewell!" And with these
> words the three goddesses rose into the sky and flew away.
> Kim Yusin prostrated himself before the departing goddesses
> and then returned to the sleeping spy. Early next morning
> Kim Yusin woke him and said, "Look. We started on our long
> journey to a foreign country in such a hurry that I forgot my
> purse and left it at home. Let's go back and get it before going
> any farther."[75]

Back in Gyeongju, Kim had the spy arrested, tortured, and executed. Having been a teenager, I can think of another reason to get
raging mad and kill your friend when three girls disappear on you,
but we just don't know the friend's version of the story. The rest of

Kim's story, as far as we know, is true: He conquered Baekje in 660 and Goguryeo in 668 with the help of the Tang armies, then had to give the Tang the Manchurian half of Goguryeo.

Modern nationalist historians have criticized Silla for relying on China's help in the first place, saying that it set a historical pattern whereby Koreans instinctively call on outside powers to help solve internal problems. That may be so but more important, Silla represented the first flowering of what can be identified as a distinctive Korean culture.

By 675, when the Silla-Tang war ended, Korea had a more advanced civilization than any in Europe, which was falling into the chaos of the Dark Ages. It was creating a centralized state, establishing educational institutes, and boasted impressive cultural, scientific, and technological advancements such as the Cheomseongdae astronomical observatory.

It is estimated that a million people lived in Gyeongju at its height, which would have made it one of the most populated cities in the world. It was a center of great learning and creativity. Choe Chi-won, a preeminent scholar and the man in charge of drafting royal proclamations, wrote twenty volumes on his experiences in China. This collection is the oldest surviving Silla document. Seol Chong, the son of the monk Wonhyo, developed a Chinese phonetic writing system for the Korean language. Silla's cultural legacy is evident in the stone pagodas, bronze temple bells, and royal tombs scattered around Gyeongju and in the nearby Bulguksa Temple and Seokguram Grotto, which features a ten-foot granite Buddha.

Silla was the last Korean political entity to accept female rulers (two followed Queen Seondeok) until Park Geun-hye became the South Korean president in 2013.

Although Silla may have adopted a relatively liberal attitude in allowing women high status, it otherwise operated under a stifling social order. Its bone-rank system, as it was known, would eventually prove to be its undoing.

Bone-ranks, or hereditary bloodlines, governed everything from the job you had to the house you could occupy, the clothes you could wear, and the utensils you could use.

By the time of the Unified Silla Kingdom, the highest rank of

Hallowed Bone had disappeared and the monarch and the nobility came from the True Bone class who lived off land rent and taxes. Head Ranks six to four represented the hereditary elites who held government posts. Below them were merchants, artisans, fishermen, farmers, and a substantial slave class.

Social status based on birth still has echoes in modern Korean society. One stark illustration is the *songbun* system in North Korea by which the population is divided into three main categories—core, wavering, and hostile—and about fifty sub-grades. *Songbun* determines access to education and employment and even the type of punishment an offender can expect to receive. It is based on a family's political, social, and economic background. Those whose families fought with North Korean founder Kim Il-sung against the Japanese before and during World War Two have the highest status; former landowning families have the lowest. The *songbun* system has been blamed for North Korea's faltering economic development because it prevents the state from rewarding its most productive people.

The same problem applied to the bone-rank system in United Silla. Take the story of Jang Bogo, for example. A man of humble birth, he created an extensive maritime shipping empire and briefly established the country as an important regional trading center with China and Japan in the mid-ninth century. As his wealth grew, Jang sought to acquire political power by marrying his daughter to a Silla king he had supported in a brief civil war. The marriage, which violated the sacred bone-rank order, proved too much for the aristocrats, who sent an assassin to kill him in his island fortress off the southwest coast. Jang is now celebrated in popular culture and in 2014 South Korea's second Antarctic research station was named after him.

By the late 800s, United Silla was being internally challenged by renegade aristocrats who had become regional warlords seeking to revive the earlier glories of Baekje and Goguryeo. One of them, Wang Geon, who represented the Goguryeo faction, defeated all challengers and in 936 established a new unified state he called Goryeo. He located the capital in his birthplace of Kaesong in what is now North Korea.

Wang Geon, who renamed himself Taejo (Great Founder), favored a policy of peaceful assimilation for his defeated foes and was kind enough to marry the daughters of as many as twenty-eight local rulers. Goryeo also incorporated parts of Balhae, an independent kingdom to the north, after the rest of it had been conquered by the Khitan tribes emerging from Mongolia.

This pushed Goryeo's borders northward to the Yalu River, creating a single state that had roughly the same boundaries until the peninsula's division in 1945.[76]

In 943, Wang Geon issued what would be considered Goryeo's founding document, the Ten Injunctions. These rules would have a major influence on the governance and structure of the kingdom during its lifespan of nearly five hundred years. Buddhism was essentially given the status of a state religion while Confucianism was formally endorsed as the source of principles for managing state affairs.

Although both Buddhism and Confucianism had come from China, Wang Geon also sought to raise awareness of a distinct Korean identity by embracing the shamanistic and geomantic elements of Korea's native culture. "Our country occupies a different geographical position and our people's character is different from that of the Chinese. Hence, there is no reason to strain ourselves unreasonably to copy the Chinese way," he declared.[77]

While Wang Geon was willing to absorb the Silla and Balhae elites into the new bureaucratic order, he harbored a grudge against those from the former Baekje region. The Ten Injunctions specially barred government posts to people from the region because Baekje suffered from negative geomantic and cultural features, he explained. This declaration would establish a tradition of discrimination against those from the southwest part of Korea that has lasted until the present day.

Among the reforms in the early days of Goryeo was the selection of government officials by state examinations, a concept borrowed from China and which introduced a meritocratic element diluting the influence of the Silla bone-rank system.

The flowering of Goryeo's Buddhist culture, along with the native shamanistic and geomantic influences, produced some of the country's greatest achievements including celadon pottery which Chinese connoisseurs believed to be the most beautiful in the world.

The Buddhist establishment also pioneered advances in printing that would eventually lead Korea to create moveable metal type, the key to mass printing, two centuries before Johannes Gutenberg, who is regarded in the West as its inventor. Monks produced some of the world's earliest extant examples of woodblock printing, one indication of the high level of the country's literacy. By the tenth century, an early version of the Tripitaka Koreana, a set of eighty thousand wooden blocks that contained the text of nearly the entire East Asian Buddhist canon, was being made. This led the way to the world's first use of moveable metal-type printing in 1234.

As the power of Buddhism grew, it posed a political threat to Goryeo's rulers. In the early twelfth century, a charismatic monk called Myocheong convinced King Injong to move the capital to Pyongyang. The king's advisers eventually dissuaded him, cautioning trickery, and he cancelled the transfer of the capital. In response, Myocheong fomented a rebellion that was crushed after a year by forces led by Kim Busik.

This episode led the central authorities over the next centuries to regard the Pyongyang region as a potential source of trouble. Kim Busik, a descendent of the Silla royal family, sanctioned the writing of *The History of the Three Kingdoms*, the first great court record, which emphasized the role the Silla had played in the country's pre-Goryeo history. Thus the regions continued their ancient struggle within the unified structure.

Goryeo also saw the emergence of the *yangban* (two orders) system under which high officials were divided into civilian and military classes. With marauding tribes harassing the northern border, military officials had gradually gained political influence. In 1170, after a civilian official slapped an army officer in front of the king, enraged officers staged a coup. The rebels placed a new king on the throne and the military effectively ruled the country for the next century until the Mongols invaded.

When the first invasion began in 1231, the Goryeo court fled to the island of Ganghwa, off the country's west coast and near present-day Seoul. And while the court remained relatively safe in its sanctuary, the Mongol hordes roamed freely through the rest of the country, abusing the populace and destroying cultural artifacts.

In 1270, after the last military strongman behind the throne was assassinated, the king sued for peace.

The Goryeo kings would continue to enjoy semiautonomy as vassals, but their Mongol overseers largely dictated policy. In 1274, for example, Goryeo was enlisted in the Mongols' disastrous attempt to invade Japan by building boats for the invasion fleet and supplying troops. Future Goryeo rulers were required to marry princesses from the Mongol Yuan Dynasty in China. This reflected a more widespread trend that was affecting the general population, with DNA evidence suggesting that a sizeable number of Korean women bore children fathered by Mongol conquerors. Korean culture from food to language was also influenced by the Mongols.

The Mongol rulers demanded "tribute women" from Goryeo to serve as their concubines. Some ascended to the highest levels of the Yuan court. The best remembered is Lady Gi, who came to Beijing and caught the eye of the Chinese emperor. She rose in rank to become the emperor's primary consort and, as Empress Gi, was regarded by many as Yuan China's unofficial ruler. From this position, she exercised her influence to have her family assigned to important posts in Goryeo, where they soon became a target of hate for their lavish lifestyle, venality, and abuse of power.

The decline of the Yuan Dynasty allowed King Gongmin, the last Goryeo king, to purge the Gi family, but it also created chaos, making Goryeo vulnerable to attack by rebels in China known as the Red Turbans from the north and by Japanese pirates from the southeast. This set the stage for the rise of the military leader Yi Song-gye, who would overthrow the Goryeo rulers and establish what would turn out to be the country's longest ruling dynasty.

THE QUEST FOR PURITY

Failure to bow was a hanging offense.

By the end of the fourteenth century, scholar-officials were embracing a neo-Confucian doctrine and siding with small-scale landowners to break the power of the Goryeo court elite, landowners, and their Buddhist supporters.

The outcome of that ideological conflict is felt today, coloring many aspects of the country's culture. The prominent historical figures who appear on South Korea's four currency notes all date from the first two centuries of the Joseon period and include two neo-Confucian thinkers.

Neo-Confucianism began in Song China in the eleventh and twelfth centuries and influenced the Mongol court in Beijing, where it was adopted by visiting Korean scholars looking to revive and refashion the classical texts of Confucianism and systemically apply them to solve social and political problems.

The new interpretation reworked Confucius's original teaching

about reciprocal responsibilities between ruler and subject to emphasize obedience for the sake of social harmony. Filial piety became the
core ethic. This is the version of Confucianism espoused by modern
regimes from China to Singapore.

The neo-Confucians gained an important ally when Jeong
Do-jeon, one of its leaders, met General Yi Seong-gye, who had been
successful in repelling the Chinese Red Turbans and Japanese pirates.[78] Both men came from relatively humble backgrounds and
harbored grievances against the Goryeo elite.

In 1388, the king sent Yi off to attack China, a mission he disagreed with because his new neo-Confucian friends considered the
Ming Dynasty to be the home of Confucian civilization. The dis-
gruntled general turned his troops around at the border and marched
back almost unopposed to the capital. The tearful king was placed
on a horse and sent off with his queen and a concubine into internal
exile and a replacement installed, with General Yi in de facto control. In 1392 he stepped out of the shadows and declared the end of
Goryeo after 456 years. In its place he established his own Joseon
Dynasty and adopted the title of King Taejo.

Along with a new name, he decided to move the capital to present-
day Seoul, which has remained the political, economic, and cultural
center of Korea ever since.[79]

King Taejo's neo-Confucian thinkers, led by Jeong Do-jeon,
restructured the bureaucracy and society. Joseon became the most
orthodox of such dynasties in East Asian history.

It is widely believed that the zeal to out-Chinese the Chinese
came from a survival strategy as the Koreans sought to raise themselves from inferior barbarian state to younger brother to the Middle
Kingdom. In fact, the new rulers saw themselves more as partners in
maintaining the values of a greater Confucian civilization.

To do this, they took steps to centralize power. Land taxes, for
example, flowed directly into the central government's coffers, while
the population was subject to military and labor service. Increased
state control over the economy hindered the growth of private sector
capital in contrast to the trends in Europe at the time that were laying the foundations for Europe's growth.

Joseon was particularly intolerant of the perceived abuses of the

Buddhist establishment and sought to curtail, if not destroy, it. Even though some kings maintained a private faith in Buddhism, the religion was restricted and state and family religious ceremonies were replaced with Confucian rituals. Under the new utopianism, politics became the supreme pursuit. This predominance of power interests is still a notable feature of the Korean mind-set today.

In keeping with the modest background of its founders, the new regime also introduced measures to benefit the common people, mainly through land reform. All current ownership was declared invalid, land near the capital was given to officials according to rank and the rest became state property. This measure destroyed the powerful nobles and undermined the Buddhist establishment, but strengthened the livelihood of the peasantry, who were given new tenancy guarantees.

Early Joseon was an ascetic country. Conspicuous consumption was abhorred and no one of high social background would engage in it. Social stability, not development, was seen as the measure of successful rule. The neo-Confucians thought the perfect society began not with the system, but with the personal morality of the monarch. They believed that immoral leadership caused instability. Looked at the other way around, instability was indication of a flawed leadership, even when no obvious flaws were visible. The wise king knew to select learned bureaucrats both for his own education and for the implementation of virtuous policy. The most important means for ensuring the best talent for these positions was the extensive use of examinations to select officials, which had been pioneered during the Goryeo Dynasty. The most important was the civil service examination, which tested knowledge of Confucian classics, history, and literature.

As Confucian education was all about ethics, the state was in theory ensuring that it recruited its most ethical young men as the future decision-makers. These notions behind the arrangement of fifteenth-century bureaucracy still have strong resonance in modern Korea.

Naturally, in Joseon, the establishment of schools was a priority. Young boys were educated in the ethics with regard to the five relationships of Confucius: a son's filial piety to his father, a subject's loyalty to his ruler, a woman's obedience to her husband, deference of youngsters to their elders, and honesty between friends. These first two were especially important and failure in this regard meant dishonor worse than death.

Neo-Confucian doctrine also gradually reduced the social status of women. The adoption of Confucian family law meant an adherence to a strict patrimonial system, with eldest sons favored over their mothers and sisters.

Scholar-officials were given the responsibility to ensure that the state charted a politically correct course. One innovation was the introduction of offices to monitor and prevent arbitrary decisions and abuse of power by the king or other officials.

However, the failure of practice to match theories about filial piety were evident from the beginning of the Joseon Dynasty. One of Taejo's sons, Yi Bang-won, ordered Jeong Do-jeon's death because the esteemed scholar favored one of the prince's brothers as the successor. The king was so distraught that he abdicated in 1398, clearing the way for Bang-won to assume the throne as King Taejong two years later.

Despite this turmoil in its first decade, Taejong is credited with placing the new kingdom on a secure footing. He established the basic administrative setup of a High State Council and six government bureaus that would last until the late nineteenth century. He instituted travel identity tags to control the movement of the population. His goal was to create the image of the monarch as an authoritative Confucian sage.

That ideal was personified by his son, King Sejong, who is so highly regarded by South Koreans that they have attached the suffix "great" to his name. He is their Washington, Jefferson, and Lincoln rolled into one. His name is on everything from universities to infrastructure projects and his face adorns the 10,000-*won* note.

Sejong's reign (1418–50) was a time of peace and prosperity. But his reputation was built on his innovations. A scholar, he set up a research institute called the Hall of Worthies, where great minds developed scientific devices such as rain gauges, sundials, and water clocks. Sejong introduced scientific farming methods from China, including wet farming associated with the paddy field as well as rice transplantation methods that allowed farmers to reap two crops a year instead of one.

But his greatest contribution was the creation in 1443 of the Korean alphabet. This system, known first as *jeongeum* (correct sounds) and renamed *Hangeul* (great letters) in the twentieth century, is striking, coming as it does from a country within the Chinese cultural sphere where the complex writing system of characters allowed the elite to keep the masses illiterate. As in Spanish, but in contrast to English, one symbol refers to one sound and there are only minimal anomalies. You can learn it in no time. It has been called the most scientific alphabet ever created.[80] And, deservedly, it has its own holiday, October 9 in South Korea and January 15 in North Korea.

Although historians debate how much credit should be given to the Hall of Worthies in developing *Hangeul*, it is said the king designed some of the twenty-four letters himself by studying his wife's mouth and tongue as she formed different sounds.

But the story of *Hangeul* also illustrates how neo-Confucianism limited development. The moveable type that in theory made Korea the global leader in printing was not widely used, since printed texts consisted of complex Chinese characters. The invention of *Hangeul* gave the country a "killer app" that lent itself to mass printing a decade ahead of Johannes Gutenberg. Unfortunately, though, neo-Confucian scholars opposed *Hangeul*. The king saw its potential for promoting values, printing tales of dutiful children who sacrificed for their parents, or wives for their husbands. But the scholar class, schooled in Chinese, viewed it as a threat to their elite status. They called it *eonmun* (vulgar script) and used their bureaucratic power to block its widespread adoption.

The fate of *Hangeul* highlights Joseon's rigid, castelike structure. There were five classes. In contrast to the earlier periods, when Korea was dominated by the nobility, the country was now run by a scholarly *yangban* class of civilian and military officials. They represented the top 10 percent of the population. They saw their primary purpose as a devotion to learning and self-cultivation, and the only employment they aspired to was government service. For good measure, they were actually banned from farming, commerce, and other jobs. Geography was also important. There were almost no *yangban* from the northern and eastern parts of the country. The *yangban* elite married within their class and lived either in separate parts of the capital or in separate villages. Professionals such as doctors and translators, and lower functionaries such as clerks, were from the *jungin* (middle people) class. Despite the apartheid-like classifications, in practice there was some fluidity between these top groups, as those in the middle were eventually permitted to sit the civil-service exams, as some peasants became rich, and as the numbers of impoverished *yangban* without government office increased.

Over half the population was of the *sangin*, or commoner class. They were also known as *yangmin* (good people). These were the farmers, fishermen, merchants, and craftsmen. There were degrees of goodness, with craftsmen the most highly regarded. Merchants and businessmen were widely looked down upon and as a measure of their lowly status they were forbidden by law to use the language of the *yangban*. Peasants were restricted by law from leaving their land and had to carry identity tags at all times. In addition, peasant households were organized into groups of five, with members responsible for keeping an eye on one another. A similar system still exists in North Korea as an important means of political control.

The next class was less euphemistically called the *cheonmin*, meaning lowborn or inferior people. These were folk in certain hereditary professions—such as grave digging, shoe making, tanning, and butchery—that required the *yangban* to hold their noses. It also included bark peelers and basket makers (perhaps because these were jobs often done by moonlighting butchers). They lived in separate villages or existed as wanderers. Lowborn men were forbidden to twist their long hair up into a bun, or topknot, as the higher classes did. They had to bow and grip themselves in a cringing, inferior manner when approached by a person of higher status.[81] Failure to bow was a hanging offense. So was giving their children too high-sounding names, such as *ui*, which means "righteousness." They could not smoke in front of other people; they had to use honorific speech, even toward the children of commoners; they couldn't tile the roofs of their houses, which had to remain thatched; they couldn't wear silk clothes or straw shoes.

Included in this class were shamans, exorcists, entertainers, and the female *gisaeng*, the Korean equivalent of the geisha, who often ended up becoming *yangban* concubines. Children from these relationships were classified as middle people. These women were highly trained in poetry and the arts in order to provide stimulating company for *yangban* men.

Coexisting with the lower class were slaves, owned by both the government and private individuals. This is a feature of Joseon society that Korean historians tend not to dwell on because it does not fit the more modern nationalistic view of Koreans as victims of foreign powers. Slaves did not have surnames and often women of the lower classes were not even given a first name. In 1650, prostitutes were made government slaves. The number of slaves declined from a high of four hundred thousand in the early years of the dynasty to around half that number by the mid-seventeenth century. In 1800, government slavery was technically abolished, but *yangban* families maintained their own slaves until the turn of the twentieth century.

The *yangban* had clan books, enabling them to trace their lineage back as far as the Silla and Goryeo dynasties. Compilation of these genealogies became an urgent consideration after the Japanese invaded in the late sixteenth century and destroyed records, leaving many *yangban* unable to prove their status and their eligibility to sit the civil-service exams. Aristocrats searched old census records and documents, official histories, and civil-service rosters to prove their pedigree. The clan books trace the family through the father's line as far back as possible. The man it stops at is identified as the lineage founder. Daughters are either excluded or registered by their husband's name. These books are still updated and handed down from father to eldest son. Forgery and bribery was a significant factor behind the rather unusual rise in the *yangban* from 10 to 70 percent of the population during the eighteenth and nineteenth centuries.

The king himself was considered sacred. His likeness could only be painted after his death, and for five months after his death no one was allowed to wear silk, marry, stage shows, slaughter animals or, one small mercy, execute prisoners. When he was alive, no other man could touch him. Or wear glasses in front of him.

Such weirdness makes you wonder how many of the monarchs might have been mentally ill. Some clearly should have been on medication. The tenth king, Yeonsan, killed a tutor, beat two of his father's concubines to death, and cut off the chief eunuch's limbs. He trawled the provinces for women and did not discriminate between the married and unmarried. If a married woman brought into the harem continued to look dejected, he would have the head of her husband brought to her to really give her something to complain about. His last offense was the rape of his own widowed aunt, who committed suicide. This was a rash move. The aunt's brother was the commanding general of the royal Tiger Brigade unit. He led a lightning coup of government officials, soldiers, and ordinary citizens, who rushed the palace, drove out the king, executed several loyalists, and emptied the jails. Yeonsan was sent off under guard into internal exile.

Another nasty character was Gwanghae, a seventeenth-century monarch, who is believed to have slipped poison to his father to avoid losing his position as crown prince. He then murdered two of his brothers. This king preferred partying with his concubines to running the country. That's understandable, but this royal also heard noises. The ghosts bothered him. He had his father's tomb dug up and the bones buried on another hillside. He upset the Confucian orthodoxy by inviting shamans to the palace to scare off evil spirits. Eventually, an army of six thousand commoners staged a coup and placed a royal nephew on the throne.

The eighteenth-century crown prince Sado was so tormented by his father's abuse that he often had violent outbursts. He beat his favorite mistress to death, cut the heads off eunuchs, and killed doctors and fortune-tellers who upset him. Egged on by courtiers, his father the king became convinced Sado was plotting a coup and had him sealed in a wooden rice chest, where he died a slow, stifling death after eight days.

Given the restrictions, you also wonder what kind of mental baggage ordinary people carried about in those straitjacket centuries when junior was required to be filial and obedient. Confucius said senior had responsibilities but the neo-Cons went light on him. A woman was to obey her father, serve her husband, and obey her sons; nothing about anything in return. A husband owed zero to his wife. She, however, had to contain her jealousy of the concubines and *gisaeng*, and if she were lucky she'd be allowed out after dark to see her female friends (when men were not allowed on the streets). Such traditions took time to break. One elderly man told me about accompanying his mother as a boy in the 1930s on a visit to a recently married sister. He recalled it because it was his first trip in a car. His mother cried all the way there and back, but wouldn't say why.

Women in old Korea were not allowed to speak to their husbands until after the wedding night. These women would go through the wedding looking at the ground and couldn't say anything while being undressed later that night by their spouses, knowing that female relatives and servants were spying through a paper window— the trick, in case you come across such a scene and want to join in, is to lick your finger and touch the paper and you can kind of see through it. One old book recounts a story, which may have been a contemporary joke, about a man who bet his friends he could get his wife to talk on the wedding night. After several failed efforts, he said out loud that the astrologers who'd predicted he'd marry a mute were right, but that he was not going to accept it, even though there was no way to annul. That did it. "My horoscope is even worse," she said. "The astrologer foretold that my husband should be the son of a rat, and he was not wrong."[82]

If a thief broke in, a woman was wise to say nothing because whatever terror she had experienced, all anyone else would care about was that a man had seen her, in which case she was dishonored. If, God forbid, a woman were raped, she was advised to kill herself. Some carried a small dagger for the purpose.

The system of justice in the Joseon period was unfair, chaotic, and often vicious. Prisons were seen as "infernos of human suffering" where torture was the norm for the convicted felon, the professional criminal, the first-time offender, and even the witnesses.[83] Prisoners were subjected to flogging, dislocation of limbs, sawing of the flesh with coarse ropes, gouging by a wooden axe, and branding. The officials responsible for carrying out punishment often received no pay and lived on bribes from victims' families.

How did such egregious inequality and violent justice exist unchallenged in a state whose central vision was of the virtuous ruler presiding over the perfect system? In Confucian Korea, it is possible that many of the *yangban* believed the lower castes to be born to their station, and that they had an inferior *ki*, or essence, which precluded them from becoming morally upstanding. Such a view limited empathy. A similar restricted empathy is at play today in North Korea, where the regime does not feel responsible for the bulk of the citizenry that it classifies as "wavering" or "hostile" by virtue of ancestry.

Although the Joseon regime was harsh, it ushered in a period of stability that lasted two hundred years until 1592 when an estimated 160,000 soldiers landed near present-day Busan, triggering what has become known as the Imjin War, the most cataclysmic event on the peninsula prior to the twentieth century. The invasion force was led by Japanese warlord Toyotomi Hideyoshi, who had recently united his country and now wanted to conquer Ming China. Hideyoshi launched his attack after Korea refused to cooperate. As his defenses collapsed, King Sunjo and his ministers abandoned the capital and headed north. Slaves in Seoul took advantage of the government's flight to torch the offices where the slave registers were kept. Japanese troops took the capital without firing a shot.

At this point the regional naval commander in Jeolla, Admiral Yi Sun-sin, stepped to the fore. Yi launched his specially designed turtle-ships, boats covered with spiked iron plates over the deck to prevent boarding. They were equipped with cannons and clouds of sulfurous smoke poured out of the dragon-shaped bow of the vessel to both spook the enemy and provide protective cover. Admiral Yi defeated the Japanese at sea within weeks of the invasion and cut their supply routes. He is regarded as the country's greatest hero.

At the same time, "Righteous Armies" of gentry and peasants, often under the leadership of local aristocrats, sprang up to defend their villages and harass Japanese communications and supply lines. As this suggests, Joseon was not as centralized and strong as it seemed. Nor were popular loyalties guaranteed. Actually, the idea of nation did not really start to catch on with ordinary Koreans until the twentieth century. Before that, rulers were judged according to whether they were good or bad, not where they were from. The invading Japanese in fact provided food for locals and in return were helped. This is not a popular point with historians.

Nor is the fact that quite possibly the decisive factor that halted the Japanese was not the turtleship but the intervention of military forces from Ming China, who defeated the Japanese at the Battle of Pyongyang in 1593 and helped the Joseon armies to push the invaders down to the south coast by 1596. Fighting stopped for a year under a truce.

During this lull, Admiral Yi fell victim to the factional struggles that plagued the government, a prime cause of why Korea was initially unprepared to meet the Japanese threat despite warning signs that they were ready to invade. He was jailed, nearly executed, and only recalled to service when fighting with the Japanese resumed in 1597. The death of Hideyoshi in 1598 led to the complete withdrawal of Japanese forces from Korea. In an attack on the retreating enemy, Admiral Yi was killed by a stray bullet.

The Imjin War had caused terrible devastation, especially in the southeast. The population fell drastically, two-thirds of arable land was left fallow and historical records, national treasures, and cultural relics were looted and destroyed. Even a present-day visitor to Seoul who wants to see the former Joseon palaces will find that almost all are reconstructions dating from between the seventeenth and nineteenth centuries.

One particularly nasty image from this period resurfaced in 1982 when a scholar discovered a tomb containing twenty thousand Korean noses in a place called Bizen in Japan. The invading troops had been under orders to send them back as proof of death. An estimated one hundred thousand were sent in batches, pickled in salt, and buried. In 1992, they were returned to Korea. Controversy flared when it was proposed they be buried at a temple that was a memorial to Admiral Yi. Locals feared that the angry, humiliated spirits of the mutilated soldiers would cause trouble. One year later they were finally laid to rest in the town of Puan, where three thousand soldiers had died in a battle in 1597.

An unintended outcome of the Imjin War was the increased influence of Korean culture on Japan. Hundreds of Korean craftsmen went to Japan where they developed ceramic and textile traditions. The Japanese also adopted neo-Confucian ideas of political organization from Korea, especially those of the school that emphasized self-cultivation and learning from experience.

Korea's woes did not end with the withdrawal of the Japanese. The substantial drain on the resources of China during the Imjin War weakened the Ming Dynasty and made it vulnerable to renewed attacks by the barbarian tribes of Manchuria, this time the Manchu.

The Manchu threatened to invade Korea as part of a broader strategy to conquer Ming China. The Joseon king initially agreed to cooperate with the Manchu but his overthrow by a pro-Ming faction triggered the first Manchu invasion in 1627. Peace was achieved after the Koreans agreed to remain neutral. In 1636, however, the Manchu launched a second invasion after Korea refused to recognize their sovereignty over the Ming. There was a humiliating capitulation ceremony on the banks of the Han River. Although the destruction was not as severe as that by the Japanese, Korean hostility toward the new Ching Dynasty established by the Manchu lasted for a century. The final downfall of the Ming Dynasty in 1644 underscored the belief of the Joseon elite that they were the last bastion of the true Confucian order now that the barbarians were ruling in Beijing.

The Japanese and Manchu invasions instilled a sense of historical victimhood among elite Koreans. They would forever feel they had been assaulted and humiliated by inferior races.

Joseon Korea spent the following decades recovering from the invasions, with the long forty-five-year rule of King Sukjong contributing to increased stability. This monarch has been compared to King Henry VIII of England with a personal life that caused intense court factional struggles even as his military and agricultural reforms strengthened the country.

The story even has its own Anne Boleyn in the form of Lady Chang, the subject of many movies and TV dramas. The king had married Queen Inhyeon after assuming the throne, but after she was unable to produce a male heir he fell for one of the concubines, the exceptionally lovely Lady Chang. When she bore him a son, the king decided to divorce his queen, marry Lady Chang, and name their boy crown prince.

The marriage created dissension among the high court officials, who regarded the treatment of Queen Inhyeon as shameful. She was seen as embodying the best aristocratic virtues of grace and dignity, while Lady Chang was seen as manipulative and rather common (she came from a *jungin* family, her father having been an interpreter and trader). Bowing to pressure, King Sukjong eventually agreed to remarry Queen Inhyeon and demote Lady Chang. When Queen Inhyeon died in 1701, Lady Chang was accused of having put a shamanistic curse on her and was executed.

The story illustrates the influence of sex and money over Confucian virtue at the time. The low-status *gisaeng* courtesans of the *yangban* scholar-officials were bearing illegitimate sons who would eventually create a sizeable pressure group demanding social recognition, while Lady Chang's monied background eased her entry into the court as a royal concubine. The neo-Confucian aristocracy stepped in to make sure that the concubine descendants and rich merchant families along with military officials and mid-level professional bureaucrats were kept in their place.

The political stability established by King Sukjong continued under the long reigns of his successors, Yongjo (1724–76) and Chongjo (1776–1800), whose rule constituted what is regarded as the golden age of the Joseon Dynasty.

The eighteenth century saw much intellectual ferment that challenged the strict and conservative dogma of neo-Confucianism. Those challenging the system were followers of what was known as the Northern Learning school, established by scholars who had visited China on tribute missions and were impressed by the social and economic progress made under the allegedly barbarian Manchu rulers.

The Northern Learning scholars argued for pragmatic policies rather than strict obedience to what they saw as the outdated principles of neo-Confucianism. They proposed reforms in agriculture, government administration, and the military and offered a new vision of the ideal state: an agricultural sector consisting of free and self-employed peasants who owned and worked their own land, while encouraging the pursuit of private wealth with the development of commerce and manufacturing based on Western scientific teachings. They proposed the abolition of class distinctions, and promoted equal opportunity in education, and selection based on merit. The program of national renovation would reverse the country's decay, which they blamed on a backward economy.

These proposals were anathema to the neo-Confucians because they placed the material over the spiritual.

Although Northern Learning scholars received a favorable hearing from King Chongjo and several were appointed to the prestigious Royal Library, their school eventually failed to make a major impact on governance due to the persistent opposition of the bureaucracy. Whatever progress the reformers did achieve ended with the king's death in 1800.

The resulting crackdown on modernist ideas included the suppression of Catholicism, known as Western Learning, which had recently arrived via Jesuit missionaries to China, with some of the leading Northern Learning scholars converting to the new faith.

Popular discontent turned violent in the nineteenth century. There were major rebellions around Pyongyang in 1811 and in Jinju in 1862. These were triggered by protests against the corruption of local officials. The life of the peasant was tough. Thousands died when the harvests were bad and many became so impoverished they left their homes and became vagrants. At the same time, the central government was weak. With a series of boy monarchs after the death of King Chongjo, real power was wielded by regents more interested in promoting their family interests than implementing efficient policies.

The most significant threat to the government came from *Donghak*, the religious movement among peasants in southern Korea. Although conceived as a bulwark against foreign influence, *Donghak*, or Eastern Learning, was a doctrine that ironically set in motion a chain reaction paving the way for Western imperialist powers to come crashing into Korea. After the founder, Choe Che-u, was executed in 1864, his followers bided their time before mounting a challenge against the government several decades later.

Meanwhile, the crackdown on Catholicism continued, a reflection of the deep fears in the Korean court about the looming threat of Western imperialism that was finally reaching the shores of Korea after the British, French, and the Dutch had conquered much of the rest of Asia, including India, Southeast Asia, and parts of China. Until the 1860s, little was known about Korea in the West. Its secretiveness had given rise to the term Hermit Kingdom.

From the early part of the nineteenth century, Western nations had sought contact. British trading vessels and warships had appeared off the coast, French warships had also tried to deliver a diplomatic letter to the government, and some Koreans had been killed in an encounter with Russian vessels. China and Japan had already opened their doors to the West, the Koreans were aware of the subsequent humiliation of their neighbors and were wary. Their resistance to the outside had deeper causes. As the upholders of strict Confucianism, Koreans thought they were superior and had no room for foreigners. The ruling elite saw the Japanese as uncultured, and Westerners, with their horrendously long noses, different hair colors, and round eyes, as barbarians and monsters.

In 1864, a new king, Gojong, took the throne. He was destined to oversee one of the most disruptive periods in Korea's long history. Since he was only twelve years old, effective power was first exercised by his father, who was known as the *Daewongun*. Faced with internal rebellion and the specter of foreign intrusion, he introduced a series of measures designed to strengthen the authority of the throne and reject all contacts with the "barbarians of the ocean." This movement was known as "uphold orthodoxy and reject heterodoxy."

In 1866, an American trading vessel, the *General Sherman*, sailed up the Taedong River to Pyongyang in an effort to forcibly open trade relations.[84] The crew kidnapped a local military official as a hostage to try to pressure the Koreans into conducting trade talks. Locals attacked the vessel, set it afire, and killed the crew.

In the same year, the French mounted an invasion to revenge the death of French priests who had recently been executed. When the French spread rumors that they planned to kill a thousand Koreans for every martyred Frenchman, the populace panicked. The palace was reportedly besieged by hundreds of shamans offering to use their supernatural powers against the enemy. Seven French warships anchored off the coast and seized part of Ganghwa Island before they were eventually repulsed, although they carried away priceless cultural artifacts that have been only recently returned.

The Americans' turn at retribution for the destruction on the *General Sherman* came in 1871 when five American warships sailed into Korean waters and landed marines on Ganghwa Island. The ensuing clash killed hundreds of Korean soldiers at the expense of only a few American casualties. Accounts of the fighting recorded the bravery of Korean soldiers. The Americans were astounded to see wounded Koreans take their own lives rather than surrender. Some jumped from cliffs and others feigned death to be buried with the bodies of the dead. "We were moved to tears when we saw them motioning us to stab them to death," one officer wrote. "We have never seen or heard of such tough and courageous fighting men. They were either the most patriotic soldiers in the world or imbued with a firm warrior spirit unknown to the Western world."[85]

The impression from these accounts is of a fine fighting force with good communications, but poor weaponry. But there appears to have been an almost effete disinterest on the part of the throne, both in terms of communication with its troops and in the outcome of battle.

The Western attempts to open Korea up and secure influence did not go unnoticed by a would-be imperialist closer to home—Japan— whose leaders started to entertain the idea that control over Korea would strengthen their own defense against Western imperialism.

In 1873, the *Daewongun* was forced to retire and King Gojong began to face the inevitable question of how to deal with the outside world. The king was lobbied by a new generation of scholars, led ironically by the official who had ordered the attack on the *General Sherman*, and who now argued that the policy of disengagement was no longer working and that Korea needed to adopt Western-style reforms to survive. The influence of what was called the Enlightenment movement first became apparent when the king agreed to open formal trade relations with Japan in 1876. The treaty identified Korea and Japan as independent sovereign states, thereby undermining Chinese claims over Korea.

The king soon sent officials to Japan and China to study modernization. In the face of opposition from Confucian conservatives over any dealings with the West, Gojong asked the Chinese to mediate a treaty with the U.S., which was signed in 1882. In the following year the king, wrongly informed that the wording of the agreement meant that the U.S. would guarantee Korea's sovereign independence, is said to have "danced with joy" when told that the first American diplomat had arrived in Korea.[86]

Treaties followed with Britain, Germany, Italy, Russia, France, and Austria-Hungary. At this time, too, the first Protestant missionaries arrived. Within a few years, they were to have tremendous impact on the Koreans with the establishment of the first modern schools and medical institutions.

Meanwhile, the throne faced domestic unrest. Many neo-Confucian intellectuals viewed this opening with fundamentalist alarm. Domestic debates about reforms soon became entangled in the wider rivalry between China and Japan over which would exert control over Korea and gain dominance in Northeast Asia.

In 1882, there was an uprising by soldiers who had not been paid for over a year and who resented the growing influence of the Japanese. The rebels allied with the *Daewongun* and burned the Japanese legation. The Japanese responded by sending troops into Korea, which in turn prompted China to send troops of its own. The Chinese took the *Daewongun* back to China under arrest.

In 1884, a group of intellectuals called the Progressives, who favored equality and modernization along Japanese lines, launched the ill-fated Gapsin Coup with Japanese support that was subsequently suppressed by Chinese troops. Between 1884 and 1894, the Chinese assumed greater influence over Korean policy, supported by the pro-Chinese Queen Min, even as both China and Japan withdrew their troops from the country.

Meanwhile, Russia was expanding its influence, a fact that alarmed the British government, which sent a naval force to occupy a strategic Korean island called Geomundo. As the sharks circled, the powerful queen and her Min clan took more and more control of state affairs.

The combination of poor economic conditions and exploitation by a stifling social hierarchy triggered the return of the *Donghak*. Believers began to petition to clear the name of the martyred founder. Protests escalated into a crusade against official corruption and foreign influence and, in April 1894, exploded into an armed peasant revolt in the southwest. In June, Korea called on China to send in troops and put down the rebellion. Japan then dispatched its own army to counter the Chinese.

By July, Japanese troops had occupied Seoul and the Japanese envoy demanded the Korean government introduce reforms. When the government hesitated, the Japanese seized control of the royal palace and installed the *Daewongun*, who, despite his antiforeign attitude, saw the Japanese intervention as an opportunity to overthrow the power of Queen Min and her family. He agreed to help lead a Deliberative Assembly that the Japanese set up to assume sweeping government powers and which included aristocrats and lower-rank government officials.

In August, Japan declared war on China and succeeded in expelling Chinese troops from Korea. In the peace treaty, China agreed to recognize the full independence of Korea after centuries of regarding it as a vassal.

While the defeat of China represented a shock to Korea's elite Confucian class, it was welcomed by the Western-oriented reformers. Even as the Japanese were putting down the *Donghak* movement, the Deliberative Assembly pushed through a wide-ranging modernization program known as the Gabo ("1894") reforms that signaled the end of Korea's centuries-long subordination to China.

Among the key measures was the abolition of slavery. As noted earlier, slavery had been based on hereditary status that was tracked through meticulous government records and although it had been gradually dying out, it had by no means disappeared, especially in wealthy city and country households. Given the stigma attached to the lowborn, many of the former slaves adopted aristocratic Joseon names, such as Kim, Park, and Lee to hide their origins. This history explains the prevalence of these three surnames today—at this writing, for example, among the 299 sitting lawmakers, there are only 56 surnames, and 118 are Kims, Parks, or Lees.

Other reforms sought to turn Joseon into a constitutional monarchy with a cabinet leading the administration. One rule required officials to come to work in the morning. Previously, they would arrive in the afternoon, bringing their bamboo pipes with them. The upper class didn't actually work and commerce was disdained. There was an attempt to end the *yangban* practice of holding government posts for brief periods simply to enhance status.[87]

The reformers also introduced modern monetary and banking

systems. Taxes were to be paid in cash, not goods, and restrictions were lifted on merchants in order to encourage the development of capitalism. In addition, a modern police force was introduced, civil-service exams were scrapped, torture was banned, and a modern court system introduced. Widows were permitted to remarry and minimum marriage ages were set at twenty for men and sixteen for women.

The king introduced some changes of his own, including the adoption of the Julian calendar and the establishment of modern elementary schools and post offices. His most controversial decree required men to cut their topknot and wear their hair short, in the style of the Westerners. He had his own cut by his minister of agriculture and commerce, who sobbed as he snipped.[88] During this epochal event, the wailing of *yangban* echoed through the palace. How could they appear at their ancestors' graves with short hair? Mobs of Confucian purists attacked and killed several bureaucrats over this issue.

Many of the Gabo reforms, however, were not implemented due to anti-Japanese protests after Queen Min was assassinated in October 1895 at the behest of the Japanese. The king and the crown prince, disguised as court ladies, fled shortly after to the Russian legation to take refuge. The reformers were hounded by mobs. Many fled abroad.

The turbulent events of the late 1890s underscore the challenges the court faced as it tried to undertake domestic reforms to strengthen itself while struggling to escape from the imperialist clutches of the neighboring Japanese and Russian powers, now that it no longer enjoyed the traditional protection of China.

In 1897, the king sought to elevate his country's status and establish its autonomy and legitimacy among the great powers by declaring itself the Great Korean Empire. The transformation of the monarch to an emperor was accompanied by moves to centralize the administration, through such means as overhauling the household registration system and establishing a national land survey to provide the government with better means to mobilize resources for economic development.

The imperial government had ambitious plans to modernize the economy, following the model established by Meiji Japan for its industrialization. It introduced a streetcar system in Seoul and the nation's first railway between Seoul and Incheon in 1899; a railway from Seoul to Busan was completed by 1904. Korea relied on foreign capital and technologies to achieve these projects and support the establishment of various industries ranging from mining and textile companies to telephone and telegraph operations.

But Emperor Gojong was not ready for democratic reform that would limit his authority. An initial challenge had come from a group of young intellectuals who established the Independence Club in 1896, whose name was intended to signal independence from both outside powers and Korea's traditional ways. They published Korea's first modern newspaper, *The Independent*, and erected an Independence Gate (which still stands) in Seoul, to uphold the spirit of the Gabo reforms.

Gojang ordered the club suppressed and the newspaper closed in 1899 because of suspected republican leanings, ending any turn-of-the-century hopes that Korea might become an independent constitutional monarchy.

12

BEING SECOND CLASS

"All Koreans wanted only one thing: freedom—
a golden word to those who know it not."

As the Koreans savored change and the promises of a new century, the whales in their vicinity started once more to fight. This time the shrimp was in for a bad bruising.

In February 1904 Japan, alarmed by Russia's invasion of Manchuria, declared war on Russia, quickly dispatching troops to the Korean Peninsula and occupying Seoul. A treaty followed, legitimatizing this action. In August, a second agreement granted Japan the right to "advise" the Korean government in foreign, financial, and military policy.

After Japan's victory over Russia the following year, this control over Korea was strengthened by the peace agreement. Mediated by U.S. President Theodore Roosevelt, the Treaty of Portsmouth firmly placed Korea in Japan's sphere of influence.

In November 1905, Korea became a protectorate, with a Japanese resident-general in charge of implementing policy in the areas designated in the earlier treaty. When the emperor's ministers refused to sign the documents Japanese soldiers marched into the foreign ministry, seized the seal, and signed in their stead. Emperor Gojong continued to resist and tried to secure foreign diplomatic help. In 1907 he sent a delegation to the World Peace Congress in The Hague to have the protectorate declared invalid by the international community. The plea was ignored. The Japanese were so infuriated they forced Gojong to abdicate. A revised treaty gave them the power to appoint all senior officials in the Korean government. Gojong was succeeded by his son, Sunjong, who was so inept that historians have described him as an imbecile.[89]

To reduce possible organized resistance, the Japanese disbanded the Korean army. As a result many displaced soldiers joined the latest reincarnation of the Righteous Army, which began staging guerrilla attacks. In the biggest engagement, several thousand rebels marched on Seoul and were repulsed by two divisions of the Japanese army. More than 17,000 guerrillas of varying types, including criminal gangs that were taking advantage of the chaos, were killed between 1905 and the annexation of the country in 1910.

The most famous act of resistance against the Japanese was the assassination in 1909 of the first resident-general, Ito Hirubumi, shortly after he stepped down from the post. Ito was a former prime minister and one of the main leaders of the Meiji Restoration that had modernized Japan. Ironically, he had opposed the plan to annex Korea, favoring instead the protectorate status that would have allowed Korea to otherwise maintain its integrity. His assassination, however, resulted in a decision by Tokyo to go ahead with this plan and assert formal control over Korea. Despite this disastrous consequence, the assassin, An Jung-geun, is now revered by Koreans as a national hero.

And so in 1910, with the appointment of a governor-general to rule over 14,700,000 Koreans as Japanese subjects, the Joseon Dynasty came formally to an end.

For some, the loss was a crisis beyond comparison. Many surrendered whatever life or privileges they might have enjoyed and devoted themselves to the nationalist cause. Aristocrats Yi Hoe-yeong and his five brothers, for example, fled to the forests of Manchuria and ploughed their entire fortune into a military academy, disguised as a school, to train young men to fight. When South Korea was finally established, the only surviving brother, Yi Si-yeong, became the vice president.[90]

One trainee at the academy was Jang Jirak, who went on to join the Chinese communists. He would be unknown today had he not met the American journalist, Helen Foster Snow. In interviews with her, Jang articulated the passion and complexity that characterized independence activists of all ideological stripes:

> All Koreans wanted only two things, really, though they differed in how to achieve these: independence and democracy. Really they wanted only one thing: freedom—a golden word to those who know it not. Any kind of freedom looked divine to them. They wanted freedom from Japanese oppression, freedom in marriage and love, freedom to live a normal, happy life, freedom to rule their own lives. That is why anarchism had such appeal. The urge toward a broad democracy was really very strong in Korea. This is one reason we did not develop a strong, centralized system of political parties. Each group defended its right to exist and its right to free expression. And each individual fought to the end for his own freedom of belief. There was plenty of democracy among us—but very little discipline.[91]
>
> . . .
>
> Nearly all the friends and comrades of my youth are dead, hundreds of them: nationalist, Christian, anarchist, terrorist, communist. But they are alive to me . . . They failed in the immediate thing, but history keeps a fine accounting. A man's name and his brief dream may be buried with his bones, but nothing that he has ever done or failed to do is lost in the final balance of forces. That is his immortality, his glory or shame. Not even he himself can change this objective fact, for he is history. Nothing can rob a man of a place in the movement of history.[92]

Jang was executed during one of the many internal purges by his Chinese comrades, his remarkable voice silenced.

Despite such examples and even though the Koreans had maintained a distinct identity for centuries, the loss of independence must have been, for the ordinary person whose loyalties at that time were more tied up with family and lineage than with nation, a bewildering moment, all the more so because it had not involved any kind of fight.

The Japanese justified the takeover as a "civilizing mission" to prevent Korea from disintegrating and creating a dangerous political vacuum in its backyard. Some Koreans agreed with this and believed the Japanese were introducing necessary reforms. Many provincial governors and other Koreans appointed to senior posts in the Japanese colonial government had been supporters of the Gabo reforms and had fled to Japan after 1896 when the reform movement was crushed. There were collaborators among the elite—one such was Yi Wanyong, a relative of the royal family who signed the 1910 annexation agreement—as well as from the lower classes, such as the members of *Ilchinhoe*, a society that thought the Japanese would liberate the common people from an oppressive central government.

In their rule over the Koreans the Japanese retained a residual core of such local supporters, at least until the late 1930s, as they introduced modern financial and banking systems, built transport and communications networks, and established schools and hospitals. Although many of these projects were primarily meant to help the thousands of Japanese migrants flocking to Korea following the annexation, they benefitted Koreans as well.

But in another way, for most Koreans, the annexation was a major step in forging a strong sense of national identity. The conviction spread that their own lack of national consciousness had rendered the country helpless.

Although the Koreans experienced the arrival of their neighbors as an aggressive usurpation, the Japanese were in many ways acting out of self-defense. By seeking membership in the imperialism club, they actually sought to avoid becoming its victim. They were latecomers as colonialists, and unusual in that they colonized their nearest neighbor and developed its industry, rather than making it simply a source of raw materials.

Unlike the Chinese, who from ancient times knew how to run a vassal state, and unlike the modern imperial powers, which had learned from experience, the nearest thing the Japanese had to colonial experience was their management of Okinawa and the other Ryukyu Islands since the 1870s, and Taiwan, acquired from China in 1895. An insular people, the Japanese lacked a philosophy for dealing with others. Their methods were informed by a long antiforeign tradition.

Unfortunately for their new colonial subjects, the Japanese had no sense of the Christian notion of individual responsibility as a check on the behavior of the men in authority. Their homegrown cult, Shinto, turned into the state religion, directing ancestor worship and other spiritual elements toward a central nationalistic statement— that the emperor was divine. In addition, a moral code called *bushido* was adapted to encourage acceptance of one's social lot and instill vigorous self-discipline. As a martial code it would soon find happy comradeship in the West's totalitarian camp and allowed for horrendous atrocities without disturbance of the conscience. For this reason, and in contrast to their society today, the Japanese of that time were governed, despite an appearance of sophisticated modernity, by violent undercurrents.

In order to justify their need to take over and civilize their neighbors, the Japanese frequently offered disparaging racist assessments of the Koreans despite the close racial links they shared. "If you look closely," said one Japanese politician, "they appear to be a bit vacant, their mouths open and their eyes dull, somehow lacking . . . Indeed, to put it in the worst terms, one could even say that they are closer to the beasts than to human beings."[93]

A Japanese travel writer, in a not untypical description, wrote that the seven major products of Korea were "shit, tobacco, lice, *gisaeng*, tigers, pigs, and flies." He referred to Seoul as the "shit capital of the world" because Koreans allegedly tended to relieve themselves wherever they felt like it.[94]

The Koreans appeared to the Japanese as coarsely superstitious. Newcomers were advised, for example, after an epidemic of scarlet fever in 1914, not to keep cats as pets. Burying cats was one of hundreds of Korean shamanistic prescriptions for tackling disease.

Over a hundred Koreans were arrested for killing Japanese-owned cats.[95]

The constant bombardment with such negative propaganda led some Koreans to conclude that their reputed backwardness was the result of a natural inferiority. What had their slothful, dependent, superstitious, and diseased ancestors ever produced that was worth preserving? With the Japanese control over modern education, the young lost touch with their heritage and accepted Japanese assumptions.

It is difficult to overemphasize the depth of this intellectual assault on the Korean mind. This was Korea's introduction to the real world, the civilized world of trains and telephones and electricity that had hitherto passed them by. Coming into it, they found their position: at the bottom.

During its first decade in Korea, known as the "military rule" era, the colonial government approached its job with fundamentalist zeal, intruding deeply into every aspect of Korean society with all the advantages of the modern police state.

The initial aim was to annihilate the Korean identity in order to absorb and assimilate them into a greater Japan, albeit as second-class citizens. Japanese became the official language, with Korean taught as the second.

Seoul became known as Keijo (Kyongsong in Korean). The colonial authorities destroyed 85 percent of all the buildings in Gyeongbok Palace, the main royal residence, and erected their own government office in front of the palace grounds with deliberate geomantic intent.[96] Viewed from the air, this and the city hall building half a mile away were shaped to form the word "Japan" in Chinese characters. They constructed tall buildings in the capital, such as the Chosun Hotel and the Bank of Korea, to dominate the cityscape.[97] There was a Japanese Shinto shrine on Namsan Hill in the city center and monuments erected to Japanese heroes.[98]

The bureaucracy under the military governor-general was dominated by Japanese, who throughout the period occupied almost all the highest positions and even a majority of clerical jobs.[99] They lived as first-class citizens and enjoyed rights not extended to Korean subjects.

They divided the country administratively into provinces, counties, cities, and townships. The governor-general appointed the chiefs of these units. Officials, and even teachers, wore swords as symbols of their authority.

In the first years of its rule Japan conducted a nationwide survey of land ownership. Many small landholders who failed to register lost their land. The Japanese also invested in road, rail, and communication networks to serve their strategic interests.

The police had wide-ranging powers, among them the right to pass judgment and punish minor offenses. An announcement that complaints could be lodged against corrupt police was at first welcomed, as policemen under the control of corrupt Joseon Dynasty officials had routinely extorted confessions and money from suspects and their families. But this reform soon fell into the same muddy pit when police chiefs found they could fire unpopular officers and pocket their salaries until they were replaced. It also became common for the families of suspects to be able to bribe police officials for the release of family members—a tradition that continued until the recent democratization. In some cases, men would offer their daughters as concubines or their sons as servants to police chiefs to spring a family member.

Many policemen were Korean, usually from the lower classes and often with old scores to settle, and they frequently treated suspects more harshly than the Japanese policemen did. In fact all the people I have met with stories of abuse by police during the occupation said their torturers were Korean. In another tradition that continued until recently, police routinely tortured suspects to force confessions. One technique was called the "crane" or "airplane," and involved tying a suspect with his arms behind his back and hoisting him above the ground with a rope, whereupon he was beaten with sticks. Other forms of torture included pouring water laced with hot pepper down a person's nose to make him choke, forcing a person to drink large amounts of water and then placing a board across his stomach and jumping on it, and pushing bamboo wedges under a victim's toenails and fingernails.[100] It took a special kind of commitment for people to continue in the independence movement knowing this to be their likely fate if they resisted.

One significant frontline of Korean transformation during the Japanese rule was the work of Protestant missionaries. In contrast to Japan, which had earlier rejected Christianity, and China, which fought against Christianity because of its refusal to accommodate ancestor worship, Koreans took to this new faith in a way that was to have a great impact.

The loss of national independence offered a compelling impetus to accept the Western faith: Confucianism had failed the Koreans, and this Western religion stood in opposition to the Japanese. Conversion was therefore acceptable both as a kind of penance for Korean failure and as patriotic commitment to a better future. Churches were also effective. Until the eve of World War Two, they remained the only institutions not subordinated to the Japanese.

Christians soon came to the forefront of the nationalist movement. Despite Japanese suspicions, Christian churches themselves were not dedicated to political goals; furthermore, they were supported by Japan's foreign allies. Suppression was not a simple matter. The first clash, however, was not long in coming. In 1912, over one hundred Christians were tried on charges of conspiracy to assassinate the governor-general. On appeal, all but six were released. Despite the arrests and torture of individual Christians, this incident actually clarified some of the misperceptions of the role of missionary and church, and church-government relations improved.[101]

But the suppressed anger over Japanese rule could not be contained. It erupted in 1919 in the aftermath of World War One with Koreans living overseas taking to heart U.S. President Woodrow Wilson's call for national self-determination.[102] Korean students living in Tokyo, who enjoyed much more academic freedom than their compatriots at home, issued a demand for independence. In Korea itself, the followers of the *Donghaks*, who had renamed their religion *Chondogyo*, planned an independence appeal in alliance with Christian and Buddhist activists.

The plan was to use the occasion of the funeral of Emperor Gojong in early March 1919 as a platform for nationwide protests and draw the other mourners into political action. Christians insisted that the demonstrations be nonviolent and it was decided that a written declaration of independence would be the best way to appeal to the international conscience.

On March 1, the thirty-three signatories met in a restaurant in Seoul, read the declaration aloud in the city's Pagoda Park and promptly surrendered to the police in a gesture of nonviolent resistance. The Japanese were taken completely by surprise as citizens paraded through Seoul, shouting "Long Live Independent Korea." The police began hauling demonstrators off to jail and arresting Christian ministers. The next three days were calm. On March 5, high school students were due back at their desks, but none turned up. Instead, at 9 A.M., hundreds of boys swarmed out of the shops and alleyways in front of the Seoul Railroad Station, chanting for independence. Girls joined the march as it made its way through the city gate toward the palace. They got about half a mile before they were charged by police with drawn sabers and many killed.[103]

Koreans today all know the story of a schoolgirl, Ryu Gwansun, who traveled from Seoul to her hometown in central Korea to rouse support for independence. She was captured, and killed in prison.[104] They also know the story of Jeam village. Japanese police called the men to a meeting at the village church after the murder of a policeman. One lady, Chun Dong-ne, recalled what happened next: "They said they wanted to officially apologize for having beaten a villager. The men all went to the church. Then they nailed the door shut and set the church on fire and shot anyone who tried to climb out of the windows." Twenty-three people died in this massacre, including her young husband. Mrs. Chun was still in the same village when I met her in 1985. She said her bitterness had evaporated a few years earlier after an emotional encounter with some young Japanese seminary students, who had visited her to apologize for the atrocity. The students later donated money for a new church in the village.

The demonstrations erupted into a nationwide protest movement, the likes of which Korea had never seen. Even old *yangban* diehards, who had been bought off with offices by the Japanese, joined in. At this point the Japanese administration showed its true colors and weighed in with violent suppression. Peaceful demonstrators were shot, bayoneted, clubbed, arrested, and tortured. The Japanese claimed that around five hundred protesters were killed in the following six months, but other estimates have as many as seventy-five hundred dead and forty-five thousand arrested.[105]

Although meticulously planned, the protests lacked leadership. In fact, the leaders were arrested on day one. Koreans had hoped for a response from the major international powers, but none came. Politically, the independence activists had misjudged the enemy's resolve, and overestimated the willingness of foreign powers to commit to their cause. Nevertheless, the unity of the nationalists involved and the mass support behind the call for freedom was itself sufficiently remarkable for many historians to conclude that the March First Movement represents the birth of modern Korea.

The uprising demonstrated more than a rejection of Japanese rule. It also marked the rejection of monarchy. The royals were nowhere to be seen during the protests. The crown prince had married a Japanese woman and lived most of his life in Tokyo. The revival of the monarchy was dropped as an option forever.

After the protests were subjugated, a new governor-general, Admiral Saito Makoto, a sophisticated diplomat, gathered an experienced team and consulted with leading Koreans and even foreign missionaries, before launching an altogether more palatable and subtle approach known as the "Cultural Rule" policy. Saito recognized that the previous harsh measures had been counterproductive and sought to co-opt Koreans into the colonial system by allowing them to pursue social, economic, and cultural activities more freely and develop a sense of their own stake in the country's development. The adoption of Cultural Rule in Korea also reflected the period of liberalization in Japan during the 1920s known as Taisho Democracy, which took its name from the reigning emperor.

Moderate nationalists were permitted to form organizations and publish Korean newspapers, albeit under continuing censorship. Two modern dailies, the *Chosun Ilbo* and the *Dong-A Ilbo*, began in 1920 and became a magnet for young, patriotic intellectuals. More schools were built, the teaching of Korean was expanded, and literacy increased markedly. Whipping was abolished as a punishment and some governmental responsibilities were decentralized. Policemen and officials no longer wore military uniforms. Economic incentives were introduced and investments were made to increase production of rice for shipment to Japan.[106]

The agricultural measures reduced the status of many Koreans to that of tenant farmers as their land was bought up by the Japanese, but other Koreans took advantage of the changes to make money as middlemen supplying rice to Japan. Regulations were also changed so that companies could be freely established by Koreans without the need for government approval. Korean companies, such as the Kyong-song Spinning and Weaving Company, pioneered the development of the family-owned conglomerate model that would later dominate the economy of South Korea.[107]

The fact that a Korean commercial elite would benefit from Japanese rule while mainly poor farmers suffered created a deep social and ideological division that still permeates Korea, with the left-wing factions now accusing some of the rich of having been collaborators.

Urban development also proceeded apace with the expansion of communications and transport networks. This growth of cities and a blossoming urban culture undermined the values that had been the product of a rural-based society. With the old upper class no longer in charge, the caste lines rapidly blurred. For example, over 90 percent of those classified as butchers escaped their hereditary caste. During the 1920s, the thirty-three thousand or so remaining butchers started lobbying for their rights, such as equal access to schooling for their children. Despite many instances of being barred from attending, by the mid-1920s, some 40 percent of butchers' children were in school, a much higher proportion than for other castes.

With the failure of the March First Movement, some nationalists turned to Russia for inspiration. The Korean Communist Party began secretly in Seoul in 1925, with the associated Korean Artists Proletarian Federation engaged in cultural activities to win the support of peasants and workers.

Admiral Saito expanded the police, which became more sophisticated in gathering information, and infiltrating and subverting opposition.

Moderate nationalists took a pragmatic and gradualist approach toward independence. Since direct confrontation with the authorities had proved unsuccessful, they favored the methodical development of a national consciousness to raise awareness of the people's economic and cultural potential and to foster future leaders. Korean newspapers and magazines played a key role in this regard as they took advantage of the Cultural Rule policy. Publications had to be careful to not offend the authorities. But they served as the main outlet for a cultural renaissance among authors, who celebrated the country's traditions and past achievements and at the same time focused on current social issues. Newspapers were also instrumental in launching literacy campaigns in the countryside, which included teaching the Korean alphabet.

The media sponsored publicity campaigns for organizations wanting to improve social conditions. One was a campaign to raise money to establish a university and the other, called the Korean Production Movement, was launched to attract entrepreneurs and was essentially a "Buy Korean" drive. Both fizzled out due to infighting, corruption, and attacks from radical nationalists. Leftists, in particular, held the view that business was itself a tool of imperialist oppression. The disputes were so heated and the disagreements so vehement they split nationalists into two broad camps and eventually into two rival countries. Although the left was fragmented, its vigorous resistance enabled it to be more deeply associated with the patriotic cause. This explains its profound appeal in postcolonial Korea.

Meanwhile, the Great Depression devastated the Japanese economy and led to a rise in militarism and an aggressive policy in East Asia that started with the invasion of Manchuria in 1931. The pressures of a growing population on limited arable land, unrelieved by emigration, provided impetus for expansion into China.[108] Koreans followed events in Manchuria and the establishment of the Japanese puppet state of Manchukuo with great interest since there was already a large Korean population in the region. A vast expanse, rich in untapped resources, Manchuria was linked to Korea in the great Japanese development plan for Asia, grandly called the Greater East Asian Co-Prosperity Sphere. The military invited Japan's big conglomerates, the *zaibatsu*, to develop Manchuria's natural resources and create an industrial base. This policy served as the blueprint for South Korea's postwar economic development model under Park Chung-hee, who served with the Japanese military in Manchuria.

In 1935 schoolchildren and government workers were ordered each morning to bow toward the east to honor the Japanese emperor.

Then the launch of the Sino-Japanese war in 1937 ended the Cultural Rule and ushered in the most traumatic chapter in modern Korea's history, one that did not really end until the Korean War armistice in 1953. When Koreans talk today about the Japanese colonial period and its horrors, they are mainly referring to this later part, when their grandparents were mobilized to support the war effort, first in China and then against the Western powers in East Asia and the Pacific.

With a total war economy in Japan and under a new governor-general, former Minister of War Minami Jiro, Koreans were now required to participate fully in supporting the war effort and subjected to a policy of forced assimilation.[109] Mass mobilization resulted in the uprooting of millions of Korean workers, further obliteration of the Korean culture, and the effective destruction of the moderate nationalist leadership.

The idea behind forced assimilation was to suppress the Koreans' distinct identity and turn them into loyal imperial subjects. It began with an order that they worship at the Japanese Shinto shrines, which provoked conflict with the influential Christian community. Thousands of pastors and believers who refused to comply were arrested and tortured. All foreign missionaries were expelled in 1942.

The use of Korean was banned in the classroom and in 1940 the screws tightened further with the closure of the *Chosun Ilbo* and *Dong-a Ilbo*, the two main vernacular newspapers.

The ruling that caused the most widespread anguish was the demand in 1940 that all Koreans adopt Japanese names.[110] Koreans lined up outside police stations and government offices, many in comatose disbelief, to register their new Japanese names. Some old people, in befuddled resistance, refused to choose and had names selected for them. For a people who could trace their male ancestry back centuries and whose fundamental sense of meaning in life derived from the imperative to continue their lineage, this was the final humiliation. For generations, a destitute Korean father above the slave caste had at least been able to bestow his name on his child. Now even that was taken away. Some submitted their new names for registration wearing black armbands and went afterward to pray at their ancestral tombs. Parents begged their bewildered children to forgive them, and a new generation of nationalists discovered themselves in the crucible of their parents' misery.

In a fictionalized account of his own experience, the writer Richard E. Kim describes a young boy queuing up with his father to register their new family name, Iwamoto:

> The long line of people is still standing outside, hunched and huddled, rubbing their ears and faces, stamping their feet in the snow. My father pauses for a moment on the steps, one arm around my shoulders, and says: "Look."
>
> Afraid, bewildered, and cold, I look up at his face and see tears in his eyes. "Take a good look at all of this," he whispers. "Remember it. Don't ever forget this day."[111]

During this period, the Japanese also sought to organize Koreans into ten-family units of the Neighborhood Patriotic Association, which had a dual purpose: to increase surveillance and to extract material resources needed for the Japanese to fight the widening Pacific war.

With Korea functioning as an important supply base for its expansion into Asia, Japan pushed industrialization. Factories sprang up, particularly in the northern part of the peninsula, to produce armaments, chemicals, machinery, and fuel. Although these factories created new jobs, workers were subject to a regimented existence that would create an aggrieved proletariat class. Meanwhile, farming families were left destitute as food was confiscated to feed the troops, another factor that added to the political agitation after the war.

Between 1937 and 1945, 360,000 Koreans served as either soldiers or civilian employees in the Japanese military. Contrary to present assumptions, the young men in uniform were, until 1943, volunteers—with pressure to "volunteer" intensifying as the war went on because so many refused to respond at first. It is interesting to note, however, that of eight hundred thousand who did volunteer in this period, only seventeen thousand were actually accepted. Conditions were tighter for Koreans than for Japanese, both because the loyalty of the Koreans was questioned and also because it was feared that if the Koreans were accepted in large numbers to fight for the emperor they would likely, after the war, demand equal treatment. One condition of enlistment, for example, was language ability, which exempted many Koreans—only about one quarter of whom spoke Japanese fluently—from having to serve.

Full conscription began in 1944. The Japanese government says that 131,955 Koreans died in war-related service. These include the twenty-one thousand commemorated at the Yakusuni Shrine in Tokyo and some thirty thousand killed in the nuclear bombing of Hiroshima and Nagasaki.[112]

Far larger numbers were drafted to fill labor shortages in the munitions factories, shipyards, mines, and construction sites in Korea and Japan, and in Manchuria and on Sakhalin Island. Estimates of the overall numbers mobilized range from 4 to 7.82 million.[113] Some 750,000, for example, were sent to Japan to work in mines and in other war-related industries. By 1944, four million Koreans, that is one out of every six, were living in Japan and Japanese-controlled territories in Asia. Organizations for mobilizing workers were created and the dirty work of fulfilling quotas was undertaken by fellow Koreans, who were seen as collaborators.

The most notorious aspect of this forced-labor policy was the rounding up of young women for work in military brothels, or "Comfort Corps," as the Japanese called them. The Japanese had decided on this system of military prostitution in response to the outcry over the 1937 Rape of Nanking, when their soldiers went on an orgy of rape and killing in the Chinese city. The military had other motives to manage brothels, similar to those behind the German military brothels in occupied Europe in World War Two. These were to control disease, prevent spying, and to keep the troops content.[114]

The first so-called comfort stations were filled with Japanese prostitutes but the foreign ministry in Tokyo was not amused by the use of these women overseas on the grounds that it was bad for the country's image. Women were then recruited from the colonies. Many were tricked into believing they were going to work in factories. In conquered territories, recruitment was more forced. Many of the brothels were frontline, where the women were required to service a huge volume of soldiers who believed that sexual release would enhance their performance in combat. There is no clear evidence of the numbers of women enslaved, but estimates vary from 80,000 to 200,000. More than half of them were Korean. Treatment seems to have varied from station to station. In some cases, women who caught diseases were left untreated. Some were executed. Those who survived the war went on to suffer anonymously, ashamed and often reclusive.

Their story was unearthed thirty years later by Kakou Senda, a Japanese journalist and author. But it was not until the early 1990s that activists in Korea persuaded some elderly survivors to recount their heartrending stories and started to pressure the Japanese government to confess, apologize, and compensate survivors. Some 238 former comfort women registered with the Korean government.

The Japanese government issued its first public apology in 1995. Regarding compensation, it argued that it had paid all victims of its colonial rule when relations were normalized between the two countries in 1965. As the Korean government's choice at that time had been to direct the funds into national projects rather than pay individuals, the implication was that survivors should take it up with their own government.

Some former comfort women in other countries have accepted the apology and some payment from a fund set up by Tokyo with private contributions, but the Koreans continued to demand more sincerity than the Japanese government has been willing to express. For the Japanese government, this is one of those cases where the more it argues about technicalities—we've already dealt with this issue and it wasn't the military who rounded the women up but subcontractors—the more it slips into the moral slime. At the same time, the issue is more complex than the activists would have us believe. That much is evidenced by the fact that it took fifty years for it to come to light. The awkward truth is that such abuses were more the norm in early and mid-twentieth-century Korea, and that the men in power in Korea were no more likely to single out comfort women as a special case than the Japanese. Also, much of the trafficking was undertaken by Koreans. It's tempting to brand them simply as collaborators and traffickers, but to do so only dodges the complexity. In fact, many of the women were encouraged, if not sold, by their families in areas where local governments were called upon to fulfill quotas.

The difficulty is that when activists in a sophisticated, democratic society hold up a twenty-first-century mirror to a fascist pre-democratic enemy, as in this case, they also catch the reflection of their country's own premodern past. This makes truth seeking all the more complicated; however, it cannot be denied that, for modern Koreans, there is no better example of the barbarity of the treatment during Japan's colonial rule. The effort to gain redress continues to this day. I hear it, just a stone's throw from my office, every Wednesday at the comfort woman statue in front of the Japanese embassy in Seoul. This protest has been going on for twenty years.

The comfort women are not the only ones who have continued into the twenty-first century to seek redress for wrongs suffered during the occupation. An organization called Donginhoe, formed in Tokyo in 1955 by seventy Korean men, has been lobbying the Japanese government for sixty years. The cause of these men seems unlikely and even somewhat outrageous because they were all former prisoner-of-war camp guards who were convicted of war crimes. In addition to the young Korean men who volunteered or who were later conscripted into the Imperial Japanese army, 3,012 were recruited as civilian guards by the Japanese military for work at allied POW camps in Southeast Asia. Although ordinary people, their work was the sort that brought out the beast. Their treatment of prisoners was so bad that, of the sixty thousand British, Commonwealth, and Dutch men who worked on the notorious Thai-Burma Railway, sixteen thousand died.[115]

Most of the 148 Koreans found guilty of war crimes were camp guards.[116] One of them was Lee Hak-rae, a seventeen-year-old post-office worker from Boseong county in the southwest. He had quit his job after losing someone's salary in the mail and having to pay for the loss out of his own pocket. The local mayor alerted him to this new opportunity. Off he went. Lee's Japanese name was Kakurai

Hiromaru. Prisoners nicknamed him "Lizard." He was initially sentenced to death at an Australian war tribunal in Singapore, but after eight months on death row and an intervention by his defense lawyer, this was commuted to twenty years. He came out after serving nine, stripped of his Japanese citizenship by the Treaty of San Francisco that ended the colonial rule, and as a Korean facing the double stigma of war criminal and collaborator. He formed his lobbying group with others in a similar predicament. In 1960 they created a taxi company in Tokyo. Japanese authorities have consistently rejected their claims for compensation. The Korean government, however, has been more friendly. In 2006, South Korea formally cleared 83 of the 148 Korean war criminals and recognized them instead as victims of Japanese imperialism and forced mobilization.[117]

I've given this matter much thought, but I'll admit I was not amused when this decision was announced. It brought to mind a gentleman I had last seen at my father's funeral in England in 2000. Geoff Williams had worked in the same bank as my father. He was a restrained man who spoke curtly, but who had a well of mischief in him that bubbled over from time to time. Years earlier, after I'd been in a school play, he'd taught me how an actor can make himself fall over onstage. He'd clip one foot with the other and over he went. He was much older now, already in his eighties. After some words of condolence, he asked if I was still living in Korea. I was. By that time, Seoul had become more familiar to me than England.

"What do you think of the Koreans?" he asked.

I waxed lyrical about the Irish of the East. After a minute, I knew I had lost my audience.

"Maybe they have changed from my time," he said.

"What do you mean?"

Then he told me his story. Like thousands of other young British and Allied soldiers in World War Two, he had been captured in Southeast Asia. The Japanese were unspeakable in the treatment of defeated soldiers. I worked in London once with a man who had, as a POW, witnessed guards executing a lineup of Australians with a bayonet up the rectum. Mr. Williams alleged that the Koreans were worse than the Japanese. "Horrible people," he said.

"What made them so bad?"

"When the camp commander was angry about something, he'd berate his officers," he explained. "The officers would take their frustration out on the Japanese privates, and they would take theirs out on the Korean guards. The Koreans would then take their anger out on the only people beneath them. That was us."

I've never had the heart to tell my Korean friends this story because I know they would have no idea what it has to do with them.

The eighty-three war criminals forgiven by the Korean government had received sentences from one-and-a-half years to life. They were not tried as soldiers or POW camp guards who had done their jobs. They were tried for overzealousness, for decisions and actions over and above the call of duty. They were the brutes, the most horrible of the "horrible people."

The Truth Commission on Forced Mobilization under the Japanese Imperialism had been set up with good intentions, but had failed to think through the moral basis for its inquiry. The reason the commission drew the line at eighty-three was that it considered people to be collaborators only if they were in certain positions or over a certain rank. In overturning the Allied war tribunal judgment, it proposed to replace individual responsibility with a defense of nationality. Such skewed morality led to the crimes against the lowest class—"prisoners"—in the first place. People who commit crimes against humanity are not innocent by virtue of being Korean any more than Japanese who brutalized Koreans are innocent by virtue of being Japanese.

I do think the guards deserve forgiveness, and indeed Mr. Lee did reconcile with a former Australian prisoner. But I wished that in taking this case into consideration, the Korean authorities had considered the victims, the prisoners brutalized by those convicted war criminals and, as they wish for their own, stepped with greater sensitivity on their graves.

On the themes of victimhood and collaboration, not all Koreans suffered during the total war period. Companies and rural landlords grew rich by supplying materials and food to the armed forces. Many born after the annexation in 1910 were more naturally inclined to accept Japanese domination than their parents and indeed identify with Japan's "crusade" in Asia. For example, Japan's creation of

Manchukuo enjoyed a measure of public support because Manchuria was seen as part of Korea's ancestral homeland, the traditional source of "barbarian" invasions and an emerging frontier for Korean immigrants in the late-nineteenth and early-twentieth centuries.

The novelist Yi Kwang-su and the poet Choe Nam-seon, who had helped create a modern Korean cultural identity through their writings—Choe had come up with the word *Hangeul* for the Korean alphabet—urged Korean students to join the "Greater East Asia Holy War" against Anglo-Saxon colonialism under Japan's leadership.

After the war, the new nation was not able to lay the controversies over such figures to rest after the war. The American Military Government that ruled Korea from 1945 to 1948 saw itself as an occupation force and focused on immediate stability without any attempt to address the collaboration question. A special prosecution committee was formed by younger lawmakers when the country became independent in 1948 to look into the collaboration question and clear up the past. The poet Choe was in fact arrested but the trial was suspended, as were almost all the other cases. Despite its wide-ranging powers, the special committee's work foundered on the rocks of changing priorities as the authorities engaged in a bloody struggle to deal with the challenge from the political left. Accused collaborators found a good defense in accusing their accusers of being communists. This shift was best indicated by the reluctance of the first president, Syngman Rhee, himself a veteran anti-Japanese activist, to purge collaborators. He did not exactly block the committee but he urged that it focus on "mending past wrongs" and not in "unnecessary vengeance and retribution." On top of this, or perhaps as explanation for Rhee's caution, the police, which the Americans had kept virtually intact from the Japanese time, fought against any such investigations. At one point a man turned himself in claiming he was part of a police plan to assassinate lawmakers on the committee. When the chief prosecutor tried to have a senior police officer arrested, the police lobbied the president and the prosecutor was demoted. Three days later the Korean War broke out and the country's leaders put the collaboration issue on the back burner.[118]

In 2005, during the presidency of Roh Moo-hyun, the government passed two laws to provide legal backing for an investigation into collaboration and the confiscation of wealth earned by "pro-Japanese activities." This attempt to rectify the past led to a list of 1,005 collaborators and confiscation of some assets, but with the arrival of a new government in 2008, the budget was withdrawn before the project was completed. A private group drawing on donations issued its own list of 4,389 figures in 2009. Among them was the former President Park Chung-hee. But the lack of government support meant the attempted reckoning was seen as partisan and lacked broad public acceptance.[119]

The failure here may be explained because of a prevailing idea that history is science and that the historian's job is to brush the dirt off the goggles and reveal it in its one correct version. That may work with old tombs. But not much else.

The prevailing narrative about the Japanese period taught in schools and enshrined in museums in Korea is: We were brutally exploited, our farmland seized, our rice stolen, everything Japanese was bad, so-called modernization policies distorted Korea's development, and the assimilation policy was a form of genocide. Some historians, on the other side, try to argue that colonial rule modernized Korean society in a way that probably would not have happened otherwise. They believe the extent of Japanese land ownership is exaggerated and that the rice was exported not stolen. It's not hard to point out the modernization of Korea under Japan; it's harder, though, to argue that Koreans would have developed on their own because the Japanese did not interrupt any development plans when they took over. A third approach to this history avoids the nationalistic argument by simply narrowing down on social change and the arts during the period.[120]

I have found it interesting that many people who actually experienced the occupation, while being as patriotic as anyone else, seem to be less fiercely opposed to the Japanese than those born after independence. A classmate of the politician Kim Dae-jung told me that he first noted his friend's political skills when Kim gave an impromptu speech at school during the war urging them all to have confidence that "we" were going to win—"we" meaning, of course, Japan. I knew Kim well when he was an oppositionist, and often went around to his house. But, unfortunately, by the time I heard this gem he was already in the Blue House and I was never able to ask him about it. I am sure he would have said: "Yes, that's embarrassing. Like everyone else, I didn't know any different then. How times change."

Young people like Kim were influenced toward the end of Japanese rule, as the economy expanded and the wartime environment opened up opportunities for employment and careers that previously didn't exist for Koreans, and because many of their elders had given up nationalist resistance and either become open collaborators or else resigned themselves to what seemed like permanent Japanese rule.

Koreans today tend to play down the extent of such acquiescence before and during the war and have trouble accepting at what point it became true collaboration. I should say that this is more of a dilemma for intellectuals assessing the past than it is for each citizen. People appear to understand that progress is wrought by the few and that the vast majority just try to make the best of life and shouldn't be taken to task for not espousing a cause they don't know anything about, like democracy, or for not putting themselves and others at risk in the interests of an uncertain future. Of course, when things change, they'll convince themselves they were always for the better new thing, be it independence or democracy.

To back up the false image of a nation in resistance apart from a few collaborators, the nationalist narrative tends to focus on independence movements that were established in China and other places outside of Korea as a sign of national resistance. This narrative unfortunately does not take us very far because many of these groups descended into factional infighting and collectively they were ineffective in ending Japanese rule and bringing about the country's liberation.

While moral and emotional judgments cloud an accurate assessment of the colonial period, it is clear that it laid a foundation for the coming development—bumpy as it would prove to be—that would transform the Korean people forever.

The bumpiness of that road ahead points to the main reason Koreans have yet to come to terms with the Japanese period: the nationalistic lens through which they perceive it prevents them from reconciling that forty-year period of colonial rule with the forty years that followed—seventy years and counting in the case of North Korea—during which Koreans suffered far more at the hands of fellow Koreans than they ever did under the Japanese.

For, regardless of how you look at the humiliation and tragedy of the Japanese period, worse was to follow.

13

BROTHERS NO MORE

"They shot them. One-two-three-four. Like that. It was at that point that I realized the communists were not our brothers."

For a thousand years the Koreans lived in a single state roughly along the border of present-day China. Then, in 1945, their homeland was split, creating what today is the one thing that almost everyone in the world knows about them: They come in two versions—North and South.

There was, at the time, no neat way to cleave the peninsula. The two American officials who drew the dividing line, on August 10, five days before World War Two ended, did so on short notice, without consulting any Koreans or experts in the country. Using a National Geographic map, they simply picked the 38th parallel, a line that in real life crossed the sea, went up and down mountains, and sliced through villages.

Their intention was to make a convenient halfway point for the Soviet and American armies to meet and assume control from the defeated Japanese army. As these liberators had opposing aims, they favored rival figures among the returning exiles of the independence movement.

For the next three years there were efforts at unity, including a proposed five-year U.S.-Soviet trusteeship that was rejected by Koreans, and elections sponsored by the newly formed United Nations that were rejected by the communist North.

These failures led to the split and formation, in the autumn of 1948, of two separate states, the pro-Soviet Democratic People's Republic of Korea in the north, and the pro-American Republic of Korea in the south.[121]

In 1950, the North invaded the South in an attempt to force unification under its terms. It failed, at terrible cost.

Even half a century later, the governments on both sides keep their people under strict controls and forbid private exchange. For decades after the end of the Korean War in 1953, no people, letters, trucks, trains, or goods of any kind crossed the demilitarized zone (DMZ), the border that separates the two countries and armies. Only commandos, defectors, propaganda broadcasts, birds, bullets, and, very occasionally, negotiators have made the trip.

Two-way trade began in the late 1980s, mostly through third countries, but some of it was direct, by sea. In the late 1990s, in a breakthrough of sorts, South Korean tourists were permitted to sail the few miles up the east coast of North Korea on highly controlled trips to the Kumgang mountain resort. In 2003 the DMZ itself was opened to allow foreign tourists to go through by coach. All of this was halted by South Korea after a tourist walking on a beach was shot and killed by North Korean guards.[122] At the western end of the border zone, South Koreans regularly crossed into the North to the nearby city of Kaesong, where, since 2005, 120 South Korean firms have employed over 50,000 North Korean workers. In early 2016, all work at these businesses was suspended by South Korea in protest over North Korean nuclear weapons testing.

The DMZ itself is supposed to be four kilometers wide. Some years ago, though, the North unilaterally decided to take a step forward, so in some places its guard posts are just a few hundred meters from the central line. As part of DMZ eeriness, this violation is treated as if it never happened and all references to the DMZ—

including foreign press reports—confidently report its official, not real, width.

At the DMZ itself an eerie, surreal silence permeates, though it is often broken by propaganda broadcasts from both sides. This was stopped some years ago, but started up again in 2015. On a blustery day, the North's maniacal preaching is snatched by the wind and only reaches the other side in unconnected phrases. The South Koreans, as you would expect, have better equipment. One student who did his military service at a DMZ guard post in the late 1980s said they used to have great fun blasting Michael Jackson's *Thriller* album at full volume across to the other side. A North Korean defector who had also served as a soldier, on the other side of the DMZ, said he had been moved one winter by the haunting sound of what he later learned were Christmas carols wafting over from the southern side. On one visit to North Korea, I could see a sign in the south through binoculars telling northerners that every South Korean owned a Hyundai. My guides didn't believe it.

Could the Koreans have prevented their own division? This question is not asked in Korea, and the suggestion that they might bear some responsibility is not appreciated. Again, this is in part due to the fact that Koreans are accustomed to seeing themselves as victims. They feel, and rightly so, that they were helpless pawns of superpower rivalry. Their particular weakness was the inability of their leaders to cooperate with one another. Since its founding in 1919, a Korean Provisional Government based in Shanghai had not been recognized by a single government, not even by those fighting Japan. It wasn't that the Korean nationalists had no voice. The problem was they had too many. So many rival organizations created a din at a time when the main powers were committing millions of troops across the globe to the common cause: the fight for the survival of freedom and for huge geopolitical interests. The Korean nationalists were so fractious they had neither the good sense nor the ability to create a cohesive contribution to the allied war effort, or offer a consistent, unified voice in allied forums. This raucous group went on to form over fifty political parties in the south, which was under an American Military Government. For international communists the word "Korean" had become synonymous with factionalism. Such disunity became a factor in the national division. But it's not one that what experts now call victimhood nationalism has room for— any negative trait like this is Japan's fault.

It is unfortunate for the Koreans that the Allies did not impose independence. The next problem for the Koreans was that the Soviets were on the allied side and were offered control over the northern half of Korea even though they had played no role in the Pacific War. (The Soviet Union had declared war on Japan only a week before the capitulation.)

An American Military Government was established in the southern zone. In contrast to their occupation of Japan, for which they had planned for some years, the Americans were remarkably unprepared to administer the Koreans, and had a tendency to see them as low-class Japanese. The Americans arrived on the peninsula to find that local "people's committees" under the leadership of a moderate leftist called Lyuh Woon-hyung, had already combined to form a Korean People's Republic. Although leftist-dominated, it was sufficiently broad to attract a conservative exile, Syngman Rhee, as its chairman. The Americans, however, viewed many nationalists as pro-Soviet communists, refused to accept the new republic, and set about dismantling the committees. They also sought Japanese advice on administration and hired many ex-officials and ex-policemen who had worked in the hated colonial bureaucracy.

In the North, meanwhile, the Soviets appointed Kim Il-sung, a guerrilla leader who had fought in the Soviet army, letting him rule while they issued instructions in the background. Within a few months collaborators had been purged, and land reform overturned the ancient ownership structure once and for all. At the same time, the communists sidelined moderate nationalists and began crushing religion, at first through united-front tactics, and later more directly. The labor camps began filling up. Christians, ex-landowners, and committed anticommunists who could moved to the South.

In South Korea, 1945–50 saw a chaotic and violent struggle for control between left and right. Before the opposing camps hardened, the ideological shades of gray suggested that much of the resistance could have been avoided had the Americans been better prepared to embrace the people's committees.

The most extreme case was on Jeju Island, where a full-scale uprising in April 1948 erupted after heavy-handed suppression of a protest that began when a little boy was knocked over by a policeman's horse. It pitted local communists opposed to the UN-supervised general elections scheduled for May against the police who were seen as pro-Japanese collaborators (because they had been). Rebels gained widespread support and were joined by soldiers from a locally based regiment. They took over village after village, frequently being chased out by day and returning at night.

At this point, the authorities turned to the Northwest Youth Association, a seventy-thousand-member group of refugees from the North, whose leaders had been members and followers of the Democratic Party of Korea. They fled south when their party founder, Cho Man-sik, was rejected by the Soviets in favor of Kim Il-sung.[123] When the police chief went to Seoul and invited the thirty-three-year-old head of the association, Moon Bong-jae, to dinner, the older man prostrated himself, touching the floor with his forehead, and begged for support. He admitted that the police were not trusted by the local people and that they had lost control. A group of two hundred volunteers headed for the island, receiving some basic instruction over the course of their two-day journey. They arrived believing that the island was in communist hands. Later several hundred more men were mobilized. Together, these militias augmented the army and police units and suppressed the revolt with horrendous violence. Armed sometimes only with bamboo spears, they approached the chaotic guerrilla conflict, where it was impossible to distinguish friend from foe, civilian from combatant, with a terrifying rigor that would be used again by Korean troops fighting in Vietnam. Entire households were wiped out, and innocent victims selected for the most gruesome executions.

In one incident in 1948, troops recaptured a village on the island's northern shore, which had been occupied for several days by rebels. The commander lined villagers up on either side of the road, and then faced one of the lines of peasants:

"I want you on this side to say that all these people on the other side collaborated with the communists," he ordered.

"But they didn't," some people objected.

"If you don't, you'll get what they're going to get," the commander said. After a while, the villagers reluctantly gestured as they had been instructed. The commander ordered the fifty or so accused peasants to be taken away. A small boy clung to his mother as she was being led away.

"Ya! Run off or I'll shoot you, too," the commander yelled, and the boy ran off down the road. The adults, meanwhile, were marched off into a field and executed.

In this fashion, the island was pacified. A government commission reported in 2003 that there had been 14,373 confirmed murders, 86 percent by the security forces and 13.9 percent by rebels. It estimated the total death toll might have been as high as thirty thousand, a statistic foreshadowing the carnage of the Korean War. The horror was buried. People never talked about it. Patrick McGlinchey, an Irish priest who settled on Jeju in 1954, and who recounted the above story of the villagers, said he had heard of it only by chance, as the result of a philosophical debate.

"I'm driving along in a jeep with this fellow having this argument. I'm saying that people are basically good and motivated by love and he's saying people are selfish and motivated by survival," he recalled. "The other man was getting insistent. Then he stops the jeep and tells me this story. He had been a medic in the unit and witnessed the whole thing. In the end, he said dramatically that this field was where they were killed. It was all to make the point about the small boy being more strongly motivated by his survival than his love for his mother. I was completely amazed and had forgotten all about the argument. But he says, 'There, you see. Survival.' That's the only reason the story came up. As a way to prove his point."

The anticommunist victors went on to rise in the establishment and others remained on the island. The military commander, Song Yo-chan, for example, later became a prime minister. The leader of the first group of Northwest volunteers, Choi Chi-won, became a national assemblyman. A Northwest leader was made commander of the local regiment on the island and twenty-four other members joined the police and settled there, too. Later, more refugees from the North were housed on Jeju. They had a very real fear of communist subversion.[124]

As well as fear, guilt haunted the survivors, especially where they had been forced to conspire with executioners in the way recounted above. But people had to survive, and to do so they buried the pain and got on with life.

"My mother died in 2014 at age one hundred and one, and she taught me all her life that I should never take revenge, but that I should love people," said Kang Joong-hoon, a poet who was eight years old when his father, uncles, and teachers were killed. "I think that event drew people together, even if it was in silence." In some villages on the island, when people perform ancestral rites on the days their forbears died, every family holds the ceremony on the same day.

Against such a backdrop, the new republic was not created amid celebration and expectation. Furthermore, the new country was an economic shambles. Bungled policies had led to spiraling inflation, food shortages, and near collapse.[125] Syngman Rhee, who had become the first president, was an elderly nationalist who had lived in America for decades and who lacked the vision for economic growth. Around 70 percent of the industry built up by the Japanese was in the North. Half of the South's energy had come from the North, which belligerently cut it off in May 1948.[126] The population in the South grew over five years by 25 percent, as millions returned home from Japan, or fled from the North.

Per capita income in South Korea in 1948 was eighty-six dollars. By this reckoning, the UN rated Koreans on a par with Sudanese. It was reasonable to assume that fifteen or even fifty years later, these peoples would still keep the same company on the UN statistics lists, that is, below Indians and Pakistanis.

"Korea can never attain a high standard of living," wrote a U.S. military official in Seoul, giving the typical assessment. "There are virtually no Koreans with the technical training and experience required to take advantage of Korea's resources and effect an improvement over its rice-economy status." He reckoned that by 1949, when the occupying American forces were to withdraw, the country would become a "bull-cart economy."[127]

Many Americans thought that nature should be allowed to take its course, and—when they pulled their forces out in 1949 and indicated they did not intend to defend the South—it did. Kim Il-sung sought and received permission from the Soviet leader, Josef Stalin, to go to war and on June 25, 1950, his army invaded.

The North Koreans swept southward, rolling over the lightly armed South Korean forces and taking Seoul in three days. They pushed on down to the south coast "liberating" towns and villages, organizing supporters, executing opponents, and taking thousands of intellectuals, and others they considered useful to their cause, back north.

The U.S. came to the rescue of South Korea under the flag of the newly formed United Nations.

It was the first major-power conflict since World War Two and was feared at the time to represent the start of World War Three, between the communist and democratic camps.

The first Americans arrived ten days after the initial attack. As they marched north to engage the communist forces, fleeing peasants stood to the side of the dirt roads and clapped. But the North Korean drive was relentless. The Americans and South Koreans were pushed back and soon all that remained of the Republic of Korea was the area around the port city of Busan.

Men of the British Commonwealth 27th Brigade landed in Busan in late August, and were soon followed by units from Australia, Belgium, Canada, Colombia, Ethiopia, France, Greece, Luxembourg, the Netherlands, New Zealand, the Philippines, Thailand, and Turkey.[128] Korea became known to the outside world through famous battles, such as Bloody Ridge, Chosin Reservoir, Heartbreak Ridge, the Imjin River, the Iron Triangle, the Punch Bowl, and the Busan Perimeter. The most famous of all was Incheon, scene of the bold, amphibious counterinvasion conceived by the UN forces' American commander, General Douglas MacArthur. Despite a thirty-five-foot tide on the west coast, MacArthur landed a massive invasion force that pounded its way to Seoul and dissected the North Korean army.

MacArthur's courage, rhetoric, and flair for the dramatic made him so difficult to deal with that his own president eventually relieved him of command, but the legendary American soldier won the profound admiration of a generation of Koreans. When he retook Seoul, MacArthur staged a ceremony formally handing over control of the city to the Korean president, Syngman Rhee, in the bomb-damaged capitol building. "By the grace of a merciful providence, our forces fighting under the standard of the greatest hope and inspiration of mankind, the United Nations, have liberated this ancient capital city of Korea," he began. He ended by inviting the participants to say the Lord's Prayer. At that moment, bits of glass crashed to the floor from the building's broken glass dome. No one was hurt and, typically, MacArthur did not skip a beat in his prayer. With tears in his eyes, Rhee grabbed MacArthur's hand. "We love you as the savior of our race," he said.[129] No phrase better sums up the feelings toward Americans that lie in the hearts of South Koreans who experienced the war, all mixed in with their suffering, the shame at their own weakness, and their resentment against authority and big powers.

UN and South Korean forces swept into North Korea, took Pyongyang and marched to the Yalu River. Meanwhile, Chinese forces then entered the war in massive numbers to rescue the defeated North Koreans. They pushed the UN forces back again. Hundreds of thousands of refugees fled the advancing communists in the bitter winter weeks of 1950–1. After enemy soldiers were discovered infiltrating disguised as refugees, American planes strafed columns of fleeing peasants, killing hundreds. Vigilante squads from the villages on the refugee trail robbed the wealthy and killed suspected communists. The new South Korean army often fought courageously, but it suffered from inexperience and corruption. Funds for the five-hundred-thousand-strong National Defense Corps were misappropriated and supplies never got through. That winter, several hundred recruits are thought to have died from starvation and thousands more suffered from exposure. Leaders of the corps were tried and executed.[130] The refugees didn't stop until they reached Busan, where they piled into squalid camps and built shacks on the hillsides with mud, stones, and flattened drums.

Despite this chaos, the South Koreans recovered their dignity and hope. Schools quickly resumed and officials and flag-waving schoolchildren turned out to welcome foreign troop ships. Perhaps the most telling symbol of their hopeful dependence was the construction in Busan along the airport road of hoardings to conceal the squalor of the refugee camps from visiting foreign officials.

Amid the violence of the civil war and the reprisals, as one side and then the other took control, any lingering ideas of Korean brotherhood disappeared. The perception among intellectuals of one united, victimized people had been honed by Japanese oppression and was not easily changed. Many Koreans thought the communists were just another political party until their occupation of the South.

"I thought we were brothers and that we disagreed in our politics, but in our hearts shared the same love of the fatherland," said Han Joon-myung, a Christian minister from the North Korean city of Wonsan. "Actually, the communists began oppressing Christians as soon as they took power. Many from Pyongyang had already escaped. But in Wonsan, the atmosphere was different. I myself was not afraid of them because they were fellow countrymen. If they [had been] Russians, we should be afraid, I thought, but we were the same people."

Han was to learn a stark lesson in how nasty brothers can be to each other. A few days after the Korean War began, he was among several hundred intellectuals arrested and put into a prison barracks. In October 1950, when North Korean forces were in retreat, guards began taking prisoners away. Unknown to Han, they were being executed. At first they tied rocks to prisoners and threw them in the sea, but some bodies floated back up. They decided the next day that it would be more efficient to shoot them. They selected a tunnel in a hillside not far from the prison.

"They took us from our cells and tied our hands behind our backs," he recalled. "Four prisoners were tied together. I remember the other three with me. The young man on the left was called Kim Yung-nok. He was an electrical engineer. Next to him was an elderly doctor, called Oh Myong-nyang. Then me, and on my right, a tall farmer called Kang. We thought we were being relocated. After many hours waiting we were told to walk up the hill. The rows of prisoners were twenty steps apart. We'd walk a certain distance and then guards would tell us to stop, then we'd walk some more. I still didn't really understand what was happening and I still had no bad feeling toward the authorities. Actually, it was very cold, and I thought they were taking us to the cave for warmth."

Eventually the four men reached the entrance of the tunnel, which cut into the hill about six foot high and ten foot wide. Inside, an oil lamp lit up one alcove, where Han saw bodies in piles. A soldier in a navy blue uniform was shooting the prisoners two rows ahead of Han. Another was reloading a gun. The next row stepped forward and knelt on the bodies of the previous line of victims and the soldier went behind them, shooting each person once in the back of the head.

"They shot them. One-two-three-four. Like that. It was at that point that I realized the communists were not our brothers. I was suddenly shocked and afraid," Han said.

Incredibly, Han survived to tell the tale of this loss of innocence, thanks to a bad leg. He couldn't kneel, and so he sprawled on the corpse below, which was still twitching. "My mind was so clear. I could take everything in. In my heart I felt such anguish. Mr. Kim fell forward. His face was kind of blown out. Then Dr. Oh was shot and collapsed. At that moment, the head of a young schoolboy in front of me jerked up. 'Look at that,' the guard who was loading the gun said to the other one. They were surprised. The other one stepped up, treading on my head, and shot the boy again. Then he shot farmer Kang. The blood went all over me and he slumped down. The guard doing the reloading called for the next four to come. He'd shot the four bullets and forgotten about me."

Another group of men climbed on top of him and the bodies of three of his companions. After they were shot, the alcove was boarded up. Later, Han heard the noise of the executions being resumed. Some victims sang in loud, bold voices. At the end, he heard women crying. They were the last to be shot. Then the mouth of the tunnel was blasted. Guards joked, telling their mates preparing the dynamite to be careful not to blow themselves up.

Five others survived the killing—two high school students, a young girl, a farmer, and a doctor. Two days later, chance American bombing of the area opened a small hole in the tunnel. One of the boys clambered out. The others, fearful that there were still communists around, stayed put. The following day, UN troops, hearing there had been a massacre, came and opened up the tunnel. They counted 289 bodies, including 28 women and several children.[131]

The South Koreans similarly dispatched those they believed to be enemies. Allied soldiers were shocked at the cruelty the South

Koreans displayed towards prisoners and noncombatants, and some-times intervened to stop killings. One correspondent wrote:

> Less publicized (than North Korean atrocities), naturally, were the excesses of the (South Korean) side, who also shot prisoners in considerable numbers, because it was in certain circumstances a bother and a difficulty, or perhaps a danger, to escort them down the line, and who rid themselves sum-marily of refugees because among them there might be, and frequently were, infiltrators and guerillas. It was all singularly loathsome.[132]

In the early weeks of the war South Korean authorities con-ducted widespread massacres of suspected leftists. A governmental Truth and Reconciliation Commission, formed in 2005, was able to confirm 8,468 cases and said it believed this number to represent around 5 percent of the total.[133]

The war ended with a truce in July 1953. It had been the bloodiest episode in Korean history. The statistics are staggering. As many as 3 million Koreans are believed to have died from causes related to the war. In addition, there were 900,000 Chinese dead and wounded. Over 55,000 Americans were killed or wounded, and 1,000 British and 4,000 soldiers of other nationalities were killed. According to South Korean figures, 129,000 civilians were killed during the North Korean occupation of the South, 84,000 kidnapped, and 200,000 South Koreans press-ganged into the northern military.[134]

The economies of both sides were pulverized. The North was flat-tened by U.S. bombing and industry everywhere was wrecked. Here is a human and economic damage assessment for South Korea: about 5 million homeless, 300,000 widows, 100,000 orphans, millions of families separated; increased population pressure with the influx of 1 million North Korean refugees; tens of thousands of schools and other buildings destroyed; 3 billion dollars (1953 rate) in damage, 43 percent of manufacturing facilities and 50 percent of mines de-stroyed or damaged; inflation accelerated as the currency in circula-tion increased from 71,383 million *won* at the end of 1949 to 650,153 million by 1953; wholesale price index (1947=100) grew from 334 in

1950 to 5951 in 1953 and the retail price index (1947 = 100) rose from 331 in 1950 to 4329 in 1953.[135]

After all this, the border had hardly changed.

What had changed was the division was now sealed in blood. Incredibly, Kim Il-sung avoided blame. A master at the art of turning disaster into victory, he actually strengthened his position by claiming the Americans had started the war and by presenting himself as the hero who brought the great power to its knees, begging for peace. Within the ranks of his fellow communists, who knew this game, he accused his South Korean comrades of misleading him to believe there would be a popular uprising in the South, and had their leader executed as an American spy. With Soviet and Chinese aid, he began to rebuild the North.

In the South, a measure of defiant normality returned. Barbers set up their chairs amid the mud and rubble. Refugees from the North worked as market traders. Women cooked up soup and noodles in street-side shacks. So many struggled daily for food. Until the early 1960s, peasants boiled grass and bark to make it through the spring when the barley crop was harvested.[136] Each year, people died of starvation. Today older Koreans remember how they were constantly hungry. The common greeting of "Hello, did you sleep well last night?" became "Have you eaten rice today?" which is still used today.

Beggars squatted on street corners. In fact, a mentality of mendicancy pervaded all levels, from the streets to the top, with the president rattling his can in front of the American government.[137] Half the country's budget derived from foreign aid.

Ever since the Korean War the two rival sides have continued a form of mortal combat. Almost seventy years later there is still no peace. South Korea has one of the strongest military forces in the world and while North Korea's is weaker and outgunned, it has a nuclear weapons program, a formidable special-forces contingent, and more soldiers per population than any other country. All men in both countries have military experience and millions are eligible for conscription.

Over the years, North Korea has been the more belligerent of the two. Despite the failure of the war, it remained committed to forcible unification. A clause in the ruling Workers' Party constitution calls for the communization by whatever means of South Korea. On a reporting trip to Pyongyang in 1992 with my newspaper's editor, we asked about that. The North Koreans knew I had drafted the questions, and let me know that particular one made them suspect I was a South Korean spy. (The question had actually been suggested to me by a friend who was a South Korean foreign ministry official: "Ask the bastards about that," he recommended. So I did.)

The North has made at least four attempts on the lives of South Korean presidents.[138] Four invasion tunnels have been discovered under the DMZ and sixteen more are believed to have been built. There have been numerous terrorist and commando incidents. In 1987 two North Koreans planted a bomb on a Korean airliner, killing everyone on board. It is believed to have sent numerous spies and several political agents to the South. In 1992, officials tried to put a figure on this activity, saying there might be as many as forty thousand northern agents operating in the South. It was admittedly a wild guess, calculated on the grounds that on any given day in South Korea up to a thousand mysterious electronic signals were being detected. The assumption was that the noises were coded broadcasts by spy cells reporting back to their masters in North Korea, and that each cell consisted of three people who were required to report twice a month.

But if the real number was even one thousandth of this, the results from the North's political-subversion program appear to have been quite useless. Although there have been surprising cases of North Koreans operating in the South, they all appear to be rather trivial. In 1996, for example, newspapers reported that a Filipino Muslim called Mohammed Kansu, who taught Middle East Studies at Dongguk University in Seoul, had been arrested as a North Korean spy. It turned out that his real name was Chung Soo-il and that he was a Chinese-Korean who had gone to North Korea after experiencing discrimination in the Chinese diplomatic service (where he learned to speak Arabic). His alleged role was to wait for destabilization and help nudge along a South Korean revolution. He was also alleged to have faxed information out of the country. Assuming the facts of the case as reported by the Seoul government were true, it is not difficult to imagine that North Korea was proud of this spy before his capture. However, the so-called top-secret material he was sending was apparently just newspaper articles and other information in the public domain.

Experts at the South Korean intelligence agency interrogate North Korean defectors to weed out possible agents, but the main focus of this questioning is to distinguish genuine defectors, not from spies, but from Chinese-Koreans seeking asylum, and ultimately citizenship, in South Korea.[139]

No agents appeared to have been in place in the city of Gwangju in 1980 when the citizenry rebelled against troops enforcing martial law. But there are indications that, subsequently, Kim Il-sung took steps to put people in place to take advantage of possible future disturbances. In 1992, it was revealed that a top North Korean official had lived in Seoul under a false name throughout the 1980s and established chapters of the (North) Korea Workers' Party. The seventy-year-old woman, Lee Son-sil, was never caught, but more than sixty people connected to her were arrested and tried. One was Chang Ki-pyo, a dissident who admitted meeting Lee when she had donated a photocopying machine to his political party. He said he had no idea she was North Korean. Chang was cleared of spying but jailed for a year for not reporting the meeting.[140]

It's hard to know what to make of such cases, which may seem trivial. But they also smell of overzealous prosecution by an intelligence establishment with dubious standards. An acquaintance employed there told me that until the 1990s anyone suspected of anything to do with North Korea was tortured as a matter of course. The fact that before the presidential election in 1997, this agency secretly requested the North Korean army to create an incident on the DMZ to bolster support for the government candidate in the December presidential election, gives an idea of the level of virtue.[141]

South Korea used to carry out intelligence-gathering missions into North Korea, but is believed to have stopped these because so many agents were caught, and because the American intelligence overflights of North Korea provided sufficient data. The terrestrial missions were extremely risky ventures in part because North Korean society is too rigidly organized for agents to penetrate. The story of one secret unit, the Headquarters Intelligence Detachment, came to light in the 1990s. In 1971, a group of civilians recruited by the air force for a retaliatory mission to assassinate the North Korean leader Kim Il-sung rebelled against their harsh training—four had been beaten to death already for complaining—and commandeered a bus to make their grievances public. Around twenty were killed in a shoot-out and four survivors were executed. A popular movie in 2003 was based on this episode. The government now admits that almost eight thousand men sent on secret missions died or remain missing.[142]

Both countries have waged intelligence warfare in third countries and have kidnapped each other's citizens, or otherwise persuaded them to defect. A South Korean disappeared in the 1970s in Oslo, apparently after a taxi driver took him to the North Korean embassy by mistake. A young member of the North Korean elite in the 1980s, apparently intent on defecting to America, went to the South Korean mission in Geneva to ask for advice about obtaining a visa to enter the United States and was persuaded by the South Koreans to go to Seoul.

North Korean leader Kim Jong-il actually admitted and apologized to Japan for the kidnapping of thirteen of its citizens between 1977 and 1983. The Japanese government believes that seventeen people were taken, but it's possible there were many more. While some were used to train North Korean agents to pose as Japanese, some are believed to have been kidnapped and possibly murdered so that agents could use their passports.[143]

For many years there was an equal trickle of defectors in both directions, fewer than ten a year. Both sides publicized only incoming defections. With the famine in the North in the 1990s, however, the numbers of northerners fleeing south increased dramatically. These defectors are not highly regarded in South Korea, in part because their escape puts remaining family members at risk (because of the system of punishment, whereby three generations of a person's family are persecuted for the alleged crime). Some defectors' family members have been banished to the gulag. Yet there have been some cases of entire families who have escaped to the South.

To date, no defector has fired the southern imagination in the way that Solzhenitsyn and Sakharov inspired the West, with the possible exception in 1997 of Hwang Jang-yop, a former philosophy professor at Kim Il-sung University who came up with Kim's

Juche version of Marxism-Leninism and who taught Kim Jong-il. But even his reception was ambiguous because, as all South Koreans knew, his escape meant the gulag or worse for his extended family, and because the government was at that time pursuing an engagement policy.

Most of the North Koreans who escape make dramatic journeys through China and Southeast Asia to reach South Korea and Western countries. Many don't make it. There needs one day to be a monument to them. There should also be a monument to the foreign activists who try to help, some openly, some secretly. At least one, Tim Peters, who has been active in providing food aid and in the underground railroad for two decades, has been nominated for the Nobel Peace Prize.[144]

Repression in North Korea has been more excessive than that of the Japanese colonial state it claims to have freed its people from. Even showing an interest in a foreign country can be interpreted as intention to desert. An Hyuk and Kang Chol-hwan, who were in the gulag and defected to South Korea after being released, said that they were in a prison camp in the 1980s with two language students who had been sentenced for expressing a desire to visit France.[145]

It is estimated that North Korea keeps as many as 150,000 prisoners in its camps, including those who may be classified as "hostile" because they have relatives in South Korea. One North Korean history lecturer, who had burned his Workers' Party card for his own safety during the Korean War when the South Korean troops took over his town, was arrested for this crime after the war. Because of this and because some of his relatives had escaped, he was sent to a remote mountain village and forced to work as a coal miner for the rest of his life.[146]

A life term for political offenders means just that. There are camps from which there is no return. There are also children in these camps, some sent with their families and some born there to model prisoners who are permitted relationships.

South Korea has always permitted more freedoms but, before democracy, it was ruthless regarding North Korea. For decades, criticizing government policy—even, in the 1970s, criticizing American policy—was a crime. Suggesting alternative ideas about unification was interpreted as subversion. Tens of thousands of government critics were labelled pro-communist under a national security law and jailed. South Korea has kept some men in solitary confinement for as long as forty years for refusing to formally declare they were not communists.[147]

What is the reason for such sustained severity? Many must believe it to be right and justified. I used to have lunch occasionally with a man who had been the head of the anticommunist section of the Defense Security Command, a military intelligence body that investigated antigovernment suspects. He didn't keep a jar of human fingers on his desk. His justification for denying rights of suspects and withholding democracy generally was that too many rules and too much social freedom would have diminished his ability to do the job. It is remarkable the extent to which a person's profession fashions his outlook: My promotion, my ability to do my job properly is more important than the lives of non-people. When you meet such defenders of tyranny, the motive that seems to most consistently emerge is fear. It is difficult to appreciate the existence of fear, because it is not visible. It is a still, dark river over which people build their bridges. Fear of instability, chaos, collapse, fear for their own necks, fear of career failure, unemployment, and humiliation. There is also fear of the unknown, and in an authoritarian culture the idea of permitting individual freedom is a great unknown. Where there is fear, there is a kind of wartime morality in which violence is seen as justifiable force.

The two Korean governments have the same reason to be afraid: Both have presented an option for the future of Korea, and only one will win.

North Korea's regime exists on the lie that it has built a Workers' Paradise, an ideal society. For years, there was a slogan over a building in Pyongyang saying, "We are happy." The paranoia is that the lie will be exposed and the leaders strung up on the first available utility pole. In the grip of such fear, it is natural to think someone who defects really is a traitor for demonstrating that heaven isn't all it's cracked up to be. If someone reads The New York Times without permission, he is a spy because he may learn something about the outside world that challenges the lie. Indeed, a North Korean scholar did once tell me that he was struggling intellectually because he had been reading foreign press accounts of his country. "The viewpoint is so different, but I cannot see where it is untrue," he said. He could have been arrested if we had been overheard. Such is the fear of bugging that he chose to tell me this when we were walking along a street.

South Korean paranoia until recently was different: The fear was that its people would swallow the northern lie. Because it is not a complete lie. It's a half-truth. Incredible as this may seem to an outsider, the North Koreans had the better claim to legitimacy in the minds of Koreans. The Koreans' *han*, their resentment and sense of worthlessness, comes from historical acquiescence to greater power. Many intellectuals feel that, after being liberated from the Japanese, the South Koreans reverted to traditional attitudes of dependency, and willingly subordinated themselves to America as they had once done toward China. But while the South was totally dependent on American handouts and troops for protection, the North developed its own version of communism, a nationalistic philosophy of self-reliance called *Juche*, which declared that the state would depend on outsiders for nothing. The "truth" is more in the rhetoric and in the perception than in the facts, which is why Kim Il-sung had to control information so tightly. In reality, the North Korean state was saved during the war by China and rebuilt with Soviet aid. It's just that it didn't let its people know. There is, for example, a Chinese war memorial in North Korea, but only Chinese visitors go to it. Ordinary North Koreans think Kim Il-sung defeated the Americans and the South Korean "puppets" on his own (not to mention wrestling Korea from Japanese rule). But there is also substance. The North's way of getting outside support appeared to turn history around. It brilliantly played off its two allies, China and the Soviet Union, and had them competing to give aid, thereby maintaining a sense of independence.

During a lunch in 1994 I attended with some foreign journalists and other visitors, Kim Il-sung explained *Juche*:

It's anathema to me to follow others. We can learn from foreigners, of course. . . . You must chew first. If it's agreeable you can swallow. If it's disagreeable, spit it out. East European countries got indigestion because they swallowed the Soviet Union. If it rained in Moscow, people put up their umbrellas in Berlin. You have to chew first. Then you eat it. In other words, you make it your own. Otherwise, you'll get sick.[148]

Kim Il-sung, like all dictators, lived in the past. He framed his response to almost every question—after a polite apology to the three Japanese and several Americans around the table with him—in terms of the "struggle" against the Japanese and the "fatherland liberation war" against the Americans.

The Great Leader, as he was called, was in good form during this session and even cracked a dictator joke. When asked what he did for recreation, he said he liked hunting but suspected, now that he was old, soldiers were raising tame bears and pushing them out from behind trees for him to shoot when they saw him coming along.

Close up, though, I suspected he wasn't all there. As I shook hands with him on the way out, I informed him in Korean that I was the Seoul correspondent of my newspaper. As everyone else was from Tokyo, Beijing, or Washington, I thought this might be an icebreaker and that perhaps he'd call me in later to advise on economic growth and democratization. But he seemed oddly detached and did not appear to absorb this important intelligence. He died less than three months later. I was informed some time afterward that he actually spent most of those last months in bed and that he had gotten up especially for our meeting. He also struggled with flatulence. That might have explained the detached look on his face. He was probably in midstruggle when I came up to shake hands and say thanks for lunch.

The *Juche* philosophy has been described by the scholar Brian Myers as a sham.[149] I take his word for it. The two *Juche* books of philosophy I have on my shelf sit there alongside *Finnegans Wake*, unread.

Kim's own explanation says all that needs to be said: I'm not going to let my people be pushed around by foreigners anymore. Koreans had been waiting to hear this. It was the therapy they needed. Kim

Il-sung was so threatening to South Korea because this attitude was clear even in his body language. A handsome young man, Kim grew rather fat and had a waddling walk. But as a public figure he had style. The absolute power he wielded made him come across like a kingly father figure. He inhabited that empty throne in the national psyche. He was one of the few guerrilla leaders who hadn't been corrupted or defeated, and he gave the sense that his first loyalty was to his country. Until the 1980s, when the rise of his son began to complicate North Korean feelings towards the personality cult of their ruler, people would weep real tears of gratitude when they placed flowers at the foot of his statues on his birthday.

Those who were not victims of his brutal regime loved him. The brutality was justified by many as unavoidable because they felt surrounded by enemies. Even many who were victims loved him, and blamed lower officials for their persecution.

Kim was also admired because he managed to do something no other Korean politician had been able to. With boldness and vigor, he melted the myriad factions into one harmonious whole. The usual choir of criticism was silenced. The single ringing note spoke to a deep place in the Koreans, saying the mandate of heaven was his. This message was delivered into the national psyche with great Nazi-like ceremonies in which a million torch-bearing citizens marched in perfect goose step, and acrobats and card flashers performed in perfect sync. These displays were not shown in South Korea in the nervous days, but they are now.

The irony is that South Korean leaders were also very independent minded and difficult for foreign allies to work with. But their strategy was nevertheless to hitch their wagon to the U.S. To this end, they suppressed their nationalistic orneriness to the point that South Korea, both its government and people, appeared the most pro-American of American allies. When anti-Americanism finally burst out in the 1980s, Americans and other foreigners were bewildered, wondering what they had done.

In simple terms, being pro-American saved South Korea, and being pro-Soviet downed North Korea. Although more united under Kim's harsh leadership and economically stronger until the mid-1970s, the North eventually stagnated under its horribly coercive inflexibility. In the 1990s, when Soviet communism collapsed, cutting off vital food supplies, the North went into crisis.

South Korea emerged from a backward, corrupt dictatorship into a modern, industrial, democratic power. It was able to do this under the American wing. Now the world waits for the North to follow suit.

WEALTH

14

DESPERATION

"Everyone was dirt poor, everything was dirt cheap."

One summer morning during the Korean War, as the sun rose in the sky and warmed the Korean fields, James Cameron, a British correspondent who would go on to earn a reputation as one of the finest writers of his generation, experienced what would remain his number one impression of the ravaged country: number two.

The reek of night soil was so bad, he wrote, that it rose "almost visibly" off the fields, filled the air and hung there "as a background for all other sensations." Cameron was no beginner to poor countries, but he'd not come across anything quite so ghastly: "I have never known a country where there was a more lively and thriving commerce in human excrement, even throughout the continent of Asia, which always seems to Europeans excessively reluctant to part with its sewage."[150]

That same summer morn over three score years ago, my wife's grandfather was defecating in his field as usual when a white man with a notebook walked by. My future relative looked up and said to his wife, who was wading in the paddy beside him, "I bet that foreigner writes for a British tabloid. I can't think of a job based on a more lively and thriving commerce in human excrement, even throughout the continent of Europe, whose inhabitants always seem to Asians excessively compelled to makes jokes about toilets."

Actually, I just made that last bit up. No, I did. Kind of like Cameron did. He was exercising that skill characteristic of many highly respected British journalists of sacrificing truth for style. And style can be very seductive. Who is not convinced by the claim of thriving commerce? Cameron, it saddens me to note—because he never came back—had seen the South Koreans at their worst and did not consider them worth British lives. As a man of the pen, he just couldn't resist dumping on them, so to speak, when the right image presented itself. But, he should have. What he wrote was mean-spirited—although that's not a crime in journalism—and exaggerated to the point of untruth—which is. My night-soil sources tell me the good stuff was not plopped in the paddies fresh. By the time it was used, gasses had been taken out. It stunk some but certainly not enough for the genteel traveler to have to hold her hanky to her nose until she was safe inside the Chosun Hotel in Seoul. The claim that the stench formed a backdrop to all other impressions is crap. Ask other foreign arrivals at that time, notably American soldiers and, in the 1960s and 1970s, Peace Corps volunteers, and they will tell you that the standout features of Korea were the barren, treeless landscape and, in the towns, the pervasive smell, not of household waste but of burning wood and coal briquettes.

But, this is an objection over degrees of distaste. Korea at that time, when my friends who are now retiring were growing up, was harsh and makeshift to the point of being repulsive to many a foreigners. "Everyone was dirt poor," said Peter Bartholomew, who arrived with the Peace Corps in 1967. "But then, fortunately, everything was dirt cheap."

Fifty years later—and Bartholomew is still in Korea, as a technical consultant to the shipbuilding industry by day and an expert in traditional Korean architecture and a conservation activist by night—the first impression of visitors is that they are impressed. You've got the modern cityscape, the ubiquitous Wi-Fi and all that, but top of the list in my ongoing survey is the friendliness of the Koreans themselves. For some years now, male foreigners in sunglasses have been telling me they spy more attractive ladies walking past the deck of the coffee shop than in any other country in Asia. These same men used to be scathing about unfashionable Korean men. Now, though, they've gone quiet. So many Korean men are stylish and in shape. They work out, coordinate their outfits, and use makeup. Lots of women, and some men, have plastic surgery. The ethics of this do not appear to be an issue. Others react according to how you appear to them. So why not give them a good experience? Win-win.

That the grandchildren of the war generation have become the beautiful people is a postindustrial thing. In between there has been an economic revolution.

And I mean revolution.

Think of the night soil man and consider this: South Koreans are a nation of early adopters, they have the fastest, most extensive mobile broadband networks and the highest penetration of smartphones in the world (97.7 percent for eighteen- to twenty-four-year-olds), they're banking and shopping on their mobile phones—and whipping out the credit card more than anyone else, and they're a test bed for new products; as land space doesn't change beyond a spot of reclamation here and there, they remain way down—109th in the world—in size; but in population they're twenty-sixth with 51 million; in all things economic they punch above their weight—thirteenth economy, seventh exporter, ninth importer, the fourth- and sixth-largest trading partner respectively for the world's top two trading nations (China and the U.S.), and the fifteenth consumer market; number one country for university entrance (70.9 percent in 2014); number one in shipbuilding (with the top four firms) and in TVs, home appliances, and displays, and second in mobile devices and semiconductors; Samsung's name keeps coming up—it's the world's seventh most valuable brand and eighteenth largest global company; three of the world's top ten LED makers are Korean and LG is pioneering OLED lighting; they're fifth in a lot of things—ranking on the 2015 Forbes list for large global companies, R&D spending, iron ore imports, POSCO for steel production (it was top in 2010), Hyundai-Kia for autos, Hyundai Mobis for auto parts, and in the medals count at the 2012 London Olympics; thirty-eight of the top hundred women golfers are Koreans; and Korea was top (and has been eighteen times) at the 2013 World Skills Competition in Leipzig with gold medals in CNC (computer numerical control) milling, carpentry, confectionery, construction metal work, floristry, IT software solutions for business, jewelry, manufacturing team challenge, mobile robotics, refrigeration and air-conditioning, web design, and welding; Hanjin is the eighth biggest company plying the oceans; Korea is second for liquefied natural gas imports, and has the world's third, fourth, and fifth largest oil refineries; it's ninth in electricity generation, fourth in nuclear power production (with the third and fourth largest nuclear power plants); the seventh offender for greenhouse gasses, it has the second biggest carbon market (after the EU), imposing caps on emissions from over five hundred of its biggest companies; the biggest tidal energy installation in the world is at Sihwa Lake, south of Seoul, and there are plans for even bigger ones at Incheon on the west coast and Garorim Bay; OECD statistics for 2012 showed Korea first in R&D "intensity," spending 4.36 percent of GDP; it ranked first on the Bloomberg Global Innovation Index of countries in 2014, with high marks for patent activity, manufacturing capability, high-tech density, tertiary efficiency, and R&D; a big future focus is anything with "smart" in front of it, like smart factories, smart city service, smart home development, smart grid security, and smart car service; they're developing electric and driverless cars; Korea has the largest indoor amusement park in the world, is the seventh-largest entertainment market and second PC online games market; although the fifteenth consumer market in the world and a test bed for stuff, they've been held back for the sake of exports and are just warming up as consumers; as I said, they are big in plastic surgery—half of local women in their twenties have had some procedure or other; and before we forget the night soil, did I mention Korean men are the biggest users of skincare products in the world?

All in all, the economic transformation is a phenomenon. Korea and Taiwan are the only two countries—let's say it, Taiwan is a country—in recorded history to have managed 5 percent growth for five decades, a feat that emerging-markets expert Ruchir Sharma says earns them a joint gold medal among nations.[151]

There are complex explanations for why some countries thrive and others don't. If the Koreans had remained poor, analysts could have blamed other countries, history, colonialism, absence of natural resources, lack of appropriate education, lack of work ethic, lack of democracy, too much democracy, racism, sexism, something in the kimchi, night soil in the rice—because the Koreans in 1945 had all that and more. But their success exposes such explanations as excuses.

So, what happened? Or, to avoid getting lost without a map in policy country, what is the most important thing that happened?

I've seen many explanations that add to the bones of the lacking-resources-the-South-Koreans-focused-on-exports-with-capital-from-a-guilty-Japan-and-aid-and-tutelage-and-market-access-from-Americans theme. They are spot on, of course, identifying wise policy choices. But a more intriguing and fundamental question should be asked before we look at policy: What drove the South Koreans to the wise choice, and when their choices failed, to wisely change tack and do something equally wise? The analyst, being wise, tends to think, "Because they went to Harvard, like me." But a lot of poor countries have government ministers with PhDs. The answer is more elusive and it takes into account more than just economics. The Koreans, I would say, were angry, dislocated, and desperate. So many were hungry, not knowing where the next meal would come from; the threat of renewed war hung over their heads; all were desperate to exchange the present for a better future. They had to succeed. Ask anyone who has ever started a business, however big or small, and they will get this point immediately. Statistics show that most new businesses fail, and the key to those that do succeed, according to bankers who learn to look out for the right stuff, starts with the right energy, the desire to do well, and the will and means to sacrifice everything else to that end. Second, the energy must be harnessed purposefully, in the right way. This depends, of course, on people, instinct, and luck. The Koreans had been poor but then were made poorer and more wanting and more upended by independence from colonial rule, by returnees, national division, civil war, and the arrival of American soldiers, young boys who should have bowed to their elders but who the Koreans found themselves looking up to, not just because they were so much taller and in charge, but because they had things.

Desperate people prioritize differently. Lee Kie-hong, a government budget planner who joined the World Bank, got a taste of this when he went as part of a delegation to Indonesia, to discuss aid projects. He was astonished on arrival at Jakarta Airport to find no one from the government there to meet them. The bank officials caught taxis, checked into their hotel, and then phoned the state planning agency BAPPENAS to confirm appointments. No one seemed in that much of a hurry to meet them. Lee, the only Asian in the group, offered to go to the agency offices to troubleshoot.

A senior Indonesian official at the agency asked Lee where he was from.

"Korea," he said.

"What's the population?"

"About thirty million."

"We're not afraid of Korea. Our population is a hundred and twenty million." After this peculiar comment, the Indonesian official relaxed and began talking frankly and revealed the problem: The Indonesians were upset that the leader of the World Bank delegation was from the Netherlands, the former colonial power. Lee was familiar with World Bank insensitivity—many of its missions to Korea were headed by a Japanese economist, which meant Korean officials had to swallow their pride and to focus instead completely on the object at hand: getting loans.

"I know the sun rises in the east and sets in the west," the Indonesian official said. "But when the whites say it rises in the east, I say no and tell them that it rises in the west."

As I say, priorities.[152]

In 1961, the Koreans got the leader who met theirs.

15

ECONOMIC WARRIORS

"Anything is possible. We can do it."

Park Chung-hee inspired, bullied, beat, cajoled, and enticed the Koreans out of the paddy fields and to the forefront of the industrial world.

Author Mark Clifford describes him as an "economic warrior." He was "a nation builder with few peers in the modern world," Clifford writes. "None of the better-known national architects of the twentieth century—Ataturk, Nasser, or Lenin—have built a more durable and prosperous country than Park."[153]

The son of a *Donghak* rebel who had been pardoned in an amnesty and had become a subsistence farmer, Park's struggle in life began when his forty-five-year-old mother tried to abort him. Thinking she already had too many children she did what she could—drank raw soybean sauce and willow soup to poison the fetus, tied a belt around her belly, and even jumped off a wall.[154] He survived this pre-birth battering and went on to do well at school. He became a teacher and then joined the army, reaching the top of his class at the military academy in Manchukuo, the state the Japanese had created in Manchuria. The figurehead emperor, Pu Yi, awarded him a gold watch at graduation. Park then went on to attend the elite Tokyo Military Academy and after his graduation in 1944 he was commissioned a second lieutenant and stationed at Manchukuo.

This Japanese experience shaped the character of Park's rule. Not only was he exposed to Japanese-style planning, from which he developed an attention to detail and the ability to take clear and bold action, but he and his fellow Korean officers were also imbued with the Japanese attitude of placing the interests of the group and nation before personal or family interests. "As a group they had scant regard for the intricacies of etiquette, which all too often limited action in Korea," Clifford writes. "They also placed much less importance on the family and more importance on the organization—both the nation and the corporation. In this sense they were much less typically Korean than the generations that preceded and followed them. It is hard to overemphasize their importance in Korean development."[155]

Scholars Moon Chung-in and Jun Byung-joon note three other ways Park's leadership was colored by his Japanese background: his admiration for Japan's nineteenth-century Meiji Restoration modernization drive—the source of his commitment to the ideas of "rich nation, strong army" and "production promotion, exports and construction"; his emulation of the Japan he knew—the military-led period—which inspired him to see his mission as saving Korea from corrupt and incompetent civilians; and his study and benchmarking of Japan's post–World War Two economic development. "The respect for Japan's accomplishments coexisted with Park's distrust of and enmity toward Japan (as) different sides of the same coin."[156]

While Park's contemporaries could understand his pragmatism, some question today whether this past makes him a collaborator. He was the most notable on the list of collaborators published in 2009 by a private institute. Inclusion on this list of Koreans in the Japanese army and police depended on their rank rather than on what they had done. For good measure it cited a story in a Japanese-language newspaper in Manchukuo about a twenty-three-year-old elementary school teacher from Mungyeong, Korea, named Park Chung-hee, who had written an oath of allegiance in his own blood in his application to join the army.[157]

This may strike us, in our armchairs, as a clear case of emperor love. But in post–World War Two South Korea, Park suffered more for his association with the Korean political left than with the Japanese. After his older brother was killed by police in 1946 during a communist-led riot in Daegu, Park became a member of the South Korean (communist) Workers Party. He saw the left as more organized and patriotic, and less corrupt than the right. In 1948 he was arrested and sentenced to death. The sentence was commuted and he was later pardoned due to his cooperation with investigators. The Kennedy administration knew enough about Park's history to worry after his coup that he might still have been a communist. The local press (enjoying a freedom he later curtailed) gave him a Russian-sounding nickname, calling him "Parkov."

"Park Chung-hee was never an ideological communist," said biographer Cho Gab-je. "But he was an emotional communist because of his mind for independence. He thought that Japanese imperialism had been replaced by American imperialism. He was a very independently minded and practical person. His basic way of thinking was that you can travel as far as your power allows you. Power is the most important thing, not empty words. He endured the humiliation [of dependency] and wanted to build up Korean power in order that we could be independent from both Japan and the United States."

In other words, *Juche* by a more subtle route than Kim Il-sung's.

Within days or weeks of taking power, Park dissolved political parties and social organizations, dismissed thirty-five thousand bureaucrats, arrested four thousand "hoodlums" and two thousand "communist sympathizers."[158] Taming the business community took longer. Park considered the conglomerates' (*chaebol* in Korean) heads to be greedy and corrupt. After several business leaders were ordered to return "illegal profits" and pressured to donate their wealth to the government, U.S. Ambassador Samuel Berger advised Park that he needed the *chaebol* and warned the *chaebol* heads that the consequence of pushing to maintain their monopolies might end up with their companies being nationalized. This advice was taken by both sides. Banks, however, were not so lucky. They were nationalized.

As commander in chief of the economy, Park employed the same Prussian style of management he had learned in the Japanese military and which he had employed as a general during the Korean War. This involved setting objectives and giving his lieutenants broad scope to take the initiative in meeting them, promoting those who fulfilled their objectives, and firing those who didn't. In such an atmosphere there was no room for learning by failure; thus, aides learned to keenly anticipate the president's will. For example, they could tell whether he liked a project by the way he signed the plan. An upward flourish in the signature meant: I like this. Downward was ominous.

Conveying bad news also needed to be handled carefully in order to protect the messenger. The president's special assistant for audit and inspection, Hong Jong-cheol, had the authority to question any Blue House official, regardless of their rank. He made a point of drinking with no one else but the president and on those occasions got drunk to lubricate the delivery of his findings and recommendations.

At the start, Park appointed military officers as government ministers. They went to work in uniform. The result in the first three years was a revolving door with economic planning and commerce and industry ministers lasting under six months on average. Park then turned to the technocrats.

The junta picked six industries as engines of economic growth for the first five-year plan: cement, synthetic fiber, electricity, fertilizer, iron, and oil refining. The last was to be managed by the state; the others allotted to the thirteen leading *chaebol*. The objective was to create the materials at home so that manufacturers did not have to pay dollars for imports. The target was 7.1 percent annual growth with a long-term vision of doubling the size of the economy in a decade. The strategy was called "guided capitalism," with the state very much in charge, with banking functioning as a utility, and the *chaebol* doing what they were told and unable to pressure the administration for laws to be crafted in their favor.

At a time when Burma and the Philippines were seen as the promising Asian economies of the day, the outside world was not impressed with Korea's economic plans. The prevailing forecast was gloom. In 1963, a financial crisis seemed to confirm the pessimism and led to the adoption in the following year of a national strategy of export-oriented industrialization. Everything Korea did was to be exportable. Instead of establishing steel and petrochemical industries, for example, to support local production of goods like shirts and ships for export, the technocrats envisioned these industries that needed to become internationally competitive as exporters in their own right.

O Won-chol, one of Park's most important Blue House aides through the 1970s, described this moment in 1964 as the setting up of a "base camp" to get the country up the mountain.[159]

Camps One to Four were marked by annual exports: 300 million, 1 billion, 10 billion, and 100 billion dollars. The successful ascent took only thirty years, the most rapid ascent to developed status in world history.

It went like this: The first focus was light industrial goods like shoes, clothes, and wigs made mostly by unskilled women being paid low wages by small and medium companies. Camp One was reached by the end of 1967. Per capita GDP was 150 U.S. dollars.

As the government during this time had encouraged firms to buy modern machinery to upgrade the quality of their goods, exports grew. Camp Two was set up in 1970. Per capita income was now 250 dollars. The climb to Camp Three started.

On May 30, 1972, Park closed the monthly export expansion meeting at the ministry of commerce and trade, and wandered over to look at the new export items exhibited in the conference room. "How precise is this?" he asked. He had picked up a piston pin. Nobody in the entourage knew. Finally, an auto industry association official spoke up, saying it was 1/100mm. "Hmm, that's about as precise as the M16," Park said.

O Won-chol remembers this well, not so much for Park's question or the surprise of everyone else at his comment about the M16, but because that afternoon Park called him in and asked him another question: "Mr. O, what industry should we develop to reach the ten billion dollars in exports mark?" That simple question would eventually lead to the construction of the heavy chemical industry.[160]

Exports were at 1.8 billion and Park wanted to get to 10 billion and Camp Three. During that climb, iron, steel, and petrochemicals developed, along with machinery, electrical goods, shipbuilding, and autos. One of O's proposals apparent even today was the idea of developing industrial clusters, such as Changwon-Masan on the south coast. (Interestingly, this idea was also picked up by the North Koreans who consulted with O Won-chol via Japanese intermediaries during the 1970s.)

In 1973, a global crisis sent oil prices way up and threatened all the plans. O Won-chol knew the Japanese were knocking on the door of the Middle East and suggested a strategy to the president: The previous years' rise in export manufacturing had turned construction into a significant domestic industry, so, what if Korea were to turn this expertise into a dollar earner? Korean military officers and civilian contractors had gained experience in Vietnam during the war, working for the Americans. In addition, technical high schools were now graduating fifty thousand students, mostly men, each year. Why not put them together—skilled workers led by people experienced in American military management? And so began the Korean rush to overseas construction, most notably in the Middle East. The economy now shifted from unskilled female to skilled male labor.

Camp Three was reached in 1977. Per capita GDP was now one thousand dollars. Camp Four was reached, after Park's death, in 1990. By that time, Park's "compressed economic development" ascent was complete, the industrial foundation for future growth firmly set.

In his public speeches, Park used statistics to get the message across. For the 1964–70 and 1973–80 periods, he set the overall goals of 1 billion and 10 billion dollars and said the country should achieve 40 percent annual export growth to make it. This would mean that everyone could eat rice, and that the country would be able to defend itself against North Korea. "Anything is possible," he would say. "We can do it."[161]

Exporting was the priority and would become a patriotic duty. The mantra of growth soon became "export good, import bad."

As a consequence of Park's use of statistics, helped along by the media, Koreans developed a high level of economic literacy. They know what GDP means and why it's more important than the price of beer, which is more than you can say about half the electorate in some countries.

Companies were given export targets by bureaucrats. Firms that reached these targets gained preferential credits, tax benefits, and the grateful support of bureaucrats, who were being held responsible by the all-powerful Blue House for the results. Firms that failed to meet their targets could get into trouble and even find themselves under orders to be taken over.

It would be a mistake to see this process working from a well-thought-out blueprint from the start. Park had a vision of a strong state that could defend itself against North Korea without depending on the U.S., and he and his fellow officers understood the factionalism and fractiousness of Korean society well enough to know they had to keep firm political control. But implementation involved ideas that came from the bureaucracy and were tested in a process of trial and error. At the same time, the junta's own factional issues got in the way and colored the future. Early on, for example, the KCIA arrested some North Korea–born members of the junta's Supreme Council of National Reconstruction who served on a Committee for Prosecution of Illicit Profiteering for allegedly favoring business leaders from the North. The net effect of this incident was that *chaebol* from the southeast and central provinces, where Park and his chief lieutenant, Kim Jong-pil, came from, became favored.

A key element of Park's economic strategy was normalization of ties with the old colonial enemy. This came with a useful five hundred million dollars in loans plus three hundred million in compensation for the colonial period, which Park used for economic projects rather than as direct compensation to victims. The signing of diplomatic relations offended many Koreans, for whom the memories of occupation were still fresh. Students protested so vehemently they almost brought down the government. This experience put Park on notice that he needed economic growth not just to build his nation, but also to legitimize his regime.

Busan was the port nearest to Japan and key to the country's future as a trading nation. Park wanted to build a modern express-way to link it with the industrial Seoul-Incheon region in the north-west. The World Bank advised against it, and the National Assembly refused to approve it, thinking Park would bankrupt the country. He ignored them. There is a story that after a few months' work the cement ran out. "I don't care," Park is alleged to have said. "Finish it anyway." Within three years, 80 percent of the country's vehi-cles would be using the expressway and the area it serviced pro-ducing almost 70 percent of GNP. If the story of South Korea's remarkably rapid transition from agricultural backwater to mod-ern industrialized state in one generation is recalled a millennium from now and reduced to a biblical-length verse or two, this slightly apocryphal episode may do. It tells of a particular miracle that typified the bigger miracle of growth. Like the biblical loaves and fishes, the cement was there, somewhere. The miracle was that people were persuaded to produce it. They were persuaded by a leader with a vision of development and the ability to push it through.

In the early 1970s Park started the Saemaul (New Village) Move-ment, which through a combination of self-help projects and govern-ment funding sought to modernize agriculture and raise rural living standards. This program began with a cement surplus in 1970. Park ordered that every village be given 335 free bags. The following year, villages that had been deemed to use them well (about half), were given another 500 bags and a ton of steel. Park issued an eleven-point memo containing such wisdom as: "Projects forced upon villa-gers by the government are doomed to fail." The movement spread to cities.

Few believed the economic development would last. The North Koreans denied it was happening and, to convince themselves, stopped releasing their economic statistics in 1965. A wonderful story illustrating this denial comes from the first ever North-South talks in Seoul in the early 1970s. The southern delegation was led by Lee Bum-suk, a man of rare humor. (A fluent English speaker, Lee often cracked jokes about his own name. Once at a press meeting, a foreign journalist politely pronounced his name in full with the cor-rect Korean pronunciation—*Ee bomb sock*. "Just call me Bum-suck,"

Lee said.) Lee accompanied the head of the northern delegation in a car from the border point of Panmunjeom. As they drove into Seoul, the North Korean got his first look at the city, which had been rebuilt since the war and was bursting with construction and traffic, somewhat different from the North Korean propaganda images of bombed-out Korean War scenes, streets filled with beggars, prostitutes, and American GIs. But he was not fooled. He could tell by the flowers along the roadside even before they reached the city that the South's propaganda machine was in overdrive.

"We're not stupid, you know," he said. "It's obvious you've ordered all the cars in the country to be brought into Seoul to fool us," he said.

"Well, you've rumbled that one," Lee deadpanned. "But that was easy. The hard bit was moving in all the buildings."[162]

Of course, the propaganda machine was in full swing. Houses along the route from Panmunjeom to Seoul were bigger and better. Obviously the cavalcade with the North Koreans did not swing through the red-light areas, nor the poor districts, nor past the huge American military base near the city center. These were features, but no longer the illustrative features of what was really happening in South Korea. After a decade of Park's rule, the country was on the move.

Through the seventies and eighties, as job opportunities expanded, people poured into the cities from the villages. From 1960 to 1970, Seoul doubled its population to over five million and by 1990 the population had doubled again. Once known for their indolence, the Koreans were turned by the opportunity and pressures—by Park's carrots and sticks—into phenomenally hard workers. Freed from the farm, they invested in education so their children could escape the factory. They saved, too. For those with the money—banks didn't do mortgages—a 139-square-meter (1,500-square-foot) apartment in the new Banpo Complex in Gangnam cost around 7 million *won* (around 27,450 dollars) in 1970. (By 1990, it would cost over 500,000 U.S. dollars and in 2015 well over a million.) Wives took on the role of family banker. They would take their husband's salary each month and allocate him pocket money. They kept an eye on apartment prices and moved their families every so often to bigger, better flats. The families who own those million-dollar apartments never had the salaries to buy them through savings and mortgages. They started off in tiny two-room places and made strategic moves every two or three years. For the first move they would go out on the street on the moving day, flag down a passing blue-goods truck, pay the driver a few thousand *won*, and pile the few things they had on board. Twenty years later, there was much more to move and the whole process became more sophisticated and expensive. As prices rose, their less savvy neighbors found themselves unable to upgrade from tenancy to ownership, and pushed to the edge of town.

In 1972 Seoul experienced its worst flooding in almost fifty years when 17.8 inches of rain fell in one night, causing landslides and widespread havoc that left 200 people dead and 127,000 homeless. After this catastrophe Park built dams upstream to manage the Han River. It would flood again, but 1972 was the last time riverside residents saw houses—with cows, pigs, and chickens on the roofs—floating past their apartments.

Park understood the importance of the American alliance for Korea's growth. Indeed, the rise of South Korea may be viewed, without offense to Koreans, as an American success story, too. After its initial bungling, including its responsibility for having divided the country, the U.S. government stood by its ally, providing a security shield against possible renewed conflict with North Korea, and a market for Korean products. There have been tensions and difficulties, but the benefit to Korea was that it was both in American strategic interests and a natural consequence of American values as a nation born in opposition to imperialism, that its client state grow economically and politically from near-total dependency to equal partnership. America did not start the growth. But it continued to provide a security umbrella enabling growth to happen. It also demonstrated by its own wealth and freedom what Korea could become.

After Park, another military coup-maker, Chun Doo-hwan, took over after a brief period of uncertain civilian rule. Chun continued the top-down management style of Korea, Inc. after allowing himself to be tutored in economics by two brilliant advisers.[163] The economy continued to boom during his 1981–8 rule.

South Korea's industry should have been restructured or reformed in the late 1970s or early 1980s in keeping with the natural shift from labor intensive to capital intensive. Chun failed to do this because he did not want the risk of social turmoil. He came to power through a brutal suppression of pro-democracy protesters and did not want to provoke unions and ordinary citizens into antigovernment comradeship with students. So he continued the Park tradition of suppressing wages in the interest of growth through exports. Another failure was an unwillingness, due to fear of inflation, to invest in social infrastructure and build the ports, roads, and rail connections needed. As a result, in the 1990s transport costs (as well as labor costs) rose dramatically, pushing up the price of Korean products and eroding the nation's competitiveness.

In 1988, when Chun's successor, the democratically elected Roh Tae-woo, opened the Summer Olympics in Seoul, the rest of the world had its first good look at modern Korea. Although Western correspondents had been reporting on the economic changes for years, the greater emphasis had been on the absence of political development. Images of student protests and labor unrest and the "dark side of development" conveyed the sense of a still backward nation. The Olympic Games brought in the largest influx of foreigners since the Korean War and most of them—athletes, officials, and sports writers—had little interest in political demonstrations and sweatshops. To them, the modern stadiums and facilities and the ability of the Koreans to organize what at the time was generally recognized as the best games to date, was nothing short of astounding, compared with what they had been led to expect. This was a developed state as far as most were concerned.

In many ways, this event marked the moment of South Korea's ascendancy over North Korea in the minds of all Koreans. Southerners continued to be paranoid beyond a reasonable level of fear about the North, but the contest was over in terms of which system would win. The telling measure of this was the decision by the North's East European allies to participate in the games, ending a run of Olympics marred by boycotts (Moscow in 1980 and Los Angeles in 1984).[164] The Chinese, participating for the first time, refused to join a North Korean boycott and received a stirring welcome when they entered Jamsil Stadium.

There was more than sports and symbolism in the Eastern Bloc decision. Beijing had already developed a significant trade with Seoul, and other states were taking a particular interest in how South Korea had grown so remarkably under strong authoritarian government. There were lessons to learn here. Within four years of the games virtually all socialist and former socialist states had developed full diplomatic relations with Seoul.

The Koreans had, in the global economic race, emerged from behind and were now running as the pacesetter for the pack chasing the leaders.

16

THE SMELL OF MONEY

"He was an uneducated truck driver but he had passion."

When she was little, Kim In-sook and her sister shared their bedroom with two large rice sacks stuffed with cash. "My mother hated the smell of money. That's why she put it in our room," she remembered.

Two men would come in the morning to empty the sacks. In-sook would step into the backyard of the house and open the gate to her father's soap factory. The sound of the workers chatting and yelling filled the small plant. In the center, animal fat boiled in a gigantic kettle two meters high and six or seven meters long. The hardened product went to the military and the soft residue was sold to traders and neighbors who queued outside each morning. By 1 P.M., the soap was sold and the sacks of money full again.

That was in Daegu during World War Two. By the time of the Korean War, her father, Kim Sung-kon, was running a small textile operation in Anyang, just outside Seoul. One day, the factory took a direct hit and everything was destroyed, except for several tons of cotton recently imported from Texas, and stacked outside the plant. As North Korean forces approached, he evacuated the family to Daegu and looked for a way to get the cotton south. At the time, road haulage was impossible, and the railroad was reserved for military use only. By good fortune, the head of the Anyang railroad station was an old school friend. He arranged for the cotton to be shipped in boxes coupled between containers of military supplies.

Back in his hometown, which was a center for textiles and outside the area controlled by the North Koreans, In-sook's father quickly restarted his business.

Over the years, as Korea developed, that business morphed into a conglomerate, or *chaebol*, called SsangYong with interests as far-ranging as construction, cement, paper, automobiles, refining, engines, presses, leisure, and finance.

The Kims' story typifies the family-run businesses that have dominated the Korean landscape for the past five decades. It is a story of energy, instinct, and turns of fortune, such as having a friend in the right place, all given broader purpose by nation-building political leadership.

"To develop a chaebol, you needed to work really hard and have a sense about where you could make money," said In-sook, now a retired professor of criminology. "But I think it was fifty percent luck."[165]

For the family to retain control of a growing empire requires something more: acceptance from their own society. When sugar millers like Samsung and car repairmen and builders like Hyundai added on ever larger affiliates to make ships, autos, and electronics, they could no longer rely on bank loans. They started offering equity. When it reached the point where the family no longer had majority ownership, they deployed a complex system of cross-shareholding whereby their affiliates all owned shares of one another. It was as if the owning family owned the smallest drum and it owned a little bit of the next one and so on, ensuring they effectively had the whole kit to play with how and when they chose. Society has accepted this until now thanks to the conviction—part truth and part myth—that the Korean economy needs the harmonizing presence of the owning families in their respective *chaebol* to ensure continued national growth.

As testimony to the extent this is accepted, it did not seem to bother anyone that for several years before he was incapacitated in 2014 "Chairman" Lee Keun-hee of Samsung hardly ever worked, and held no formal title in any Samsung company.[166]

As of this writing, there are sixty-one such groups composed of two or more companies and with combined assets of five trillion *won* (4.37 billion dollars). That qualifies them as *chaebol*, and has made them subject since 2014 to cross-shareholding restrictions between affiliates. These groups have around seventeen hundred affiliates in all. These are in over half of all business sectors, are the lead players in one-quarter of all sectors, and account for around one-third of all sales.[167]

The four largest groups—Samsung, Hyundai Motor, LG, and SK—generated value added in 2013 equal to almost 10 percent of GDP.[168] The giant of these giants, Samsung, which alone accounted for almost 5 percent of GDP, has sales of over three hundred billion dollars and its listed affiliates make up one-fifth of the Korean stock market. Their flagship, Samsung Electronics, accounts for 14.4 percent of stock-market capitalization, generating 43.5 billion dollars in value added in 2013, the equivalent of 3.1 percent of GDP.

These global brands are a source of national pride, admired for their contribution to the country and their standing in the world.

Today's *chaebol* have their roots in the period of Japanese rule, when Japanese business was dominated by large family-held conglomerates called *zaibatsu*.[169] (Doosan is the exception. It started earlier.) More were born after World War Two, when the assets of Japanese companies operating in Korea were confiscated and sold off at exceptionally favorable terms to Korean businessmen. Others, such as Daewoo, began in the 1960s.

At first, Park Chung-hee actively supported certain companies, but these almost all failed. He then generally created an environment in which creative and energetic entrepreneurs could succeed. Park strapped a rocket to these businesses, but it was up to the tycoons to light their own fuse.

Park wanted firms that could compete internationally with the

Japanese. He thought that, as Koreans were not traditionally hard-working and as businessmen and politicians were corrupt, a few loyal and capable lieutenants would be more effective than a vast army of small and medium businessmen. There was a risk. Large, powerful groups could become power bases for ambitious tycoons to challenge his authority. It was precisely this fear that was behind Chiang Kai-shek's unwillingness to foster large firms in Taiwan. But Park Chung-hee thought he could control his businessmen. (In 1992, the political establishment was directly challenged when the Hyundai founder, Chung Ju-yung, formed a party and ran for the presidency. Chung lost, and the winner, Kim Young-sam, removed similar ideas of grandeur from other businessmen by prosecuting the septuagenarian Chung on charges of violating election-funding rules. The Hyundai man was given a three-year sentence, suspended out of consideration for his age.)

Going the Japanese way also posed a risk of another kind. The Korean business culture is characterized by an extremely low level of trust between people outside the same family. From this point of view, it would have been more natural to foster small- and medium-size family firms, and for the state to create the large corporations in sectors where size is necessary.

The scholar Francis Fukuyama has introduced this notion of trust as an underlying factor in business success.[170] He notes that Japanese, for example, can do business more easily with, say, Americans, than they can with their neighbors and cultural cousins, the Chinese. In some countries, rational and fair legal systems and business practices underlying economic behavior work because they are underpinned by a high level of trust between people. This trust may be strengthened by democracy and good, fairly enforced laws, but ultimately it derives from cultural factors. Germany, Japan, and Britain, and some parts of America are examples of "high-trust" business environments; Taiwan, China, France, and Italy are "low-trust." In high-trust societies, you see businesses ranging from small family firms to huge conglomerates that endure through several generations of management. In low-trust societies, most businesses are small, and family-run, and lucky to survive through the third generation because young owners seldom have the same interest as their grandparents, and the family can't make the leap of trust to introduce professional nonfamily members into management. Such societies can develop economically when the state steps in and creates big corporations at the other end of the business spectrum.

For Fukuyama, Korea is an anomaly. It has massive corporations and a highly concentrated industrial structure just like a high-trust society. Yet it has a low-trust culture. What is unusual is that the state has consciously promoted gigantic conglomerates as a development strategy. "The Korean case shows . . . how a resolute and competent state can shape industrial structure and overcome long-standing cultural propensities," Fukuyama observes.[171]

The Korean government controlled companies through a complex licensing system, through subsidies, and protection in the domestic market from foreign competition. But the key lever of control was the restriction on the financial sector. In contrast to the Japanese *keiretsu*, which developed around a bank, the *chaebol* were forbidden to own more than an 8 percent share of a bank. Korean businessmen looking to borrow money to start or expand their businesses had to go to state-directed banks and gain government approval for loans, even for overseas loans. In this way, finance was directed into productive nation-building endeavors like shipbuilding and steel, rather than restaurants and mortgages. The bankers did not have to take responsibility for bad loans: given that the government had approved them, the government would bail them out.

This mechanism of control served as a whip, driving credit-led companies to go boldly into completely unconnected types of business. But it was also a restraining leash. The presidential Blue House yanked when displeased. For example, credit was withdrawn from the Kukje Group, causing its collapse in 1985, in part because it was known to have provided funds to the parliamentary opposition party and to have failed to provide corresponding, and sufficiently large under-the-table donations to the Blue House. The economic planners in the bureaucracy who favored pushing the *chaebol* out to the mercies of market forces also yanked at the leash from the Kukje Group, which was bankrupt and poorly managed. Letting it go would send a signal to the others to shape up. The same signal went out after

Daewoo was allowed to flounder in the wake of the Asian crisis, much to the astonishment of its founder, who had thought the government would help with the debts he thought he had incurred for the sake of the nation.

Actually, that was not an unreasonable assumption, given the purpose for Korean companies in the Park era. Unlike, say, American companies, which run on a model of increasing shareholder wealth, Korean firms existed initially for nation-building. In addition, for as long as Korea lacked a social welfare system, big business accepted the unofficial duty of absorbing the huge numbers entering the labor market. *Chaebol* were given quotas of students to employ. Labor laws made it almost impossible to fire workers and the government set pay guidelines that saw a dramatic rise in labor costs in the second half of the 1980s. At the same time, the stock market was opened in imitation of the Anglo-American system, but without any protection of the small stockholders. Owners started floating their companies, but still conceived of them as their own. People who bought shares were seen as gamblers without any rights, rather than co-owners.

Thus, Korea appeared capitalist on the surface, but socialist in practice and attitude in terms of the strength of central control. In fact, Korea up to the Asian crisis could be described, in a century of failed experiments, as one of the world's most successful centrally planned economies. (The closest sensation I have ever had of a workers' paradise was not in North Korea but in the 1990s in the South Korean cities of Ulsan and Pohang, which were so dominated by their resident *chaebol*—Hyundai and POSCO respectively—they struck me as the kind of fiefdoms that Marxist planners in communist countries could only ever dream about.)

Many of the first-generation *chaebol* leaders were truly charismatic overachievers. The undoubted master was Chung Ju-yung, the founder of Hyundai Group.[172] A peasant from North Korea, Chung left school at the age of fourteen and began picking up odd jobs on building sites. After a stint as a dockworker in Incheon, he moved to Seoul, where he got a job delivering rice. Soon he had his own business, but it collapsed when the government introduced rationing. Then he went into car repairs. His first workshop burned down and he started again. After independence in 1945, he opened another garage, called the Hyundai Auto Repair Company.

Five years later he started the Hyundai Construction Company. Thanks to a brother who spoke English and had good relations with U.S. military engineers, Chung won contracts to build facilities for the U.S. army. Although a tough boss, Chung was not aloof. He used to roll up his sleeves and work on sites alongside his men and, for relaxation, would challenge them to wrestling matches.

"He was an uneducated truck driver but he had passion," said O Won-chol, the presidential economic secretary who called Chung in to execute new ideas such as spearheading the expansion of Korean construction companies to the Middle East. Chung first came to Park Chung-hee's attention when he agreed to build a set of barracks for officers near the DMZ, for a budget all the other builders had rejected as too low. "He showed the others what was expected of them," said O.

Later, Chung took his group into electronics and shipbuilding. The scale of these operations was breathtaking from the start. The Ulsan yard was the biggest in the world, but it was being built by a company with no experience in shipbuilding. The first ship was built there while the yard itself was still under construction. In order to progress payment, the Hyundai workers spot-welded the keel and invited international certifiers in to approve it. They completed the welding later.[173]

Chung survived the arrival of the new dictator, Chun Doo-hwan, in 1980. Like other *chaebol*, Hyundai paid millions to the presidential Blue House in political donations. Among other donations to the national cause, Hyundai funded Seoul's successful bid in 1981 for the 1988 Olympics. In the later part of the decade, Chung led the charge of Korean business into Russia and China. In 1989, he became the first prominent South Korean businessman to visit North Korea, where he was permitted to return to his home village with a convoy of vehicles bearing gifts. When he stepped down as honorary chairman in 1991 at the age of seventy-five and launched his bid for the presidency, his younger brother, Se-yung, took over.

Another business figure who went more successfully into politics was Park Tae-joon, the man who developed the country's steel industry. A former army officer, he inherited some aspects of American management training with its emphasis on rationality and efficiency. As an aide to Park Chung-hee, Park Tae-joon was put in charge of the plan to develop a steel industry.[174] After being turned down for World Bank and U.S. Exim Bank loans, he used personal connections in Japan and an argument that the Japanese were honor bound to atone for the occupation by helping the Koreans. He got the loans he needed in 1969. By the mid-1980s, his Pohang Iron and Steel Company (POSCO) had turned the small fishing village of Pohang into the world's single biggest steel-production plant. Ten years later, after new plant openings, POSCO had become the world's biggest steelmaker after Japan's Nippon Steel. Originally conceived for weapons manufacturing, the Korean steel business soon began to make a name for itself. Much of its product was taken a few miles around the coast to Ulsan, another small fishing hamlet that had become the site for the huge Hyundai shipyards and car factory.

Park Tae-joon had the same single-minded capacity for hard work as Chung, but he was a perfectionist. He later became a leading political figure who opposed the nomination of Kim Young-sam as the then-ruling party's presidential candidate for the 1992 election, and wisely moved to Japan after Kim won to avoid retribution. He returned to politics in 1997, as an ally of Kim Dae-jung, who became the president in 1998.

Another phenomenally hard worker was Kim Woo-choong, the founding chairman of the Daewoo Group. Unlike Hyundai's Chung, whose sons were parachuted into top positions, Kim could not be accused of nepotism. He could be accused of neglect, though, along with a million other Korean men of his generation. He was a fifteen-hour-a-day, seven-day-a-week man for three decades. It is said he took his first day off work in 1990, at the age of fifty-four, when his son was killed in an auto accident.

His family story illustrates the combination of suffering and solidarity that lies behind so many successful Koreans. When he was a boy during the Korean War, Kim's father was taken off by North Korean soldiers and never seen again. Still in his early teens, he became the breadwinner, selling newspapers. He wouldn't come home until he had made enough for the family to eat the next day. His mother and younger brothers waited till he got home before they had dinner. "I was so happy, and we really enjoyed those meals," he wrote. Sometimes they would already be asleep by the time he arrived. On those occasions, he realized there had been only enough rice for one bowl and that they had saved it for him. His mother would fib and say they had already eaten. He would fib and say he had eaten out that night. "We were obviously lying to each other and we both knew it," he wrote. "We were materially poor, but rich in heart."[175]

On the paper route, he competed with others boys to poach customers. He learned to outdo his rivals by running as opposed to walking around his route, and delivering the newspapers but returning later for payment. This kind of street-smart mentality is typical of the first generation. In Singapore once, armed with fabric samples from Hong Kong and Vietnam, Kim claimed they were Korean-made, secured 300,000 U.S. dollars in orders, went home and had the clothes copied and made.[176] He broke into the U.S. market after buying a range of American shirts and having them taken apart stitch by stitch and copied.

Daewoo ("Great Universe") began as a trading company with a 5,000 dollar loan in 1967. Three years later, it had export sales of 4 million dollars. Kim expanded from selling into manufacturing textiles, and soon gained the attention of Park Chung-hee, who had been a pupil of his father at Daegu Normal School. With this political connection and his own energetic business sense, Kim branched into cosmetics, shipbuilding, construction, electronics, automobiles, and other sectors. He did this by taking over existing companies, often at the government's request, rather than starting new businesses in the Hyundai style.

Kim Woo-choong was something of an upstart among the older *chaebol* chiefs in the 1960s and 1970s. He was also unusual in that he did not drink or smoke and had little time for formalities. Indeed, he was reputed to be almost vulgar in his eating habits, slurping his noodles at breakneck speed and finishing before the others at the table had finished the toasts. These bad manners reportedly upset the North Korean leader, Kim Jong-il, when the Daewoo chief visited Pyongyang for business talks.[177] They also created a bad atmosphere once in Italy, where he offended a local businessman who had prepared an elaborate meal that Kim wolfed through in a few minutes.[178]

It's easy to be impressed by these legendary characters. But, in the end, you have to ask yourself what exactly it was that they were so good at. When Daewoo collapsed in 1999, it had debts of 80 billion dollars. A friend who ran a small business responded to this news saying, "Now I see how these *chaebol* grew—if the government lent me eighty billion, I'm sure one or two of my companies would turn out okay." Kim fled abroad to avoid the inevitable corruption investigations. At the time, it was the largest corporate bankruptcy in history. Thirteen other top-thirty groups, including Kim In-sook's father's SsangYong conglomerate, met the same fate. Hyundai lurched under a debt load of almost 50 billion U.S. dollars, but survived.

17

THE CHAEBOL PROBLEM

*"My mother always told my brothers to tip waitresses well.
'That's where the rumors start about your character,' she'd say."*

The *chaebol* have always been a visible and convenient target for the broader complaints of Koreans about the corruption, unfairness, and powerlessness they experience. Mindful of this, the politicians, an even bigger target, routinely seek to deflect potential criticism by addressing the "*chaebol* problem."

Governments have been declaring since the 1980s their intention to rein in the conglomerates, yet they haven't, or couldn't. ("Economic democratization," code for *chaebol*-curbing, was a key issue in the 2012 presidential election.)

In essence, the *chaebol* problem refers in business to the inequalities and bullying that occurs everywhere else in a society that, for all its straining to be different, cannot stop viewing people hierarchically and therefore as fair game for abuse. Thus a large company in Korea means something different from a large company in an egalitarian place like, say, Australia. Status allows for different rules.

That was why the business community in 2013 saw the four-year sentence given to Chey Tae-won, the chairman of the SK Group, for embezzling company money for his own investments, as harsh. Unfortunately for Chey, the court was influenced at the time by public disgust at the easy fines, suspended sentences, and presidential pardons that *chaebol* chiefs normally enjoy because of their jobs as vicars in the church of the national economy.[179]

Getting into a *chaebol* is not easy, and requires a rigorous application process that used to rely totally on credentials but which is now becoming more creative. But still, as the instinct is to hire and instill loyalty and to worry later about competence, a noticeable feature of the *chaebol* is the difficulty they have in recognizing and rewarding talent. It is not always the high performers who rise to the top.

"I was quite astonished [by what] seemed to be a policy of promoting young people . . . who were notable for their mediocrity," said one American research fellow who spent several years with one of the conglomerates. "I figured it was connected to the growing authority of the chairman's son. The people around him [in senior positions] had to be young but not too brilliant."

This type of environment in which capability is subordinated to political skill—not of course unique to Korea—helps explain why Koreans prefer the more predictable practice of subordinating capability to age. In other words, promotion by seniority alone, which is the default preference in Korean companies and even among Korean staff in many foreign companies.

At the dizzying heights of *chaebol* chairmanship we find an atmosphere of power the ordinary Westerner would find peculiar. Not so much because of the power-wielding—many Western companies have an authoritarian culture and their people are nervous around bosses—but more because of the rituals that signal such power. In some companies, for example, even the top executives stand to attention when the chairman walks in.

I used to have an office on the same floor as the top executives of the Dainong Group. On the first day back from New Year holidays, the big boss would assemble his staff and yell at them for half an hour. "It's just a pep talk," my secretary would tell me. It sounded more like the regimental sergeant major on a bad day.

I once became quite friendly with the brother of one *chaebol* chairman, who had been given the presidency of an affiliate even though he was not really into business. On the executive floor, a hushed quiet prevailed. People spoke in low voices and padded around on thick carpets. No work was done here, at least not work in the sense that I knew it. The bookcases contained a decorative set of reference manuals, their spines never cracked; the desk was clear, with no evidence of paperwork. I'd always find him sitting in one of the armchairs. He liked to chat about politics to practice his English and he'd tell me how the political parties were always after him for donations. Before we went for lunch, he would press a button, then stand up and say, "Let's go. Is Chinese okay?" and then transform from a casual, rather artistic character into the corporate general, and march out of the office. The secretaries would already be standing to attention and an aide would be holding open a private elevator. I would follow, and acknowledge the aides, and wink at secretaries, pretending to be a democrat but enjoying the role as the boss's foreign pal. They probably thought I was a flake. We were ushered down the elevator, and at the bottom, the driver was waiting to whisk us off to a posh local hotel where a table lay prepared in one of the private rooms of the restaurant.

"Why do you bother with all this?" I asked him after he confided that he'd rather be playing music than doing business. "I mean, the staff just being paid to hang around you, and all the standing to attention?"

"I know," he said. "If I didn't do it, they wouldn't take me seriously."

That was certainly true. Nothing dilutes authority more than fraternizing with the troops. I can think of only one Korean boss I came across who behaved as if we were all equals. He had been a scholar, and had spent years in America, which may have explained it. He would actually chat with secretaries, as equals. Seeing a Korean man in a senior position like this, even I found it reflected weakness and inexperience. He was replaced after a while and returned to academia.

Of course, the humble folk further down the ladder aren't so humble with people inferior to themselves. It is remarkable how the harassed junior employees at big conglomerates mistreat their suppliers. Unlike the Japanese conglomerates, which tend to cultivate relations with suppliers and see them as integral to their network, the Koreans opt for abuse. Prospective suppliers are treated like supplicants. Once they win a contract, the real abuse starts. Fees may be reduced, and payment delayed. I know some public relations companies, for example, who will only work for multinational clients in Korea to spare their staff the calls at 6 P.M. on Friday afternoon, unnecessary weekend work, and general unpleasantness of working with Korean firms.

This is a matter of corporate, not national culture—the clients at the multinationals will invariably be Korean nationals—and has some logic. For example, until quite recently, suppliers were usually paid with a promissory note, a kind of check the recipient could not cash for three or six months. There's some benefit, when you've got the scale and millions due to the milkman and the plumber, to hold it in the bank for a few weeks just for the interest. (When the unofficial loan market was active up until the late 1980s, a company could lend this money it was holding back from suppliers at 30 percent interest). Thus the abuse is not just a consequence of culture. It happens because it makes financial sense. The helplessness cascades downward. Printers, who are suppliers who supply suppliers, are a highly abused business caste and have a high rate of bankruptcy.

So, the little guy in Korean business expects to be abused. Case in point: One small company spent years developing a continuous variance, or gearless, transmission for cars. (Big international firms have been working on this for decades and have not come up with a commercially viable product.) Two Korean inventors put their prototype into an old Hyundai model. I had a go in this car. The sensation of going from zero to eighty kph without changing gears and without the revs going up was unusual. (A slight problem was that it had no reverse gear, so it still needed some work.) The inventors were invited by a leading *chaebol* to use their facilities under a deal by which the *chaebol* would have first refusal on buying the final product. After a few months, the inventors discovered that the *chaebol* had registered a near-identical patent. The *chaebol's* engineers had been unscrewing the product at night and copying it.

In 2009, when Korean pop artists turned their attention to overseas sales, they found their music being pirated by a number of international sites. The biggest of these piracy sites were able to provide extensive music catalogs within minutes of release in Korea. As a result, they could generate two, three, four times the number of unique visitors and traffic that the biggest Korean music sites could manage in Korea. This meant that Korean consumers were going to these sites instead of buying the music at home through local distributors. Distribution company DFSB obtained ministry of culture funding to go after the top forty piracy sites in the world. "We ended up shutting down over one hundred sites through warnings and takedown notices," said Bernie Cho, the CEO of DFSB. Cho then discovered that two prominent Korean companies, CJ E&M and Soribada, had been supplying the foreign pirates, a claim later backed up by a 2011 Korean government investigation. That explained the scale and speed that had puzzled the industry. The motive? To screw the local, Korean distributors.

Another feature of the *chaebol* problem is price-fixing. Since the 1990s, for example, a key Samsung Electronics strategy has been to conspire with competitors to cut production and raise prices where it could. The company was fined millions of dollars for a long-standing scheme involving cathode-ray tubes in courts in Korea, Europe, and the United States in 2011 and 2012.[180]

In 1998, when LCDs were starting to replace the cathode-ray tube, the company proposed to competitors Sharp and Hitachi that all three raise their LCD prices. Years later, it paid out millions in settlements in the United States for this racket. In 2005, six Samsung Electronics executives were jailed and the company paid fines of three hundred million dollars to the American government for fixing prices for its DRAM memory chips.

While we're on Samsung, another of its standard practices is to copy other people's products. Now, let's be clear and accept there is a place for copying in business. In fact, business is like music: You learn by imitating and becoming accomplished in playing music written by others. To earn royalties, a song, like a business, needs a differentiating point. In business, this point may be small. The lady who opens the coffee shop didn't invent coffee, cups, ambience, or anything, and maybe even got the idea for everything from the name to the menu color from other places. But hers is the only coffee shop for miles. That's her point of differentiation. The leaders in this game tend to be those who make the more significant changes, the category changers if you like. Their innovation may be protected by patents, with the legal and reputational risk for those who violate them. It's here, though, where Samsung is most guilty. It is a shameless copier of other people's ideas. A European court, for example, found Samsung had copied Sharp's flat-panel technology; the US International Trade Commission said Samsung had stolen Kodak's digital imaging technology.

The highest profile and most egregious example was the ripping off of the Apple iPhone in 2010 and the tablet computer in 2011. Apple sued and, as part of its muddy-the-waters strategy in this extremely complex tech sector, Samsung countersued, claiming Apple had copied its patents. The clash cost the two sides over a billion dollars. Courts found for Apple in Germany and the United States, for Samsung in the UK and Japan, and for both in Korea.

As Samsung is by far the biggest *chaebol*, these cases beg a question: What does it take in Korea to get to the top and stay there? I would suggest Samsung remains at the top because it insists on being the best in whatever it does. Where it can't, it withdraws, as it has with retail, automobiles and, in 2015, defense. Being the best in the Korean environment requires a tooth-and-claw approach to business: It's a vicious world out there, so to win, you have to be the most vicious.

This goes back a ways.

When Lee Kie-hong was assigned as a section chief in the planning bureau of the ministry of reconstruction at the end of 1956, he hired English-speaking graduates of North American universities, and his team—who included a future deputy prime minister and future governor of the Bank of Korea—was given the job of dealing with the U.S. embassy to allocate raw materials imported under the U.S. aid program.[181] They were young, inspired, and, most important, from well-to-do families and, therefore, did not need to engage in the kind of leveraging of their discretionary power for gain, an endemic evil in those days when bureaucrats' salaries were not enough to live on. U.S. aid at that time was a special boon for companies because the exchange rate was fixed at 500 *won* to the dollar, while the market rate was anywhere between 800 and 1300. The pressure on the bureaucrats dealing with the Americans was relentless and the temptations hard to resist.

> The industrial lobbyists were usually very personable. Every morning they would come to greet us and sit down in the office so naturally [as if they belonged there] it was difficult to get them out. They behaved as if they were members of the family. It presented quite a strange scene. They often invited me or my staff out to high-class restaurants. A single lunch could cost more than a month's salary. They would also quite frequently invite us to dinner at a gisaeng house. The cost was more than several years' salary in my case. I accepted these invitations because it was a good opportunity to hear the background stories of the respective industries.
>
> I suggested to the representative of the sugar industry, which was experiencing explosive growth due to U.S.-financed raw-sugar imports, to provide lunches to my staff of ten. Our salaries were not sufficient to eat lunch. I arranged to have my staff eat lunch at a nearby restaurant every day and at the end of the month the bill was paid by the industry association. Yes, this was corruption. There is no question of that. But I took comfort in the thought that this was less evil than taking bribes individually. The free lunch boosted the morale of the planning section. But good things don't last. Colleagues in other sections of the ministry complained about unfair treatment. My assistant Chung suggested discontinuing the free-lunch program. And so our short period of "corruption" came to an end.[182]

One of Lee's team, Yoo Ho-sun, was responsible for agricultural products in the American aid program. A graduate of the Harvard Kennedy School of Public Administration, he would find himself on the receiving end of Samsung ruthlessness as a result of a decision made by Lee, who was the ministry's representative on the joint committee between the U.S. embassy and Korean government.

In setting priorities I proposed raw cotton, wheat, and fertilizer be given priority over sugar. Though sugar was regarded as essential in rich countries, I thought that as we were poor we should not waste the U.S. aid funds on it. Those who could afford it should be made to pay the market price. In other words, my argument was that allocation of the fund for sugar imports at the rate of 500 *won* meant we were subsidizing consumption of nonessential commodities. My counterparts (on the U.S. side) strongly supported my position and Yoo also agreed. I reported to the planning director and the minister. They simply accepted it, without comment. We cut the (annual) allocation of $12 million in half. At the time the sugar industry was rising at an explosive rate and the three sugar refineries grew into a conglomerate headed by Samsung Sugar Co, the founder of today's giant Samsung Group. From their perspective, we had committed an unforgivable error. Though we agreed not to divulge information on how the decision was made, the culprits soon became known.

The ruling Liberal Party was the beneficiary of generous political funding from the sugar industry. Minister Kim was pressured to restore the allocation, but he firmly opposed any change. Six million dollars was a huge amount at the time when Korea's total exports were a little over $20 million. We two became marked men. Critics called us puppies who did not fear a tiger. In June 1958, Yoo was fired on exaggerated corruption charges and jailed. As the agricultural products section chief he was technically responsible for raw sugar, but I was the real culprit. He had just followed my instruction. But by the time of his arrest I was already in Bangkok working at the UN Economic Commission for Asia and the Far East, a safe haven from political persecution. [A senior colleague] warned me not to visit Korea. Once targeted by Samsung there was no escape for Yoo. In those days it did not matter whether you committed a criminal offense or not, just being summoned by the prosecutors almost always destroyed a person's social and professional standing and it would certainly have ruined me. Officially, Yoo's crime was receipt of bribes from a friend in the silo business. Actually, the person in question was a mutual friend and, as such, he gave us a little cash occasionally. Although this could be interpreted as bribery, given the realities of that time, it was not really considered as such. His government career ruined, Yoo became a professor at a university in Seoul.[183]

The year after Lee shared this fifty-year-old story with me, I had my own, albeit milder, experience of the same Samsung bulldozer in modern form. In a satirical newspaper column on Christmas Day 2009, I decided to list up some spoof Christmas gifts. Like, Korean President Lee Myung-bak sent world leaders gift packages of Korean food. I know, it's hilarious.[184] I also made a couple of topical cracks about Samsung, one to do with the promotion of the chairman's son, Lee Jae-yong, and another to do with revelations by a whistle-blower about the extent of corporate gift giving to the establishment.[185]

None of this seemed so funny a few weeks later, when a prosecutor asked me to explain it in a tediously drawn-out interrogation that lasted five hours.

"When you said that Samsung sent photographs to its employees, did you research to see if it was true?"

"No." He was going through all fifteen or so gifts in the column and with each response spent an age typing into his computer. In the interest of time, I was being monosyllabic.

"So, you admit you did not research?"

"Yes."

"So, you wrote it not knowing if it was true or not?"

"Correct."

"In fact, you wrote it knowing it was not true?"

"Yes."

When he reached the last unfunny joke, which was about the North Korean leader sending his South Korean counterpart a gift of Kopi Luwak coffee beans, those rare and expensive ones that are extracted from the feces of the palm civet, which is a kind of Indonesian cat, I added: "It's satire."

"What?"

"Satire. It's funny because it's not true. But there's a half-truth in there."

"What do you mean?" He wasn't typing this.

"Let's say Koreans are really annoyed with America over something and you write a humorous column saying that President Lee shook President Obama's hand and kneed him in the groin. That would be funny. Because you can see why Lee would want to do it but you know he can't. You know it could never happen."

"It's not funny if it's not true," he declared and resumed typing.

Either way, the whole experience wasn't that funny. Samsung took out a civil suit demanding one million dollars in damages. It was withdrawn after I apologized. But this prosecutor thought he had a criminal case and took me separately to trial after I rejected a summary judgment of five thousand dollars. The judge threw it out.

For this book, I became curious about the man who had blown the whistle on Samsung's corporate gift-giving. I went to Gwangju, where he now works, to talk to him. Kim Yong-chul, who had been Samsung's legal counsel, explained that prosecutors had investigated his charge that Samsung made regular payments to prosecutors and others but claimed they could find no evidence.

"It was strange," he said. "I made the list of prosecutors to receive money myself. I also personally delivered some of it. I gave the investigators lists of high-ranking officials who accepted the money." The going rate for such payments before he quit in 2004 was 5 to 20 million *won* for prosecutors and 20 to 50 million for tax officials.

So why was nobody prosecuted? Kim's explanation comes from his own experience, before he joined Samsung, as a prosecutor.

"Prosecutors and senior officials are afraid of being isolated," he said. "It's well known that colleagues who disadvantage Samsung get demoted." It's a well-founded fear that goes back to Lee Kie-hong's experience in the 1950s.

The payments are not considered bribes by donor or recipient but rather function as gift-giving. Samsung, Kim said, is somewhat sophisticated in that it makes payments to officials in keeping with traditional practice. For example, donations at funerals, birthday presents for the wife of an official, a "congratulations" donation to a new arrival at the tax office. Hyundai, on the other hand, he said, just gives one-off larger amounts.

The purpose behind this multibillion-dollar annual endeavor is quite simple: to secure popular and institutional support to maintain the family control over their *chaebol*.

This is important because, as we have seen, *chaebol* family shareholding is typically very low. The average is just 4.3 percent.[186] But this stake shoots up to 60 percent thanks to investment between group affiliates and by executives who are beholden to the family; thus, the families maximize their power with minimum investment in a system that is not tolerated anywhere else in the developed world.[187]

The champions of cross-shareholding are the Shins of Lotte. Their group has annual revenues of seventy billion, making it the fifth largest. But the Shins themselves own only 2.4 percent. They manage it all through a web of 416 circular investment links between affiliates. Similarly, the Samsung Lees own just 1.28 percent of their empire but cross-shareholding boosts their effective stake to 47.29 percent.

"To keep control of Samsung," Kim Yong-chul said. "The Lee family needs acceptance from the National Assembly, politicians, Korean people, and the media."

As everyone knows, Samsung makes very good products and a lot of them. Indeed, as I have said, Samsung tends to excel at everything it does. It doesn't quietly own a bunch of different brands. Rather, for Koreans, the Samsung name, whether it's the hospital or insurance company, means excellence.[188]

But in these pages, I wish to underscore the more problematic side of such *chaebol* because they represent serious issues from both ethical and business points of view.

The *chaebol* vision and competence has served the nation well, and has for their shareholders been a multibillion-dollar winning approach. But it is not sustainable. No one loves them. That means society will drive them to change and clean up their act.

One way to achieve this is to bring to Korea the competition its companies face abroad.

Because national development has been a process of catching up with developed countries, it has involved imitation, not innovation. Foreign companies were deemed useful for as long as their technology was needed. While making money out of foreigners—i.e. exporting—was considered virtuous, there was a collective revulsion at the notion that foreigners should be making profits in Korea.

One of the worst manifestations of this attitude a generation ago involved the American company, Amway. This highly successful company was no stranger to controversy. Its multilevel marketing method of distribution was frequently attacked in other countries and it was often associated with dishonest and predatory "pyramid" companies. Amway gained approval to enter the Korean market in 1991 after a request by then–U.S. president, George H. W. Bush, during an official visit. Multilevel marketing, whereby independent salespeople received commission on the sales of other salespeople whom they recruit, was new to Koreans but perfectly suited to their relationship culture. Distributors could operate independently and avoid the stifling hierarchy of a normal company and, second, they could recruit and sell through their large circle of family and acquaintances. Seventy percent of Amway's distributors were women, who soon started to threaten the established order of the conglomerates which controlled the distribution and labor markets.

Early success with its soap and detergent products led to attacks in the media and bureaucratic delays, especially in customs clearance of key product components, which were prompted in part by business rivals.

Two years later, prosecutors began investigating pyramid sales. Two American executives and several Korean staff were held in jail and interrogated by prosecutors for allegedly infringing rules on distributor training. The company president, David Ussery, was kept behind bars for nine days with his hands often bound. "I wasn't badly treated, but the Korean staff were knocked about a bit," he said. The company was later found guilty of violating a provision in the law that was later revoked. By 1996, Amway's annual sales represented almost 40 percent of sales in the multilevel-marketing sector. In 1997, the Korea Soap and Detergents Association, a grouping of eighteen rival companies, launched an attack. It took out advertisements alleging that one Amway product was a major cause of water pollution. The National Council of Consumer Protection Organizations, funded mostly by the government and *chaebol*, formed an anti-Amway committee. Reporters who included Amway's position in their stories got angry calls from this organization accusing them of taking bribes from the American company. As a result, during the year, sales dropped by

64 percent and half of the 140,000 distributors stopped working. Finally, the Fair Trade Commission ruled against the Korea Soap and Detergents Association, which was forced to apologize.[189]

Ten years later, the foreign whipping boy was Lone Star Funds, an American firm that specialized in buying distressed assets—companies, buildings, or loans whose owners were bankrupt—and turning them around. This company endured tax and criminal investigations as a direct response to negative public sentiment whipped up in the media after a group called SpecWatch formed by activists and a handful of workers who had been laid off when Lone Star bought the bankrupt Korea Exchange Bank. One of these former employees had actually held a knife to the throat of the bank president, an act that the media and others seemed to consider evidence of passion—naughty, but irrelevant to the big picture in which the evil Americans stood to make a multibillion-dollar profit from Korea when they sold the bank. Media were also incensed that, as the company was registered in Belgium, Lone Star could benefit from a bilateral agreement and avoid paying Korean tax. The prosecutors went in with no evidence but with the idea, as the Korean saying goes, that "beat a coat and dust falls out"—i.e., everyone is guilty of something.

Sure enough, there was dust. The investigations were so intense, with staff being called in to explain things about the business that prosecutors didn't understand, that the fund's business was effectively brought to a halt. The first crime that came to light, which the fund's own lawyers found and reported to prosecutors, was that its Korean head had stolen twenty million dollars from his employer. His successor was eventually jailed to take responsibility for an announcement by the bank's board of a plan which caused the share price of the bank's credit card unit to fall and then followed it a week later with an announcement that the fund would buy up the unit's shares. This move was interpreted, without evidence, as deliberate share price manipulation. (Later, when Lone Star was looking for buyers for the bank after it had been turned around, consultants found a secret compartment in the office of the bank's American president, complete with computer, monitor, and live camera trained at the monitor on his desk. A search for anyone in the company who had requested more than one IP address turned up a bank director who had set it up during remodeling of the office in order to get inside information that he could sell to potential bidders.)

The pattern holds ten years on. In 2015, for example, when IKEA, the Swedish furniture maker, opened a store, local furniture associations moaned and, miraculously, a study was commissioned that found that some of IKEA's products were more expensive in Korea than in other countries. As pathetic as this sounds, this is a typical starting point for regulatory moves against a company.

Such issues arise as a consequence of the willingness of bureaucrats and politicians to prioritize political factors, including public sentiment and personal relationships, over the law. A call from a journalist to a prosecutor asking what he is doing about company X is enough for the latter to feel pressured to do something. This could change, for as of this writing, in the first ever investor-dispute case involving Korea at the International Centre for Settlement of Investment Disputes of the World Bank, Lone Star Funds is suing the Korean government for $4.6 billion, the amount it claims to have lost because the financial regulator violated its own rules in refusing to let the fund sell its assets in Korea until the court cases were completed.

If the government loses this case, it will learn to follow the law even if it hurts.

I should point out that Koreans are not as antiforeign as these stories may suggest. Absent a domestic competitor or source of complaint, the foreign player is welcomed. But where there is local competition, the deeper relationships usually mean the foreigner is disadvantaged. Consider, for example, that the government looks for every opportunity to slap Google around even though it has only 4 percent of the market, and yet the local competitor, Naver, which has 75 percent, is left alone. Such blatant bias comes from fear.

"Koreans are afraid of foreigners because they lack confidence in their own ability to compete," says lawyer Jeffrey Jones. "This applies less to the younger generation but it's still there." The government, for example, fears that despite its small share Google will somehow find a way to dominate the "less capable" Korean-owned company.

The most blatant example of the unfair disadvantaging of foreign business involved the Visa credit card company. In 2008, it accounted for 64 percent of all card transactions in Korea. In that same year, the local telecom, KT, acquired a company called BC Card and didn't like the low market share. It's easy, with long-standing relationships with the establishment, for local executives to moan about this type of situation, "We're getting killed by the foreign players. It's not right." One or two lawmakers raised the issue of "excessive fees" by market-dominant foreign players and the regulator came up with specific guidance to banks to stop issuing foreign cards. The regulator, the Financial Supervisory Service, even wrote the marketing script that banks were to read to customers advising them to choose domestic cards. As a result of this campaign, Visa's share dropped thirty points in three years.

This, however, is an exceptional case. If anything, the reality is that foreign and Korean businesses alike find it challenging to do business in Korea.

When Richard Hill was appointed the CEO of Standard Chartered Bank in Korea, he found the bank subject to the same type of over-scrutiny by regulators as local banks.

> In my last year in man-hour terms, we had eighteen hundred days of auditing. The regulators have such blanket power to demand information that they effectively paralyze operations. When you consider that there are billions of transactions a year, there are bound to be some mistakes but whether these mistakes are material or intentional is not taken into consideration. This starts with the Blue House. . . . At the time of the *Sewol* ferry accident we were under investigation for data leakages, but there was an attitude emanating from the Blue House that banking had to pay for something and it magnified the pressure on the regulator to find guilt. Issues became massively exaggerated. This is the most challenging thing for business, foreign or local, in Korea. The uncertainty of the relationship with government officials makes it impossible to plan ahead. They lurch, it seems, from crisis to crisis. Why? Because that's the state people feel most comfortable with. Drama is the most comfortable place for people to be in Korean society—the hierarchy works, roles are crystallized and people see what they have to do.

For foreign firms, antiforeignism is an easy one for the foreign CEO to argue with his bosses, but it is more of an excuse than a real explanation for why things go wrong. Foreign companies are more likely to get into trouble because the foreign CEO knows nothing about the market and does not have the right support to plug the gap.

In the twenty-first century, Korean companies no longer function as alternatives to welfare, although the government taps them on the shoulder from time to time.[190] That notion has shifted to "corporate social responsibility"—the public relations and goodwill things a company must do to be liked.

At the same time, the conceptual function of the company has not shifted from nation-builder to one of creating wealth for all shareholders. The institutional investor is viewed as an outsider and the mom and pop investors are just putting their money in the company instead of the bank. That is not to say the purpose has not changed from nation-building. The real purpose of the Korean *chaebol* company is now to build wealth for the controlling shareholder and allow them to maintain their exalted lifestyle as the real owner.

As a measure of the success of this objective, the wealthiest people in modern Korea are indeed mostly second- and third-generation *chaebol* owners.

Their relationship with their homeland is a complex one. Koreans do not believe the rich have earned their wealth fairly and legitimately. Rather, given the extent of government control and corruption, it is as if they have been allowed to get rich because it was useful for the country for them to do their thing, while your average Mr. Kim wasn't. Put another way, the rich do not belong to a class whose path to wealth is accepted. If PhDs, for example, earned twenty times more than average, Koreans might understand and accept it. But the *chaebol* families were just tossed around like everyone else, by division, war, and revolution, into the lottery bowl and tumbled out randomly not quite knowing where they stood. (Kim Sung-kon, the SsangYong founder, for example, found himself kowtowing to his former driver. The man had left him to join the army during the war and by the time of Park Chung-hee's military coup was in the group calling the shots.)

Ironically, traditional family ethics aggravated this resentment. In old Korea, a successful person was duty bound to take care of his extended family. A businessman, for example, would provide support, tuition fees, loans, and jobs for relatives. But such consideration did not extend to neighbors. There was no obligation to society. This containment of benevolence, so to speak, has created a bloodred vein of envy in Korean society.

That is why *chaebol* families don't let their hair down at home. "When we're overseas, you'll see sports cars, actress girlfriends, and expensive wine," said one *chaebol* family member. "But, we are very cautious in Korea."

The risk of offending public sentiment became clear in 2014 when a daughter of the Korean Air chairman flipped out on a plane at John F. Kennedy International Airport after being served nuts in a bag instead of on a plate and ordered the pilot to taxi back to the gate to expel the cabin crew chief. Such was the reaction back in Korea that she was given a one-year sentence for violating aviation safety and her father, also the chair of the 2018 PyeongChang Winter Olympics Organizing Committee, had to come out and apologize to the nation for being a bad father.[191]

It would be *chaebolist*, however, to portray all scions thus. Most are in fact, rather like European royals, highly educated—the third generation now invariably at U.S. Ivy League schools—and taught to be nice.

"My mother always told my brothers to tip the waitresses well in the room salon," Kim In-sook says. " 'That's where the rumors start about your character,' she'd say."[192]

Ironically, the worst behavior tends to be between members of the same family. There is hardly a *chaebol* where, in the second generation, the sons do not fight over money. After the Hyundai founder, Chung Ju-yung, died in 2001, for example, the group split into three parts, each controlled by a son; the sons of the Unification Church founder, Moon Sun-myung, were already squabbling over assets of his Tongil Group and its international affiliates before he died in 2012; sons of the Daesung Group founder were still in court a decade after his death in 2001; the staff of two sons in the Kumho Group, who had offices on different floors of the same building, reportedly kept in communication to make sure the brothers did not accidentally bump into each other.

The scariest moment for the *chaebol* families came in August 2015, when a biblical Jacob and Esau–like battle between the two sixty-year-old sons of the ninety-three-year-old founder of the Lotte Group spilled out into public and led to calls for reform. As the Shins have the most complex cross-shareholding structure, the reform is obvious—further restrictions. Fortunately, for the other *chaebol*, though, the main public issue with the Shins, who are a Japanese-Korean family, was the realization that their mother was Japanese and that they couldn't even speak Korean very well. Phew.

The indications are that the second-generation leaders, in keeping with national trends, will opt for more equitable shares for their children and so minimize the ugly squabbling. In Samsung, for example, it looks as if the third-generation son, Lee Jae-yong, will take control of the IT and finance affiliates, while daughters Boo-jin and Seo-hyun will take the resort/hotel and fashion sectors respectively.

Besides the family issue, the main reason for the dislike of the *chaebol* is what can only be described as their unpleasant corporate culture. They're actually not very nice to work for or deal with.

But that could be changing. On the eve of a government decision over a duty-free shop position, Lee Boo-jin reportedly told employees that if the company's bid was accepted, it would be down to their hard work; if it wasn't, it would be her fault.

Tell that to the earlier generation of employees and they won't believe you.

18

WORK, WORK, WORK

*"In the showers, I saw that everyone was completely black
with bruises down their back as far as their knees."*

Like many political and social leaders in Korea, the magazine editor
was unexpectedly small, almost fragile, in real life. He kept ahold of
his words. Young reporters imagined his inner life to be a rich debate
on the ethics of issues and policies they struggled to grasp.

Until the first company dinner, that was. Then, after a few drinks—
and he wasn't "strong," as the Koreans say, so it didn't take many—
the inner manager came out.

"As for you fuckers," he said, while waving a drunken arm in the
direction of the three interns, "Don't think for a minute we're going
to do you any favors."

This champion of the left was referring to their chances of a job
at the mother paper, where openings had just been announced. For
the past year, the interns had been applying for all the main media
jobs and had lost each time in the biannual employment stampede
of thousands. Just that week, the magazine had run a story claiming

that its own media group was going to do things differently and hire by a process that emphasized aptitude over credentials. Their three-month internship on the magazine's special investigative team now represented a huge advantage.

No, it doesn't, he cruelly warned.

Crushed, the three innocents sat in deferential silence until about 1 A.M. when the gods intervened and the editor fell asleep. After he was bundled into a cab, workplace etiquette freed them to go home. My sister-in-law told me this story. She was one of the three. In fact, it was her second internship at the same publication. During the first, her byline ran under two cover stories and the leader of her team had won an award for their reporting, but she and the other interns received no thanks. She saw the same prospects with the new project and quit, much to the astonishment of the fully employed who had already learned that the strategy for advancement was to put up with shit.

She swapped stories with friends culled in other mass applications for the same jobs. One had found a place with a prominent plastic surgery clinic in Gangnam. As a junior nurse, she lived in fear that she might forget some routine task or that she might—and this is common—be ordered to do something new that was not explained and then be reamed out for not doing it well.

"The atmosphere in the surgery is really bad sometimes," she said. "The doctors often get annoyed and throw things around. One threw a surgical knife during an operation and it stuck in the wall. They're always swearing at us. Sometimes they swear at the patients as well." They, of course, have the advantage of being anesthetized.

Such episodes are common, and illustrate what young Koreans can look forward to when they leave the bosom of college and family and strike out in the world.

These days, stories of slapped faces and nasty bosses circulate on social media and cause outrage. The most egregious case of exploitation in recent memory involved salt-farm workers on the islands off the southwest coast, who lived as little more than slaves.[193]

"Extreme. Intense. Extraordinary. There are not enough adjectives to describe the mistreatment of workers at the bottom of the South Korean employment hierarchy," wrote Koo Se-woong, the editor in chief of the online publication *Korea Exposé*. "The question, though, is why this state of affairs continues unchallenged."[194]

That's a good question, and that it gets asked marks progress. It means things will change in time, once society figures where to start. Perhaps when it decides, Case No. 1 could be the bureaucrat in the ministry who is ordered by his superior at 5 P.M. on a Friday night to spend the weekend drafting up the let's-be-nice-in-the-workplace guidelines and then on Monday morning gets the papers thrown back in his face.

Victims tell themselves that when they get promoted they will behave differently. Thus civility creeps slowly in. But there is something in the culture that makes the mental roughing up of juniors more the norm than the exception. One well-known journalist who has spent his adult life lecturing society admitted to me that when he hears a North Korean or Chinese accent spoken by a waitress in a restaurant, he finds himself addressing its owner more rudely for it. Why? "Well, the other serving staff with normal accents could be students," he said.

Around thirty-seven million, or 73 percent, of Korea's fifty-one million people are of working age. Of this number, six million are contract workers, who do the same jobs as salaried workers but are easier to fire and get paid less. Around 6 percent of the workforce is in agriculture, nearly 17 percent in manufacturing and the remaining 77 percent in what is loosely referred to as "services."

Tough labor action hasn't done much to change the fact that work is stressful. From observation, it strikes me that this is the result of a vicious convergence of factors. One is the producer orientation of the Korean form of capitalism, a theme I will come back to. Also, absent alternative sources of satisfaction, the intense struggle for promotion creates high degrees of stress that impacts everyone. Bosses have bosses, too, and they are annoyed a lot of the time.

Another factor is the absence of leverage. Consider: The shopkeeper needs the customer's service; the supplier needs the *chaebol*'s business; the employee needs his boss's approval. In a democratic environment, such distinctions are underscored by the notion that all people have equal value. (Not everyone agrees, but you know what I mean.) In the Korean case, though, value runs up the ladder.

The person on the lower rung has zero leverage because he both needs the approval of the superior and, both agree, has less value. (For people who don't desperately need the job or can find another, however, there's the option of quitting. Dislike of bosses is the most commonly cited reason for people leaving jobs.)

Even more strange, workplace bonding leads to rudeness and cruelty. An interesting and positive feature of work in Korea is that people make an effort to fit in. Before I left England I heard many people proudly declare that they never socialized with the people they worked with. But in Korea colleagues eat lunch, go out at night, and even go on trips and vacations together. Here's how this warm camaraderie with peers is developed. The story is a little old, but it still applies. When the *Segye Ilbo* newspaper launched in 1989, journalists and editors built up their files and prepared dummy editions for several months before the actual daily edition was started. Timothy Elder, an American hired for the international news desk, found an unusual routine during the months prior to publication:

> There wasn't actually so much work to do. So from our desk, everyone except the editor used to go out drinking together at night. They would end up getting home at four or five in the morning. They'd be at work at nine, and somehow manage to drag themselves through the morning. At twelve, they'd go off for lunch and then spend the afternoon together in the sauna. They'd come in later in time to clock off and then they were all out for dinner and more drinking. This routine went on day in, day out for months. The editor didn't join in because his peer group was the other editors. And I didn't need to go out with them because I'm a foreigner. I couldn't figure why the company would pay people whose pattern of work was like this. And why people would endure such an arduous lifestyle. Then it occurred to me that this was their way of bonding. Later, when the paper began, of course, there was no time to do this. In fact, people worked very hard. But they were able to do so because they felt part of a group that had bonded.

In this bonded group people call themselves by familial terms: "older brother" or "older sister" for anyone slightly older. The problem with intimate relations is that, if you're not careful, familiarity breedeth contempt. Stressed managers get annoyed with their charges as they would with kid brothers and sisters. And, as Koreans don't hold back, it comes out. "As for you fuckers . . ."

As language changes according to the relative level of the person you are speaking to, low forms amplify the contempt. The medicine here is to throw out the low forms and treat everyone with respect. This was the experience of Ahn Cheol-soo, a popular politician admired for his thoughtfulness and demeanor. Growing up, his parents addressed him in the high form of language—extraordinarily unusual in Korea, where the opposite is the norm.

As you would expect, the extreme cases of workplace abuse come from testosterone central—the military. Again, the intimacy of Korean relationships is a factor here in that it used to be considered normal for older brothers to knock the younger ones around. This behavior was institutionalized the army, which inherited from the Japanese the idea that systematic beating drives the girlishness out of a man and makes him a fearless warrior.

In the first year of Pyo Wan-soo's military service in 1969, soldiers on their second year burst into his barracks one night and herded all the men outside naked and set about them with planks of wood. "This went on night after night for quite a long time," said Pyo. "When we were all in the showers, I saw that everyone was completely black with bruises down their back as far as their knees." In his second year, after he was promoted, he took the road less traveled and forbid the men under his command from continuing this tradition.[195]

Hahn Dae-soo, the folk and rock musician, similarly refused to beat people when he served in the navy in the early 1970s. "I was the only one who wouldn't do it. They said these new recruits were pussies because of me," he remembered. "In the first two years, we were beaten with baseball bats regularly. Some people suffered permanent damage to their backs. A few could not take it anymore and jumped into the sea. It was a dictatorship, so the military just told the families they'd died doing their duty." He found the strength to go on after reading *The Gulag Archipelago*. "When I realized Solzhenitsyn went through worse every day for years, I thought that I could survive this ordeal."

This systematic barbarism has been outlawed but the underlying notion that it is acceptable in the workplace to be unpleasant to inferiors remains. Barracks bullying continues but is more random, said Lim Tae-hoon of the Center for Military Human Rights, a nonprofit group that, among other things, investigates cases of abuse on behalf of victim's families. "You see it in some units and not in others. Even different barracks have different cultures. It depends on who's in charge." Given this, it is no wonder that parents with the means help their sons evade compulsory service.[196]

In 2015, police arrested an academic named Jang and two students on charges of terrorizing another student. All worked at Jang's nonprofit institute. The abuse included beating the man with a baseball bat and forcing him to eat human feces. This last part was videotaped. The victim reportedly put up with it because Jang had promised to help him get a university teaching job.[197]

At work, Koreans refer to one another by title. There is an emerging preference to use names among people of equal rank, but generally in an office you won't hear, "Hi, John, how's it going?" It's, "Honorable office manager, did section chief Lee call you this morning?" Thus, promotion not only means more pay but also a better title that may be used generally in society. Therefore, the difference between section chief and office manager is as important as that between corporal and sergeant. Each promotion means a whole new batch of folk who salute you. Koreans are surprised when I tell them my experience in British factories of workers turning down advancement because they did not want the extra responsibility.

When people behave toward one another on the basis of rank, the symbols of power become extremely important. Something like, say, arranging the telephone extension numbers in an office becomes a concern because numbers denote hierarchy. Similarly, getting the right office is not so much a matter of having the nice view out of the window as avoiding the locations deemed lower in the hierarchy. In one place where I worked, we tried to get around this visual hierarchy by arranging desks in an H-shape. But the Korean staff figured that the person who got to sit with his back to the door, in the horizontal line of the H, would be seen as the most junior and so subtly argued to avoid that place.

You will find when you walk into a Korean office that you can immediately tell who is in charge. If there is ambiguity it may indicate some ambiguity in the office politics. In some joint-venture operations, for example, you may find that two people seem to have similar offices and similar-size furniture. This could be a case in which the boss from the operational viewpoint is a foreigner, assigned by the head office, while the titular boss may be a Korean.

Woe betide a foreigner who tries to mess with symbols of power. In one news bureau, a foreign correspondent was asked by the head office to find a new office and recommend staff salaries. He saw this as an opportunity to signal to his Korean colleague, who was called "bureau manager" but who did little actual work that he, the "correspondent" (lower title), was the real boss. Familiar with the culture, he ordered a larger chair and desk for himself. The bureau manager said nothing but stopped coming to work, which said a lot. After a week, the correspondent went to the man's house and told him he was adjusting the furniture. Problem solved, and everyone went back to work as if nothing had happened.

In preparing this book, I asked several management consultants to name one Korean company they admired, not for performance, but for values. Some said none. Others noted one or two, such as the pharmaceutical and chemicals company Yuhan whose founder in 1926 was a patriot who gave his firm a purpose to live by—for Koreans to be able to reclaim their sovereignty, they had to be healthy. For most companies, though, the corporate philosophy is something that doesn't have any relevance outside the About Us section of the Web site.

I don't wish to overstate the question of workplace unpleasantness but the fact my analysts had to really think to come up with a company they liked reflects its prevalence.

One way companies signal their values is through hiring practices. In Korea, there seems to be little to distinguish them. Korean companies, I would say, have a great deal of difficulty assessing value—in this case, the value of people. The larger companies especially seem to make zero effort to understand how keen or competent a candidate might be. The prevailing view is that students are not ready for work and so those who make it through the hiring process will be trained and in the first year or two the company will figure where to put them. Hiring, then, tends to be on the basis of credentials. This has the added advantage of appearing to be objective. This is the reason for the obsession not with a good education but with good schools.

It also explains widespread résumé fabrication. It's remarkable how many curricula vitaes (CVs) show candidates studying at prestigious international universities that fail to make it clear that they didn't actually graduate. I know one professor of religion at a top university who claims to have a doctorate from Harvard. I found this out by chance—an American visitor had been in her class and revealed she had actually failed and been given a "booby prize"—i.e., a lower degree. Another friend's wife claimed to have studied at his university in Europe when in fact she just used to visit him there for romantic weekends. I warned him about increased scrutiny of fake CVs after a high-profile scandal involving a lady who had falsely claimed to have earned a PhD at Yale. He told me his wife had in fact upgraded the false claim to Cambridge. The point that slips between the cracks here is that the fakers do perfectly well at their jobs, thereby proving that the organizations who hired them needn't have bothered erecting such high-credential hurdles.[198]

Another way of signaling corporate culture is through expressed values and charitable projects that appear to embody them. In the twenty-first century, it is kind of de rigueur for a large company to have "core values" and engage in "corporate social responsibility." Many Korean firms unintentionally demonstrate the shallowness of such postures by allowing every new CEO to reinvent them.

"I had three bosses in three years," said Todd Sample, a Korean-speaking American who was hired by the public utility KEPCO to advise top management:

The company did not reflect a consistent management principle—it was just, follow the boss. The first boss introduced five tenets. There was no interest in manifesting the sentiment or philosophy behind them. The new tenets generated a lot of work. People negotiated with designers and printers to create posters with the tenets on them. There were lectures we all had to attend to hear about them. But no one had to interpret them for their own work. They just did what they were told. It was just work, not the application of any change in the way of doing things. Then he left, and the five tenets vanished.

Sample's next CEO preferred the populist touch:

He would hold monthly meetings, which all fifteen hundred employees were required to attend. These were a new waste of time. He saw this as a way to get closer to employees. His staff would collect the names of everyone who in that month was having a birthday, getting married, or who'd had a family member who had died. All these names were put into his presentation for that month. Then at the event the slides flipped by so fast you couldn't read any of them. Another thing he liked to do was personally congratulate people who were being promoted. You might have two hundred employees at all levels who that year were to be promoted. He had them line up and then individually mount the stage where he would shake hands with them. It was like a graduation. It took two and a half hours. We were cynical but there was nothing we could do.

The third CEO was more grounded and less full of himself. With each new arrival, everyone adjusted themselves in the interests of self-preservation. That, and not the random mottos, of course, reflected the real culture.

One characteristic that typifies Korean firms and which explains why many do so well is that they are very results oriented. In fact, the result is always considered the most important aspect of work. Workers are ultimately judged by their ability to achieve the results required at their level. Given this, the new mottos and pointless meetings are critical, but only for those tasked with organizing them. For everyone else, they are simply a waste of time and energy.

Another common workplace characteristic is that the rewards for success are minimal and the punishment for failure to achieve results severe. It's no surprise then that workers are highly averse not just to risk-taking, but even to putting up their hands.

"In many companies, it's all about not being noticed," said Peter Underwood, another fluent Korean-speaking American businessman.

The emphasis on results leads inevitably to cutting corners. Rules are bent everywhere. This became horribly apparent in the *Sewol* ferry disaster and has put the country on notice that firms must look for better ways to do things.

This includes drawing on the best of foreign practices, but this is easier said than done. In 2008 LG Electronics executed a first for Korean business by engaging foreign executives as chiefs of supply chain, marketing, procurement, strategy, and human resources. Two years later, a new Korean CEO ended the experiment. At the same time, SK hired an American human-resources expert and promoted her to head of Global Talent at SK Holdings. She also lasted two years.[199]

In another contemporary experiment, some companies tried operating in English. They soon gave up, highlighting the unfortunate fact that the approach to language teaching at school guarantees that most students will end up not being able to speak it. Falling back on Korean is of course natural. Unfortunately, though, the language has served in an international setting as a door closer.

"They have been operating like the Navajo code talkers," said Sample, referring to the Native Americans employed by the U.S. Marine Corps in World War Two. "They can function with foreigners but there's a point where they switch to their own language and it functions like an undecipherable code."

The impetus for change is most likely to come from a new generation of expatriates who speak Korean. These will come either from the Korean studies programs overseas or from the rising numbers of foreign students in local universities.[200]

But the aspect of business that Koreans most desperately need to address, whether the lesson comes from overseas or not, is productivity. It's widely believed among Koreans that success comes primarily not to those who are smart and make good choices, but to those who work hard. And hard work means putting in the hours. There has, therefore, long been a certain nationalistic pride in the statistics showing they have longer working hours than most other countries.[201] Around one-third of workers don't take their vacations.

Recently, though, the government has been doing the math. The hourly productivity of Koreans has been put at 29.75 dollars against an Organization for Economic Co-operation and Development (OECD) average of 44.56 dollars. If you were to allow Koreans more leisure and average the working hours of OECD nationalities, their economy drops from thirteenth in the OECD to twenty-seventh.

Given the desire to improve and the will to work hard, you would think the Koreans would have cracked the productivity question a long time ago. But it is a heavy elephant to push up the mountain. Michael Kocken, a human-resources specialist who worked for a Korean firm, believes the military-like hierarchy credited for the country's early success now represents a problem, in particular because it requires that bosses at all levels be briefed all the time.

"The constant cycle of *ad hoc* reporting ensures that there is little strategic work and movement within a company," he wrote. "Instead, the corporate environment feels like a fire department, where teams are always on call for spot fires, and need to be ready to respond to unexpected problems immediately."[202]

The military culture is also a prescription for dishonest feedback, another time waster, as leaders have to keep going back to the drawing board after the failure of plans that could have been better prepared with more honest feedback and thoughtful input.

Another issue is a form of perfectionism. One of the flip sides of fear of speaking out is the yearning for small pats of affection that come with prettifying documents and presentations. My team once prepared a document for a CEO and was advised by one of the traffic cops along the boulevard of power that it was wrongly formatted and in the wrong font. Apparently, all documents going to the boss had to look the same. When I asked why, no one had an answer. The corrections wasted a day.

Other drags on productivity include the fact, already mentioned, that new hires are totally unprepared for the workplace. University education and, in the case of men, two years in the army, is great for random knowledge and mental gymnastics—how do you spell the capital of Iceland backwards?—but doesn't prepare them for work.

Another comes from the lack of trust within companies. *Chaebol* employees, for example, tend to exhibit a weak sense of loyalty to their companies. Instead, loyalties form around subgroups, such as departments or the informal group of people who entered in the same year. Indeed, different functions in a company often treat one another as the enemy, with those subgroup loyalties the only way of breaching the barriers erected. In other words, the PR and sales teams get along right now because their respective bosses joined in the same year.

Then there is the whole issue of actual time wasting, which, if we're going to be thorough, we need to divide into "real" and "perceived." For example, hangovers caused by office partying and smoking breaks are real time wasters. Talking, on the other hand, is a perceived time waster because bosses consider it to be frivolous. As a result, it's normal for employees to sit in silence for hours at their desks looking busy. When they need to talk with colleagues, even the colleagues sitting next to them—and often they don't need to talk but just want to—they do so by online messaging and mobile phone. This helps explain one common motive for not taking that vacation—people who don't actually do much work fear their secret will be exposed if they are away.

The issues I have described so far are things that typically lead to expatriate warnings of imminent economic collapse. But Korea moves so fast these may soon be in the past.

Consider, in terms of management experience, where the country has come from in just two generations. In old Korea, commerce was for the lower classes. There were no large-scale nonbusiness organizations where Koreans could learn how to manage large numbers of people in complex tasks.

During the Japanese period, Koreans were in low positions and gained little actual management experience. After World War Two and the ousting of the Japanese rulers, Koreans began studying American management principles. The first to do this were army officers. Hundreds of U.S.-trained officers took executive posts in state-run companies and organizations.

Americans were looked up to because they were more powerful, wealthier, freer, and better organized. Koreans loved, but found it very difficult to import, the American way of displaying authority. Individual Americans in powerful positions are often so untypical of the Korean (or even the European) idea of leaders, and seem to many Koreans who deal with them to combine professionalism and informality in a way that is at once engaging and confusing, for it is so distinct.

The Korean management style—highly formal and not always so competent—often seems to be the exact opposite of the American. Back in the 1980s, when the U.S. military introduced simulated war games, the Korean generals were so reluctant to participate that the American commander himself had to sit down at the console and jolly them along: "It was 'Uh-oh, General Kim, you just blew up your own side. Hahaha. Never mind,' " an American official said. "Once they realized they were not going to be criticized for making mistakes, they learned so fast they became better than our guys. Those Koreans are so focused."

The Korean system displays real weakness with its decision-making. In smaller corporations still run by their founders there is only one decision-maker. For larger organizations, the process is more complex. Companies vary, but in general there is a sort of consensus approach with consultation between varying levels of management. In government bureaucracies, there is more of a Japanese-type process with the ideas emerging from the bottom.

Another characteristic of decision-making in business that typified companies during the development period and which can still be seen in practice is the lack of long-term vision. It's possible that in the days of the dictators this came from an uncertainty about who would be in power next year, what rules might change, which of the company's assets might be seized, and so on. The scholar Mark Setton told me some blame lies with child-rearing habits:

The focus is on immediate gratification of the child's demands, particularly the male child, not only during infancy but also during childhood when the sense of time and space is in a critical stage of development. . . . Consequently, in adulthood, short-term sacrifice for a long-term payoff is not the popular way of doing things. So even if there is vision, the self-discipline needed to push it through comes in short supply. From this perspective, Korean companies might do better if they were managed by women. They used until recently to be given much more rigorous training by their mothers under the principle that they are required to serve in the home, and this could be the reason why they appear to have twice as much self-discipline as the men. Unfortunately very few women as yet have policy-making roles, and Korean organizations are full of impatient males who want things done "yesterday" for results "tomorrow," irrespective of what may happen the day after.

Of course, no discussion of the Korean workplace would be anywhere near complete without mention of the labor movement. Right now, very few workers belong to unions. Membership as of this writing is only 10.3 percent of the workforce but labor is more relevant than this statistic would suggest because the membership tends to be in the big and prominent companies. It is also important because of the historical contribution of labor leaders—many of them exceedingly courageous and committed—to the modern workplace, even if it is one where their services are no longer required.

The political and *chaebol* leaders of newly emerging Korea were haunted by the fear that labor unions would become a political force and ruin the new nation they were building. This was not an unreasonable fear. Not only because of a history of manipulation of labor unions—by communists before 1948 and by the government since— for political ends, but also because of the relative classlessness of Korean society. Any differences between boss and employee were scarcely a generation old. The relative difference in their fortunes was seen as accidental and perhaps even the result of leverage. It would therefore be natural for workers to exercise their own leverage if allowed to have some.

The result was a system of worker control that "inflicted humiliation on the very people who produced the economic miracle."[203]

For example, involvement of third parties in labor disputes was illegal, which virtually precluded efforts by labor specialists and political activists to advise workers and negotiate on their behalf. The government recognized only one union per company, though some companies refused to allow unions at all. They were centrally controlled through the Federation of Korean Trades Unions, an umbrella group with about twenty-four hundred affiliated unions. Intelligence officials used to sit in on its meetings. Management in small firms could intimidate workers so that labor organizers could not find the minimum thirty employees necessary by law to agree to a union being formed. Those they could not prevent, they tried to tame: In companies that were unionized, the union leader's position was full time and came with privileges and a salary paid by the company. Strikes were suppressed by riot police, often violently.

Such control rested on three assumptions that would from the late-1980s begin to be vigorously overturned. They were: Foreigners bought Korean products because they were cheap and therefore keeping wages down was crucial to maintaining competitiveness and growth; workers were lower on the ladder than owners, managers, and officials, and should defer to their decisions; and, collective action by workers was most likely evidence of the presence of communists.[204]

The first assumption provided the rational argument while the other two explain the emotional bias and thus the force with which authorities crushed any labor action. When George Ogle, an American who taught industrial sociology at Seoul National University in the early 1970s, was arrested, these hidden assumptions manifested in his interrogator almost as a kind of demonic possession. Ogle was being held because he had spoken out publicly on behalf of eight men who had been accused of being communists and sentenced to death:

Around eleven o'clock that night I was taken to the office of Lee Yong Taek, chief in charge of the KCIA's sixth section.

"You have been in Korea a long time, Mr. Ogle, but obviously you still don't know much about Korea. And you know nothing about communism. You have violated our anticommunist law, but because you are a foreigner, we are going to be generous. I am going to prove to you that these eight men are indeed communists."

Lee then repeated to me the exact same accusations that had come out in the newspaper. The only piece of evidence that he showed me was what he said was a copy of a speech made by Kim Il Song [sic], the Premier [sic] of North Korea. One of the eight condemned men, Ha Chae Won, had listened to the North Korean radio and copied down Kim's speech and then showed it to some other people. Otherwise, Lee Yong Taek appeared to have no support for his case against the accused.

Then an amazing transformation took place. Instead of a cool, calculating man reciting alleged "facts," Lee switched over into an emotional monologue.

"These men are our enemies," he screamed. "We've got to kill them. This is war. In war even Christians will pull the trigger and kill their enemies. If we don't kill them, they will kill us. We will kill them!"

What was going on? Lee was transformed in front of me. His eyes were afire. His face clenched with hate. He marched in small, tight circles. His emotional high was far beyond any evidence of guilt against the condemned men. Here was a man locked in mortal battle with Satan. The world depended on him. He would save his nation from communism even if it means executing innocent people.[205]

Labor responded to such harshness with its own extremism. Many activists were willing to die. The ultimate expression of frustrated will, this also functioned to replace fear of the inquisitor in the hearts of the general populace with outrage and sympathy. Another key aspect of the labor movement was that moral support and education—teaching workers they had rights—came not from political activists but from Christians.

The willingness to die most notably began with a young man named Chun Tae-il. He was one of around twenty thousand (mostly women), who made clothes in the sweatshops of Seoul's Peace Market.

One day Chun read a copy of the Labor Standards Act and found that, among other things, work over forty-eight hours a week was considered "overtime" and should be paid at time and a half. Employers, he found, just ignored this and other parts of the law. After an appeal to the government was met with silence, Chun and some friends staged a protest. Police beat them up. During the second protest, Chun poured gasoline over himself, set himself alight, shouting, "Obey the Labor Standards Act! Don't mistreat young girls!" His last words were to his mother: "Now you are the mother of all the workers!" This act remains a symbol of resistance to this day.

In the 1960s and 1970s, a number of labor conflicts involved the Urban Industrial Mission, a largely Protestant group. One day, one of its members, Reverend Cho Sung-hyuk, was helping unload a truck when he got into an argument with the driver.

> The [driver] was on top of the load lifting the wood down to other men below. Instead of taking his time and lowering it carefully, he threw the wood down as fast as he could with some force and cursed the guys when they missed. After getting his head jolted by a missile from above, out of pure anger Sung Hyuk yelled, "Do that one more time and I'll come up there and knock your teeth down your throat." The truckman cursed him soundly, but did as Sung Hyuk told him. Through that mundane experience . . . it dawned on him that . . . religion and salvation were not a sermon or a ritual, but a fight with a truckman to ease the pain of the man at the bottom.[206]

Let me interpret: It's okay to use violence because we're nice people and they're not.

Despite these efforts, though, the Korean worker saw no significant improvement in pay and conditions. Safety standards were appalling. Between 1964 and 1994, 39,000 workers were killed and 2.9 million injured in accidents at work. Even as recently as 1994, for every 10,000 workers in Korea, 118 were involved in accidents, compared with 80 for Taiwan and 39 for Japan. The losses that year were estimated at 6.3 billion dollars. Over 52 million working days were lost through accidents, which was 39 times more than days lost through strikes.

Then came the pro-democracy protests of June 1987. Almost immediately, the lock on its cage snapped, the beast of labor frustration leapt over the heads of the middle-class democracy protesters. The first wave of strikes pressed for recognition of new unions created illegally by workers in opposition to the existing "pro-management" unions. In the few weeks after the lifting of political restrictions, over three thousand strikes paralyzed car plants, coal mines, shipyards, electronics and textile factories. Employees struck at over two-thirds of Korea's big plants employing more than one thousand workers.[207]

In Ulsan, twenty thousand strikers from seven Hyundai plants took to the streets to demand the resignation of the chairman Chung Ju-yung, who had refused to recognize a new union. In an incident typical of its kind, goons acting for the company had snatched documents the unionists planned to submit to register the union. In the end, the government ordered the documents returned and the registration announced. Chung, humiliated by the change in government attitude, continued to oppose union demands. Hyundai shipyard workers dressed in protective clothing and welding masks marched through Ulsan behind forklifts and cherry pickers. Several hundred went on a rampage, setting fire to cars and wrecking the city hall. Hundreds of riot police took up positions by the Hyundai-owned Diamond Hotel and drenched the rioters in tear gas. Eight thousand workers took over the Hyundai shipyard. Similar scenes were played out at the Daewoo car factory at Bupyeong outside Seoul. In two massive predawn blitzes, thousands of riot police invaded the two sites and arrested the strikers. The police were in full riot gear and carried fire extinguishers in case desperate strikers set themselves alight. They placed mattresses around buildings to prevent protesters from making suicide leaps. Several tried to immolate themselves but were overpowered and at least two strikers were injured jumping out of a window.

In the next wave, workers began pressing for more say in management, improved conditions, and better wages in almost all sectors. It seemed that everyone with an issue demonstrated. I remember watching with some amazement a march of chanting publishers protesting Korea's signing of an international copyright agreement, and demanding the right to pirate foreign books.

The country ever since has braced itself for the spring wage negotiations.

Today, unions are still active, but do not enjoy the broad support for the adversarial posture they once had. Society expects them to work with, rather than against, management and government.

POWER

19

AT LEAST PRO THE RIGHT KIND OF DEMOCRACY

"Hey man, do you speak English?"

When foreign protesters are stomping over your flag but are otherwise nonviolent, the mature reaction is to put your fingertips together like a literature professor and ask what they're upset about. But that's hard. Because the torn cloth is alive with meaning, the boots on its pattern are studs on the faces of your teachers, your heroes, and your children, down your street, across the lawn, and onto your grandma's apron. The Korean protesters knew that, of course. That's why they did it. By the time fifty thousand demonstrators were done, the Stars and Stripes was a shredded mess.

But it was a symbolic victim and a small mess, in their view, weighed against the crime committed against them when a U.S. military tribunal on a U.S. military base in their country tried—and acquitted—two U.S. soldiers who had been driving a U.S. military vehicle on a public road in Korea and had run over and killed two local teenagers.

Koreans thought the men should have been tried in a Korean court. But the commander of U.S. forces in Korea had rejected a justice ministry request for jurisdiction, as was his prerogative under the agreement by which U.S. troops are stationed in the country. The charge was negligent homicide, which is less than murder but still criminal, so the public was hopeful. The tribunal found no criminal intent. Legally and rationally, it was hard to argue with this. The men had been operating a fifty-seven-ton armored vehicle-launched bridge during maneuvers. Such monsters were allowed during exercises on public roads and the driver did not see the girls crouching down against a wall covering their ears because of the noise. He did not deliberately hit them. The whole terrible thing was an accident.

On this day, I found one of my Korean colleagues in a state of rage.

"What a joke. Being tried by their friends," he said.

He showed me a local newspaper commentary featuring a cartoon of Osama bin Laden in front of a jury of twelve men with beards.

"Do you think they were guilty of negligent homicide?" My question annoyed him. It sounded like the setup for one of those typical American technicalities used to evade responsibility.

"Whatever that means, they were guilty."

"Why?"

"Because they killed those little girls." He had tears in his eyes.

"But it was an accident."

"I don't care. That is not the point. They should have been found guilty."

"But why? If it was an accident."

"To assuage the feelings of the people."

I found it hard to believe that this highly educated man thought in this way, but he did, and his views were representative. The nation was furious. Even a young rapper called PSY smashed a toy American tank on stage over this, something he later had to explain when he became famous in America.[208]

In Korean decision-making, such public sentiment matters. The people were angry. The soldiers were guilty. No one would say it aloud, but if the pattern held, the soldiers would have been released early after the public focus had moved elsewhere because everyone knew that—actually—it was an accident. In other countries, particularly those familiar with how the main story in the New Testament ends, people equate this approach with mob rule and see law as an electric fence between it and a defendant to ensure justice. But not the Koreans. Their inclination is to see the mob as "the people" and responding to its will as the essence of democracy.

A few days after the flag stomping, some commentators in the U.S. media suggested the U.S. should withdraw its troops if they were not wanted. This suggestion, a masterful and democratic tempering of American hurt with good sense, prompted a fresh round of criticism from protest organizers in Korea. But this time, the theme shifted in a somewhat surprising direction. After years of attacking the U.S. for having supported dictators, for pressuring Korea to open its markets, and for "crimes of American soldiers," anti-American demonstrators now charged the United States with something altogether new: failure to understand their anti-Americanism.

This new sin was not well-explained. In fact, it left foreign diplomats and journalists in Seoul, who had to report on this, quite bewildered. Just because we set fire to your flag and get tens of thousands of people protesting against you and your soldiers doesn't mean we are protesting against you and your soldiers. We want them here. But we want you to change your attitude. And what attitude would that be? *Not letting our courts try your soldiers. Acting as if you are better than us. Being superior. Because that makes us feel inferior.*

I realized then that the anti-American protests were not about military exercises on public roads, or crimes of American soldiers, or even about America. They were really about how Koreans felt they were being made to feel about themselves.

And that led to a revelation: You have to approach these issues like a therapist, not a policy analyst.

This may sound flippant and condescending, but it's not meant to be. I had spent twenty years trying to understand things, then something inside me relaxed and I stopped trying to be right. I accepted I had been trying to turn Koreans into Americans and then I stopped. In marriage, this surrender moment is necessary for real, deeper love. No more wriggling inside the onion to find the core and coming out empty-handed and in tears. No more judgment or moaning. I just observed. Like, at that second round of anti-American demos, I observed as Roman Catholic nuns in the newly named "Peace Square" near the U.S. embassy innocently pinned "Fucking USA" badges on to their habits. No longer would I add this to the list proving Koreans were wrong. A Fucking USA badge is a Fucking USA badge is a Fucking USA badge. It was color on the canvas. I was no longer an analyst, but an artist. (In case you're wondering, it was a song title, although it could have been a mistranslated reference to the new phenomenon of Korean Christian missionaries going forth and multiplying in the United States.)

I point out this change of heart to underscore how difficult it actually is, when you've been in the middle of all of the junk and broken pieces in the tsunami of Korean democratization, to step back and grasp how truly inspirational and impressive it has been.

While dreams of democracy began with some Koreans at the end of the nineteenth century, the real and practical start of popular democracy began when Koreans met their first Americans and aspired to be like them. That was in 1945, at the height of American influence and power in the world. We might forget but Americans back then exuded something intangible that was wonderfully attractive. My father, a Royal Air Force officer, saw it in the sloppy way the GI saluted his officer. Civilians saw it in the friendly way in which soldiers threw chewing gum, Coca-Cola, and chocolate to them from army trucks. I remember feeling the same at Checkpoint Charlie in Berlin back when communists and dinosaurs roamed Eastern Europe. The American soldiers just looked different. They were so friendly. Free and unharassed, they had, it seemed, in their freedom, chosen to be friendly. I dare say that no other people has ever been so admired on such a scale.

As an occupied people, of course, many Koreans had bad experiences with the rude, drunk, priapic young American men in uniform. But youngsters especially were taken by them. Those they helped became fans for life.

"Hey man, do you speak English?" a young soldier called out to Lee Kie-hong one morning in September 1945. The U.S. occupation forces had just arrived and were billeted in schools. Lee was walking past one, carrying an English-language newspaper. [209]

"Yes," he said. "I can speak English." He had taken what was then the unlikely subject of English literature at a school in Hiroshima and had sneaked back home a few months earlier, after students had been ordered to stop studying and work in a munitions factory. A group of Americans came out and surrounded him.

"They were like the white people we had seen in movies and books," said Lee. "But we had never seen so many before. It felt as if we had been taken to some fairy-tale world."

"What is your name?" one asked

"Where do you come from?" asked another.

"How did you escape the atomic bomb?" That was when he learned that his college town had been incinerated.

When Lee went back the next day to tell his new friends he wanted to be an interpreter they helped him find a position on the staff of General Archibald Arnold, the military governor and number two man in the occupation forces. One day in October, Lee found himself guiding the famous independence figure Syngman Rhee—who had just returned after forty years in exile—to General Arnold's office.

"The old man looked very gentle and benevolent, not like the wicked figure maligned by the leftists," Lee wrote. "He was patting my shoulder with grandfatherly affection, saying, 'Be a good man.'"

Rhee became the first president of the Republic of Korea in 1948. He and other authoritarians imitated democracy; the real thing came in 1987 with people power. Now, thirty years later—and here's a thought—the Koreans are such fast adapters I wouldn't be surprised if they end up teaching America and other mature democracies a thing or two about transparency and participation and how to reduce the importance of that scourge of modern history, the professional politician.

Because the concept is so broad, all of this could happen under the flag of "democracy." With return to monarchy out of the question, democracy was the aspiration of almost all Koreans since their separation into two states in 1948. The leaders of both Koreas knew their respective state had to be accepted as the true and legitimate "democracy" of the people. The North Koreans even put the word in their name, the Democratic People's Republic of Korea. Until President Roh Tae-woo in 1988, the rulers of South Korea—with the exception of Chang Myon's short-lived government in 1960–1—were not accepted internationally as democrats. North Korea's leaders, of course, remain dictatorial to this day. They claim to act in the interest of the people, but do not permit free elections to test the claim, thus ruling it out as a democracy in the free-world definition.

This point may seem self-evident. But it's not easy to argue with true believers. I once tried to explain to a tourist guide in the North Korean capital, Pyongyang, that the elections he was telling me about were not democratic.

"What do you mean? They were elections and people could vote," he said.

"But all the candidates were from the same party," I said.

"That's what elections are," he said.

"In some cases there was only one candidate," I said. "Also, everyone by law has to vote. No wonder they got a hundred percent."

"Well, we have elections laws, like you have election laws in your country. They are our laws."

"But there are no opposition candidates."

"Why should there be opposition? We're not opposed to each other."

"Well, I mean, a different viewpoint. Candidates from a different party."

"Why do you need different parties when the Workers' Party represents the people? Anyway, you can have different views in the same party."

"Yes, but—"

"Anyway, these were candidates all chosen by the Great Leader."

"Well, there's your problem."

"What?"

"They couldn't take a different position from him. The Great Leader would have them shot."

"Only traitors are executed. You don't allow traitors in your country, do you?" At this point another guide intervened and explained to the young man in Korean that my lack of understanding was because in Britain we are not united like North Koreans and that's why we have rival political parties. I hadn't looked at it that way.

As I say, South Koreans also told outsiders they were a democracy, even in the darkest days of dictatorship. President Chun Doo-hwan's foreign-press spokesman, who had been jailed as a student protester under the previous regime, invited a small group of resident foreign correspondents to lunch one day during a period of antigovernment demonstrations in order to give us the government's views. We were sitting at a circular table in a private room of a restaurant. The opposition party had walked out of talks on constitutional reform and called for street protests. The presidential spokesman knew this move had created a measure of moral confusion among Western diplomats because the regime's allegedly democratic opponents were abandoning the democratic process for the streets, where there would be violence.

"The opposition has taken this undemocratic decision," he said, reasonably. "But we hope they will return to the table." He went on to explain at length about the government's commitment to democracy and respect for human rights. After a few minutes of this, I became aware of motion in my peripheral vision. The journalist seated on my left was holding out his hands and sliding them up and down a rather large imaginary pole in an extremely vulgar gesture which everyone pretended was not happening, but which effectively ended our host's pretense.

When countries are criticized for the absence of democracy, it is often pointed out in their defense that democracy takes a long time to develop. This is certainly true, and it is quite an acceptable point, unless it's coming from the people with the power to help it develop. Democracy is a political system that involves governance by popular consent, whose introduction involves a humbling of political authority. As much as we may take it for granted once done, it is difficult to accomplish. In fact, it is almost unnatural in light of the way human society has been ordered for most of history. Surely it is too much to expect the powerful to be gracious and generous? It is more natural for them to feel they are special, or even indispensable, because by some miracle of heaven they have been put in charge, or by their own force of will they have put themselves there. In more basic terms, as anyone who has been the head of the parent-teacher association or the village council knows, when you have power, it is a horrible feeling to lose it on terms not your own. It is unreasonable to expect a leader to voluntarily relinquish power any more than a middle-aged man would voluntarily give up his job mid-career to give a younger person a chance.

If there's a threat that your successors might arrest or kill you, it amounts to foolishness to subordinate this personal risk to a national benefit that can only be imagined and which may be dubious. Democracy is, of course, a system that is greater than the leaders wrestling with these matters. The problem, though, is that the leaders introduce the system, and they need to be forced along sometimes. But like economic development, once the model is established somewhere in the world, it is possible for others to imitate it and catch up.

The Korean political culture was not conducive to democracy. Nor were the circumstances. The security threat from North Korea and the ideological anticommunism hindered the pursuit of democracy. Sometimes, to a general, a democratic suggestion such as "let's talk to them" came across as lunacy or, worse, treason. Many foreign observers, especially those opposed to communism, could justify authoritarianism in South Korea. However, it is important to note that for South Koreans themselves, culture and security may have been explanations for the absence of democracy, but they were never ultimately accepted as excuses.

We can identify three basic issues that dominated South Korea's politics over the decades. The first was the issue of succession. Once in power, the first presidents quickly seemed to have become possessed by the conviction that the nation would be doomed without them. They responded by manipulating constitutions, parliaments, and elections to make sure they remained seated at the head of the table. It took forty years to achieve the first peaceful transfer of power. A second issue was corruption, both the temptations of power and the use of anticorruption drives to disarm opponents. This elusive monster still haunts the loch. A third, and critical one, as we will see, was elections. Democracy allowed them to become less violent, freer, fairer and beyond government manipulation.

The first president, Syngman Rhee, was very familar with American democracy. But circumstances, and his own shortcomings, prevented him from truly being democracy's champion in his own country.

"Few heads in international politics have been battered longer or harder than his," biographer Robert Oliver, wrote in 1951 of Rhee.

"During a political career that began in 1894, Dr. Rhee has spent seven years in prison, seven months under daily torture, and forty-one years in exile with a price on his head. He has directed a revolution, served as president of the world's longest-lived government in exile, has knocked vainly at the portals of international conferences, and finally shepherded his cause to success only to see his nation torn asunder by a communist invasion."[210]

Rhee was born in 1875, and educated at a school run by American missionaries. He converted to Christianity. He wrote for *Maeil Shinmoon*, the first daily newspaper in Korea, and organized protests against corruption and against Japanese and Russian designs on Korea. He was jailed in 1897. For seven months, his head was locked in a wooden weight, his feet in stocks and his hands cuffed. He was beaten with rods and had oiled paper wrapped around his arms and set on fire. "His fingers were so horribly mashed that even today, in times of stress, he blows upon them," Oliver wrote.[211]

After his release and the Japanese takeover of Korea, Rhee went into exile in the United States. He earned his doctorate at Princeton, where he studied under the future U.S. president, Woodrow Wilson. He was one of the main leaders in exile and lobbied for decades for Korean independence. He married an Austrian woman, and by the time he returned to Korea after four decades, he seemed to his fellow countryman to be more a foreigner than a Korean.

Lee Kie-hong's grandfatherly impression of the man notwithstanding, Rhee was a divisive character. Moves by civilian advisers in the American military government to sideline him were blocked by military officials. When the journalist Mark Gayn met him, he was more than unimpressed:

> Rhee has a Master's Degree from Harvard and a doctor[ate] from Princeton. Yet his English is labored and he puts his sentences together with effort. I wondered by what inner strength he had impressed his ideas on General Hodge and men of the Military Government. Listening to Rhee, I thought he was a sinister and dangerous man, an anachronism who had strayed into this age to use the clichés and machinery of democracy for unscrupulous and undemocratic ends. I had been in Korea

only seventy-two hours, and it may well be that my impressions are wrong. But I have begun to think that it is not Hodge who is the most important man in the U.S. zone, but this old, pale man with half-closed eyes.[212]

If you subscribe to the theory that politicians continue to fight the battle that raged at the time of their political awakening—Kim Il-sung was still going on about the Korean War forty years later—then Rhee's "struggle" against Japan was framed in his own mind as a struggle against ineffective monarchy. To be victorious, he positioned himself as the good "democratic" monarch. General Hodge's political adviser reassured Gayn that Rhee was not a Fascist. "He is two centuries before fascism—a pure Bourbon," he said.[213]

The imperious Rhee saw himself as the leader of a country that was half held by communist rebels. He was preoccupied with the big picture of national division, but was not able to reunify Korea during his twelve-year rule. He was incensed that the United States had not repelled the Chinese during the Korean War and he refused to sign the 1953 armistice. Such posturing deeply frustrated the Americans, but there was some method to it. When Rhee opposed the truce agreement, he refused an invitation by U.S. President Dwight Eisenhower to discuss it—pretty ballsy given the circumstances—but he let it be known that he would keep his mouth shut on condition the U.S. agree to a mutual defense treaty, modernize the Korean military, and keep its navy and air force in Korea. By this shrewd stubbornness, he secured the American backing that became the crucial factor behind the country's recovery and eventual growth. This achievement illustrates Rhee's understanding of the United States and ability to play his country's weak hand to its best advantage. Gong Ro-myung, who joined the foreign ministry in 1958 and retired as the foreign minister in 1996, believed Rhee to be the most talented diplomat among the seven presidents he served under. "He was a very rare figure with deep insight into international politics," Gong told an interviewer. "He highlighted the importance of taking an independent stance based on patriotism."[214]

Rhee's threats to "march north," though never backed with military movements, were at first taken seriously. Again, on the face of it, such behavior was so pesky that the U.S. government entertained removing him. But there was a simple logic. If Rhee had been reasonable, the real power figure in the country would have been the U.S. ambassador.

South Korea at that time was a poor, agricultural country whose people were preoccupied with where their next meal was coming from. Rhee had no economic vision and, just as he had lived off friends and supporters for most of his life in exile, without a thought to paying his debts, so the country lived off American handouts. In 1957, U.S. officials warned the Korean economic team that Congress was tiring of Rhee and would reduce aid. They suggested the government make some long-term development plans to preempt such a move. As a result, the ministry of reconstruction developed a five-year plan and in December the minister, along with his counterparts from finance, agriculture, and trade, presented it to the president. Rhee listened for an hour before opening his mouth: "You ministers are talking about five-year plans," he said. "That sounds like Stalin's idea." And that was that. Economic plans became a taboo subject.[215]

Labor unions in Rhee's time were used as a political arm of government. Teachers were pressured into joining the ruling Liberal Party and required to investigate the political leanings of their students' parents. High school and college students had to join the Korean Student Corps for National Defense and receive military training and anticommunist indoctrination. The press was relatively free, although one leading newspaper, the *Dong-A Ilbo*, was closed down for a while because the Chinese character for "puppet" was once used instead of "president" in reference to Rhee, apparently by mistake.[216]

Rhee considered himself above the fray of politics, which was unfortunate in the time of left-right conflict and the chaos of war, and meant that his underlings took it upon themselves to provide the firm hand that was needed. As we have seen, Rhee was surprisingly forgiving of collaboration. Had he expressed this approach in terms of the need for reconciliation, and paid attention, such a policy might have been acceptable. The Americans had set the precedent for this in 1945 by agreeing to a request by the outgoing Japanese colonial officials to help the five hundred thousand or so Japanese military and civilians in their sector leave the peninsula unmolested. (The one million Japanese departing Manchuria and three hundred thousand leaving North Korea were not so fortunate. Many were rounded up and put in detention camps and others suffered random acts of retribution.)[217] However, Rhee either did not care about the presence of serious collaborators, most especially in the police, or thought it sufficient that he forgive their collaboration because he was thinking big picture and needed them in the battle against communism without selling the idea to the people. This failure to engage left a stain on the memory of the country's democratic foundation.

The police, thus forgiven, now acted with vigor against suspected leftists. The randomness with which such zeal was expressed on the ground had heart-wrenching consequences. One colleague told me that in the late 1940s her mother and uncle, then barely out of their teens, were denounced by a neighbor in Seoul as being leftist sympathizers and were arrested by police and imprisoned without trial. Her grandmother went to the prison and successfully offered herself up in their stead. A few days later, the family heard that prisoners were being moved and rushed to see their mother, who was in a line of people roped together and being marched down the street.

"Did you bring any food?" she asked. They had rushed so quickly to see her they had forgotten to bring any food, not realizing the prisoners were surviving only on what relatives brought them. They never saw her again, and don't know what happened to her, and lived with this wretched guilt all their lives. Had Rhee been a more engaged leader, such unfairness may not have run so terribly rampant.

Another friend of mine, Peter Hyun, arrived in the United States around this time on the eve of the outbreak of the Korean War, only to find that the State Department had mixed him up with another Korean of the same name who was believed to have been a communist. He was given two weeks to leave or risk deportation. "If I'd been sent back to Korea by Americans on the grounds that I was a suspected communist, I'd have been dead. There'd be no need for a trial. It would be enough that the Americans thought I was a communist."[218]

Rhee may have been above all the politics on the ground, as opposed to directing it, but when he saw that he was not going to be reelected in 1952 he rolled up his sleeves and got his hands dirty.[219] At the time, the president was elected by the National Assembly, which Rhee threatened to dissolve if it did not approve a constitutional change to allow for presidential election by popular vote. He treated opponents as if they were enemies of the state. When assemblymen voted to have martial law lifted in Busan, Rhee had half of them arrested. After a staged assassination attempt, police began to investigate alleged links to the opposition.

Police claimed that an assemblyman called Chang Myon was working with assassins paid by North Korea to depose Rhee. Under this type of pressure, the Assembly voted 160 to 0 for Rhee's constitutional amendments.

Rhee's vice-presidential running mate, Yi Pom-sok, who as home minister controlled the police, was behind much of the maneuvering against the assembly. Lee was a nationalist who had graduated from the Chinese Military Academy and fought the Japanese in China. He had held a general's rank and served on the staff of the nationalist Chinese leader, Chiang Kai-shek. In 1946 he formed the Korea National Youth Association, which had the support of the U.S. Department of Defense, and which he saw as the foundation of a future Korean army. This group soon claimed 1.3 million members. Pro-Western and anticommunist, its members supplemented police units and fought against leftists. On the day before the election, Rhee, who was feeling threatened by his running mate and his large youth group, suddenly ordered his supporters to vote for a different vice-presidential candidate, who won.

Another constitutional amendment allowed Rhee to run for a third term in 1956. He won again. One opposition candidate died of a heart attack just before the election, but still received about 20 percent of the vote. Another, Cho Bong-am, won 22 percent. Cho was a former communist who had split with his old associates before the war over their subservience to the Soviet Union, and had later served as Rhee's agriculture minister. He argued that the way to defeat communism was to strengthen democracy and that it would eventually be possible to win peacefully in an all-Korea election. Leaders of his Progressive Party were arrested in 1958 for allegedly contacting North Korea. Cho was charged with spying and sentenced to five years for contacting a North Korean agent. An appellate court sentenced him to death. He was executed in 1959.

Rhee, now in his eighties, became more isolated, his administration more inefficient. In 1960 he ran a fourth time and won 88.7 percent of the vote. Twenty people were killed in election violence and many injured in protests against widespread vote rigging. These protests erupted into full-scale demonstrations and after student protesters were shot and killed in the streets of Seoul, Rhee resigned in disgrace. He lived the rest of his life in exile in Hawaii.

Did Rhee contribute to democracy? He argued for liberal democracy at a time when most intellectuals were inclined to socialism with authoritarian East Asian characteristics. He forged deep ties with the United States and his republic did hold elections. It survived. But, despite the war and the poverty, Rhee could have done so much more, especially given his vast experience with democratic countries, and his mandate for vigorous action, particularly as he had to deal with leftist guerrilla subversion, left-right violence, and a civil war. However, as he saw his own victory as being more important than the process, he failed to institute the basic traditions of democracy of reasonably fair elections and a tradition of peaceful democratic succession. Had he lost to Cho Bong-am in 1952 or 1956 and stepped down in a dignified manner, or retired and let another candidate run, he may be remembered today with more affection.

Rhee's presidential system was replaced by a parliamentary democracy under Premier Chang Myon. This was the kind of government that advanced countries love to see among their developing world allies, because of the promise of something so much better for the people and because it removes the criticism that comes with having to back friendly dictators. Chang was by all accounts a pleasant and sophisticated man and had opened the Korean embassy in Washington as his country's first ambassador. A Roman Catholic, he went by the name John. As a leader, he was way ahead of his time but his administration was breathtakingly weak. In his outbreak of freedom after Rhee's departure, campus activists formed a Student League for National Unification, which advocated reconciliation with North

Korea and the withdrawal of foreign powers. Thanks to Rhee's manipulations of elections, a heavy-handed police force, and poor economic leadership, young citizens did not feel their country was much different from the North. Just seven years after the end of the war, among the young, the fantasy that the northern leaders were their brothers was already replacing the horrors inflicted by the North's attempted takeover.

When the students called for a conference with North Korean students, rightist groups protested in nationwide rallies, raising fears of a return to the left-right violence of the late 1940s. Hundreds of teachers went on a hunger strike when the government declared a new union illegal. Students demonstrated in sympathy after some of their teachers collapsed in class, and decided to stage a march to Panmunjeom.

When they heard the military wanted to end the chaos they began to tone down their activities, but it was too late. The leftist agitation had provided what one scholar has called "useful justification" for a military coup.[220]

Park Chung-hee drove his tanks into Seoul at 5 A.M. on May 16, 1961, and seized power unopposed. The prime minister hid in a convent. Citizens adjusted to the new reality, but not without nervousness. The uncertainty was perhaps best characterized by a joke that circulated at the time. It tells of a soldier on guard duty on the Han River bridge on the day of the coup. He was—typically—asleep in his hut in the early hours of the morning, when General Park's convoy rumbled onto the bridge. Awakened rudely by mutineers who burst into his hut, the guard paused and made an instant assessment of his predicament. He thrust his arms into the air and shouted in welcome, "*Inmin-guk Mansei!*" (Long live the North Korean People's Army!)

The seeds of the coup were sown by military involvement in Rhee's last election. Young officers had started talking about removing corrupt military leaders and when one of them, Kim Jong-pil, was discharged for his role in this effort, he started planning a revolution with his relative, Park.[221]

It is possible that Park interrupted a real opportunity at this stage in Korea's history for economic development under parliamentary democracy, yet some doubt the civilian politicians would have been capable of it. Even today, many people believe Park did the country a favor. He had little respect for civilian politicians and brought many military officers to run government and state corporations.[222] Conservatives welcomed the change because they feared pro-North elements might take advantage of the apparent instability. Bureaucrats also welcomed it because they had fewer politicians to worry about. They had been spending half their time coaching senior ministry officials to handle the endless questioning in the National Assembly by politicians who they felt were just using them to score points. Two of the worst offenders were young politicians Kim Dae-jung and Kim Young-sam, both future presidents.

Park claimed to have democratic goals. Fortunately, despite his personal preference for communism before the war, these were for democracy as understood by the free world; however, he had arguments for postponing his goals. Korea, he said, was in the "topknot and horsehair hat stage of old" and couldn't be changed overnight by the institution of Western European–style democracy, which he believed to be unworkable. The weakness of the Chang Myon government backed up this viewpoint. For democracy to work, Park said, it would first take an industrial revolution. What he proposed instead was "Administrative Democracy."

"The goal of the revolution is to weed out corruption, strengthen the autonomous ability of the people, and establish social justice. Therefore democracy should be established by administrative means, not by political means, during the transition period," he wrote.[223]

The transition period he was referring to then was that between the 1961 coup and elections, which came in 1963. Park of course ran in those elections and continued to do so, changing the constitution and fiddling with the results when it was necessary. In effect, the transition period lasted until his assassination eighteen years later.

Park earned respect during his first two terms of office, up until 1971. Had he stepped down at this point, as the constitution required, he would have done democracy the favor of having both kick-started the industrial revolution necessary to underpin it and of having established a precedent for a peaceful transfer of power. However, events conspired to convince him that he was indispensable.

Fear of North Korea mounted in the late 1960s after Kim Il-sung in Pyongyang put old guerrilla comrades in charge of his South Korea policy. In 1968 North Korean commandos on a mission to kill Park reached the Blue House in Seoul before being stopped. Park wanted to parachute South Korean forces into Pyongyang, but the Americans refused to permit retaliation.[224] Two days later, an American spy ship, the USS *Pueblo*, was captured fifteen miles off the North Korean coast. Its eighty-two crew were taken prisoner. And as the United States was at war in Vietnam, it was not prepared to retaliate and risk a second war in Korea. A few months later, North Korea landed over one hundred commandos on the South Korean coast. In another incident, a U.S. Navy reconnaissance plane was shot down by North Korea and thirty-one crew were killed.

After U.S. President Richard Nixon decided in 1970 to cut the strength of U.S. forces in Korea by a third—down to forty-three thousand—Park became increasingly doubtful about the reliability of the United States as an ally. This lack of U.S. resolve also reflected on Park himself. South Koreans felt secure in the American embrace and confident that North Korea would not launch a full-scale attack as long as it feared it was going to war not only against the South but also against America. Park's argument as to why he was indispensable was that he was the man who could maintain this "special relationship" with the United States. When Park learned that it was actually the U.S. Congress that called the shots, his aides began a program of corrupt lobbying and gift giving that ended in the "Koreagate" hearings in Washington in 1978, which took bilateral relations to an all-time low.[225]

As his second term came to an end, Park forced through a constitutional change to allow him to run again in 1971. He nearly lost that election. His opponent was Kim Dae-jung, a surprise compromise candidate between opposition factions. There was cheating on both sides. As Park had enormous funding and all the resources of the state at his disposal, Kim Dae-Jung's campaign team had to be creative. One of their tricks was to knock on doors pretending to be from the ruling party and hand out small gifts to voters. Later, others would follow—these "officially" from the Kim campaign, and bearing more expensive gifts. Such tactics are, well, naughty, but the man who came up with them was so endearing—he chuckled like a child when he told me this one—and so forgiving of his opponents—he even laughed dismissively after describing how the goons of the next dictator had hung him upside down and beaten the soles of his feet—that he converted me to the idea that democracy is a messy process to ever-better fairness and integrity and, far from being dismissed for impurity in the early stages, should be expected to start muddy.[226]

I'm not sure the tricks helped, but Kim Dae-jung managed to win 45 percent of the vote. Park was not impressed with his own performance and realized he needed to do something to stop Kim or another "wrong person" from winning the next time.[227] He started planning a new constitution that would allow him and his Democratic Republican Party to rule unchallenged.

In the following year, talks began with North Korea, and the two rival sides signed a historic agreement pledging to end their hostility. This process was treated internationally as if there had been a breakthrough. This was not the case. Korea's problem was not to be solved by peace; it was a zero-sum game and, as both sides knew well, there had been no significant power shift toward one side or the other. The reconciliation was just a temporary lull. Ironically, the exposure to the North Koreans, as described to him by the intelligence chief Lee Hu-rak who had travelled to Pyongyang to set up the talks, made Park more nervous. Kim Il-sung had built up a powerful communist personality cult and ruthlessly suppressed dissent. The result was, to his South Korean opponents' way of thinking, enviable. Instead of seeing the extent of coercion and the latent threat in the anger and resentment it had caused, they saw unity, which gave the impression of total strength. Dissent in the South gave an impression of weakness to both the North Korean leaders and to Park and his followers.

Three months after the agreement with North Korea, Park introduced a new "Yushin" (revitalizing) Constitution and had himself reelected for a six-year term. Kim Il-sung took this as a betrayal of the spirit of the agreement and in the spring of 1973, three North Korean commandoes tried to assassinate Lee Hu-rak in a beach hotel. One was shot dead, another went back into the sea and disappeared, but the other was captured and revealed the plot.[228]

From this point, Park's rule degenerated into repression. He even made it illegal to criticize the new constitution.

His chief lieutenants were younger officers who had played key roles in his coup. Most outstanding among them was Kim Jong-pil, the brains behind the coup. His wife was Park's niece. Kim combined qualities that do not always sit well together but which made him a persuasive leader: He was pensive, but purposefully so, and he was capable of courageous action. His winning, open smile made him stand out against some of the thugs around Park. I believe Kim was a genuine democrat and, indeed, Kim Dae-jung appointed him prime minister in 1998. But he also knew the harshness of reality and could see what was needed in terms of policy development, committees, and structures to push things through. He set up the Korean CIA and tried to build up the ruling Democratic Republican Party along the lines of the all-powerful Kuomintang in Taiwan, as a body that could go beyond the factionalism of Korean politics, earn public support, and rule for as long as possible. It was he who negotiated the 1965 normalization treaty with Japan and then stood up in front of critics and argued for it. (That type of bold leadership is lacking in modern-day Korea where politicians dodge debate.) Kim had his ups and downs with Park and went into exile when opponents tried to convince Park he was plotting to be his successor. Kim was also artistic. He once sat at the table I was hosting at a foreign press party when the trot singer Ju Hyun-mi came on the stage and sang her hit "Night Rain under Yongdong Bridge," an old-fashioned ballad about lost love. Unlike most politicians at his level who are too self-important to admire others and who seem to forever have aides whispering in their ears, Kim was lost for the moment in her performance, like a weepy drunk in a bar.

Another lieutenant was Park Chong-kyu, who became known as "Pistol Park" in 1974 after he shot at a gunman who tried to assassinate the president in a crowded theater. The gunman, a North Korean agent, killed the First Lady. He and Cha Ji-chul, the chief presidential bodyguard, increasingly controlled access to the president. On one occasion, when Park Chung-hee visited a province, the local governor went to light the president's cigarette with his lighter flame unintentionally set at high, which startled Park. After the meeting was over Cha is said to have stayed behind and beaten up the governor.[229]

Such thuggery indicates the assumptions at the time that overrode the purported pursuit of democratic values and practices. One was that the president was the state, that his word was law, the raising of his eyebrow open to interpretation, and his anger license to violate niceties. Another was that opposition to Park and the ruling party was the same as communism. Another was that those with power had the right to physically and verbally reprimand those below them. This happened at all levels. For example, Park was angry that some of his senior party officials opposed the change to allow his third term. No instructions were issued but, chief among the opponents, Kim Sung-kon, the head of the SsangYong group, was picked up by KCIA agents who held him down and mindlessly plucked his moustache from his face.

The KCIA had sweeping powers and, under various directors, expanded and intruded into every sector. Its main task was to guard against North Korean subversion and in the 1970s, after North-South talks began, this effort became quite sophisticated. The agency quietly developed and gathered detailed data about North Korea. At North-South meetings, for example, agents took samples of North Korean cigarette packets, glasses, bottles, tableware, and anything else they could lay their hands on, which they then used to analyze North Korean manufacturing processes. Its domestic departments, however, investigated government opponents, devised plots to undermine them, controlled the media, spied in colleges and churches, and coordinated policy between government ministries. Under Lee Hu-rak, KCIA agents kidnapped Kim Dae-jung from a Tokyo hotel in 1973 in what appears to have been a murder plot designed to look as if it were committed by North Koreans. The American CIA, alerted by Kim's supporters and by a former KCIA director, Kim Hyong-wook, intervened to save him.[230] Kim Dae-jung was dumped outside his home, shaken but unharmed, and barred from political activity for the rest of Park's term. (Kim Hyong-wook, the former KCIA director, testified against Park Chung-hee at the Koreagate hearings and later disappeared in Paris. It is assumed he was murdered by KCIA agents.)

In October 1979, opposition leader Kim Young-sam was expelled from the National Assembly and protests erupted in the cities of Busan and Masan, his political base. At a dinner, Park Chung-hee scolded the KCIA director, Kim Jae-kyu, for failing to control the demonstrators. Kim said to do that they would have to kill three thousand of them. Park responded by saying that the Shah of Iran, who had recently been ousted, had failed because he was not prepared to kill enough of his own people. If necessary he, Park, would kill thirty thousand. Park's bodyguard, Cha Ji-chul, joined in the criticism of the KCIA chief. Kim had been frustrated for some time over his difficulties managing the politics of his job as KCIA chief, and over Park's criticism of his performance and Cha's interference. He left the room and returned with a pistol, shot Cha and then shot Park, killing both men.

Sensible assessment of Park is hindered by political labels, and by his progress through different phases. He was, in turn, a Korean nationalist in a Japanese uniform, a communist officer in the rightist South Korean army, and an anticommunist nation-builder. The labels get so confusing they wear thin and peel off. Park was a pragmatist, not an ideologue. Ironically, if he had not been so closely allied with the United States and if he had played up the revolutionary, interventionist, and collectivist features of his rule, he may have received a better hearing in the court of the international left. He employed dictatorship in order to transform the economic base of society. But he failed to see class warfare within society, believing that, among the classes of nations, Korea was a proletariat. In order to become strong, its workers had to be dedicated, and its producers favored in order that they produce.

From the point of view of democracy, though, while Park contributed greatly to the creation of a middle class, he obstructed political development in practice. Two decades after Rhee's departure, democracy had regressed. Park's state was more repressive than Rhee's had been even during the Korean War. From this perspective, his gift to democracy after two decades of industrial growth was his sudden departure from the scene.

Two million people turned out in the streets of Seoul to watch the journey of his coffin to the national cemetery, and wonder about the future. Their leaders were still not elected fairly and there was still no peaceful method of power transition. Park did not have a successor. The dictator gone, Koreans found themselves back in 1960. History was about to repeat itself.

20

POWER SHIFT

"Democracy for us Koreans means the right to choose our own dictator."

The man who took over as acting president after the murder of Park Chung-hee was the prime minister, Choi Kyu-hah.

Acting is the operative word here. In the Korean system, the prime minister gets to bang the gavel sometimes but the main role is to make the president look better. He—or, once in 2006, she—finds himself out of a job as things go wrong and the president hits the refresh button. That's quite often. There have been ten or eleven each decade since Choi, so many that the Korean people don't pay attention. To test this thesis, ask a Korean friend to name the current prime minister. As of this writing, I can't. Nor can my wife. (Real-time confession—five minutes ago, I googled him and I've forgotten again.)

Occasionally, the post is filled by a member of the power group who will add some weight to the office. But Choi was a bureaucrat, a political lightweight who lacked the character and the political power base to grasp the historical moment for democracy. In one of my first small-group press lunches, a year or so after the critical events described below, a senior American diplomat referred to him as a "feckless asshole." It struck me as being a little rude. But apt. There is no excuse not to deploy your finger in the dike and to try to stop a disaster when the hole is right in front of you.

The day after being made president in December 1979 by an electoral college, Choi abolished Park's Emergency Decrees which had banned political assembly by students, demand for constitutional reform, and circulation of rumors. The following day, he released Kim Dae-jung from house arrest and allowed newspapers to mention Kim's name again for the first time in years.[231] Choi had a large face, protected later in life by heavy jowls you would think could have absorbed a few slaps for democracy. But his first bold moves did not change the fact that he was like a schoolboy shoved on the stage and, knees knocking, expected to act presidential.

The real power in the country was Chung Seung-hwa, the martial-law commander. Another army general, Chun Doo-hwan, who headed the Defense Security Command, the military intelligence agency investigating Park's assassination, thought there were unanswered questions about Chung's own involvement in the assassination. Chun had other issues with Chung.

Like Kim Jong-pil, Chun Doo-hwan was a character, bold and not one to be manipulated. But he lacked Kim's thoughtfulness and his charm. He looked more miserable than mean. The source of dourness may have been the prematurely bald pate that sat atop his face. Koreans are rather rude about such things and always joked that the oversupply of head made Chun look Japanese. Still, he was leader of the officers of the Korean Military Academy's eleventh class, the first group of professional army officers who had completed a full four-year course. Older officers were either Japanese trained or had graduated from the Academy after only a brief period of training. The eleventh class members, who had graduated in 1955, were seen as the older brothers of subsequent graduating classes and commanded intense loyalty. This group's members felt they had been deliberately denied promotion and held back by the generation Chung Seung-hwa represented. When they heard that Chung planned to remove their leader, Chun, from his powerful post and reassign him to a field command, they mutinied.

On the night of December 12, 1979, Chun arrested Chung and troops loyal to him came to the assistance of the martial-law commander. A gun battle broke out in the streets of Seoul, and several soldiers were killed. One of Chun's group, Roh Tae-woo, ordered troops under his command down from the DMZ, leaving a gap in the defenses against North Korea. After this act of mutiny, there was no turning back. Fortunately for Chun and Roh, younger officers stood by them and they were able to take control of the military, including those loyal to Chung.

Like Park Chung-hee, Chun Doo-hwan had grown up poor.[232] His story contains the familiar ingredients behind the Korean achiever: devoted mother, pro-independence father, poverty, and the helping hand of heaven. Chun was the seventh of ten children. He came with portents. Two brothers had died before he was born and his mother was desperate for another son. Three years before his birth, she had a dream in which three majestic men and a woman walked down a rainbow to her house. In the dream the second man had a crown on his head. She went on to have three boys and two girls. One of the girls later died. The second son was Doo-hwan. When a wandering monk said, except for her protruding teeth, she had the face of the mother of a great man, she smashed her teeth out against a log pillar. Chun's father once hurled a Japanese policeman who had insulted him down an embankment and nearly killed him. After this, the family thought it prudent to flee to Manchuria. While they were hiding on one occasion from bandits, Chun's baby brother, Kyung-hwan, started to cry. Neighbors whispered that they would have to strangle him otherwise they would all be discovered and killed. One was about to do it when the baby stopped.[233]

After this experience, the family returned to Korea and lived in Daegu. Chun was a good athlete and a natural leader. He joined the Korean Military Academy in 1951, where he captained the football team. In the army he was nicknamed Lieutenant Principle for his alleged uprightness. Two soldiers once offered him cigarettes as a bribe and he thrashed them with a pole. That's seen as a good thing, by the way. He married Lee Soon-ja, the daughter of the academy's chief of staff. In 1959, he went to the United States to study psychological warfare and went through ranger training with three fellow officers, one of whom was Cha Ji-chul, later to be Park Chung-hee's stroppy bodyguard.

The day after Park's coup in 1961, Captain Chun allegedly demanded to see Park to confirm that he was not just another corrupt general. According to the account in a later hagiography, Park agreed to explain himself, telling Chun he opposed the corruption and incompetence of the government and that he planned to develop a "nationalistic democracy." Satisfied, Chun persuaded the military academy faculty and students to support the coup and led an unprecedented march of eight hundred cadets into central Seoul where they were greeted by Park.

From 1970 to 1971, Chun commanded a regiment of the 9th (White Horse) Division. During combat duty in the Vietnam War he is said to have ordered his men to always wear clean underwear, saying, "Do you want your enemy to see your dead body, should you die, in dirty underwear?"[234] Chun believed that internal disunity was the source of South Vietnam's vulnerability to the communist North. He apparently wrote in a letter to Park that South Korea needed a "Koreanized democracy" to avoid the same fate.[235] Chun became a general and commanded the First Airborne Special Force. He was later the assistant to the presidential security chief. In 1978, he was appointed the commander of the First Division. Chun apparently introduced the personal touch and managed to shake hands with each of the ten thousand men under his command, and oversaw the construction of a strategic defense wall near the DMZ and the discovery of a third North Korean invasion tunnel under the DMZ. In March 1979 he was assigned to command the Defense Security Command, the intelligence agency that polices the military.

The day after the "12.12" incident, as the struggle between the generals became known, it was business as usual as far as the rest of the country was concerned. President Choi was still in charge, and martial law was still in effect, but Koreans still enjoyed a sense of new freedom. In February, the civil rights of opposition leader Kim Dae-jung and almost seven hundred other dissidents banned by Park were

restored. With the new academic year in March, students formed associations and took to the streets. Workers staged strikes to press their
demands. The period came to be known as the "Seoul Spring." But all
was not well. In parliament, politicians argued and held up the rewriting of the constitution. The economy was reeling under the effects of
a global recession. The president did not appear to be in charge. In
April, Chun appointed himself head of the KCIA. In May the campus protests against martial law gathered momentum and tens of
thousands of students engaged in furious warfare with police. The
scale of these events exceeded the "chaos" that preceded Park's coup
two decades earlier. On May 16 the ruling party leader, Kim Jong-pil,
joined in the call for an end to martial law. But it was too late.

On May 17, 1980, Chun informed the cabinet he was taking
over and imposed his stricter version of martial law. Political activity
was banned, leading politicians were arrested, media censored, and
universities closed. Troops arrested activists and went on to campuses to prevent students from gathering. Highly trained special forces
units were assigned to Seoul National University, and Chonnam and
Chosun universities in the city of Gwangju, the capital of South
Jeolla province. This was not the first time these elite troops had
been used for police work. Park had used them to put down the riots
in Busan and Masan the previous October. On that occasion, they had
clubbed and beaten demonstrators, but not more severely than a protester would expect, not in daylight anyway. Nighttime was a different
matter.

In Gwangju, it was to be different. The special forces behaved in
broad daylight with such brutality that the citizenry erupted in rebellion. Soldiers beat and bayoneted demonstrators and rampaged
through the city, barging into coffee shops and storming onto buses
and beating young people of student age. Troops even used flame-
throwers on protesters. The hospitals began filling up with dead and
injured.

Amid a general news blackout, the rest of the country was unaware of what was happening. Rumors flew that those directing
the brutality were from Daegu, the capital of the rival North
Gyeongsang province. It was easy to believe they were being made
an example of out of regional prejudice. Gyeongsang people found

various reasons to dislike Jeolla. The region's politicians had been the reactionary landowners who had opposed Syngman Rhee. Leftist guerrillas fought from mountain bases in the province even after the Korean War. The people were friendly, artistic, but couldn't be trusted; you get your money from them up front. Under Park, this prejudice had become more exaggerated. As a result, Jeolla was far behind the rest of the country. Its people's resentment was feared.

Tens of thousands of protesters piled on to the streets and fought back. A strategic maneuver by the city's taxi drivers forced the troops to retreat. Rebels assaulted the prison where leftists and guerrillas from the conflict of the 1940s and 1950s were still being held. As Shim Jae-hoon, a veteran reporter of the Vietnam War and Korean correspondent for *The New York Times*, approached the city, he told me he wondered if he'd get out again:

> There was smoke rising from several places in the city. There were long lines of refugees with bundles on their heads, escaping the city. Rebels had machine guns on trucks and were using walkie-talkies. They had been in the army so they knew what they were doing. There were armed citizens guarding places and snipers on the roofs wearing helmets. They had taken over a factory which made jeeps and trucks. It was civil war. I knew they'd get slaughtered.

The city mayor and a committee made up mostly of bureaucrats appealed for calm and persuaded citizens to return their weapons. But passions were still running high. Militants pretended to cooperate, joined the committee and, once they had gained a majority, took over.[236] The radicals called on young people to take up arms, and held military drills. A young man called Yun Sang-won emerged as their chief strategist and another, Park Nam-son, led the armed rebels. Yun was an organizer in Gwangju for an antigovernment group called the National Democratic Workers League. His plan was to resist for as long as possible to force Chun's regime to either surrender or to kill them and thereby demonstrate its barbaric nature. He wanted the United States to intervene and protect them from Chun's troops, but was not hopeful. In the end about 150 armed rebels remained, knowing they would die.

"We think the United States as an ally can exercise its influence on the Korean government. Since it hasn't done so, we suspect the U.S. might be supporting General Chun Doo-hwan," Yun told foreign reporters.[237] The Americans were not exactly supporting Chun, but neither did they use their leverage to restrain him. The rebellion was quelled and the city retaken after an assault by paratroopers. Yun's body was among those found at the city hall building, which the militants had made their headquarters. The final death toll for the nine-day event was over two hundred.

Government propaganda, media censorship, and popular prejudice against Jeolla created confusion for years about what had actually happened in Gwangju. The fear of North Korea was played up, and there were charges that the rebellion had been directed by communist agents. Yun's associates, however, say there was no such evidence, and that Yun himself was very critical of North Korea.[238] I once asked Kim Dae-jung about the possibility of communist agitation during the uprising and he noted that throughout, rebel citizens were still reporting suspected North Korean agents to the local office of the KCIA. One writer has claimed that the uprising was actually an invasion by six hundred North Korean special forces.[239]

The military claimed it had American support for its actions in Gwangju. The Americans were not able to credibly defend themselves against this charge, not because it was true but because they were no longer believed. Both the special forces units, whose brutality caused the revolt, and the paratroopers who quashed it, were outside of the Combined Forces Command: Chun did not need U.S. approval to move them. For the Americans, this legal point limited their responsibility. To the Koreans, however, such arguments about law were technical sophistry. Power politics is what counts. The Americans could have stopped Chun but didn't.

Where the Americans did act, though, was to save Kim Dae-jung. With baffling judicial logic, Chun's junta found Kim guilty of having masterminded the Gwangju protests, despite the fact that he was behind bars at the time. A court sentenced him to death. In the face of criticism from the Carter administration, the junta delayed the execution until the November 1980 election of Ronald Reagan, who they felt would be more sympathetic to an anticommunist ally. They planned to execute Kim before Reagan's inauguration.[240] Carter officials met with Reagan's incoming national security adviser, Richard Allen, and conspired to save Kim's life. Allen met with Chung Ho-yong, commander of the special forces and a member of Chun's junta, and offered Chun a state visit in exchange for commuting the death sentence. Chun, who by then had himself elected as president, accepted the deal and became the first Korean head of state to visit the newly inaugurated American president. This deal was never made public and as a result, media images of Chun and Reagan together convinced dissidents that the Americans had been backing Chun all along. This perception prompted anti-American protests that lasted a decade.

I first heard of this deal during a dinner with three dissidents in 1983, hosted by a close aide to Kim Dae-jung. One of the guests, a prominent antigovernment lawyer, assumed I was an American and was distinctly frosty toward me. He shook hands coldly and responded to my English in laconic Korean. I didn't understand the origins of anti-Americanism in those days and perceived it as a kind of racism. I had a policy of not pointing out that I was British simply to squirm out of the line of fire. What's more, I was writing for an American newspaper, so if not the enemy himself, I was a willing collaborator. The host recounted at length this story of how the White House saved Kim Dae-jung. In his telling, there was another condition Chun had been forced to accept: That he would step down after his seven-year term of office was over, as the constitution required. The host described, with actions, how just before entering the room to meet Reagan, Chun was handed a piece of paper with these conditions written out in Korean. He nodded and was ushered in, the host said, giving a little nod and imitating Chun waddling in with his arm outstretched in greeting.

"How do you do?" the host said in exaggeratedly poor English. "So, you see, Reagan saved DJ's life," and added confidently that: "Chun will step down in 1988."

As this tale unfolded, a cloud of resentment lifted visibly from behind the eyes of the lawyer. He leaned over the table and, with a warm smile on his face, held out his hand to me.

"I am very, very sorry," he said in flawless English. "I had no idea about this."

"Oh, don't worry," I said.

"He's British anyway," the host said.

I began to understand that anti-Americanism emerged as a necessary part of the Koreans' raging against their past. They were throwing off their own historical habit of dependency, rather than making valid comments about any particular American offenses. As an essentially emotional issue, it lent itself, as politics so often does, to great ironies. One for me was that during the height of anti-American protests by students, the American military commander in Korea was the antithesis of what you would expect the chief representative of an imperialist oppressor to be. William Livsey was commanding general of U.S. forces from 1984 to 1987, and was also commander of the combined forces, the arrangement under which the bulk of the Korean military fell under American command. At the time, Chun Doo-hwan's dictatorship could only have survived with American support. Livsey, then, was one of the most powerful men in Korea. If the roles were reversed and a Korean commanded such a position in America, he would have the biggest car in Washington and swan into the White House as if he owned it. But Livsey was a farmer-general. "Farmer" is being polite. By British standards, where we are accustomed to generals being posh, Livsey was a peasant. A friendly, spontaneous, and informal man, he sometimes played the buffoon. At press meetings, we always tried to get him to admit the political importance of his role, but he never would. His public-affairs officer would mutter a prayer for divine intervention to prevent the general from saying something that would end up on the front pages and cause riots. But, he'd just smile mystically and say in a Georgia accent: "Ah'm a simple soldier. Ah don't understand these things but ah know what you guys are tryin' to git me to say, an' ah won't say it. Every morning, I jus' wake up and look myself in the mirror and say, 'Livsey, look north.'" We correspondents loved our sessions with this man. He would get tears in his eyes talking about his soldiers. He used to appear in advertisements on the American Forces

Korea Network, which was a TV channel widely watched by the Korean public, advising the men and women in his command on safety and fitness. In one, he hammed it up, bouncing into a car, snapping on his seat belt and, turning to the camera, said: "Buckle up! Ah do!" In an ad encouraging fitness, he began with the memorable line: "If you ain't fit, these hills in Kor-riya'll kick your butt!"

Throughout Chun's rule, students protested continually. But this generation of campus activists was different from its seniors. The appearance of a new dictator, and the apparent ease with which democratic America backed him, swayed students away from American political values. Through the 1970s most young intellectuals had sought freedom, democracy, and human rights. In the 1980s they turned to socialist revolution. I had my first brief taste of this in the student refectory at Yonsei University, where I went for Korean lessons. One lunchtime, a student came up to me and asked what I knew about the Russian Revolution. He was talking about 1917. I said something to the effect that I wouldn't wish communism on my worst enemy. "We think it's a good model for us," he said. I guessed he was an isolated crazy. This was a mistake. Had I had the good sense to make friends, I might have developed some real insight, and sources in the student movement. Throughout the decade, foreign correspondents dismissed as propaganda the government claims that the students were communist. But sometimes dictatorships don't need to make stuff up. Campus notice boards were plastered with revolutionary slogans, and the thrill of the total cause, where ideology and action fit with tight certainty, energized thousands. Some of them spent more time protesting than studying and guilt-tripped professors to pass them. Riot police, most of them young men on military service, became a permanent feature outside certain university campuses. With advanced warning from police spies of demos, they'd pull on their padded uniforms and protective masks and, once the demo got going, fire canisters of tear gas into the university grounds to prevent protesters from getting off campus. Police "grabbers" in anoraks, gym shoes, and helmets would try to grab student leaders. When protests were planned in the streets, the police posted men at subway stations and in the city center. They would stop young people and check their IDs, and go through their bags to see if any were carrying leaflets. In the 1980s, residents became so accustomed to the sight of riot police that they forgot what a militaristic and often frightening impression they give to foreign visitors.

The footage from that time was dramatic, but it gave a false impression. In London once, I represented Korea at a meeting of an international foreign press association and was astonished when I was treated as if I had come from a war zone, even by reporters from the Middle East. I had to correct them. Yes, Korea was at a serious point. The state was like a police bus being rocked back and forth by protesters. It was almost tipping over. But nobody was trying to kill the people inside. It looked as if they were, but they weren't. Injuries were accidental. The Molotov cocktails were specifically fashioned to flare up on landing and not to set fire to the target. They were for TV. There was a famous photograph of a lady walking in front of the main gate of a university engulfed in flames. Eyewitnesses told me the flames were out in a split second and that the woman just carried on walking. Swivel the camera away from the action and the chances are you would see people shopping.

The police became the best riot-control force in the world, able to clear a plaza full of protesters in a matter of seconds, by driving in from two sides pumping tear gas and making sure to give the students an escape route.

The smell of tear gas hung almost permanently over the major campuses—and they used a mix of it so strong it was illegal in other countries. Downtown, you could twitch your nostrils like a cocker spaniel, hold up a wet finger like a scout, and guess where the demo was. (Actually, I didn't trust my nose any more than my own political analysis, so I'd ask the photographers.) For a day after a street protest, it would hang in the air like an invisible layer of pepper. Citizens learned not to rub their eyes and noses but to let their tears and mucus wash it out. Students seemed to develop a cockroachlike immunity and made it a point of honor not to wear gas masks (which were illegal). They would put toothpaste in their nostrils and under their eyes to cut the effect of the gas.

These students were remarkable for their selfless innocence. They had gained entry to university with the sacrifice of their families behind them. Before they did their military service, most of them were virgins. They drank and smoked but they did not take drugs. Most could not afford to go to discos and buy fashionable clothes. They did not have nihilistic or self-absorbed views of life. They had emerged from a childhood of hard study and now felt responsible for their country. One I got to know well was Lee Yong-ho, who was one of the top-scoring students of his year. The son of a construction worker, in 1983 he entered the economics department of Seoul National University, the leading college in the country. Then he gave it up to become an underground radical and work as a laborer.

"At the time I was too young to know about Korean society," he said. "I saw police on the campus, fighting with students and beating them. I was very shocked. I looked for seniors to explain about society. I felt I knew nothing. A high school friend introduced me to a senior and I joined his group studying about social science, history, and economics."

Lee had joined an illegal "circle" and in the second year studied economics texts, some of which explained Marxist and neo-Marxist theories:

These kinds of theories were not even studied in universities. Some of the books were blacklisted and if you were caught with them you'd be charged with spying. I'd heard a story about a drunk who had shouted "Long Live Kim Il-sung" as a joke and been arrested for spying, so I was careful. We didn't really have any set program or even know how to approach these books, so we just read them and passed them round. I was not a radical being inspired by radical texts, but an intellectual trying to understand things. I'm not sure about my friends, but it was the lack of freedom that radicalized me. Some people were more intellectual and others more political. If someone had read a book that no one else had, it gave them a kind of power over others. So group leaders would read books strategically and not hand them around. It's ironic because we studied about freedom of philosophy and thought, but the way some people used it was contrary to this freedom. Most of these circle members were the intellectual leaders of the student movement.

Lee worked for three months in a factory, concealing his identity
as a student, and then did his twenty-seven months' military service
before returning to university. After graduating in 1990 he moved
to Incheon, where he worked as a welder and in a factory.

I was in a circle of old friends. Some were from my underground student circle, some from other circles, and some
were laborers. We passed around books and talked of our
philosophy and strategy for the labor movement. We didn't
have a political strategy. There were other underground
workers but we had no contact with them. In those days
the government could catch nationwide organizations easily, so we didn't make one.

At that time, I read about Kim Il-sung's *Juche* theory. One
Seoul National University law college student had written it
down from North Korean radio broadcasts and distributed it
to friends. One of my friends was a key member of his group.
My impression was that real North Korean spies would have
no way of finding out about these groups and contacting them.
At that time, Korean nationalism was very popular among
students and *Juche* emphasized strong nationalism. But all the
time I was studying it I was haunted by the feeling that it was
not logical. I couldn't understand the logic of the emphasis on
the leadership. I struggled with my friend about that point.
He insisted, "Just believe and follow." I felt it was comical for
him to say this, but I couldn't say what I felt because others
were taking it so seriously.

I stopped the factory work after eighteen months. I tried
to be a laborer but couldn't be successful, so decided to quit.
I was an educated intellectual, very different from workers. I
can do more for society and myself as an ordinary educated
man, not an underground man. I found I didn't like workers.
This was not a class feeling. It's just that the culture of laborers was not mine. I didn't like the hard physical work because,
when you're doing it, you cannot think of anything except
work. Normally my mind was always thinking of things, but
I couldn't think when I worked. Also, I felt isolated among

workers. Our group didn't really try to make unions, we just gave them ideology. I felt I was useless, I couldn't do anything for them.

Lee became a chartered accountant and later an auditor for Samsung. His old friends became lawyers, politicians, and businessmen.

The value of it all was that we had freedom of speech and thinking within our own group. . . . We couldn't change society by ourselves. You cannot take away people's freedom and no one should take the freedom from others. That's my basic thought. It's the conclusion of my ten-year activism. The thing we have in common is that we still share a feeling that we want to work for society. We still talk about the need to live a righteous and meaningful life and help society.[241]

Some campus protests in the 1980s escalated into massive events. On several occasions students occupied campus buildings and at Sungkyunkwan University, declared some buildings a "liberated zone." Eventually riot police retook them. After a siege at Konkuk University in Seoul, fourteen hundred students were detained and thirty-four of them jailed under national security laws. In 1985, radical students took over the American cultural center library in Seoul for three days. Diplomats would not permit riot police to remove the students by force, and international TV cameras set up across the street. The boldness of this event released a pent-up resentment, which most of us covering it at the time were unaware existed. Many of the Koreans walking by seemed more impressed than shocked. This was just the first of numerous assaults on American targets through the decade.

Despite all this activity, though, the students were remarkably ineffective. Demonstrations seemed to be ritualistic, rather than strategically designed to make a point. Citizens did not criticize students, despite the constant tear gas and blocked streets. But neither did they support them. Student leaders seemed to be pursuing their own political careers and fantasy revolution, unaware that with their radical slogans and violence they had little backing from the populace.

But one issue would not go away. That was Gwangju. Every year in May, memorial rallies were staged in the city and on campuses around the country. The ghosts of murdered protesters haunted Chun Doo-hwan throughout his rule.

There were often lingering reasons to hate Chun. In 1980, he had conducted communist-style purges. Over eight thousand officials were removed for alleged corruption or other offenses, or simply because their names had been put on the lists. Almost sixty thousand were picked up in a drive to "eliminate social evils." Two-thirds of them were sent to "purification" camps, where at least fifty died. Media organizations were forced to close or merge, and several hundred journalists lost their jobs. Under new rules, newspapers were not permitted to have reporters in other cities and had to rely heavily on the state-controlled news agency.

In 1982, Kim Dae-jung was released and allowed to go into exile in the United States. Seoul had won its bid for the 1988 Summer Olympics, which gave it a focus for political development. The country had to be ready for this crowning glory. The economy had picked up again. In 1985, Chun released many politicians from a ban, and while Kim Dae-jung was in America his faction, and that of Kim Young-sam, combined to form an opposition: the New Korean Democratic Party. This party won an impressive number of seats in the National Assembly. It began to press for a constitutional change to replace the electoral college system for electing the president, which the government could manipulate, to a direct popular election.

However, the National Assembly itself was a pretense. A proportional system was in place whereby additional seats were allotted to each party according to how many seats it won in the election. The way these were allocated allowed the ruling Democratic Justice Party to enjoy a clear majority, although it won only a third of the vote. The ruling party agreed to the opposition's demand for talks on constitutional change to allow for more democracy but with its majority had no reason to concede to any demand. To create the necessary power shift to force a democratic change, the opposition politicians had to use other means. They took to the streets.

It would be a mistake to portray the struggle for democracy as a battle being waged by noble civilian democrats against a corrupt and brutal military regime. Opposition and government were part of the same authoritarian political culture. It was really this culture that was being rejected, and no single figure or party clearly represented the democratic alternative.

Chun had no fans. Even those who could justify his usurpation of power found his dourness, and financial scandals associated with his family members, reasons to dislike him. I used to marvel at receptions where he would make a grand entry into a hotel ballroom flanked by security, stand at the front holding a drink, and start talking about something. A few people would go to the front and listen, but the rest carried on their own conversations, completely ignoring him. Nevertheless, dislike did not translate into support for opposition. The government may have been disliked but it had significant support, as it was capable of managing the economy and the defense against North Korea, skills the opposition had never been in a position to develop.

But then things started to change. In January 1987 a twenty-one-year-old linguistics student from Seoul National University named Park Jung-chul died in police custody. Police had been dunking his head repeatedly in a bathtub and, in their zeal, smashed his windpipe against the side of the bath. They tried to cover up the incident, but details leaked and inflamed the populace against the regime. Protests and memorial services were held throughout the country. It was a tipping point. After years of indifference to student demonstrations and opposition-party antics, the death of this young man touched ordinary Koreans deeply. Chun now had a new and fearful enemy—the mothers of Korean students. In a few months their voices would be heard.

In April, Chun announced that the talks the opposition was boycotting on constitutional change were off permanently. Any further discussion, he said, would threaten the peaceful transfer of power at the end of his term in 1988, and the Olympic Games later in the same year.

Around this time, in the foreign media, we began to have our own problems with the police. Korean and Japanese photographers had often run into trouble covering demonstrations and antigovernment events. We complained officially after one or two of our members were beaten. The authorities obliged by issuing armbands for specific events which identified us as foreign journalists, and police were told to allow us to do our job. Then the photographers and TV crews, who were almost all Korean nationals, began to notice strangers with "foreign-press" armbands. We realized the government was issuing foreign-press armbands to police cameramen, who could get close-up photos of individual demonstrators. Students realized it, too, and at least one photographer was mistaken for a police agent and man-handled by students. At this point we decided to distribute our own armbands, with each person's Seoul Foreign Correspondents' Club membership number and strict rules about not lending them to other people. The authorities did not appreciate this initiative. In a yelling match, an assistant minister of culture and information accused a small delegation I had taken, as the club president, to explain the decision to him of violating Korean national sovereignty. We used the armbands anyway for a ruling-party event the following day at which Roh Tae-woo was to be nominated as the party's candidate for the December 1987 presidential election. It was a timely mo-ment, for that night the fiercest and most sustained—and finally, meaningful—period of rioting began.

With the electoral-college system, in which people voted for around five thousand worthies who elected the president, Roh was to be a shoo-in. The opposition was in disarray and students had lost popular support. People had accepted that Chun had overcome his predecessors' weakness for perpetual rule and would actually step down. But this was no longer the issue. The problem was that he was afraid to allow a free vote and was putting his best friend in his place. An organization of religious leaders and dissidents called for pro-tests. At 6 P.M. that night, June 10, 1987, drivers were asked to sound their horns in solidarity.

Several journalists were sitting in the bar of the press club, talk-ing about our armband victory. A photographer walked in reeking of tear gas, saying there was a little demo going on somewhere. At six, we opened the windows to see if people driving home from work had responded to the call to sound their horns. At first, there was just the sound of traffic. But after a minute, it seemed that the normal erratic noise was taking some shape, as if an orchestra tuning up was, section by section, starting to play. A long line of cars in convoy came down the boulevard to the city plaza, with their horns at full blast, and the rush-hour traffic picked up the theme. Meanwhile, on the other side of the plaza, a cloud of tear gas appeared between the buildings. It was the little demo. Thousands of people were already in the streets.

I drove around downtown with another Western reporter. Seoul had been the scene of several large-scale protests before, but nothing quite on this scale. The debris of street warfare was everywhere. Ripped-up paving stones and rubble, powder scars where tear-gas canisters had landed. We rescued two young women who were choking on tear gas, and dropped them at a subway stop. At one point, a crowd of several thousand was making its way along the broad road between the Namdaemun Gate and City Hall. The car was completely surrounded by people and only inching along. People slapped on the hood and shouted. These were not only students. One or two people in the crowd gave us baleful looks. North Korean agents, fanatical anti-Americans, nutters who get drawn to mobs? A large man in a suit knocked on my window. I lowered it wondering what he was planning.

"The horn," he said in English. "The horn." Of course, the horn.

I jammed a fist, palm down, on the horn and the crowd around us erupted in joyous applause. I took my *waeshin gija* (foreign reporter) armband out of the glove compartment and held it up to the windshield. The people roared again and slapped the car in support.

The protests spread to cities all over the country and lasted for days and days. Some students occupied the Myeongdong Roman Catholic Cathedral in the city center. Riot police were positioned around it and the siege became a focal event. After a few days, it became apparent that these were more than student demonstrations. I found a coffee shop on the second floor of a building that afforded a view up the street to the cathedral and hung out there, shielded from tear gas. One lunchtime, I watched a line of riot police block a man carrying a briefcase from going down a narrow street, probably back to the bank where he worked. He went berserk and in his outrage looked as if he would take on the entire South

Korean police force single-handed. He was manhandled away. On another occasion, three or four policemen bundled a businessman, who must have been rude to them, into a doorway and were themselves set upon by some middle-aged ladies who flailed at them with handbags. This was a middle-class revolution.

After *The Washington Post* reported this theme, the minister of culture and information came to the cathedral to take a look for himself, and suffered the indignity of being chased down the street by angry demonstrators. Chun knew he had a problem that was not going to go away. He held separate talks with opposition leaders. When Kim Young-sam came out of a Blue House meeting and told the world that Chun was still not prepared to concede, the riots intensified and the government debated whether to introduce martial law and bring in tanks. But the ghosts of Yun Sang-won and the others killed in Gwangju were also in the demonstrations. The ghost of the future also haunted Chun. The Olympics were only a year away and Chun envisaged their opening by Roh Tae-woo, who would then be president, with himself sitting by his side as the elder statesman, a tribute to his achievement of the first peaceful, democratic transfer of power in Korean history.

The only way to break the impasses was to concede. On June 29, Roh Tae-woo made a dramatic announcement calling for a rewriting of the constitution to allow for presidential elections by direct popular vote. The country was jubilant. On July 1, Chun approved. The opposition was back in business. Kim Dae-jung was released from a political ban. Kim Jong-pil had returned and formed his own party.

Most people you asked wanted Kim Dae-jung, Kim Young-sam, or Kim Jong-pil to be the next president. Foreign correspondents believed them and predicted that the winner would at least be called Kim. But a scholar warned me not to assume that a ruling party victory by Roh Tae-woo could happen only if the election were rigged.

"Democracy for us Koreans means the right to choose our own dictator," he said. His point was that when it came down to the vote, people would want a person they thought was capable of ruling and who had the backing of the military.

In the end, this is what happened. The opposition did the government the big favor of splitting the antigovernment vote. The alliance between Kim Young-sam and Kim Dae-jung broke and they ran against each other. The government pulled out all the tricks. It controlled media. Pretending to report equally, it always began each news item with a report on Roh's campaign because his candidacy number was '1'. Gift giving occurred on a scale the opposition couldn't match. There was also a convenient reminder of the threat from North Korea: A terrorist who had planted a bomb on a Korean airliner was caught in Bahrain and brought to Seoul on the eve of the election.

The opposition had more committed support and could produce more people at its rallies. Election workers tried to convince media of their own crowd estimates. Kim Dae-jung had the biggest rally of the whole campaign, on the Yeouido Plaza in Seoul. He asked me for my crowd estimate and looked disappointed when I said "over a million." I found out later his aides had told him the crowd was nearer three million. That's what aides are for.

Large crowds gathered also for Kim Young-sam, and though Roh's looked abundant, when you were in them you could do your tai chi moves without touching anyone. A lot of his ralliers were reluctant. A friend from Samsung told me he had been ordered by the company to go to a Roh rally. He took his headphones with him and, while Roh addressed the masses, he got nostalgic with Jimi Hendrix.

In the absence of credible polling, I was going on intensity and size of crowds as the measure of support. I thought Kim Dae-jung would win. But in the week before the election, all those people who didn't bother with rallies and were noncommittal when you asked them who they were going to vote for, like my landlord and other neighbors down the street, decided for Roh. In the end, Roh gained 37 percent of the vote, enough to win. Kim Young-sam came in second, DJ third, and JP fourth. The opposition complained of vote rigging. Dissidents tried to prove there had been a sophisticated fiddling of the vote count using computers and claimed the military dictatorship was continuing to rule. Indeed, there had been some questionable incidents. A ballot box was removed from a polling station. Voting on military bases was not secret and soldiers were pressured to vote for Roh. Candidates violated spending limits. But by the standard of previous elections, this one was an improvement. The claim that Roh had won through fraud fell flat in the face of the opposition split.[242]

There had been for the first time a peaceful transfer of power through a reasonably democratic election.

Until now, democracy had been imitated. Now, its form was in place. Over the next decade the focus would be on developing its substance, with fairer elections, expansion of individual rights, and a democratization of the culture. Democracy had begun.

21

THE FIRST DEMOCRATIC PRESIDENTS

"Culture is not necessarily our destiny. Democracy is."

That day the dictator conceded, June 29, 1987, is celebrated as the starting point of democracy. It was a conception, and as is the way with power relations, more forced than gentle. People power, you might say, had shafted dictatorship and impregnated the state. The delivery was eight months later, on February 25, 1988. That was when, forty years after the founding of their nation, twenty-five since the economic revolution, and seventy days on from the election, the Korean people inaugurated the person they had, for the first time, peacefully and properly, though noisily, chosen to lead them. They listened when he stepped up to the microphone at the ceremony on Yeouido Island in Seoul and gave a speech entitled, "We Can Do It."

It was a familiar exhortation from the Park Chung-hee era. But this time it was about democracy. And they have been doing it, since then, the Koreans.

That said, Koreans don't celebrate that moment because they see it as Roh's. But it was and is theirs. It marked the point at which Koreans changed from a people ruled by a person to a people governed by rules, sort of. It went from the country of kings, outsider power, Rhees, Parks, and Chuns, all of whom manipulated law in the service of their own power, to a country where the law ruled.

This point often gets lost. The Earth did not move. Life did not change. More to the point, many refused to accept Roh Tae-woo as a democratic president. They looked at his gray suit and saw a green uniform. Of course, the transfer was peaceful, they'd say, it was from the top thug in the junta to his best friend. He's a military guy. How could he be democratic? And please don't mention Washington and Eisenhower because this is Korea. Yes, Roh later held Chun responsible for the past, but he was forced by public opinion, and went easy, letting his buddy slip into internal exile in a temple. No, they say, the real first democratic president was the next one, Kim Young-sam, a civilian oppositionist. This claim had many advocates, most notably Kim Young-sam.

The bias is understandable. The necessary weakness of democracy is that it doesn't come with ideological commissars. The flabby rump of old thinking continues to sit heavily on the face of the electorate. It's no wonder voters can't see what's changed. The inclination remains to look to the person of the president, rather than the system by which he or she is selected and then dismissed. It doesn't help that media remains obsessed with every move a president makes. Like America, Korea's presidents are treated as if they are short-term monarchs.

The fact remains, though, that the presidency on that cold winter day in 1988 was a very changed office.

Starting with Roh, each occupant since has been required to leave after a single, five-year term. None has tried to stay. In the first twenty-five years two and a half were opposition candidates— the half being Kim Young-sam, who cunningly merged with the ruling party and won as its candidate. One was a minor player before winning his party's candidacy, one was a single woman, and one actually had a career other than politics. This short history already allows for a claim that Korea's is one of the most impressive democracies in Asia.

Indeed, it is. By their example, Koreans embody a crucial argument for the universality of democracy. Millions in China and elsewhere are convinced by the arguments in defense of authoritarianism and collective rights made by Asian intellectuals and politicians, pointing to Western social ills and blaming democracy for what they see as Western decadence. They argue for a different type of democracy, one more relevant to family-based heritage, a democracy with Confucian characteristics. The result is either the postponement of democracy or an arrangement whereby the same party wins democratic elections and seems to rule forever. The Koreans are subject to the same intellectual temptation but refute it by example, not because they're moral philosophers but because they know what people who seek power are up to.

Kim Dae-jung, the third democratically selected president, said it best: "Culture is not necessarily our destiny. Democracy is."[243]

This democracy is a fertile paddy, some sections of which have sprouted more thickly than others. Elections, for example, have improved each time. The 1987 campaign was measured in outdoor rallies, many of them characterized by stone-throwing. Roh and then-oppositionist Kim Young-sam, both from the southeast, were pelted by mobs and driven from venues when they ventured to Kim Dae-jung country in the southwest; and when Kim Dae-jung went to their territory the spirit of revenge was in the air, but he knew the limits of this violence—it was not intended to really hurt anyone—and was prepared. At a rally in Daegu, bodyguards stood on either side of him intercepting stones with Plexiglas shields, as he orated without flinching.

I had a taste of this when I was recognized by one candidate at a rally and invited to sit with the candidates at a table set up in a school playing field—being friends with the foreigner was a way to score points. One by one the rivals went to the mike to deliver their sermon. At some point in an opposition speech, someone at the back started throwing pebbles. Some of them bounced off our table. We all pretended it wasn't happening and nobody identified any offenders or complained. I'm surprised nobody lost an eye or had a hole made for a third one.

Nowadays, candidates walk through markets to hug grandmothers and shake the hands of babies for TV. The whole process is less exciting, which is how it should be.

Another improvement is the acceptance in principle of protest and its consequent evolution from Molotov cocktails and tear-gas exchanges to something less newsworthy. Take a walk through downtown Seoul on any day and you will usually see at least one person with a placard outside the main government building, sometimes a group with red headbands—which are incidentally made by a company that supplies protesters—outside the tax office, larger groups outside the district offices, and unionists outside corporate headquarters and, if not protesters, then a line of police buses protecting the U.S. and Japanese embassies. Occasionally something occurs on a larger scale and with it an unnecessarily large police presence.

On the slow front, some attitudes and ways of thinking seem to have hardly changed. Consider this pattern: Each of the first five democratically elected presidents has gone through the near-exact same popularity pattern, a lurching descent after election from enormous approval ratings to an end point of political leprosy, so contagious his own party's candidate shies away from his support.

This drop in popularity poses each time as a response to failure— the arrest of aides for corruption, policies, or lack of them—but like much political conviction it is more gut than reason. The electorate swims in a gathering current it cannot explain. People criticizing the president change tack when you come back at them. Getting to a rational explanation can be like catching the proverbial bar of soap.

Kim Dae-jung (1998–2003) had it bad. He was unfortunate in that the *Dong-A Ilbo*, one of the three most influential papers and previously one of his supporters, made a strategic decision to join forces with the others against him. The publisher calculated that it would be better for business. That meant, apart from one out on the left, all the main media were shooting from the same trench.

I went down to Kim's home island during this time and found that, even there, in the tiny community two hours by ferry off the southwest coast, they'd turned against their boy.

"We expected he'd do something for us," the owner of an old-style *tabang* coffee shop moaned. A mainlander, he'd been a photographer and decided to stay after a visit years earlier.

"But he's the president of all Koreans," I said. "If he did something for you, that would be favoritism, maybe even corruption. In fact, don't you admire him for not favoring you?"

"I know what you mean," he said. And he did know what I meant. But he just felt critical.

The reason, I would suggest, was that Koreans had not, on February 25, 1988, or thereafter, adjusted their view of what the presidency actually was. They knew, but didn't really get, what had changed in terms of what a president could or could no longer do. The ghost still occupying this space in the national psyche is our old friend Park Chung-hee, and he's whispering: "Look at this fellow. Does he have what it takes? Has he built up an industrial base from nothing to protect us from North Korea? The whole National Assembly is yelling at him. The people are protesting against him in the street. He's useless."

On the face of it, any comparison with Park Chung-hee is absurd, especially considering that it takes a year to learn the job and that the last year is lame-duckery. This leaves the modern Korean leader three years to accomplish anything, not the eighteen Park had, and usually it's against an opposition-held parliament and in the face of a highly critical media. What's more, how do you compete with a nation-builder when the nation is already built and able to defend itself against its enemies with or without American help?

The failure to articulate the limitations of the democratic presidency falls most squarely at the feet of the presidents themselves. It's hard for them to think about, let alone do, because in the hierarchical society, democratic limitations are not a source of strength to boast about, and to go on about them risks sounding like an excuse. In other words, these new presidents share the old idea of how the office should work: They think they're Park Chung-hee—for the first few days, at least.

Kim Dae-jung, for example, set himself up for failure at his inauguration. He had been elected during the Asian financial crisis and had a perfect opportunity to pull a Winston Churchill and make the people smell the toil, tears, and sweat ahead. Instead, he promised he would turn the country around and recover in three years. Despite an impressive national turnaround, three years later the bureaucrats had to be creative to pretend they had achieved everything they had set out to do. But it didn't work. Kim got more criticism than credit.

Lee Myung-bak (2008–13) tumbled into the same boiling pot. As the electorate in late 2007 braced for a tidal wave from the U.S. financial crisis, he campaigned under the slogan "747 Economy," which promised 7 percent growth, doubling per capita income to 40,000 dollars, and making Korea the world's seventh-largest economy (it was fifteenth). The country bounced back and even found itself taking a center stage role, chairing the G20, the new global leadership body. But what did people see? His failure to get even close to the 747 vision. He should have promised them blood, toil, tears, and sweat.

It's as if the external posture of a newly elected leader is: "You, the people, have chosen me. An excellent choice, if I may say so. Now, here's what I'm going to do. You just sit back, put your seat belt on, enjoy the movie, and I'll see if I can fly this plane."

Confidence is one thing and competence another. Roh Tae-woo knew what he didn't know and allowed himself to be scripted in almost everything. At a rare foreign-press event in the Blue House, as we waited at circular dining tables, we were advised of the S-shape route he would take through the room. When he sat down at our table, a secretary placed the table plan in front of him and, without looking at anyone, he spoke.

"Mr. Breen, it must be difficult being the president of the foreign press," his interpreter said.

"Yes, it is, Mr. President. But I'm sure it's much harder being the president of a country," I said. Everyone was too uptight to roar at this rib-tickler. Roh was already consulting his sheet.

"Mrs. Tunney, it must be difficult being a woman in the foreign press," the interpreter interpreted.

"Yes, Mr. President." Kelly Tunney, the AP bureau chief, who had reported in Vietnam during the war and was married to a son of the boxer, Gene Tunney, was too much of a lady to be anything but sweet.

And so it went through the whole meal, as if we were voice actors who didn't need to make eye contact.

Roh's instructions and comments at cabinet meetings were similarly prescripted. When the ministers realized this, they had their aides get together in advance with the scriptwriters and the meetings would go off swimmingly, with no surprises.

While Roh was at least humble—perhaps because he'd been good at something else, as a soldier—his successor, Kim Young-sam (1993–8), suffered from the conviction that what he didn't know couldn't be important. "We had to get briefings onto one page. Otherwise, we'd lose him," said Kwon Tae-shin, a finance-ministry official who was in and out of the Blue House under four presidents.

I admired Kim for his sheer, stubborn determination. He had wanted to be president since he was a boy, but I had the impression he didn't know why. He should be credited as much as Kim Dae-jung for democracy, but in foreign estimation he tended to be overshadowed because he was less articulate.

At one lunch in 1986, one of my colleagues asked him what democratic reforms he'd introduce if he were to one day be the president. As the question was interpreted, he looked to his right, then to his left, where his party's vice presidents were seated, for support. They looked away: You're on your own, mate.

"If I am elected, Korea will be a democracy," said the interpreter.

Now it was our turn to look at one another. Huh? Who's going to ask the follow-up?

The same reporter asked, "What I mean is that you say that Chun is not a democratic leader. So if you were the next president, what changes would you make?"

"Mr. Kim says that as he is a democrat, if he is elected, it means that the country will be a democracy," the interpreter said. People said that YS was not a thinker—he once got nuclear weapons mixed up with nuclear power—but I never held that against him. I don't believe a president needs to be exceptionally articulate or clever. It's the instincts and strategic sense and the ability to choose good people around them that make them good leaders, I thought. But this was freaky. It was like policies were something for aides to pick, and coach him on before interviews.

Kim had a face that was made to smile and arched eyebrows that gave him a look of innocence. He had gray hair, distinctive in a society where even eighty-year-olds dye theirs black. Once I turned up to a lunch with him, shook hands with three of his aides and said something like: "How is Mr. Kim these days?" before realizing I'd just shaken hands with him. He'd colored his hair. It wasn't even black. More auburn. Something had gone wrong. The effect was to make him disappear.

Kim came from Geoje Island off the southeast coast. After serving in the army during the Korean War he aimed for politics. He was elected to the National Assembly in 1954 when he was just twenty-seven, and served nine terms. In 1960 North Korean agents broke into his family's house, apparently looking for money, and shot and killed his mother. This, and his army service, put him above suspicion as far as the anticommunists in power were concerned.

In the 1970s he emerged along with Kim Dae-jung and a former rightist student leader, Yi Cheol-seung, as the new generation of opposition leaders. In August 1979 when Kim let striking women workers use his party's headquarters for a sit-in, police assaulted the building, killing one of the women, and badly beating several lawmakers. Four years earlier, Park had promised Kim that he would introduce democracy, but he asked that this pledge be kept confidential. Kim obliged, but in his outrage at this attack on the strikers, he told *The New York Times* in an interview that Washington should stop supporting Park. It was this that led to his expulsion from the National Assembly and prompted the chain of events that led to Park's assassination.

On his first day in the Blue House Kim's first guest was his widowed father. No problem there, but I always had the sneaking suspicion it was to ask his dad a desperately private question: So, Dad, I've been working on this for forty years. What do I do now?

To his credit, one thing he did do immediately was address the issue of prisoners of conscience.

To mark his inauguration, Kim conducted an amnesty for about forty-two thousand offenders. This type of thing happens on major national holidays. Prisoners get early release, pardons, parole, reduction of sentences, restoration of civil rights, removal of past offenses of corruption from the records, and waiving of drunk-driving and speeding tickets. Much as these amnesties are welcomed by those involved, they typify the overruling of the judiciary by the executive. But that's another point. This one was the biggest to date and was designed to underscore the arrival of real civilian democracy.

That day, I drove down to a prison near Daejeon, a city in central Korea. It was wet and chilly. Outside, thirty students from a local university awaited the release of some friends. They watched as criminals, mostly young men, came out and were greeted by family members, who were happy but embarrassed, and slipped away. This went on all morning. Then a tall, scholarly man in a crumpled blue suit and, incongruously, a pink chiffon scarf tied around his neck, walked out of the prison gate. Beside him was a short, stocky man almost eighty years old with dark patches around his eyes. He didn't look well. These were the men I had been waiting for. Someone explained to the students that they were long-term prisoners. The students weren't expecting them. They applauded politely and asked the old man to say something.

"Thank you for coming to meet us," the stocky man said. "I'm only an old man. There are younger men who should be released because they still have their life to live. I feel guilty in front of them." He bowed and the students applauded again.

"Grandfather, how long were you in there?" a student shouted out to the man with the pink scarf.

"Thirty-seven years," he said.

The students gasped in disbelief.

The two men walked down the road with their family members.

One of the human-rights activists, Suh Joon-sik, who had also just been released, pointed at the man with the pink scarf: "His name is Hong," he said. "Often in prison you find a person who seems to forget about himself and takes care of others. He was such a person. He was in the cell opposite mine. Once I was brought back to my cell after being beaten. I felt so wretched and in despair. We were not permitted to talk. He stood at the door and watched me for hours. I could feel that he was willing me to feel courage. This was how I began to recover my spirit."[244]

The two men were among a group of prisoners of conscience virtually unknown to the general public, jailed on charges of subversion or spying for North Korea, and kept in prison indefinitely because they had refused to recant.

Another in this group, Lee Jong-hwan, was being released after forty-two years. We found out that, as he had no relatives to greet him, he had been taken out a back gate by prison guards and driven to an old people's home about fifty miles away. The activists got the address.

We found Lee sitting in his new room, a little bewildered. He had a lean, wiry body, color in his cheeks, and a lively sparkle in his eyes.

"It hasn't sunk in yet that I've been released," he said. "I saw in the papers that they were going to free people who were over seventy years old, but I wasn't sure if I would be included. Even this morning the guards didn't let me know. They only told me as they opened the gate. Then I was driven here. I'm not sure if this is still a prison. I've been told I can't go outside the grounds without permission."

"Don't worry," Joon-sik said. "That applies to the other people as well. It's because the management is responsible for your welfare."

What does a man think of in those first moments?

"I felt gratitude to dissident and church groups lobbying for the political prisoners and regret that all the long-term offenders were not released," he said. Among those still in was Kim Sun-myung, who had been arrested in the same month as Lee, October 1951, during the Korean War. He would eventually be freed in August 1995 after almost forty-four years in prison.[245]

Kim and Lee were South Korean–born communists. Kim had been a private in a reconnaissance unit in the North Korean army when he triggered a booby trap and was captured by American soldiers. Lee had been a political operative, picked up by U.S. forces as he crossed the border coming south. Both were sentenced to fifteen years as "collaborators" by a military tribunal. The following year, they were retried as "spies" and sentenced to life. Ahn Hak-sop was another soldier in the North Korean army. In 1953 he was captured in a battle with South Korean troops. In prison, it was discovered he was actually a South Korea–born volunteer. He was badly beaten and charged with collaboration. Family members, meanwhile, were unable to get permission to visit him because they lived in a restricted area near the DMZ. A relative finally obtained the necessary pass, but it was too late to plead for leniency. A military court had, a week earlier, sentenced him to life imprisonment. The relative was told that, had she arrived before the trial and paid a few dollars, she could have obtained his release.

These men were jailed less than halfway through Syngman Rhee's term as president. They were kept for the most part in solitary confinement through the rule of Rhee, Park Chung-hee, Chun Doo-hwan, Roh Tae-woo, and into the administration of Kim Young-sam.

"In the fifties the prisons were not fit for humans, just beasts," said Kim Sun-myung. "There'd be from fifty to a hundred people in a large cell. Many were near starvation. When an inmate died, we tried to put him in a sitting position so he looked alive and after roll call we got his ration." For ten years after the 1961 military coup, all visits and letters were banned. It was during this period that the prisoners disappeared from public knowledge.

Ideological offenders were given an opportunity to change sides. In a system the Japanese had used to great effect against independence activists, and which was formally adopted by South Korean authorities in 1955, they were able to swear loyalty to the country and be pardoned. Kim, Lee, and Ahn declined because they saw themselves as POWs. In 1972, when the Yushin Constitution was announced, there was a new policy of persuading inmates to convert. They were required to sign two conversion documents, one a declaration regretting past activities and the other an oath of allegiance to South Korea. Compliance entitled a prisoner to basic privileges and made him eligible for parole and amnesty. By this time, the numbers of ideological prisoners had increased. Some were captured North Korean agents. Others were antigovernment leftists accused of being pro–North Korean. They had various reasons to resist. The North Koreans knew that if they converted, their families in the North risked loss of status or worse. Li In-mo was a North Korean war correspondent who had been treated as a guerrilla because he had been captured in 1952 in the mountains with partisans left behind after the communist army retreated. In Pyongyang, his wife had privileges as the widow of a war hero. When I met her there, she told me she had only learned in 1991, three years after Li's release from prison in the South, that he was still alive. Several of the holdouts were dissidents who had falsely confessed under torture to being spies. They wouldn't recant because to do so would require them first to admit they were guilty of the crimes for which they had been sentenced.

Refusal required great courage. At least seven people died under beatings, survivors say. The unconverted were kept in solitary confinement to keep them from influencing others. (Kim Sun-myung went on to spend thirty-five years in solitary cells.) When these measures failed, more subtle means were used. Wardens brought political scientists to discuss the errors of communism and encourage prisoners to recant their beliefs. Family members were also brought in to pressure them to sign. There were also occasional day trips to a textile plant near Daejeon and for lunch at the Kum River resort run by the Hyundai Group to show how the country was changing.

Visits were restricted to family members. Since his wife's death in 1953 Lee Jong-hwan had received almost no visits. Once a relative came with some deeds of land that Lee owned and asked him to sign it over. He refused. Conditions began to improve after June 1987. After prisoners protested by kicking their cell doors, they were permitted to watch special TV programs. From 1988, recorded radio news was broadcast once a day and then prisoners who received money from their families were allowed to buy one newspaper a day. Guards stopped beating those found secretly communicating with inmates in neighboring cells.

When the story of these forgotten men was revealed in 1990 by Suh Joon-sik and his brother Suh Sung, Korean-Japanese freed after an international lobbying campaign, there were around seventy unconverted prisoners remaining, and a similar number who had converted and were awaiting release. International human-rights groups had no access to them and little was known about their cases. Amnesty International adopted them as prisoners of conscience after satisfying itself that the prisoners were not terrorists and had not committed violence.

For some, resistance was a simple matter of principle.

"I couldn't lie. I couldn't cheat my conscience," said Kim Sun-myung.

Such righteousness was not usually appreciated by prisoners' families. Four years before his release, I managed to trace Kim's brother. He was not at home but his son gave me a work address, an electronics shop he managed in the Myeongdong district of Seoul. The next day I went to see him. He seemed very embarrassed and ushered me out quickly to a coffee shop.

"No one here knows I have a brother," he said. "Even my son didn't know. But I had to tell him last night after you visited our house."

The family had come under such pressure that in 1968 he decided to register him as dead. Their mother, who was in her nineties when he was finally released, did not know Sun-myung was still alive.

"I went to see him once about twenty years ago, but he was still a crazy Red," his brother said. "He brought so much grief to the family. All he had to do was sign the form and he could have been released."

Kim Young-sam allowed the war reporter Li In-mo to return home to North Korea in 1993. But when relations with North Korea turned bad again, the decision was criticized, a sure sign that the prevailing idea among politicians in the South was not that letting Li go was the right thing to do in terms of respect for his rights, but that people exist to be exploited by government for greater ends.[246]

22

DISSIDENTS IN CHARGE

"Look at this boy. He is going to be important."

Kim Dae-jung became president after YS. Ask him why he wanted the top job and he'd give you a list of what he wanted to accomplish, one, two, three, and four. In fact, when he was a dissident I'd ring him up to ask about something and he'd give me one, two, three, and four and there was half my story written already.

Over the years he had adopted a regal habit of staring ahead while he replied to you, or as people whispered in his ear. In the hierarchical culture, such a posture is necessary to avoid being sucked in by those lower on the ladder. You only deal eye-to-eye with equals. Fail at this and you'll find yourself controlled by aides. The effect was to make him appear somewhat lethargic, dull even. An EU delegation, led by a former Swedish prime minister, and which had visited Kim Jong-il in North Korea before coming to meet Kim Dae-jung in Seoul, joked among themselves about whether they had gotten the two leaders mixed up. Surely the guy in Pyongyang is the South Korean fellow and the other way round?

I never found this dourness off-putting. At lunch or dinner at his house—our small group met regularly in the 1980s with him—I found myself getting choked up sometimes just looking at him. It was because he was the burden carrier, bearer of the sins of his age. This perspective was helped along because he had damaged hips from a road accident that he believed to be an assassination attempt, and walked with a waddle. It was also unintentionally helped along by the Chun government that ringed his house with riot police and intelligence agents who were not letting Koreans through. This just added to his importance.

That he had his flaws, there is no doubt. He was a politician. He lost election after election. You'd think a normal party would let someone more electable have a go, but after he lost to Kim Young-sam in 1992, one of his secretaries let me in on the secret. The party's monthly costs were 300 million *won* and Kim Dae-jung was the only person who could secure that amount from corporate donors with a single phone call.

He also had things to hide. Despite being a people who've come from behind, Koreans don't like rags-to-riches stories. On TV at election time, the information about candidates goes: name, party, constituency, age, and then the important stuff—hometown and university. I had a good deal going with one of Kim's congressmen once—I taught him English, he told me everything that was happening in the opposition. This man had been a shoe-shine boy and was seen as a future leader. But he had to hide the shoe-shine bit.

Kim had heavy PR baggage: raised by a single mother, a falsified birthdate, a wife who had committed suicide, subsequent remarriage, had been a leftist, had not served in the army.[247]

His birthday is officially listed as December 3, 1925, but he was in fact born two years earlier. This change was never explained but it appears to have been made when he was around nineteen by his mother, whose motive was most likely to make sure her son avoided conscription into the Japanese army.

His mother, Jang Ro-do, had been a young, childless widow who chose to strike out on her own after the death of her first husband. Her in-laws, who had a rare two-syllable surname, Jekal, had the decency to permit her to leave rather than insist she spend the rest of her life serving them, as was expected in proper Confucian society. She had a relationship with a gentleman named Yoon, before taking up with a married man, Kim Un-shik, the son of an Oriental medicine practitioner. They had three children in a not-uncommon concubine arrangement. Kim Dae-jung, the eldest, grew up with his mother and siblings, less than a mile away from the house where his father lived with his other wife and children. This background was rich fertilizer for political opponents. The spokesman for one of his rivals in the 1987 election once rather bitchily corrected himself in a conversation with me, "Kim, oh, I'm sorry, I mean Yoon Dae-jung." At a rally, opponents waved banners, "Down with Kim Dae-jung! Down with Yoon Dae-jung! Down with Jekal Dae-jung!" All, of course, referred to the same man.[248]

When he was seven, Kim was enrolled in a privately run school and scored at the top of his class in the exams. This achievement elated his mother and won the approval of the most respected man in the village. "My father used to say, 'Look at this boy. He is going to be important,'" said Kim Chun-bae, the son of the teacher. Thus, the young Kim Dae-jung discovered his path to affirmation.

In school photos he looks mystically upward and outward. Instead of putting his arm around a schoolmate and smiling at the camera, it is as if he is struggling away from the group. His apparent inner strength and solitude made others a little afraid of him, but they found that if someone voiced a strong contrary opinion, he would disengage to avoid conflict.

"I sensed he wanted to be strong and successful, but that inside he was lonely and afraid," said Chung Jin-tae, a school friend whose father was the local deputy police chief.

This style of interaction with friends would later characterize his leadership. As an opposition boss and as president his views and policies were not crafted through debate and argument in the inner circle. He studied, absorbed, and directed, shunning those who considered themselves clever and chastising subordinates with his silence. His aloofness—a trait others perceived as a quiet confidence—made him a natural boss. With subordinates it was big-brother/little-brother, a relationship code characteristic of Koreans, but which the islanders are said to possess more intensely than mainlanders.

"School days were the egg and the Blue House the chicken," said Chung Jin-tae.

At Mokpo Public Commercial School, Kim, given at that time the Japanese name of Toyota Hiroshi, most dreaded military training. One test, to instill courage, required a student to go alone and in the dead of night to a burial ground two or three kilometers away and, as proof, leave a ribbon at a specified spot. Some students ran away. Years later, he could still recall this ordeal in vivid detail:

> My legs were wobbling and my heart was throbbing. As I neared the burial ground, I heard haunting sounds here and there like footsteps on dried grass. My heart pounded.
>
> My palms were sweating. I felt like slumping down on the spot. I remembered my classmates' talk about goblins and ghosts. I hallucinated that a woman in white burial clothes with long unkempt hair and bleeding eyes was about to pounce on me and strike me with her long fingernails. . . . I wanted to quit and run away, but continued, hearing the haunting sound nearer and nearer.

Then someone, or some thing, started throwing stones. He picked up a fistful of stones and ran straight at the source of the attack, shouting: "Beast! Beast!" At which point, the teacher stepped out from behind a grave, waving his arms. "Toyota! Toyota! It's me. It's only me."

Reflecting later, he said rather humbly, "I often think I am molded in the image of that boy who had been petrified with fear and kept lunging ahead that night."[249]

At school, Kim learned memorization techniques. A military officer the boys considered especially mean announced a more rigorous training program than usual and then offered an improbable challenge: "If anyone can memorize the code of honor, his class is exempted." The section of the military manual took five minutes to read aloud. Kim volunteered and, to everyone's surprise, did it.

After the Korean War, Kim became drawn to politics and ran unsuccessfully for office. He caught the attention of Chang Myon, the

Catholic politician who became prime minister in 1960. A single father after his wife had a breakdown and committed suicide, Kim converted to Catholicism and took the name Thomas.[250] He won his first election in 1961, but before he could take his seat, Park Chung-hee staged his coup and closed parliament. Kim later married Lee Hee-ho, a Christian activist, and had another son. She was an enormous influence on him, helping shape the moral depth of his subsequent political suffering. He became the lawmaker for Mokpo and spokesman for Chang's Democratic Party.

In 1971, opposition party elders decided it was time to field a younger candidate for the presidential race and Kim Dae-jung emerged the surprise winner of a runoff vote. His near-victory stunned Park and the ruling camp, making Kim a marked man. On a trip to Japan in 1973, KCIA agents kidnapped him. Blindfolded and trussed, he was bundled onto a boat and believed he would be thrown overboard. According to him, at that moment, he felt the power of Christ, an inspiration that remained with him all his life. An aircraft buzzed the boat and, without explanation, Kim was returned to Korea and dropped off outside his home. The American CIA, tipped off to the kidnapping, had intervened to save him.[251]

Until then, Kim had been buffeted by events, but after this he deliberately took on the dictatorship, volunteering himself, its most high-profile victim.

His opponents countered by portraying him as a communist, or, in more reasonable moments, a pro-communist. As with most tarring, there was a brush of truth to justify this accusation: Kim had studied banned Marxist texts and joined an underground communist group in high school. His main activity seemed to have been to surreptitiously paste anti-Japanese posters around town. After marriage, he gave this up at the urging of his father-in-law, a businessman, and took a job in a shipping company. With the departure of the Japanese from Korea at the end of World War Two, he and other employees took over the company and in 1947 he bought a ship and started his own business. That same year, he was arrested after a local detective who did not like him claimed he was still a communist. A colleague took the policeman responsible for the case out drinking and paid a bribe to have him released.

That was the end of his communist period. His adversaries would later make something of the fact he was on a business trip to Seoul when the North Koreans invaded at the start of the Korean War, suggesting he was there to greet them, and that his escape to Mokpo and jailing there by North Korean troops was some kind of deception.

Such intelligence gymnastics were the consequence of a specific fear. Given the weak role of law and the importance of alumni and other friendly networks to a person's advancement, a change at the top would slam shut the door to opportunity for hundreds of ambitious people. The four presidents who ruled from 1961 until Kim took power in 1998 came from the southeast Gyeongsang provinces. In elections against all of them, Kim would win 90 percent of the vote from his home Jeolla provinces, and if he managed 10 percent from Gyeongsang, most were probably from expat Jeolla voters living there. Gyeongsang had double the population of Jeolla, but if swing regions like Seoul went for Kim, he could win. The Gyeongsang fear was that those resentful Jeolla folk would invade the corridors of power and dance on the rubble of long-established networks. The country might be ruined. More important than country, careers would be wrecked wholesale. Such fears, unreasonable as they were, explain how non-Jeolla Koreans so readily accepted the government's zany accusations that Kim was a communist. The threat to their well-being equated to the same thing.

The fact is, Kim was made of greater stuff than his accusers. In prison under death sentence in 1980, he told his family to pass on the message to his supporters that, after his execution, there should be no revenge. A devout Catholic, he understood the importance of breaking the cycle of fear. After his release from prison he maintained that Chun and his lieutenants should be forgiven. He did not want them to hold on to power out of fear of retribution. For this reason, after Chun and Roh were jailed by Kim Young-sam, Kim Dae-jung pardoned them.

Kim believed the desire for democracy grows out of human nature and that, as an option for national organization, it was sweeping through the world, chosen by culture after culture and region by region. It would not stop until everyone on the planet enjoyed its benefits.

As president, Kim proposed engagement with North Korea and

held a summit with the dictator Kim Jong-il. He was awarded the Nobel Peace Prize for this and for his efforts as a dissident, and remains the country's only politician to have emerged as a truly international figure, which is why, as the reader will have noticed, I have devoted more space to him in these pages than to other presidents.

"He really knew what he wanted," said Kwon, the official who had previously worked for Roh and Kim Young-sam. "He had a small notebook and would bring it out in cabinet meetings and issue instructions and write more notes in it. He was a very clever man."

Kim's "sunshine" rapprochement policy with North Korea was widely criticized after the initial thrill of the June 2000 summit in Pyongyang. Kim, though clever, was sucked in by the delusion, common to well-meaning people, that if we're nice to them, they'll be nice to us. "I feel a flood of pleasant emotions coming from inside," he told Kim Jong-il. North Korea, however, was not in the cold because of the South Koreans; they put themselves there and did not want to leave. Kim Jong-il's response might just as well have been, "I know. This Hennessy is so the best."

Unfortunately the increased exchanges did not amount to much. It later came out that the summit had been bought. Kim had Hyundai, the *chaebol* most keen to nation-build in the North, entice Kim Jong-il to show up by giving the dictator a 450 million dollar under-the-table payment.[252] Had this been known earlier, the Nobel might have been awarded to someone else.

However, in terms of our contribution-to-democracy theme, Kim's decision to opt for reconciliation broke from the past in an interesting and underexamined way: Before Kim, political leaders had benefitted from tensions with North Korea. A sufficiently anxious populace is usually more supportive of those already in power. Indeed, even today, the ruling party manipulates the North Korea situation on the eve of an election. Kim Dae-jung denied himself this advantage by aiming instead for peaceful engagement. In doing so, he purged South Korea of its instinctive fear of the North and revolutionized attitudes. The generation that had been taught in school that North Koreans literally had horns on their heads could see a personable Kim Jong-il in action. Now, when the North Koreans behave like idiots, South Koreans still get nervous. But they no longer imagine the fetid breath of Satan on their necks.

With each president, democracy became more rooted. Roh Tae-woo lifted restrictions on overseas Koreans visiting North Korea, a move that sparked a wave of noncommunist consultants and go-betweens from the U.S. and elsewhere to open the way for South Korean businesses and others to engage with the North. Kim Young-sam also started a move toward greater transparency, initially with a ban on the use of false names in bank accounts, a practice virtually all wealthy people engaged in. Under his presidency, women's rights improved.

But the biggest step for democracy was taken by the unlikeliest of these new presidents, Roh Moo-hyun (no relation to Roh Tae-woo). When he took office in 2003, the structural flaw that had provided legal backing for human rights abuse in Korea was still in place—the domination of the legislature and judiciary by the executive branch. Neither the first Roh nor the two Kims thought to weaken their own power by addressing it. Roh Moo-hyun did.

This Roh was the youngest child of a peach farmer. Born in 1946, he grew up in a village near Gimhae, a naval base in southeast Korea. In primary school he once refused to accept a prize for placing second in a calligraphy competition because he believed the first prize, won by a boy from a rich family, had been bought. This untypical reaction to a normal circumstance in a Korean school earned him a slap from the teacher, underscoring one theme that those who knew him emphasize: that he acted on principle rather than out of political expediency.[253]

To pay his tuition at Busan Commercial High School he worked during the holidays as a night watchman in a fire-extinguisher factory, sleeping at his sister's house during the day. After graduating in 1966, he could not afford college and began studying law on his own, working at a firm that made fishing nets, and briefly on construction sites at the same time. Nine years later, he managed to pass the highly competitive national bar exam.

The lessons from Roh Moo-hyun's presidency began with his selection as the candidate by the then-ruling Millennium Democratic

Party. This was achieved through an American-type primary vote. This method, used for the first time, broke the factional-boss system and left his party's leaders, who thought they were senior to him, somewhat nonplussed. As indication of their disappointment, party elders withheld election funds from his campaign and told reporters off the record that he wouldn't win.

When he started to trail in the polls, several of the party's congressmen joined a rival candidate, the FIFA Vice President Chung Mong-joon, which precipitated a decision by the two men to join forces. They agreed to a televised debate and a public-opinion survey as a formula for deciding. Chung lost and stepped aside. At lunchtime on election day, when exit polls showed Roh trailing his main opponent, his supporters conducted a massive Internet and text messaging campaign targeting young voters. By the end of the day, he had won 49 percent of the 24.5 million votes cast (70.2 percent turnout), beating the conservative runner-up by 2.5 percent.

When the party leaders congratulated Roh on election night, the body language was something to behold. The frozen smiles and inadequately deferential tilt in the bow, captured their quandary: "Is he senior to me now?" Many of them decided no, and a few months later peeled off to combine with the opposition to have the new president impeached on the silly pretext of violating Blue House neutrality by expressing support for his party before an election. This was overturned later by the constitutional court.[254]

This farcical episode points to another of the slow-changing attitudes in democratic Korea: the refusal to accept the result of a democratic and fair election. When the first three—Roh One and Kims One and Two—won, the results were accepted because the winners were powerful party or faction leaders who controlled the cash. Roh Two's election marked the end of the days of these faction bosses. Since then, the losers have seized on issues with a passion to change the result.

Most presidents, democratic or not, have sought to expand their power by having their own people head the ruling party, the police, and so on. Kim Dae-jung chose not to do that because he thought it wrong. Roh Moo-hyun took this a step further and, having survived the attempt to unseat him, took steps to reduce presidential power and gave his prime ministers more authority. He declined to use the Central Investigation Department in the prosecutor's office, which the Blue House theretofore had used to investigate opponents. He also tried—but failed—to make the intelligence agency independent and to reduce its power by splitting the domestic and international spying functions.

Before Roh, the country's political elders, both ruling and opposition, continued to operate in an authoritarian political culture. One feature of this type of rule was a high level of intervention by government ministries and the presidential Blue House in the form of ad hoc guidelines sidestepping legal passage through the National Assembly. Roh minimized this style of rule, preferring instead to allow market forces play out. Such is the effect of labels, that for this radical departure from presidential politics in Korea, Roh was seen as an anti-U.S., antibusiness radical.

Unfortunately, Roh's liberation of the judiciary and legislature from the control of the executive branch was temporary. He did it as a policy, as a matter of preference, but was unable to enshrine the changes in law because he lacked a wide political support base. As a result, his two steps forward for democracy were followed in the next administrations with two steps back.

23

TWO STEPS BACK

From "Free" to "Partly Free"

Of all presidents, Lee Myung-bak, who succeeded Roh in 2008, had the most impressive resume in the real world of business and administration. He had spent twenty-seven years at Hyundai, where he had been appointed CEO of its flagship engineering and construction unit when he was only thirty-five. He was, immediately prior to his election, the mayor of Seoul.[255]

Unfortunately, though, Lee and his successor, Park Geun-hye, the daughter of the dictator Park Chung-hee, were children of the sixties—in Korea, that is. They came to maturity during dictatorship and are of the generation that still has difficulty getting its head around the concept of freedom. They do not see it as an inalienable right; nor do they buy into the idea of freedom as a source of moral power engendering national loyalty and strengthening democracy. They tend instead to see it as a gift to be enjoyed if the coast is clear and everyone gets along—i.e., in the future, when North Korea is no longer a threat.

Unfortunately, the constitution backs them up. It allows freedom of speech, the press, assembly, and association. But, it adds: "Neither speech nor the press may violate the honor or rights of other persons nor undermine public morale or social ethics." This sounds like a reasonable insistence that freedom be exercised with responsibility, but in fact it underscores an attitude that *Homo koreanus* is a teenager, whose freedoms are awarded conditionally: "You may stay out as long as you like, but if you stay out too late, you'll be in trouble."

As a result, democracy has not been nudged along on their watch. Their instinct has been to protect their own office.

"The president is supposed to have only administrative power and the National Assembly is supposed to set the legislative agenda," said Lee Cheol-hui, a former aide to Kim Dae-jung and Roh Moo-hyun and a prominent commentator. "But the balance is broken. The president in reality is above all three branches of government."

The notable issue in the Lee (2008–13) and Park (2013–18) administrations from the democratization perspective has been the decline in freedom of expression.

"Lee Myung-bak was a catastrophe," said Lee Sang-don, a noted conservative scholar. "We were crazy to have elected him. His brain only understood money. He had no idea about democracy or the rule of law."

Before him, press freedom had improved little by little to the point that Roh Moo-hyun became the first president to resist using the levers in his reach to pressure critical media.[256]

The main laws allowing for this have been around for a long time but their use has perked up under Lee and Park. The National Security Law allows seven-year jail terms for praising or expressing sympathy with the North Korean regime. It was commonly used by dictators to suppress dissent. Another tool is defamation, which can be a criminal offense in Korea with five years in prison and up to ten-million-*won* fines.

In 2011 Freedom House, the American human-rights group, changed Korea's rating from "Free" to "Partly Free." In the same year, a United Nations report agreed that, under Lee Myung-bak, freedom of expression had worsened. It cited the case at the start of his term that set the tone for the next five years—the arrest of a scriptwriter and four producers after their television documentary prompted mass demonstrations against the president's decision to reopen the market to U.S. beef, five years after it had been closed due to mad cow disease.[257] The charges were defamation of the agriculture minister and a government negotiator. The court eventually found the defendants not guilty but the message that people who openly criticize the government should watch their mouths had been delivered.

As indication of the exercise of law to bully ordinary folk, consider the fate of Park Dae-sung. At thirty, he was preparing for university entrance exams by day and playing online games at night. In early 2008 he started posting on economic issues in an online forum. He chose the name Minerva, the Roman goddess of wisdom. Somehow, the course of the global financial crisis started to back up his prophecies and investment advice. The mysterious Minerva became a sensation. When a government-run bank planned to buy a stake in Lehman Brothers, Minerva warned it would cost 80 billion dollars. When Lehman collapsed—fortunately after it had failed to agree with the Korean bank on price—Minerva was celebrated in the media as the "Internet economic president."

This was enough for the prosecutors to announce a search to find him. This was easy, as Koreans must submit their ID when setting up Internet accounts and even when buying mobile phones. A few days later investigators appeared at his apartment, confiscated his computers and books, and took him in for questioning. Incredibly, the young man was held in a cell for 103 days. The prosecutor accused him of deliberately posting false information that had caused a two-billion-dollar foreign-currency panic, and which amounted to the crime of "malicious rumor mongering."

In the end, the court disagreed with the prosecutor and set Park free. But the values and attitude of the elite could not have been clearer: The people are too stupid to be left alone. They need our protection from imposters like Park, who muddy like uncredentialed infidels the sacred ground of the national economy.

Lee established the Korea Communications Standards Commission in 2008 to censor broadcasting and the Internet. In its first year it blocked 4,731 sites and ordered 6,442 items deleted for encouraging gambling, obscenity, violating the rights of other people, or for disturbing law and order. This last covers the hundreds of sites connected with North Korea blocked at the behest of the intelligence agency and police.[258]

In 2011 a clever fellow created a Twitter account "@2MB18nomA." You wouldn't need to have worked at Bletchley Park to figure this was code for "Lee Myung-bak, you fucking bastard." Here's how that works: "2" in Korean is pronounced "ee," the same as the president's surname (the "L" is silent), so 2MB is a reference to him, plus a neat insult of being old-fashioned—"two megabytes"; "18" translated into Korean sounds like *ship-pal* which sounds almost the same as *ssibal* (fucking); and adding the "a" to *nom* (bastard) makes it sound like that's what you're calling him. The KCSC ordered the account to be blocked. The user took the case to court but lost.

Such decisions illustrate the claim that Korea has greater restrictions on free speech online than other democracies, a distinction that sits uncomfortably with the fact it has one of the most technically advanced, and certainly the fastest and most penetrated Internets in the world.

As for traditional media, its journalists are highly educated and good at their jobs, but the media itself, although few reporters on the newspapers actually see this happening in their day-to-day work, are in the pocket of the *chaebol*. Negative news about Samsung, for example, disappears after a day without any follow-up or opinion because almost all media depend on its funding and support, in the form of straightforward advertising as well as what are referred to as "planned articles," usually features or news stories that have a reporter's byline and look genuine but which are paid for. (The going rate at one English daily is the equivalent of five dollars a word; a one-thousand-word article would bring in 5,000 dollars; three a day could sustain the paper). Similarly, with broadcast media, documentaries are frequently paid for by their subjects. Banks and government agencies also get in on this act. In 2015 the online publication *OhmyNews* acquired a list of payments made to all media from 2012 to 2014 by Busan Metropolitan Government. These ranged from 444 million *won* in 2012 to KBS-TV and 315 million *won* in 2014 to a local network, KNN-TV, to small payments of one million *won* to small publications. The total budget each year was just under three million dollars. For the large *chaebol*, it is several times this amount.[259]

The obvious consequence of such collusion is that the public does not get the critical coverage it needs, particularly about business. One other unfortunate consequence is that calls for improvements in freedom of expression never really come from the press.

President Park Geun-hye has continued the good work of her predecessor in winding things back. This has come as a surprise, not only for those who expected more from the first female president, but also for her own party colleagues.

"When she was the party leader back in 2004, she favored democratic debate and the free exchange of ideas," said one of her own party's lawmakers. "But it seems she went back to 1975–9 when she was playing the role of First Lady."

As modern history demonstrates, the electorate never really knows what a candidate is going to be like until she, or he, has been elected and takes office because, until that point, they've always been on their best behavior.

Park's problems in this regard started with her own election in December 2012, when election officials and police, acting on a tip from the opposition, found that National Intelligence Service agents had conducted an illegal campaign posting over 250,000 online messages as ordinary citizens, supporting her and attacking her opponents as pro-North leftists. This outraged many but surprised few. It is possible the intelligence service has messed with each presidential election, and was just found out this time.

Park would have done democracy and herself a huge favor had she responded to this event as if it were an attack on democracy. But she simply did the minimum and promised to get to the bottom of it. The agency chief was found guilty and sentenced to three years but the Supreme Court, citing lack of evidence, nullified this ruling and ordered a retrial.[260]

The main consequence of this treason—let's call it what it is— was the disbanding in December 2014 of the political party that had first revealed the shenanigans. The complaint against the United Progressive Party, which had five lawmakers in parliament, came after some of its members were recorded at a meeting discussing rebellion and sabotage if another war broke out. One of the lawmakers,

Lee Seok-ki, was jailed for nine years for inciting rebellion (but found not guilty of actually plotting one). A handsome man who looks more like a vicar than a scheming Bolshevik, Lee is one of those youthful radicals who remains convinced that South Korea is still a dictatorship and that what the country needs is a good, strong socialist system like North Korea's.

The constitution and the National Security Law forbid the existence of a real pro–North Korean communist party. But Lee's party claimed his views were not theirs, that their party was not pro–North Korean. It was forcibly disbanded anyway, even though the court failed to establish a connection.

"The Constitutional Court made this decision on the basis of a tendency, not on evidence," said Lee Jae-hwa, the lawyer who defended the party.

Few shed tears for Lee Seok-ki and his colleagues when the party was disbanded. Polls indicated that nearly 70 percent of the public backed the decision. But that still left many in doubt, and I found them among ordinary people—elderly taxi drivers and young professionals and students who, in my informal survey, felt more perturbed about the banning of the party than about its existence because of what it said about the state of the country's democracy.

The far-left would get even fewer votes next time now that it had shown its true colors, the ordinary folk said. So how exactly is democracy protected by driving its advocates back underground?

On the plus side, Park introduced a revolutionary anti-corruption law aimed at putting an end to the pattern of gift-giving and wining and dining of public officials in return for favors that had characterized decision-making by bureaucrats for decades. The Kim Young-ran Act, as it is known (after the Anticorruption and Civil Rights Commission head who wrote the first draft), is so tough that it even includes teachers and journalists, and their spouses, in its definition of "public official." When the law came into effect in September 2016, restaurants in business districts immediately adjusted menus so that customers hosting politicians, journalists, and officials had options under the 30,000-won-a-head limit as prescribed in the new law.

This was a welcome development, but to really clear away corruption and allow Korea's democracy to flourish and move forward, the country needs to address the parallel issue of power abuse by the political and business elite. This lesson rang out as if on cue just a few weeks after the introduction of the anticorruption law when newspapers revealed that President Park had a secret best friend who had been allowed unparalleled access and who exercised huge influence over the culture ministry and was apparently shaking down the *chaebols* to fund her projects. Although these allegations did not seem completely new—in previous administrations, it was the family members of presidents who abused their proximity to the center of power—they instantly wrecked the image of Park, who had never married and who was estranged from her siblings and therefore free of greedy relatives, and brought hundreds of thousands onto the street, pushing baby carriages and inviting the police to join them as they demanded that she step down. As of this writing, it is unclear whether Park will be allowed to serve out her last year powerless and disgraced, or be forced to quit. Either way, popular outrage has put future leaders on notice that the permission granted them by voters to rule is no longer an invitation to privilege and abuse.

And democracy is once again moving forward.

NEXT

24

THE MIRACLE OF AFFIRMATION

"Korean films make you want to call your mom and dad.
You leave the theater wanting to be a better person."

Ask middle-school girls in Korea these days what they're going to be when they grow up, and which boys would make the best husbands, and chances are you'll find them dreaming of stardom and marriage to a chef. This is hard for parents, who still think actresses moonlight as "private" entertainers for rich men. And a cook? Just a few weeks ago, it seems, chefs pretended to be something else. What happened to the lawyer, the doctor, and the dentist?

The rise in prestige of performers and artists may be all rather new. But it was predictable—although I don't know anyone who predicted it—because wealth and freedom brings artists to the fore, even if poverty and repression remain their themes. In settled capitalist democracies, the politician, the professor, and the priest move to the back and the minstrels and players take the front row of popular appeal, with experts and executives mingling with them if they're arty performers themselves. We may expect more of this.

Now that Koreans are no longer fearful and herded, and now that they have more free time, beauty and creativity will light their alleyways with meaning. Politicians will still be famous but for reasons that disappear in time; few will enter the affections, unless one pulls off reunification. The administrator pales beside the storyteller and the purveyor of dreams.

Korea today, it seems, is so caught up with beautiful people and celebrity that it claims a right over their private lives. The nation took actress Hwang Soo-jung to its heart as the ideal Korean woman for her portrayal of a classy lady in a historical drama called *Hur Jun*, then angrily expelled her after she—the actress, that is—was caught taking methamphetamines with her live-in lover, who was married to someone else. After jail for the drug offense, she hid from view for five years before sneaking back to work. The singer Baek Ji-young took a similar five-year absence after a sex tape surfaced of her with her manager. The viciousness of the fan-mob became apparent when Korean-American star Jay Park was hounded out of the group 2PM five years after some private comments to a friend about being homesick were unearthed by people online. Some even launched a petition for him to commit suicide. All he said was: "Korea is gay. . . . I hate Koreans." He has since returned as a solo artist and producer.

Money abounds now to sponsor art and with it galleries have opened all over the place. (Tip: if you want to open a coffee shop, call it a gallery and you will qualify for a local government incentive.) Korean artists are making a real impact in some areas internationally. For example, a form of protest art that emerged during the military dictatorship period that is called *Dansaekhwa* ("monochrome painting") is relatively unknown among the layman but is seen by many in the art world as the most important art movement of the late twentieth century. Around the cities now, sculptures can be found in the lobbies and forecourts of buildings (because it's required by law for a building over a certain height). Other art forms are becoming more popular and the queue of hopefuls for talent contests wrap around the block twice. Such developments, we may say, are the predictable part of widening artiness.

But there is also in the culture of new Korea something unanticipated in the making. As I have suggested, the emergence of the Koreans is miraculous because it was so unlikely and because they could have veered off course at any time. If industry is step one and democracy step two, the story is completed by culture. It is culture in the broadest sense, the arrival in foreign ports of the country's expression to a point where the world feels as familiar with the Koreans as it does with the Australians and the French, and where Korea's distinctiveness is valued and embraced.

In contrast to economic growth and democratization, which were described as miracles by outsiders, this arrival to the attention and acceptance of outsiders is more of a miracle for the Koreans themselves. For this really is the part they cannot quite believe is happening, let alone explain. But it is and it astonishes. It means their distinctness has virtue and relevance. They always told themselves they were unique but didn't know how, beyond the façade of their exclusive language. They used to describe themselves as a frog in a well. Different, alone, but uncertain of what lay outside. Perhaps, they wondered, uniqueness was a bad thing. They told themselves this when the Koreans the world knew by name were infamous—Syngman Rhee, Park Chung-hee, Kim Il-sung, Moon Sun-myung, Kim Jong-il. They still don't get that there is something about them that the world likes and admires, and that now the outsiders have leaned into the well to help the frogs climb out. It's just that the frogs don't know why. But they will learn, and this will be their affirmation.

Of course, like any other society, Koreans have long enjoyed and appreciated their own art, music, literature, movies, and TV programs and, as you would expect, when modern international culture, American in particular, impacted theirs, they made an effort to preserve their own more traditional forms. This story is fascinating and colorful. But our particular theme here is not about how Koreans interpreted life and entertained themselves. Rather, it asks how, why, and when Korean art set sail and found itself welcomed overseas.

There are three aspects to this: the business of culture—and we can see the art forms that have most impact overseas, at least at this stage, are those where big business has a hand; the government, which makes the right noises about "soft power" but is hoisting the sails for cultural exports primarily for economic reasons; and, of course, very talented artists, who, besides doing what they do so well, represent the best argument against the accusation that the local education system throws a duvet over creativity.[261]

Underlying all is a collective compulsion that drives the Koreans outward.

Take music, for example. Ever since 1992 when twenty-year-old Seo Tae-ji mixed rap with rock and traditional music and transformed the local scene, people in the entertainment industry have been asking aloud when one of their Korean acts would make it in the United States: "The British invaded. When will we?" There is an aching for achievement in this question, as common to the arts as in other fields. It's with the reporters waiting outside the house of the poet Ko Un every year when the Nobel Committee announces the literature prize—Ladbrokes had him at 20 to 1 in 2015—and when some foreigner they've never heard of is announced instead, they wonder: "Is there anyone else we can put forward?"

I should say that this asking reveals the nationalist's insecurity, and is nothing to do with normal professional ambition. It's not coming from the artists either.

"One of the main qualities required for a writer to become a world figure is a particular form of self-confidence, an intense conviction that one's writing has value," said Brother Anthony, Ko Un's English translator:

When Ko Un travels and meets other very famous writers, Nobel Prize–winners and such-like, they immediately recognize him as "one of us," even though he does not speak their language. He has that stature as a person and a writer. He is automatically an international figure. That is completely mystifying for Koreans, who are extremely aware of the foreignness of the foreigner, and immediately feel at a loss, or inferior, and give up even trying to communicate. Ko Un is a loner, as any great writer might have to be, and in Korean society someone who refuses to play the generally accepted games of social convention is an outcast, he has few or no friends.

The longing for recognition is collective. It seems lodged in the soul, although a less poetic explanation makes better sense: If we are told from kindergarten that what we do is for the nation, it follows that the accomplished will be sent forth to do battle with foreigners. Little Jin-soo with his welding gear, and Jin-ho in ballet shoes are not just their mothers' children. They are members of Team Korea whose teachers will drive them to win. (These two did—Nam Jin-soo got gold for welding in the WorldSkills competition in Leipzig in 2013 and Won Jin-ho in the 2012 Cape Town International Ballet Competition.)

Where there is desire, of course, luck and other magic can also work. Bernie Cho found this out in early 2009 after he had secured international distribution rights from Apple iTunes for Korean music. K-pop had been growing more popular in Asia. In 2006 BoA became the first K-pop act to top the Japanese charts. The following year another Korean star, Rain, had been the first to perform at the Tokyo Dome, Japan's biggest venue. The thinking, as usual, was that this would be the limit. Then the god of the unintended consequence stepped in:

> At the time in Korea, downloads and streaming were sold separately. Downloads were roughly sixty cents per song. But then a cartel of Korean music portals got together in late summer 2008 and agreed to bundle downloads and streaming music together—nowhere else in the world had done so or even does it now—which basically meant, for the price of monthly streaming music of a few dollars, downloads were included. This brought the effective price of digital music downloads down to six cents per song. Ninety-two percent of the Korean digital music market moved to this download/ streaming bundle market.[262]

This decision seemed to reinforce the view that music was no place to make a living. Foreign visitors have noted for centuries the Koreans' love of music and singing. But the purveyors were low class, *gisaeng* courtesans or wandering minstrels. One enduring form, called *pansori*, was peddled by roving singers who performed bluesy ballads over several hours to outdoor audiences. The *pansori* artist would speak—rap, you might say—shout, sing, and mumble her way through a tale. The mixture of forms was partly designed to allow the lower classes to talk about the upper classes and let off steam in a way that only the lower classes could fully understand. This old form was introduced to a new generation in 1993 by the director, Im Kwon-taek, whose movie *Sopyonje* told the story of a *pansori* singer who blinded his daughter so that she would stay with him and discover the soul of her art.

In the modern era, Western music changed popular tastes, and many Korean artists got their start performing on U.S. military bases. In the 1970s, purists leading the economic revolution figured that rock music disturbed the morals of young people—a not-unfamiliar theme in the history of rock and roll—and censored it. (For good measure, they also banned long hair on men and miniskirts for women more than twenty centimeters above the knee.) Rock icon Shin Joong-hyun was harassed after refusing to write a song about the dictator. They got him later for smoking marijuana. He was arrested, tortured, and jailed, and his music banned. Others had their careers ruined. In the 1980s, even the singers who appeared amid the lavish backdrops and dry ice on TV struggled to make ends meet. One night in 1987, a colleague and I tried to follow one well-known singer, In Soon-i, on her nightly tour, which took her from performances in two venues in downtown Seoul, out to Incheon, an hour's drive away, and back to another part of Seoul. We lost her on the expressway back from Incheon around 1 A.M. This grueling routine was all the more remarkable given that she was already famous. Wherever the money was in the industry, not much of it was getting to the actual artists.

With the rise of the Internet in the 1990s, the CD market collapsed, and the management companies began to focus on digital sales, as well as on live shows and overseas markets. In particular, music piggybacked on some highly successful TV dramas exported throughout Asia and even further afield.

But then, with that price drop in 2008, more and more artists turned to sales overseas, where iTunes downloads, for example, were ninety-nine cents. Fortunately by this time the Internet had opened up a new path to success and the artists promoted through Facebook, Twitter, and YouTube, were able to form a community of foreign fans and bloggers.

One Sunday morning in 2009, Mark Russell, a journalist who had been writing from Korea for Western music publications for over a decade, was sitting in a dingy café in Barcelona, when he heard a familiar sound. "The music was bright and poppy, in different chords than Spanish pop usually uses," he wrote. "Then I finally heard the voices: They were singing in Korean. I asked the bartender, a middle-aged Catalan man, how he could have K-pop on his stereo, and he shrugged and said he just liked it. No big deal."[263]

K-pop was on the move. The main entertainment companies, which had been spotting and training young performers—including arranging for some to study at international schools in Seoul to make sure they could sing in unaccented English—were coming out with more acts. Music exports grew from thirty-one million dollars in 2009 at almost 60 percent a year for the next five years.

The fan base among youngsters as far-flung as Peru and Finland at first went unnoticed. When tickets for a show arranged by SM Entertainment in Paris in 2011 sold out and a flash mob of French K-pop fans demanded another, pundits in Seoul in their wisdom figured that music producers had pulled a PR stunt. But, no, something very genuine was happening. Here is a glimpse through the window, courtesy of one overseas reviewer in 2015:

> Something I learned at BIGBANG's concert this weekend in Newark, New Jersey—something I've never learned from anyone else over the past twenty or so years of seeing large-scale concerts—is that to execute a successful arena show, a good idea is to play every single song like it's your last song.
>
> It helps, of course, if you are the biggest boy band in South Korea and, quantifiably, the entire world; if you possess the physical energy to execute both pristine choreography and your own improvised, gymnastic endurance; and if you are equipped with an arsenal of fireworks and confetti timed to blast off every third or so song. It helps if you have a crew of twelve backup dancers. But this quintet of very cute, very lovable, and very personally distinct fashionistos let every single

rise to a volcanic peak, building intensity with as much flash and bang they could muster, belting out every lyric and hitting every rap with precision, all while allowing the tumultuous libidos of twenty thousand screaming women and girls to boil over with subtle suggestion. (Nothing beyond a PG rating, but very expertly delivered nonetheless—they go a long way by being extremely attractive and proffering the occasional pelvic thrust.)

. . .

Though K-Pop still doesn't get the shine it might deserve, it has less of a problem breaking through in the U.S., and not just with fans who speak Korean or have some cultural ties there; BIGBANG's lyrics don't necessarily have to translate for non-Korean speakers to absorb the band's core essence, which is universal: singing and rapping flawlessly, hitting every note (mostly, but functionally, does it matter when a boy band doesn't?), and playing off cuteness in a way that all boy bands have since time immemorial. Did I mention these dudes are so cute? They're so fucking cute. I have been to multiple boy band concerts and written extensively on the issue; I can rightly tell you that in my advanced age I have never seen a group nail being a boy band the way BIGBANG did, playing up each member's individual strengths and personalities but also flawless when it came time to come together as a unit, whether on a Michael Jackson–inspired spin or a dramatic R&B harmony.[264]

Early-teen fandom is a kind of remote but intense crush that functions to open sexual awareness and identity. That's what boy and girl bands do. The Korean boy and girl bands are now doing it on a global scale.[265] Young people thus ensnared may retain affection for some performers all their lives, particularly if the music matures with them.

The performers speak to the insecurity, the compensating posing, the rebellion of young people in a world made fearful by adults. It was this part that PSY inhabited: He had been popular for over ten years and had become chubby. But when his "Gangnam Style" video burst onto the scene in 2012 and started breaking K-pop and then global YouTube records, he crossed all kinds of barriers. The French taxi driver taking me and some colleagues late one night from Nice airport to Monaco knew almost nothing about Korea but was an expert in Gangnam Style—Gangnam is an upmarket neighborhood in Seoul, he said, and two bit-part players in the video are famous comedians in Korea. (He was right. The comedians were more famous than PSY.) When I suggested to him that PSY might be a one-hit wonder, he disagreed. In the old days maybe, he said, because future success would depend on the system: "Now," he said in English, "it is the fans and YouTube. He will do it again. Maybe not as successful. But he will not disappear."

As magical and unexpected and overnight as such stories seem, they depend on a necessary economic foundation, which is why, at least before God created YouTube and reality TV, they don't pop out of the Third World. The other ingredient is hard work. With every Korean success, there is usually a backstory of focus and sweat. With K-pop stars, it's the factory system run by the entertainment companies that audition youngsters (from America and Asia as well as from Korea), train them for years, and enter into long-term contracts with the survivors. The support networks are hard at work as well. A big part of the success of Gangnam Style can be attributed to the preparation, called "seeding," whereby his agency, YG Entertainment, was able through fans of its other acts, which include BIGBANG and 2NE1, to build up a base of 2.5 million subscribers to its YouTube channels.

There is a similar story behind the movies that are coming out of Korea.[266] To start with the history, Korean movies go back to the Japanese occupation and the era of silent films. Notably, in 1926 a movie called *Arirang* (after the folk song that is considered an unofficial national anthem in both Koreas) depicting a central character tortured by Japanese police and a woman raped by a collaborator, gave birth to a decade of anti-Japanese films. This ten-year run ended when the Japanese authorities intensified their control over local culture. With the end of World War Two, liberation and anticommunism were the main cinematic themes.

During the Korean War, many in the industry either sided with the left and went north, or were forced to. In the 1950s the government encouraged filmmakers with tax exemptions and a number of their films won international awards. In 1962, after Park Chung-hee's revolution, a new law designed to boost the industry required cinemas to show three local films for every one imported from overseas. The unintended result was a raft of poor-quality movies, cranked out on tiny budgets to meet the quota. This, and censorship that restricted creativity, left the moviemaking industry unable to compete with the growing appeal of TV. It foundered in the 1970s and most production companies collapsed. In the mid-1980s, when the United States started pressuring Korea to open some of its markets reciprocally to American products, Hollywood drove a few more nails into the local movie industry coffin: By 1993, local efforts accounted for only 16 percent of box-office receipts.

The revival came in the mid- to late-1990s with a marriage between big business and a new generation of filmmakers. On the business side, this change began when the Samsung Lee relatives who controlled the sugar milling and food companies in what was called the Cheil Jedang Group (CJ Group), invested three hundred million dollars in Steven Spielberg's DreamWorks Studios, secured exclusive distribution rights for Asia (excluding Japan), formed their own CJ Entertainment division, separated from the main Samsung conglomerate, launched their own multiscreen cinema chain and, after a false start producing on their own, signed up with three production companies that would be able to compete with Hollywood. Their success inspired others. On the industry side, many young professionals had studied overseas and, on return, did not want to play the hierarchy game: stepping onto the lowest rung in a movie company ladder and spending twenty years climbing before they were allowed to direct. They wanted to do it now.

The first blockbuster to come out of this convergence was director Kang Je-gyu's *Shiri*, a 1999 thriller with the added appeal of portraying its North Korean villains in a more interesting and sympathetic light than the usual wooden baddies. The movie became a sensation, breaking all records with ticket sales at nearly six million and beating the American movie *Titanic* at the box office. This was followed in 2000 by Park Chan-wook's *JSA*, another North Korea–related drama, where the action takes place in the truce village of Panmunjeom. Other notables included *Silmido* (2003), *Taegukgi*

(2004), *King and the Clown* (2005), and *The Host* (2006). In 2015, *The Admiral: Roaring Currents*, a historical drama about the sixteenth-century naval hero Admiral Yi Sun-sin, who defeated a Japanese armada in part due to his twenty-cannon-strong warships, sold almost eighteen million tickets, outdoing the previous record holder, the superb 2014 film *Ode to My Father*, by three million.

Korean films also began to make an impact overseas. In 2002, *Oasis*, a love story about a woman with cerebral palsy, became the first to gain serious international recognition, winning the Director's Award at the Venice Film Festival. Its director, Lee Chang-dong, had switched to cinema from theater, one of the arts with very little tradition in Korea because prior to democracy authorities viewed it as more difficult to control. In 2003 Lee was appointed Minister of Culture and Tourism. In 2004 Park Chan-wook's *Oldboy* won the Grand Prix at Cannes. In this story, a man is released from fifteen years of unexplained confinement and given five days to discover why. In the same year Kim Ki-duk won both best director at the Berlin Film Festival for his story *Samaritan Girl* and the Silver Lion award at Venice for *3-Iron*. In 2012, Kim won the Golden Lion award for his *Pietà*, the first such top prize awarded to a Korean film.

The movie industry is now well established, with great diversity in the types of films produced and certain standout features from a technical and content point of view: "There is a glossy sheen to Korean films (even low-budget independent films) that gives them a distinctive look," said Darcy Paquet, the founder of Koreanfilm.org. "New technology and developments in computer-generated imagery have greatly expanded the range of tools available to today's directors. Of course, this is true of directors from all countries, but when you compare Korean films to those from other parts of Asia there is an unmistakable emphasis on the visuals."[267]

Directors in Korea wield more power than their Hollywood counterparts, and are expected to write their own scripts. Paquet notes that in their treatment, emotional directness prevails over irony and any effort to look cool:

> When I first began to watch Korean movies and TV dramas, I could feel that there was something different about them. But it took years before I figured out that the real difference was

not in the storytelling, or in the directing, but in the way that the characters express their emotions. Of course, sometimes characters hide their feelings, or find themselves in situations where they can't freely express themselves. But when they do express their emotions, it is with a directness that, from an American perspective, can sometimes feel shocking. When they feel sad, they cry openly. When they feel angry or betrayed, they shout and throw things. When they fall in love, it is written all over their faces.

Producer Kyu Lee told me he moved from the U.S. to Korea to be a part of the art scene after having watched Korean films in the United States:

With movies in the States, the actual stories are very weak and conventional. But they get away with it. . . . Korean directors on the other hand write their own stories and are very creative. They are really good at these tear-jerkers. Their films make you want to call your mom and dad. You leave the theater wanting to be a better person. The first movie I saw was *Taegukgi*. It stunned me. It's a war epic but the core story is about two brothers. It was very emotional and heartwarming. And it only cost fourteen million dollars to make. That blew me away.

Koreans have been very successful also with exports of their TV miniseries. In fact, the popularity of these dramas in Asia created the first wave of Korean culture around the region. The dramas tend to run either daily or at least twice a week, last for only one season, and are filmed just prior to screening. This allows screenwriters to be responsive to viewers' online comments and preferences. Storylines, in contrast to so many American TV series, tend to be about relationships rather than about crime and questions of right and wrong.

The 2003 dramas *Dae Jang Geum* (*Jewel in the Palace*), for example, was sold to about ninety countries and was an especially huge hit in China; the male star of *Gyeoul Yeonga* (*Winter Sonata*), Bae Yong-joon, performed mysterious magic with Japanese housewives and is single-handedly credited with attracting millions of inbound tourists from Japan who visit locations used for TV dramas and movies.

Some take the view that *hallyu* (literally, "Korean tide"), as the spread of Korean culture is called, resulted from a deliberate government focus after the 1997 Asian financial crisis. Actually, this is not true. The government did seek to encourage the development of content, which improved the flow of funding, but bureaucrats were slow to see what was happening.

In 2003, President Roh Moo-hyun and his aides were astonished at a Blue House luncheon with the visiting Vietnamese Prime Minister Phan Van Khai, when the Vietnamese delegation lined up for the signature of the actress Kim Hyun-joo, star of the television drama *Yuri Gudu* (*Glass Slippers*) which had been a sensation in Vietnam that year. It turned out that the Vietnamese had requested that she be invited to their lunch. The Korean protocol officials were not sure why, but obliged.

According to reports, the guests sat down only after the announcement reassuring them that the actress would sign all their menus.

25

FOR WIDER ACCEPTANCE

"Koreans are very quick to absorb trends from the West and mix them up in a way that seems to make them more appealing in Asia."

To their credit, instead of feeling upstaged by mere actresses and minstrels, Korean governments have been quick to recognize both the soft power and economic benefits of cultural exports.

At best, they have had the good sense to incentivize and then get out of the way; at worst, they have tried to co-opt stars to support government initiatives—like being "ambassadors" for this, that, and the other—at the risk of damaging the stars' integrity; at worse than worst, they have been unable to stop themselves from coming up with their own Korean-wave initiatives, which have all the style of your dad leaping up and doing his Mick Jagger moves at a teenager party.

One example of an initiative that keeps getting sent back to the drawing board is the promotion of Korean cuisine, precisely because it is in the hands of bureaucrats. The initial approach looked as if the heavy industry promotion team from the 1970s had been called back in. Accordingly, the first objective, set in 2008, was for Korean to be among the top five global cuisines by 2017.

First Lady Kim Yoon-ok rolled up her sleeves and got stuck into this project and a large budget was distributed to a few agencies, the bulk of it administered by the then ministry of food, agriculture, forestry, and fisheries. The logic here was that the promotion of Korean cuisine worldwide would serve to boost the export of Korean agricultural products. That was a strategic mistake because the types of products Korea specializes in, such as ginseng and *Hanwoo* beef, would not benefit. Ginseng is too associated with medicine, and *Hanwoo* can't even be exported because of foot-and-mouth disease. Other products like *kimchi* do not need Korea-originated ingredients.

The focus on exports led to a series of tactical mistakes, the most notable being a plan for the government to open its own restaurant in New York, which immediately pissed off the natural allies: i.e., the owners and chefs at the Korean restaurants already there. This plan was thankfully dropped. Two other flaws in the execution are typical of many projects in the hands of bureaucrats. One was a target of forty thousand Korean restaurants around the world in five years. This build-it-and-they-will-come approach has worked with apartments and (some) stadiums in rapidly developed Korea, but isn't always the best solution when based on zero market research.

The other problematic area has been marketing, which in some cases has been downright zany.[268] Five million dollars was used to create an institute dedicated to the soft chewy *ddeokbokki* rice cake. There have been campaigns promoting Korean milk and strawberries to Westerners featuring highly paid Korean celebrities in markets that hardly recognize them. A promotional music video was created with some odd adjectives joined to each product being promoted: Romantic Mushroom, Fit Milk, Pleasant Paprika, Fun Makgeolli. Not only did it sound awkward and Konglishy, some of the products weren't really what consumers associated with Korea. In 2014 the Texas Rangers outfielder Choo Shin-soo was featured in *The New York Times* (not the *Houston Chronicle* because no one at HQ in Seoul would have heard of it) in a much-criticized ad: "Hi, I'm Choo Shin-soo. I'm an outfielder for the Texas Rangers. Spring's here and I'm ready to play! And do you know what got me through training? Bulgogi. Try some at your favorite Korean restaurant. It's delicious!"[269]

Joe McPherson, founder of the Korean food blog ZenKimchi.com, said:

> Despite my wish that Korean cuisine would actually become a top-five world cuisine, I think it more adequately fills a niche . . . I think should be associated with a feeling, a lifestyle. Apple, Starbucks, and McDonald's don't lead with specific products. They become successful by promoting lifestyles and positive feelings associated with their brands. I think Korean food is well positioned for that. Its fun, exciting, and rustic character hits a chord with people. Its strength is its use of fermented ingredients and its rustic nature. It's also easy to cook, making it easier to adopt in global homes than other recently trendy cuisines. I think it will become more common and everyday. The exotic factor will fade, and it will be as normal as burgers and sushi.

Indeed, the cuisine is becoming more noted internationally. About time, if you ask me, although I still think that British cuisine is the best in the world, especially the type you get in Indian, Thai, and Italian restaurants and from Chinese takeaways.

The first thing visitors take to in Korean restaurants is the unusual ritual. In many places, "service" involves delivering uncooked meat and veggies to customers, who cook it themselves either in a pot of boiling stock or on a grill inserted into specially built tables. When it's done, chopsticks and, sometimes your fingers, take lettuce, sesame and other leaves from a common pile to be wrapped, fajita-style, around bits of meat and whatever else can fit in one mouthful. The feast is perked up with a section of side dishes, cloves of garlic, raw or grilled, bean paste and various types of bean, leaf, and twig. The king of side dishes is *kimchi*, or fermented vegetables. The ancient version is usually radish or cucumber preserved in salted water; the newer and more famous type ("new" meaning since the eighteenth century) is cabbage soaked in a mix of red chili pepper and other seasonings. Then there's the rice, white and sticky. In contrast to Japan and China, it is acceptable to eat it with a spoon instead of chopsticks. Many dishes, including soups, are communal. The combination of salt, spice, and sour—not much sweet, unless one of the side dishes is ginseng and honey—overwhelms any original taste. For a visitor accustomed to meat and two veggies, some items can be a little too unusual at first. Some side dishes are so spicy they can blow your face off; mysterious ingredients float in the soups; and a serving of kimchi can, on first encounter, look remarkably like a saucer of bandages, post-use. But such discomfort wears off by the second meal and the visitor soon develops an approach to eating that is hard to let go of, simply because it is so conducive to, and really made for, conviviality, conversation, and fun. Somewhat like a meal on tapas, but more filling. You're just so busy. This type of meal is accompanied by beer and soju, a local spirit made from white rice or barley. Courtesy forbids people from filling their own glass, and requires that they accept refills and swap glasses with people who want to toast them, polite customs that Westerners take to very quickly. They leave the table feeling wholesome, even if drunk, because they've been prompted by etiquette to pay attention to their dining partners.

It's this convivial ritual that I can see catching on overseas.

There are, however, a couple of downsides. One is that the eating and drinking from shared bowls and glasses is cited as a reason for the high incidence of hepatitis B. The second is the availability of dog meat, which I don't think will catch on overseas (nor is it popular in Korea—many people have never had it and don't want to, me included). Another is the flavor of the seafood. One reason I've never fully enjoyed a weekend by the seaside in Korea is because every single restaurant for miles around is seafood, and I'm not talking about fish and chips. It's more a mix of stuff that tastes like salted Wellington boots or is still squirming when it's delivered to your table. Once at a company outing, I brooded like a teenager as colleagues and children around me feasted on cephalopods and other beasts from the deep. I once tried sea cucumbers, which despite the harmless name are animals. Checking them out on Wikipedia, I see their long slimy body contains a "single, branched gonad." They actually look like octopus penis and taste like . . . salted Wellington boots. But the worst bit was the stuff that was delivered to the table alive.

The ten-year-old daughter of a colleague consigned an octopus into the boiling pot in front of us at our table and carried on a conversation, while, for the agonizing minute or two that it lasted, shoving the creature back into the cauldron each time a tentacle struggled outside to find a foothold. That's the bit of Korean dining I've never gotten used to. I am still amazed at the restaurants that display large photographs of cows, pigs, chickens, or whatever it is, outside to entice the customers in. I thought meat grew in supermarkets.

Another area where Koreans are likely to make an international impact—because they are doing so already—is in the broad field of design. This may seem counterintuitive in a country noted for the ugliness of its townscapes, the spoiling of nature with high-rise apartment complexes in the middle of nowhere, where you can get a café and a florist on either side of a tire repair shop, and with a disappointing tendency to plagiarize and imitate. But the explanation for the above is that the real decision-makers who have been determining what the country looks like have been bosses. It's routine in companies for creative folk to have to stand in front of their PowerPoints, tilted slightly forward, hands clutched deferentially in front of their groin, looking at the ground, and say: "Yeah" (Korean for yeah) as the gentleman paying for the service tells them how to improve their creation. But this is changing, helped by the government. Korea has many talented fashion, interior, and graphic designers, architects, and beauty businesses the world is going to start hearing from. The catalyst for much of this, particularly in fashion and beauty, is China.

"There is an enormous appetite right now in Asia for Korean style," said Park Jung-ah, the director of the Miss World and Mr. World franchises in Korea. "Koreans are very quick to absorb trends from the West and mix them up in a way that seems to make them more appealing in Asia."

If you look at K-pop and the TV shows, the styles all cry out: "Look at me!" There is no reservation. When they have plastic surgery, they let you know about it, unashamedly. This confidence and outgoingness appeals to the Chinese, who, Park said, "Want to know how Koreans do makeup, how they do their hair, how they manage to look so good. This is becoming a huge cultural influence as well as a huge business. People are thinking, we know now what we have to do to live to be a hundred, but when we are a hundred we want to look as if we're fifty."[270]

If I were to come up with a slogan for Seoul right now to capture its future aspirations, I would probably go for Seoul: City of Style. (Not as hip as the new one they came up with in late 2015—I. SEOUL. U.—in which the city becomes a verb. And not to mention my all-time favorite from the 1990s: My Seoul, Our Seoul.)

As mentioned, one of the challenges for the business of Korean culture is for industry and government officials to take a back seat to the artists. It is astonishing how hard this seems to be. Back in 1982, I went to a performance of the Little Angels Children's Folk Ballet, a troupe of schoolgirls that had already been acting as frontline ambassadors for Korean culture for twenty years, the kind of act the haircutting fashion police approved of. Based in Seoul at the Sun Hwa Arts School, owned by the Unification Church of Moon Sun-myung, the Angels had performed for Queen Elizabeth, President Richard Nixon, at the United Nations, Carnegie Hall, and the Kennedy Center. They are a favorite with war veterans.[271] They even performed in Pyongyang. The repertoire back in 1982 included Korean classics and some American favorites: "God Bless America" and "When the Saints Go Marching In." The cuteness and professionalism was a winning combination with foreign audiences, for these girls represented the innocence of a nation reborn. I saw retired U.S. generals choke up at the performances. Twenty years later I saw the Angels again. Amazingly, the repertoire had hardly changed. That's the problem when nonartists are in charge and even worse when they hit on a winning formula.

One area where the government has been encouraging and supportive, but where big business is absent, is literature. With Han Kang winning the 2016 Man Booker International prize for her novel *The Vegetarian*, there is expectation that Korean writers are poised to make a deep impression internationally. Charles Montgomery, a Seoul-based academic who edits a Web site called Korean Literature in Translation, said they will need to soon if it's going to happen: "Korea has the products, the films, and the food that the world is finding it likes, and the government is pushing literature," he said. "It was at this stage in the seventies that Japanese literature began to make an impact. Now Japanese literature per se is not good or bad. It simply is. I expect we will see a similar moment for Korean literature." What's not clear is which authors will become the most popular abroad. It may not be those who are most loved at home.[272]

As with movies, the modern Korean novel dates back to the early part of the Japanese occupation. When Yi Kwang-su's *Mujong* (*The Heartless*) was serialized in the *Maeil Sinbo* newspaper in 1917, people walked for miles to make sure they got their daily copy. The story itself is about a love triangle between a schoolteacher and two women, one the daughter of a Protestant minister and another, a *gisaeng*. The force of the novel comes from the first-person account of how the second woman became a *gisaeng*. Notably, the central character says that everyone must strive to make a better country. This established a path for writers to ensure their art serve the nation, and as they were forbidden from being negative about Japan, they mostly took on themes of social change resulting from modernization, and especially the changing roles of women. (The poetry from the same period was less inhibited and often dark and mournful, echoing the helpless despair of a loss of national identity.)

Most talented intellectuals of the later 1930s and 1940s were idealists convinced that the future lay with socialism. With the end of Japanese rule and the start of the struggle for control of the Korean Peninsula, they almost all assumed they should support and identify with North Korea. Many either headed north or stayed in the South to actively oppose Syngman Rhee. By the time they learned that Kim Il-sung's regime in Pyongyang was even less open to them and their idealism, it was too late.

Therefore, after the Korean War, writers who remained in the South knew they had to be positive about their government, or at least ask no questions about politics, and be morally edifying. The best they could do was depict lives and deaths marked by simple human dignity. They came to see the prewar and premodern periods as idyllic times of innocence. During the dictatorship of the 1960s and 1970s, writers took on themes of alienation from mass migration to the cities, although they were careful to avoid approaches that could be interpreted as socialist. This continued into the 1990s, when many younger women wrote about life in apartment blocks, cut off from meaningful social relationships and neglected by hardworking, unloving husbands. More recently, with the increase in wealth and the concern for well-being and quality of life, younger writers have begun producing more entertaining, humorous, magical fantasies.

Poetry, meanwhile, has mostly been seen as a search for deeper meanings and inner life, whether by focusing on the beauty of language and feeling, or by a satirical evocation of what it means to be human in a world today that often seems inhuman.

For a long time after the Japanese occupation, writers were unable to gain access to quality translations of contemporary Western fiction, and could not read the originals; their readers in Korea, too, had not learned to appreciate fiction that did not tell familiar stories in familiar ways. It is only very recently that this has begun to change. For Korean writers the role of the imagination was sublimated, with many novels sounding like autobiography, which they often are. And given the foreignness of Korea, and its complex sociopolitical history, it is difficult for translators to convey hidden meanings, and the rich contextualization of what remains unsaid.

Unaware of these shortcomings, Korean writers and their supporters are frustrated by the lack of global interest, and tend to assume their fiction fails to achieve acclaim due to poor translation (despite government support). For example, the bestselling multivolume novel, *Toji* (*The Land*) by Park Kyung-ni, is a family saga of the kind that is also very popular in India and other Asian countries where, like Korea, fantasy and suspense are less popular than the slightly melodramatic stories often used as the basis or inspiration for television soap operas. *Toji*, which took twenty-five years to complete, is regarded in Korea as a Tolstoy-like masterpiece that deserves the world's recognition as it slowly grinds its way through various individuals' experience in the course of the various stages of recent Korean history since the late nineteenth century. When the first extract came out in translation, the British novelist Margaret Drabble described it as a "major addition to world literature." This may be so. But it is apparently—I am advised of this—so full of obscure references to premodern lifestyle and events and, at six million words, so long I wonder how many people will manage to get through it if and when it is all translated.

Park, who did not plan out her work, wrote at great speed. Ko Un seems to have a similar approach, according to Brother Anthony, his translator:

> Since 1990 his main identity has been as a writer, he has poured out over 150 books of many different kinds, novels, essays, translations from Chinese, as well as every kind of poetry— lyrical, narrative, brief, long, serious, funny. . . . He is quite simply a phenomenon. His poems are not refined, polished, revised, perfect laborings. Rather they are scribbled down in rapid succession because he is so eager to move on to the next poem, to something different, something new. Even at eighty.

Brother Anthony believes that it may be some time yet before Korean writers find their place in world literature. "Korean fiction is too new, too uninformed by what [other] writers across the globe are writing, to have great international appeal," he said. Some novels do get broad attention, like Shin Kyung-suk's highly popular, million-copy seller, *Please Look After Mom*, published in Korean in 2009 and an American bestseller when it came out in English in 2014. "But a novel published by Knopf has to be seen as a commodity rather than as a work of literature," Brother Anthony said. "It was not chosen by them because it was Korean or because it was great writing but because they had had a certain commercial success with a sentimental Chinese novel about a mother, and they were looking for something similar to continue that vein of sales, centered in the American book club sales."

The great difficulty with Korean fiction is that it is, for want of a better description, too Korean. (Indeed, the English translation of *Please Look After Mom*, for example, is very different from its Korean original, with some structural change and expansions and explanations otherwise not required in the Korean. The English version of *The Vegetarian* is also different from the Korean version.) Fiction is, at the moment, going through a phase where it has become highly experimental; perhaps this is promising, and bodes well for the future of Korean literature as these writers throw off the prescriptive yoke of the past—and their responsibilities to the nation—and their creativity, at last, is allowed the freedom and confidence it deserves.

Koreans now have tremendous opportunities to promote their culture and they don't have to go overseas to do it because so many foreigners are visiting. After hosting the Olympic Games and the World Cup, the country developed an appetite to host other world-class events. Indeed, Seoul now says it wants to become one of the top three MICE (meetings, incentives, conventions, exhibitions) cities in the world. Whether it's the Asia-Oceania Congress of Obstetrics and Gynecology (in 2005), the World Conference on Lung Cancer (2007), the 10th Biennial Conference of the International Association of Women Judges (2010), or the 20th Meeting of the International Association of Forensic Sciences (2014), such events offer opportunities at home to tell Korea's stories.

Lee Charm, the former head of the governmental Korea tourism organization, said the difficulty is that the Koreans don't do this well.

Cultural communication is very weak. We Koreans are not so aware of the value of our own culture. For example, the guy giving the speech about Korean culture will say something like, "Our ancestors used metal chopsticks. This means Koreans have great dexterity. Which is why we are so good at medical research." The effect is to diminish Korean culture. The truth is that in old Korea there was a long-standing drive to understand the world. Confucian scholars observed nature in a very scientific way and set things down and tried to find principles for life. Hundreds of these scholars, called *seonbi*, wrote hundreds of books. The zeal for understanding remains part of the culture. That's one reason Koreans have risen to high levels in research. It's nothing to do with chopsticks.

Lee once visited Istanbul with a large delegation of Korean bureaucrats and elected officials. After seeing the Blue Mosque and other sites, the Koreans were astonished and deflated at the same time.

They said, 'Wow, this is real tourism. We have nothing compared to this.' But in the year 800 Gyeongju was one of the four biggest cities in the world. It was a center of Buddhism and traded with the world. There was tremendous sophistication in the art. It is quite fascinating. But they don't think highly of it.

This lack of confidence means those in the culture business focus on things such as kimchi making or having your photo taken wearing traditional *hanbok* garb. Interesting, perhaps, but not inspiring.

There has long been in the Koreans an ambition to inspire the world. It may come in some way from the idealism of the neo-Confucian period that failed to produce what it promised. But the desire was there throughout the twentieth century even when the country was among the poorest.

It is this undiscovered potential to inspire that hints at the ways Koreans may, in years to come, proudly share their distinctive cultural value with the rest of the world. Koreans will brag about their record-breaking working hours and their gold medals in welding. But such achievements ring hollow at home. It's as if they know there is something about themselves they want to really shout about, but don't know what it is, let alone how to do so. This elusive quality manifested in the way foreign religions were integrated without replacing the old; it's in their philosophical instincts for fusion, their way of mixing things up and coming out with something new; it's in their fractiousness that comes from an ease with powerful expression and intimacy, wherein also lie their instincts for harmony allowing them to put aside those parts of others that would be deal breakers in other places—the religion, the beliefs, the bad behavior—in the pursuit of the joy of the embrace. Whatever it is, it is for the artists to consider.

26

A WEALTHIER FUTURE

"A rule of the road: don't get hung up on the rules."

One or two hundred years from now, much about Korea will of course have changed, probably even its name, but some things will be, for the time traveler, unexpectedly familiar. Like kimchi.

It is possible by then that economies will no longer require the labor of citizens, tax will be something for the history books, an evil of the past like compulsory military service, and adults will occupy themselves and find meaning and prestige in ways unconnected to what we know as work. They may even have remembrance ceremonies to thank us for getting them there.

But between now and then are the small steps that we should be able to guess at. What will Korea look like in the more immediate future? The safe limit for the forecaster is ten years out, for this portrait is made with the relatively bright colors of technology already around or being developed, and also well framed by present trends.

From that starting point, we may say that the Korean economy will continue to compete and cooperate, to mutual benefit, with China, while a declining population, the rise in one- and two-person households, and the need to care for more older citizens will drive changing labor practices, government spending and consumption patterns.

Here are some of the likely new features and drivers of the Korean economy from a 2014 study:[273]

In agriculture: the development of high-rise factory farms close to urban centers and with a focus on specialized products.

In technology: 3D printing equipment, materials and software; sensors for devices to be incorporated into the Internet of Things; carbon fiber; "smart clothes" that warm and cool the wearer on request; customized 3D-printed fashion; incorporation of smartphone-type apps into spectacles, vehicles, furniture etc; electric vehicles, driverless vehicles, driverless electric vehicles, electric vehicle batteries; automobile functions; next generation new and renewable energy sources such as fuel cells, photovoltaic, and biomass; LED and OLED lighting; smart homes; nuclear power plants; medical equipment.

In services: tourism for the rapidly growing Chinese middle class is expected to keep booming. At present, the Korean offering is somewhat formulaic and the options and service rather limited. But there is enormous scope for development. The medical sector also offers huge promise for both Koreans and visiting "medical tourists" with progress in tele-medicine, long-distance care, wearable devices, biotech, molecular diagnostics, gene therapy, cell therapy products and even 3D modeling of bones, for example.

In education: while the Korean system itself is insufficient for the country's own needs, it can teach the world a thing or two about getting kids to study hard. It is possible the Korean-owned *hagwon* (study institute) could become as common overseas as the *taekwondo* school.

Current industries will not fade, in the way that, say, coal mining and textiles have. Instead, the above new industries will be an addition to, and an enhancement of automobiles, shipbuilding, electronics, and other industries currently driving the economy.

This picture of Korea's economy faces a range of challenges, any one of which could mess up the future.

The first is the workforce. Numbers are now peaking. Assuming no change, for the sake of highlighting the issue because of course something will change—i.e., assuming no increase in the birthrate, no merger with North Korea, and no significant immigration—the number of people between fifteen and sixty-four who can work is likely to drop from 35 million at this writing to 29 million by 2040 and to 22 million by 2060. That would mean fewer things being made and fewer services delivered, which means less income.[274]

The next matter is the economic structure. The Koreans were farmers who went into factories and now, the experts say, must become investment bankers. Kind of. Just as they stopped growing stuff and started making stuff to get richer, so other countries now are making the same stuff for less, which means the Koreans need to become more sophisticated—easier said than done. It is hard to get the formula right for successful development, and even harder to change it.

Here are the statistics: In 1963, 63 percent of working Koreans farmed or fished for a living.[275] The fruits of their labor that year represented 43.4 percent of the overall economy. Forty years later, this sector was down to 8.8 percent of the workforce and accounted for just 3.7 percent of the economy. The services and industry sectors did exist in the 1960s, but did not drive the economy.[276] By 2003, however, 63.9 percent of the workforce was in services (59.6 percent in terms of value) and 27.6 percent in industry (26 percent in value). As a share of the economy, industry peaked in the late 1980s and started to slip, while services continued its steady rise. This was what should happen as an economy becomes more sophisticated.

But after 2003, something unusual occurred. The manufacturing sector started expanding again, to a point where it reached 33 percent of the economy in 2010, and remained there since. Indeed, Koreans have become even better at making things.

Three features of this surge stand out: the first is that some of the larger *chaebol* made the shift from being purveyors of cheap, second-rate products to respected global brands. Names like Hyundai, LG, POSCO, and Samsung are now internationally associated with innovation and quality. Second, there has been a rapid expansion from the trusted North American, Japanese, and European buyers to China and other new markets. The third is that while they have become even more competitive in traditional areas like automobiles and ships, the Koreans are steaming ahead into new and often innovative industrial sectors like those mentioned above.

Once upon a time, the experts would have wagged their fingers. But such is the respect for Korea these days that some recognize the country to be forging a new model. "A rule of the road: don't get hung up on the rules," says Ruchir Sharma.[277]

But perhaps the real rule is not that the country should not improve its manufacturing (or agriculture for that matter) but that it should avoid depending on sectors easily duplicated by the competition. But Korea depends on manufacturing more than any other developed country.

This is problematic for a couple of reasons.

One is trade balance. "In 2013, we had a trade surplus of seventy billion dollars. In 2014, it was ninety billion," said economist Kim Joo-hyung. "If this continues, we may face problems. Trade partners may accuse us of taking their jobs and retaliate. We may also encounter huge appreciation of our currency, like Japan did in the 1980s. Ours is a small, open economy. We must live peacefully with other countries. We cannot sacrifice them for ourselves. For this reason, we need to develop new demand and raise the level of our own consumption. This will encourage imports, which in turn will create the room for exports to grow."

The other issue is jobs. Such is the impact of improved technology that the number of jobs in manufacturing is dropping.[278] With around 70 percent of the workforce in services in 2015, the government cannot keep focusing on manufacturing exports if it wants to keep people in work and earning decent salaries.

The service sector covers everything that doesn't involve working the land, digging out resources, or making things. In Korea, that means the butcher, the baker, the broker, the waiter, banker, spanker, and chef; the shopkeeper, tour guide, adman, milkman, the beautician, builder, and ref; it's the consultants of all stripes, guitarists, hairdressers, the pole-dancers, the barristers, and Internet-based every kind of thing; the dicks, the hacks, the flacks, the baristas, snappers, cobblers, plumbers, and actors; and most of their friends. Consider me one of them. While there are exports in this sector, services for the most part serve the domestic market in a country—and here's the heart of the matter—that had for decades been geared toward export manufacturing by big conglomerates, both in practical policy terms, with access to financing, incentives, and government support, and in attitude. Government officials and media have managed, thanks to the 1997 crisis, to outgrow the idea that any foreign company profiting in Korea is "stealing national wealth;" beyond that a lot of shabby thinking still hampers the industry. The idea lingers, for example, that exports=earning dollars and is therefore good, and that imports=spending dollars and only okay if it helps more exports. It is still hard for small companies to obtain loans. Every government for decades has trumpeted policies to support SMEs, but these policies largely involved tax breaks and subsidies aimed at mollifying them, because their employees account for 87 percent of the workforce. That's where the votes come from. If there is an interest in making them competitive, it's to turn them into exporters.[279]

The services sector in Korea is nowhere near as impressive as it should be, with productivity at just 56 percent that of manufacturing, whereas for most other developed countries it's roughly the same.[280]

Take, for example, the business of distributing pharmaceuticals, a market valued at twelve billion dollars, with two thousand companies supplying 31,334 clinics and hospitals and 20,890 pharmacies.[281] On the math alone, this seems okay—average revenues of 6 million dollars per company seems fine for a small business. But this is a sector that needs warehouses, systems, trucks, and a workforce. Many of the distributors supply just one local hospital, usually because it was founded by a relative. And when uncle's hospital is supplied by the nephew who gets the product from a bigger wholesaler, you find costs higher, loyalty overriding inefficiencies, and quality hard to control. Japan, by comparison, presents a more workable model—with a pharmaceutical distribution sector five times larger than Korea's but managed by around thirty companies, four of which account for 75 percent of it. What Korea's pharma-distribution system needs—actually let me interrupt myself here because the framing of the question in that way is how the mistakes start in Korea: "What we players in the sector need is a, b, and c." In the service sector, it should be about the needs of the clients (manufacturers), the client's customers (hospitals, clinics, pharmacies), their customers (doctors and patients), and the government (taxman). What they all need—which is different from what the players need—is a safe, trustworthy, and efficient system that is worth the cost. And for that, there's nothing better than competition with foreign companies who do it well, or better. A few years ago, that happened. But when foreign pharmaceutical labs asked Zuellig Pharma, an Asia-based firm they used in other markets, to handle their distribution in Korea, the local association of distributors fought a rearguard action that lasted for a decade, trying to get the government to shut down the foreign company before finally running out of arguments to do so.

Sometimes, within an industry, the government stands back as the big players bully their suppliers and abuse smaller competitors. This is the *gap-eul* (senior-junior) mentality as it plays out between companies. For example, there are around four thousand companies manufacturing and selling cosmetics. When one of them comes up with a product that consumers like, the handful of large players who dominate the sector shamelessly copy it.

A related characteristic of the Korean service sector is the extent of government interference. The financial regulator is especially guilty of this. The Korea country manager of one large investment fund expressed his frustration thus: "Such is the capriciousness of the regulator that business plans are only good for two years in Korea." You just never know what they might prevent you from doing, or pressure you to do next.

In Park Chung-hee's day, "administrative guidance"—code for a government behest for businesses to "voluntarily" comply with—was strong. Businesses were incentivized to follow. For example, the government would informally ask companies to keep the price of gas down in order to keep the consumer happy. Then when the price of imported gas dropped, the government would keep the consumer price as it was so the firms could profit. This type of informal interference is much weaker now, particularly after the Fair Trade Commission fined some companies for unfair pricing, rejecting their claim to have been following "administrative guidance" through lack of evidence. Since then, businesses have insisted that the "guidance" be on the record, which has made government officials more cautious about interfering.

Because government has for so long acted not as representative of the consumer, but as referee between producers, it has a tendency to create compromises, rather than apply principles, with the result that once a conflict has passed the restrictions put in place look strangely petty. For example, in exchange for agreeing to keep its fares low, the government makes sure the powerful taxi lobby is not threatened by competition. So when car rental companies started providing chauffeurs to customers, taxi drivers complained and the authorities stepped in. The resulting compromise was that only foreigners, government officials, the handicapped, and elderly are allowed to rent a car and a driver to go with it. For everyone else, it's illegal.

The effort to clear such petty regulations that get in the way of service industries has been ongoing since 2004 but has been fairly ineffective, in part due to weak leadership in the face of the inevitable complaints.

But the most important reason for the weakness of services and the inability to raise private domestic demand is political. It lies in the inability of leadership to fully address the main legacy of the export focus: that Korea is a country of producers. Consumers did matter to exporters, of course, but they were foreigners, Mr. and Mrs. Smith in Pittsburgh, buying their LG fridge, Hyundai automobile, and Samsung TV. They mattered, but it was not the Korean government's job to care about them. It cared about the Korean entity selling to them.

As for Mr. and Mrs. Kim in Korea, they were important to politicians as consumers not because they might want and need better quality food and furniture and the rest, but because they didn't want to pay too much for things like gas and electricity. Hence the administrative guidance requests to gas companies. That also explains why KEPCO, the country's power utility, has a 105.1 billion dollar debt.[282] One KEPCO CEO got fired for arguing for raising utility prices.

Similarly, doctors want to raise their fees, which would allow them to buy more advanced equipment and hire more practitioners. But the government, as union leader for the "consumer," says no. We could say Mr. and Mrs. Kim are in part to blame because the producer fixation was one they endorsed as being better for the national economic interest, and what they care about most is getting stuff cheap. But it is really a failure of political leadership, and such failures in Korea all stem from the inability of politicians and bureaucrats to mediate, mitigate problems, and lead.

I could go on: There's the question of how, in improving services and the lot of small and medium companies, to avoid misbehavior—bribing of officials, copying of competitor products, and the like—by the *chaebol*, which have until now been attracting the best people, the favorable policies, the incentives, and financing. Another obstacle to improvements in SMEs is the harsh bankruptcy laws, which carry criminal penalties. Bankrupt businessmen often end up in jail until they resolve things with their creditors or until creditors can be persuaded to support their release. They carry a criminal record that ensures they won't get funding for future projects.

Despite all these issues, there is solid ground for optimism. But it lies in that territory beyond economics and policy making.

Despite the tremendous changes in their lifestyle, and despite their arrival at a place where quality of life is more a focus for many than the acquisition of material things, the Koreans remain linked in one important way to their predevelopment Confucian past. The prevailing view of reality derives from relationships with other people and not so much, despite popular Christianity, from a relationship with an invisible deity. Thus, the striving to achieve a place in society and gain affirmation from others, to be seen as successful, is stronger than the other impulses that arise from within; in other words, people find greater meaning in work than in leisure. What they do is who they are. That's why, just as the English seemed to Napoleon to be a nation of shopkeepers, the Koreans are a nation of presidents. Take ten shopkeepers and the five men among them will form five associations so that each can be the president of something and be addressed as "association head" by everyone else. If there's no association, each shopkeeper still gets to be called "CEO" even if the only employee is his wife. (This may be one of the explanations behind the statistic that 30 percent of those in the services sector are self-employed, the highest proportion among OECD member nations.)

This striving of individuals with their eyes on the group makes for collective strength. The Koreans will not go down. They have climbed the ladders of poverty and backwardness recently enough and if an unlucky throw of the dice lands them on a snake and they slither down, they will immediately make their way back up.

That said, could this quality of resilience change? I've long wondered whether young Koreans might not tire of conformity and have a Woodstock moment. There is in fact a contemporary form of dropping out, of young men in particular. They are referred to as the *sampo* (three give-ups) generation. They give up on love, marriage, and children. Actually, there have always been dropouts, such as the eldest sons in large families who couldn't handle their responsibility, yet who lived at home and puttered around in the village. Every extended family seems to have its drunk. The contemporary *sampos* pull the rip cord in a school system that drives all to compete. They sponge off their parents and exist in the virtual world of computer games. To make their lifestyle fashionable, they would need to connect with one another and make an appeal to values, like the hippies who turned their back on materialism and promoted peace and love. Yet it's hard to imagine them being bothered to do this.

Still, if the *sampo* do mutate and form communities, developed Korea could handle it. Not everyone need strive for a country to thrive. That could be their motto. There is room for different levels of energy and ambition. A developed economy doesn't need every citizen to scramble upward. It just needs its fair share of finders, minders, and grinders to respectively develop, take care of, and roll up their sleeves in businesses.[283]

On a micro level, I am sure stupid policy decisions will be made, especially given the current sense that public service requires the bureaucrat and lawmaker to obey he who shouts loudest. But in a macro sense I have faith in government because—given the cultural imperative to strive for the good job and given that opportunity is open to all—the Koreans will continue to demand that their government manage the environment fostering success. They want economics first, and all the rest second.

You can see this expectation at play in the way Korean governments have responded to recent economic crises. It is worth looking at the big ones, the 1997 Asian financial crisis and the 2008 global financial crisis in some detail to make our case for optimism. We will digress a little with the first case to see how the country got itself into such a vulnerable position.[284]

Here's how the Korea Inc. operating system 1.0 was explained to me by the vice president of an affiliate in one of the top thirty *chaebol* on the eve of the 1997 crisis:

> In Korea, we have this focus on volume. This is typical of our character. We like to show off. The contents inside don't matter. . . . When you want to borrow money, you have to present financial statements to the bank. But the first number they look at is sales volume, not profit. So as a company, we never permit our sales volume to go down. If sales do not increase, you cannot borrow money, and you have to give up. If you've actually made less in sales one year, you have to lie or find some way to manipulate the numbers. Almost every company will record sales growth of ten to twenty percent a year. Ninety-nine percent of Korean companies are growing by sales volume. This means there must be something wrong. The problem here is the way the banks evaluate us. Why do they do it like this? I don't know to be honest. In the seventies it was necessary to reward the growth in quantity. But once you reach a certain volume, you have to shift from quantity to quality. But we have never made the transition. . . . Everyone knew the problem but bankers are very weak. They can't say no. If I am a government official and you are my friend in business and I ask a banker to take care of you, he will lend you money unconditionally. In return, you support me, the government official, financially. The politicians have said we must change this system, but they themselves are dependent on it. They are not going to shoot a bullet which will bounce back and kill them.

His company had outstanding loans with interest ranging from 0 to 45 percent. Sometimes to make interest payments or pay wages on time, cash was borrowed for twenty-four hours.

He wasn't alone. The average debt-equity ratio for those top thirty conglomerates was over 500 percent, way more than double the OECD average for manufacturing firms.

At this time, government deregulation to qualify Korea for entry into the OECD in 1996 had encouraged businesses to take out short-term foreign currency loans to finance their long-term investments. The finance ministry liberalized short-term over long-term borrowing to prevent losing control of financing decision-making to the banks and the *chaebol*. The result was that by 1996, 61 percent of external debt was due in a matter of months. New rules also allowed for more banks to jump in. From 1994–6, the number of short-term lending banks shoveling debt into *chaebol* furnaces grew from six to thirty.

The international financial community saw a disaster in the making.[285] Finance ministry officials were more worried about panic and kept assuring investors and journalists that the fundamentals remained sound: Growth was still impressive, the ratio of foreign debt to GDP was lower than in other developing countries, and the IMF in mid-1997 still said Korea was unlikely to be damaged by the currency crisis roaring through Southeast Asia.

Those two conflicting perspectives underscore the two explanations for what then happened: One is that the banks and *chaebol* could no longer keep pedaling and fell off their bikes; the other is that foreign investor panic fed on itself and caused a massive withdrawal from Korea that put the country in crisis. The truth is a combination of the two.

The chain of events went like this: In 1996, a strong dollar and weak yen put pressure on Korean exporters, many of whom were unable to repay loans to local banks. Japanese banks were unable to roll over loans. In the new year the steel giant Hanbo collapsed with almost 6 billion dollars in debts after the government rejected a bailout. There followed a record number of bankruptcies of small companies and some notable collapses of other large businesses such as Sammi and Jinro. In the summer, Kia Motors got into trouble but by this time a presidential election loomed, and the politicians pressured the bureaucracy to make an exception. This mixed message further alarmed foreign investors. Meanwhile, the Southeast Asia currency crisis was spreading, and foreign banks were unable to roll over loans to Korean short-term lending banks, into which the central bank started depositing foreign currency, foolishly trying to hide the problem. Once word of this got out, international investors started withdrawing their money, making the exchange rate go haywire. Further panic ensued. Rather than let the foreign exchange market fluctuate, the central bank tried to prop up the *won* by selling dollars in its reserves—this at the prompting of the finance ministry. It depleted its reserves by 30 percent (10 billion dollars), and saw the *won* halve in value in a matter of weeks. In November, one month before the election, the government put an emergency financial reform package to the National Assembly but the politicians refused to act on it. This shoved Korea over the cliff. Foreign investors immediately accelerated their currency withdrawals, forcing Korea to turn to the International Monetary Fund. Even then, it took intervention by the U.S. government to encourage international banks to roll over short-term debts and the willingness of the president-elect, Kim Dae-jung, to change his tune and accept the IMF bailout to avert sovereign default.

The IMF stepped in with a 58 billion dollar loan, its largest-ever bailout of a country. The money came with conditions.

By the end of the year, banks had stopped loaning money, even to healthy companies. In December alone, 1,226 small and medium companies went bankrupt, unable to afford the 13 to 18 percent monthly interest rates being offered by loan sharks, who had mushroomed in Seoul behind doors with signs on them like "Mountaineering Association." The figures for January 1998 represented the biggest monthly drop ever recorded (compared with the previous January): industrial production down 10.3 percent, total manufacturing shipments down 7.2 percent, domestic manufacturing shipments down 20.6 percent, consumer durable goods shipments down 23.2 percent, consumer nondurable goods shipments down 17 percent, machinery imports down 47.3 percent; capacity utilization fell to 68.3 percent, the lowest level ever recorded.[286]

The grief behind these figures ripped people's lives apart, particularly as there was no unemployment benefit or other welfare.[287] An increasing number of men left home in the morning as usual in their suits, but went off not to their offices but to the mountains, where they kept hiking gear in lockers, concealing the fact, sometimes even from their families, that they were out of work. You could also see these men in cinemas, coffee shops, and saunas. Others started driving taxis.

As they entered what they referred to as the "IMF era," Koreans went through the gamut of emotions: at first a kind of denial, and wounded pride that the country had needed to ask for foreign help. There were angry accusations that it was the previous government's fault, and a proposal to hold hearings and identify which bureaucrats were to blame. No, it was the conglomerates' fault. No, it was a foreign plot.[288]

Then people rallied. Tens of thousands got caught up in a gold-selling fever launched by KBS TV and the Korea Housing and Commercial Bank to raise money to help repay the IMF loans. They queued to either donate or sell their gold after experts had announced there was an estimated twenty billion dollars' worth kept in Korean homes. This is the most enduring memory from that period, evidence for cynics of how pliable and easily mobilized the Koreans are—did you know, they said, that those housewives drove the international price of gold down to its lowest in eighteen years?—to which, I would say, who cares about the price of gold, what have others done when their own countries have teetered? Fight their own police? Smash shop windows? Perhaps from a practical point of view the gold campaign was kind of pathetic. But when couples line up to hand in their wedding rings and old ladies surrender items of tremendous personal significance, believing they are helping save their country, it's the gesture not the efficacy that illuminates the nation's deeper qualities, which in turn gives investors renewed confidence. These people had landed on a snake, and within weeks were back up on the ladder.

The Koreans are probably more fractious and critical of their leaders than any Europeans, with the possible exception of the Italians, but when the crisis came and they were all out of work, they knew to pull together, not to smash their infrastructure.

When and if they ever lose that tendency—only then can we question our optimism for their future.

The shock of near-collapse forced the government to create a new regulatory structure and to reform the banking and corporate sectors to prevent a recurrence.

This involved closing or restructuring bankrupt firms, introducing market discipline, and improving corporate governance. A decision in 1999 to allow the collapse of Daewoo, the fifth largest *chaebol*, drove home the message. The group believed it was too big to fail and the instinct when it did was to look for political reasons for the government's lack of intervention. The scale of its failure—at eighty billion dollars, then a world-record bankruptcy—was stark evidence that the old formula was not going to work anymore.

By 2002, Korea's government had injected 160.4 trillion *won* into the banks to clean up their balance sheets. By the summer of 2003, 787 financial institutions (37.5 percent of the total) had been shut down or merged. Only three short-term lenders remained. Government loosened many of its controls and strengthened others in a way that made banks more responsible and subject to market forces. At the same time, restrictions were lifted on foreign investment in the stock market, in nonlisted companies, and in property. At IMF insistence, laws were passed to permit companies to lay off workers for the purpose of downsizing, ending the job-for-life era.

Korea repaid its IMF loan by the summer of 2001, three years before it was due. The economy, meanwhile, which had shrunk 5.7 percent in 1998, bounced back to growth of 10.7 percent in 1999 and 8.8% in 2000, shedding its old skin and transforming itself on a path to advancement.

It was in much better shape when the next big external shock hit.

This financial crisis began in the United States and went global in September 2008 with the collapse of the Lehman Brothers investment bank. In the next six months the Korean stock market lost almost half its value; the *won* weakened 40 percent against the dollar; exports shrunk by 41 percent in the last quarter of 2008; investment went down 45 percent; output plunged but then returned to normal in the next quarter of 2009. President Lee Myung-bak's administration earmarked 100 billion dollars to guarantee the foreign currency borrowings of local banks and provided 55 billion dollars to local banks in foreign currency; it also undertook separate 30 billion dollars' worth of currency swaps with the U.S., Japan, and China to ease the credit crunch.[289] Lee also approved a 23.3 billion dollar stimulus package, a 20 billion dollar bank recapitalization fund and, for companies, a 10 billion dollar bond market stabilization fund, and the extension of small and medium enterprise loans.

This was possible thanks to low state debt and high fiscal reserves. The country now had reserves of $270 billion. In addition, local banks were healthier and companies less indebted than a decade earlier.

Lee's main concern was for jobs. The government introduced a raft of preemptive measures to ensure employment. One, which I tried to take advantage of with my own, small company (we were ten people), was to take on an extra worker, with the government paying most of the salary. The condition was that current employees had to unanimously agree to a minimal pay cut—around fifty dollars or so off a monthly salary of three thousand. The only foreigner, a Korean-American, balked, and our role in the grand plan was over.

Still, unemployment was contained and recession avoided, achieved without taking on huge additional debt and without budget deficits. After growth rates of 2.3 percent in 2008 and 0.2 percent in 2009, growth in 2010 was 6.1 percent. Samsung, meanwhile, became the world's biggest technology company in terms of sales. A KEPCO-led consortium beat rival American, Japanese, and French firms to win a 20 billion dollar nuclear power contract in the United Arab Emirates. Hyundai responded nimbly and sizably increased its share of the U.S. market.

Korea is now an advanced economy. But there are fears that, like other countries once the apple of the foreign investor's eye, it might stagnate.

The evidence cited is persuasive and centers on a number of the country's weaknesses. One, for example, is that it remains more vulnerable to external shock than it should be, not so much because of reliance on exports and weak domestic consumer sector, but because of the absence of rules that would prevent aggressive speculation in times of trouble by international finance.[290]

To address such weaknesses, real or perceived, in 2013 the incoming administration of President Park Geun-hye set as its five-year flagship theme the development of a "creative economy." As with President Kim Young-sam's *segyehwa* policy two decades earlier, the announcement sparked a long debate about what this actually meant, even though people kind of know the meaning already. (*Segyehwa* turned out to mean we should internationalize in order to remain competitive in a globalizing world).

Park's underlying message is that Korea can no longer copy its way to the top, herding its corporate troops to follow the vision of a few, but must itself become advanced not just in the output but in the process, too. It must become the sum of its individual parts, necessarily adjusting systems and attitudes that will unleash the talent already apparent—in entertainment, fashion, food, industrial design (Korea has more design schools than the United States), and tech.

Innovation is one aspect of this. Even before the announcement in 2013, Korea was the highest research and development spender in the OECD, with 4.4 percent of GDP in 2012. But there needs to be commensurate change in corporate culture. For example, businesses do not trust their own people, let alone outsiders such as universities, research institutes, or consultants. Korea needs to reverse this, and become high-trust.

The creative-economy initiative may not be producing fruit yet, but it is an indication that Korean leadership is being pushed in the right direction. It's enough for me to be confident and feel that, for the foreseeable future, the South Koreans will get richer. Their economy will keep growing and when the inevitable unexpected downturns come and those dark-cloud issues seem most pressing, they'll get over them.

27

THE FUTURE OF DEMOCRACY

"The country's political mechanism should be compatible
with the economic mechanism, but it's behind."

Democracy doesn't unfold to a plan. In its first two decades, Korea's lurched, like a man on too much beer, from right to left and back again, but generally in a forward direction. In the last decade, as we have seen, our man switched to spirits. The effect—something I felt myself one night along the sidewalk in Yulguk-ro, a street in central Seoul—is a little disconcerting. The intention is still there for progress but as you move to step forward the rest of your body tilts uncooperatively, and the airborne foot lands where it took off, sometimes farther back.

No one person is in charge of this stumbling body politic. The brain seems to lead but under the microscope you find a gooey mass of politicians building their careers. It is not unreasonable to assume that Korea will end up with whatever suits them rather than what suits the country as a whole.

Some pundits predict a kind of political stagnation, with a ruling party ruling forever, like Japan's Liberal Democratic Party or Singapore's People Action Party. This doesn't mean democracy won't progress in terms of rights, but it suggests a certain accommodation with the corruption that gnaws at the floorboards of elections.

But I'm not sure the Koreans have finished with their feistier form of democracy. They want theirs to improve. Also, more practically, in presidential elections, swing voters go for personality. The ruling side may not always have the more attractive candidate.

If politics is about who gets what when, then the arguing at the core is about the ethics of the how. It's about use or abuse of power. Where power is abused by political dictators and cultural authoritarians, fear carries off the best intentions. Democracy can prevent cruelty and unfairness, and remove fear. In old Korea fear was pervasive, which is why their transformation is so monumental and liberating. Fear did not exist solely in the area of political control. It billowed through the culture. Until recently theirs was a society that whipped children, punched wives, thrashed soldiers, and herded, insulted, yelled at, slapped, crushed, abused, and exploited everyone else all the way up the ladder. So unexamined was the consequent depth of anger and discomfort that people believed life to be like this by design, and that the gods and the dead were at it as well, expecting to be appeased through ceremony and sacrifice.

Of course, Koreans were not unique in their outlook. In many other societies, people stepped out of their doors into a nasty world. But it is a mistake to see the people as victims and democracy as a process by which those with power stop being unpleasant about holding on to it. It may start there, but the citizen has obligations of his own, for he, too, was likely made nasty by virtue of his survival in a nasty world, and must also change.

I'm not exaggerating the extent of the unfairness. The foreigner is treated nicely and can miss the signs, like a tourist visiting a dictatorship. You don't get invited to torture festivals. Then, sometimes a door opens on an unlikely place, and you witness a small display, and don't know what to make of it. I remember once hearing about an all-night prayer session at a church in Seoul when some men—not intent on joining in—sneaked down to the basement to catch some sleep on the floor, among them my source and a few expatriates. At some ungodly hour, a church official strode out of an office and started kicking people. "Get up, you fuckers," he shouted. "You're supposed to be praying." Yet when he saw the foreigners he smiled and bowed in greeting, then carried on kicking his way down the corridor. The victims woke up, said, "I am sorry," eyed the back of God's messenger till he disappeared up the steps, then leaned into the wall to sleep again.

Now, a generation into democracy, there's a response: "You can't kick me! It's not right. I am somebody." Elders are now more restrained and therefore less feared. Teachers may no longer beat students, executives no longer strike their staff (although this still happens in small businesses) and although police, prosecutors, and intelligence agents still seek your confession as the easy route to conviction, they are not supposed to torture it out of you.

That's because they represent the state, and while the state may employ force against you, it may no longer use violence. Well, not directly. Such improvements are unfinished business. For example, squatters, tenants, or illegal strikers getting in the way of a company or developer making money, or of a local government office pushing a project through, risk being set upon by gangsters (officially providing "demolition and eviction services") hired for the purpose.[291]

The voice arguing for more rights remains hesitant, unsure. For example, the idea that gay and transgender people should do anything except keep quiet is relatively new. Homosexuals who have tried to highlight their case for equal treatment face a foe in Christian groups. But, despite the influence of Christianity there's a sense in society that these opponents lack the moral high ground. Many people, especially women, like homosexuals because they find them to be nice and gentle. Such attitudes now count for a lot in Korea.

In another example, the type of racism that makes it normal to discriminate against foreigners—for example, what Amnesty International referred to as "rampant abuse" of foreign workers and the forcing of only foreign teachers to submit to AIDS tests—is only now being challenged.[292] On this matter, Koreans are being pushed in the right direction by their own desire to be polite to their foreigners, and by demographics—one in twenty babies in the country now has one foreign parent—and with some help from those who care enough, and see the country's potential as a rights advocate.

"I'm waiting for a Korean hero on this," says Benjamin K. Wagner, a rights activist who successfully took a teacher's HIV case to the United Nation's Committee to End All Forms of Racial Discrimination. "Korea looks like a liberal European country from the viewpoint of the treaties it has signed and ratified. It could be a beacon in Asia on such nondiscrimination and do what Japan has failed to do. But it hasn't yet."

The trickier areas for democratic progress are those involving security. It is possible that South Korea will not fully relax and permit certain freedoms until there is peace with North Korea. On the other hand, the country has come a long way under the prolonged shadow of threat.

During dictatorships the main legal instruments for repression were the National Security Law and the Anti-Communist Law, the latter introduced in 1961 and repealed in 1991. The former remains in place. Over the years, it may have flushed out some real villains, though I can't think of one. But there are plenty of harmless defendants. In 1978, for example, some stamp collectors were arrested because they had obtained some North Korean stamps from international collectors at a stamp collector show somewhere overseas. If you haven't seen them, by the way, these stamps are beauties. There's one that commemorated Charles and Diana's wedding in 1981. Don't quote me, though, because it's still a crime to praise anything North Korean or agree with anything North Korea agrees with.

Even under democratic presidents, hundreds of government critics have been detained for allegedly being too nice about North Korea or something similar. In a crackdown on "leftists" in August 1996, police raided Yonsei University and rounded up six thousand students. Also in that year, police arrested a singer and a publisher over their songbook that apparently "praised" North Korea. The numbers of cases filed rose sharply under Lee Myung-bak and Park Geun-hye.[293]

The armed forces are another area where attitudes and practices need to catch up with democracy as understood by the rest of the country. In August 2014, the Defense Minister, Han Min-koo, issued a public apology over the death of a conscript who had choked to death four months earlier after being beaten by fellow soldiers in his medical unit. It turned out that the soldier, Yoon Seung-joo, had been humiliated and beaten so many times that the record detailing it ran to twelve hundred pages. The army told Yoon's family that he had died "after being hit" and rejected a request for a meeting with witnesses. But as a result of the publicity and outrage, it came clean, the defense minister apologized, and four perpetrators were sentenced to terms of twenty-five to forty-five years.[294]

Abuse is widespread in the military. In fact, as the Yoon case was coming to light, another victim of bullying went on a shooting rampage at a military outpost, killing five soldiers and wounding seven others.

Such problems persist because the military in Korea is not yet fully answerable to the country's civilian institutions. "The military itself represents a human rights problem," said Lim Tae-hoon of the Center for Military Human Rights. "In practice, it is outside of the law. It has the right to withhold information requested by the National Assembly and can just refuse to cooperate with authorities. The only person the generals will obey is the president, but he or she benefits too much from this arrangement to want to do anything about it."

That said, as of this writing, prompted by the murder of Yoon Seung-joo, a military ombudsman function has been mooted for legislation, an indication that the country is taking more to heart the idea that the young people it requires to serve for collective defense have, as individuals, rights that should be protected, not just for good PR but because it is those very rights that go to the core of what distinguishes South from North and makes it worth fighting for.

The military is not alone in its disregard for laws and rights it considers inconvenient. You can see in the way that people drive through red lights at night—and that the worst offenders, it is important to note, are professional drivers of buses, taxis, and trucks—that Koreans' experience with following the rules as an overall good is relatively recent and the learning curve steep.

"Our legal system is a Japanized German one which has for the last forty years come gradually under American legal influence," said Song Sang-hyun, the former president of the World Court. "This state of affairs helped generate hostility to the rule of law in general."

That history began in the late nineteenth century, when Japanese were assigned as advisers to the Korean king and enjoyed unlimited access. The changes they introduced had been borrowed a generation earlier from Germany and were imposed on the traditional system already in place. When the American Military Government took over in 1945, Lieutenant Leonard Bertsch, the political adviser to the governor, brought in U.S. laws chapter and verse, some of which were difficult for Koreans to understand and others impossible to comply with. For example, during this period political agitators deliberately set about fomenting strikes, but under the labor law the authorities were required to recognize them all as legitimate and legal. The new Korean government of Syngman Rhee passed a law making all laws and regulations from the Japanese period still operational; these then existed alongside the American laws.

Under Park Chung-hee there was a legal housecleaning with replacement laws copied from Japan. Then with economic development, Korean business became exposed to U.S. investors, who arrived at meetings with their own accountants and lawyers to negotiate terms. As the American influence increased, Korea began to adopt U.S. wording in areas such as antitrust, intellectual property, foreign investment, and trade.

"We actually have a very good system," Song said. "It is very beautifully written because it is a carbon copy of American law. The problems, though, are bureaucratic interpretation and the fact that people's general attitude is not terribly rule-of-law based. Globalization needs rule of law and in order for it to be successful it should be based on rugged individualism in the good non-egoistic sense. But still our society considers collectivism and family as greater than the individual, so there is this ethical conflict."

As a result, the law often becomes what those in power say it is.

Prosecutors once summoned a foreign consultant for having made a recommendation to a government official which had angered the prosecutor's office.

"I do not see what I have done wrong," the consultant said. "I simply made a recommendation."

"No, you requested a favor," the prosecutor said, using the word *cheongtak* and adding that this was illegal.

"Well, I said what I said to the official. So tell me the legal difference between a recommendation and a request."

"It's simple. If we like you, it's a recommendation. If we don't, it's a request."

This standard—if we don't like you, we will apply the law—is normal practice. For example, prosecutors indicted Uber, the taxi application company, in 2015, but not other limousine companies doing hotel pickup services which were guilty of breaking exactly the same regulations, because Uber had upset them.

With the enforcers so conflicted, it is difficult to persuade the dissident that his lawbreaking now makes him a delinquent. Corruption abounds, and, the dissident will note, so much of it is at the top. You can see this almost every day if you read the news: Tax officials being investigated for extortion; prosecutors and regulators for accepting bribes; lawmakers for illegal fundraising; *chaebol* heads for illegal fill-in-the-blank-here-ing. Here are a few choice examples from a random few weeks in 2014: Executives of a robot vacuum cleaner company called Moneual, a government-designated "hidden champion," are arrested on suspicion of faking claims it had exported 3 billion dollars in home theater personal computers to qualify for additional bank loans. The Korea Council for University Education found that ten thousand cover letters and teacher recommendations submitted by high school students to universities had been plagiarized and some officials admitted that more had probably gone undetected. The whistle-blowing researcher who in 2005 exposed the stem-cell fraud of scientist Hwang Woo-suk says researchers are still under enormous pressure to produce the results their bosses in government and academia want; the Fair Trade Commission reveals that affiliates of thirty-six *chaebol* had engaged in illegal price cartels in the previous eleven years, with Samsung topping the list with forty cases.

Given all this, it's no wonder Koreans don't trust their leaders. Mistrust goes back a long way. Authority in the recent past seemed to exist in order to steal people's money and make them suffer. During Japanese rule, said Roh Jae-won, a retired ambassador to China, "Fathers told their sons, 'Don't follow authority unless it's a matter of personal safety. Obey, but internally defy.'"

Somehow, such attitudes are reflected both in the plunging approval figures for presidents as well as in a popular yearning for the ethical leader on a white horse. This longing seemed as if it had been fulfilled in 2011 by Ahn Cheol-soo, an academic, and founder of a successful software antivirus company who became so popular among young people for his columns and speeches on the need for political change that he declared himself a candidate in the 2012 race. Ahn dropped out to back another opposition candidate but became a lawmaker, after which a fickle public turned its back on him—not for becoming a politician, but for not being very good at it.[295]

If democracy is to progress, party politics needs to improve. And to that end, the first question the parties must ask is whether they really represent real differences, and whether the opposition can continue to present itself as a credible alternative. As of this writing, many opposition party members come from the ranks of 1980s student and labor protesters, a distinct weakness because of their tendency toward stubborn self-righteousness. All parties are weakened by the natural factionalism that comes from recruitment by party bosses. Still, there are more lawyers and people with PhDs in the assembly than there used to be—which I think is a good sign, assuming they wrote their own theses.

Politicians need to work on their reputation with business executives, though. In 2012–3 World Economic Forum surveys asking countries to rank their own parliament, Korea's came 119 out of 148.[296]

"Sometimes I feel these guys are so stupid," said one expert who works for the National Assembly. "The country's political mechanism should be compatible with the economic mechanism, but it's behind. They don't know what they're doing. But then I can see that it's more important for the policy maker to have the public interest at heart than to have expertise in the subject at hand. A lot of them are very willing and reasonable on that score."

One of the new generation of politicians is Yoo Seong-min, a ruling-party lawmaker with a PhD in economics from an American university. He sees the discussion among lawmakers on both sides during the Park Geun-hye years as leading to constitutional change that will make her presidency the last of an era, a bookend to the modernization that began with her father, Park Chung-hee, in the 1960s.

"Lawmakers think that the powerful presidency is a thing of the past," he said. "Among politicians there is significant support for a change to a cabinet system of government but it will be difficult to argue because it has very low support among the public. Far more likely is a change to an American-type four-year term, two-term presidency. Forty to fifty percent of lawmakers now favor this change."

After reunification with North Korea, he thinks, there could be a change to a cabinet system with the addition of an upper house for regional representation.

Yoo, who is conservative on defense but pragmatically liberal on economic and social issues, believes the presidencies of Lee Myung-bak and Park Geun-hye have created a widespread desire for more democratic development:

> The people were taking democracy for granted by the end of Roh Moo-hyun's term but now see it was not so secure. . . . A majority of voters are conservative but in presidential elections they look more to the person than the party. Given the criticism of the last ten years, it is highly likely that the vote will go to opposition next time.

It is hard for Koreans to trust their leaders because, by electing them, they are in essence putting them in a position of superiority. This very dynamic soon convinces the electorate that the newly superior lawmaker no longer merits the status. Only prolonged suffering and staying power, such as that exhibited by opposition leaders under the dictators, seems to break through this mistrust. That, and external circumstances like war, which call for unity. Still, if greater trust does develop, politics will become more representative. And if politicians can be seen to represent their constituents instead of manipulating them for their own careers, they will be more trusted.

If, however, the mistrust prevails, then it is possible the Koreans might invent a new role for politicians as administrators, and deny them the spotlight to pontificate and pose as leaders. There is already an instinct for "participatory" politics with maximum community involvement. It is but one step to see this, with the aid of technology removing many decisions that politicians now argue over and putting them in the hands of voters.

As Korea's democracy improves, so the left-right divide changes from pro-democracy left versus a pro-security and therefore authoritarian right. Now the "new right" is seen as pro-democratic, with its prime concern appearing to be a broader approach to history and in particular an acceptance as legitimate the Rhee-Park-Chun roots of the South Korean republic, which the left, echoing North Korea, discredits on account of unpurged collaborators and anticommunist suppression.

The memory of civil war and fear of a repeat underlie all politics. There is, therefore, passionate conviction behind the differences in how that threat is interpreted and what it might take to achieve a resolution. The buzzword for the left is "peace" and its strategy is engagement, compromise, and reconciliation; for the right, it's "unification" and the need to maintain vigilance and tolerate tension until the North changes and the South can dictate terms. A secondary difference is between the pro-*chaebol* right and pro-labor and freer market (because it means reining in the *chaebol*) left.

Perhaps the most important question facing Korean democracy regards freedom of expression. The country needs an environment of healthy debate, as befitting the new culture that democracy brings, to replace the manipulative tactics by presidents and their staff who believe the "monarch" should not be criticized. As it stands now, government interference in media inhibits mature analysis and criticism of the presidential office.

"Intellectuals no longer watch [the main TV channels] for news. There is a huge need for a BBC-type public broadcaster with independence guaranteed," said Lee Sang-don, a conservative scholar.[297] The president directly appoints the heads of TV networks. Newspapers and news magazines are dependent on advertising and donations from government agencies, state-owned firms, and the *chaebol*. If that is not incentive enough to behave, the Blue House is not above calling publishers and editors to apply backdoor pressure. Then, of course, there is the ultimate deterrent of the defamation suit.[298]

Democracy's next task is to make the prosecutor's office independent from Blue House interference, to enshrine in practice the changes Roh Moo-hyun introduced but which Lee Myung-bak bulldozed; at the same time, prosecution responsibility should be limited to indictments and its powers of investigation taken over by the police.

Both of these changes are likely in the near future.

If democracy is to improve in the years to come, the powers of the presidency should be reduced and more powers given to the National Assembly. This can happen if the serving president cooperates, but it's possible that North Korea—again—will be the argument for a strong office for as long as it is able to misbehave.

The best illustration of outdated attitudes to the presidency, which I would say add to the argument to reduce presidential powers, is the way police are deployed in Seoul, particularly when there's a larger than usual demonstration. These days protests are usually peaceful; demonstrators know that public acceptance of violence was due to a frustration that no longer exists. Now, demonstrators have to make their point in a democratic fashion. However, police deployments remain excessive. Some protesters in downtown Seoul are entirely hemmed in by serried ranks of police buses (ironically, a system Moo-hyun introduced to replace lines of riot police so that no one would get hurt). The nearer the Blue House the more frantic the police effort. The reason for this is not difficult to grasp. If southern Seoul goes up in flames it might be necessary to wake the president, but if a single protester broke through and got anywhere near the Blue House with a placard that said "Up Yours!" the police chief would get fired.

Curtailing presidential powers would help unblock a particular problem that plagues the bureaucracy—inaction. Senior bureaucrats are fearful of taking action without clear orders from the top. Midway through a presidency, ambitious officials are already looking to align themselves with the next leadership.

If there were others sources of authority, bureaucrats would also be tasked with the longer term. As it is, in Korea, there are no plans— bar the ten-year land-use plan—that look beyond five years. Not even any planning with regard to North Korea, which is itself an astonishing failure.

If plans were made, it would help lead to a transformation in the more amorphous sphere of public sentiment. There is, as we have seen earlier, an unusual power to this notion in Korea. It is more than public opinion, more than the people or the masses; it exists almost as the life force of democracy, the energy that chased away the dictators and which now sits on their throne. It is the force the president must obey and which every politician, bureaucrat, prosecutor, tax investigator, and *chaebol* executive pays attention to, for it cannot be challenged. It can be sat out, but it cannot be fought, for it is the deity of democratic Korea.

Koreans assume the god of public sentiment rules elsewhere. For example, when a deranged student named Cho Seung-hui murdered thirty-two fellow students at Virginia Tech in 2007, Koreans in Korea braced for a backlash, not from rednecks, but from a White House and Congress, articulating what they expected to be American public sentiment. This was so anticipated that President Roh at the time offered his condolences, the foreign ministry expressed its "indescribable surprise and shock," the Korean ambassador to the United States proposed a relay fast for thirty-two days, one day for each of the victims, and Koreans lit candles in Seoul. But what came instead was a beautiful example of the wonder of America: forgiveness of the killer by Virginia Tech students who said they wished he had received help earlier. They even described him as the thirty-third victim.

This public sentiment that Koreans see—and they have a saying that, "The Law of Public Sentiment is above the law"—is a beast that needs to be put in its cage to avoid mob rule. Korea now needs leaders strong enough to occasionally go against what most people want or believe to be right.

28

TIME TO UNIFY?

"While we Germans were divided after the war because of our sin, the Koreans were divided because of their innocence."

The most commonly asked question about Korea is when will its two rival halves reunify.

One day some lucky pundit will get credit for calling it. Every analyst and consultant dreams it'll be her, just as she hopes it doesn't happen in the six months between handing in the manuscript and the book coming out.

Every correspondent assigned to Korea wonders if destiny isn't bringing him at the providential time and prays it just not when he's on the beach in France, that his legacy doesn't live on in journalism schools for the famous text from his editor, "South Koreans repel invasion, advance units head for Pyongyang. What are your plans?"

The truth about timing, though, is no one knows. When I'm asked, I try and cut the disappointment with two stories: one was an evening in 1990 with two American diplomats and two other correspondents, one of them Korean, when we each put down a 10,000 *won* note and bet on the date. I said April 15 (Kim Il-sung's birthday)

1992. Communism had fallen in Europe. I hesitated, worrying that I was being too hesitant. The most conservative prediction, by the Korean reporter, was again April 15 . . . 1995. Of course, we all lost. I don't remember what happened to the money.

The other story is about the fortune-teller I asked in 1998. She wasn't guessing. She knew. "Kim Jong-il will die in three years," she said. I like to defend her and point out she just missed the figure "1" in front of the "3." Sometime, the window into the spiritual world needs wiping.

The next question is whether it will happen at all. Most South Koreans, when polled, say they prefer delay. But this should not fool us. They say that because they know unification is inevitable. They're not being asked, shall we join like Germany or stay separate like Russia and Ukraine? Even if it's phrased like that, what they hear is, would it be better to do it now, or later? Only refugees and the people from separated families say now. The others want to be sensible. Why have the surgery before you really need it? South Korean governments could be accused of being antiunification for wanting gradualism over absorption, but they never are because voters know what they mean and for the most part agree.

Reunification is inevitable. The Koreans will want it and will not need to ask permission. No country may stand in their way. That point was nicely expressed by a German official explaining why his countrymen had needed permission from their neighbors to reunify: "While we Germans were divided after the war because of our sin, the Koreans were divided because of their innocence."[299]

Having said that, the first and more pressing need is not reunification but reconciliation. This will be the real game changer. If there is no war, and not too much loss of control, and if things go the way the two governments and most people in South Korea want—we don't know what the northerners will think—it's possible that reunification will be postponed as the final act of a long process of reconciliation by which North Korean escapees will be able to go home, or at least visit their families, unmolested, where we can drive up to Pyongyang for the weekend, and northerners can come south. Over time the types of exchanges can expand and the conditions under which they occur can be lightened.

The trigger for this reconciliation to begin will be a shift of some sort whereby the government in the North prioritizes the well-being of its people over security. This may be signaled by a dramatic moment, like the removal of Kim Jong-un, the dictator, or an understated one, like a new policy of decriminalizing the desire to emigrate. What is clear, though, is that this moment will not be of South Korea's making. It won't be something that American policy makers can prompt. Short of an international invasion to remove them, it is up to the North's leadership to make the change. The South and its American allies just have to be careful not to scare them into a reversal when the moment happens.

To return to our question of timing, if we break it down like this into power shift-reconciliation-unification, we still cannot predict, but we can outline a timetable that is both desirable and fits in the context of the argument of the Korean emergence I have been making in these pages.

Consider the fortunes of Korea in its modern period in forty-year chunks. The first forty from the protectorate treaty with Japan in 1905 to the end of World War Two were biblical years of wandering in the wilderness.

The next forty-year stretch, which you can either start in 1945 or with the formal establishment of two countries in 1948, is the foundation period for the modern nation. In this period, South Korea goes from basket case to emerging market. At the end, in 1988, it has its first presidential election under the new democratic rules and hosts the Summer Olympics, with North Korea's allies participating, as a symbolic acknowledgement of the South's ascendancy over the North.

The next forty years are a period of maturing, when the South becomes an advanced economy, with a strengthened experience of democracy, and sees its culture widely appreciated around the world. This period ends in 2028 by which time South Koreans will be settled with their international identity. There will be a new confidence. I would like to say that reconciliation should be completed and that reunification should take place at the end of this period. But that's because, like my fortune-teller, I am impatient. It may prove to be the desirable moment to start reconciliation. I say that because there is an inhibiting factor in any joining of the two Koreas that the world does not see but which both sides know so well. That is, tradition and culture. Day One will be all fireworks and live coverage on CNN. Day Two, the poor North Koreans go to the bottom of the hierarchical ladder. That is why whoever is in charge in the North owes it to its people to build up the country, reconcile slowly, and join together only when they know they will be received with civility.

In the mid-century period, the 2030s, '40s, '50s, and '60s, Korea will fully flourish on the world stage and by the end of that period the North Koreans should be part of it.

During the reconciliation, I would like to think the North Koreans could add something beyond land and people. But I cannot see how or what.

No, I think it is the South Koreans who will make reconciliation and their reinvention as a unified people such a thrilling story. And the particular quality they will bring to this union which will make it so is one they have been defiantly exhibiting for the past seventy years: the desire to be better.

A Unified Korea will not be chauvinistic, it will not police smaller powers, or bully its neighbors. Nor will it, despite today's unresolved emotions, annoy Japan. By inviting their compatriots in, and by favoring truth and reconciliation over revenge, for revenge will weaken them all, they will together continue their endeavor to be more wealthy, more educated, freer, and better, and in doing so, these Unified Koreans will make the world a better place.

ACKNOWLEDGMENTS

In the preparation of this book, I must thank my wife for encouraging me to go ahead with the project and helping me create the time to do it; my agent, Kelly Falconer, for convincing me that now was the time for a new book on Korea; and Peter Joseph and Melanie Fried, my editors at St. Martin's, for their supportive approach to editing and for catching those points in the text where the writing flagged.

For interpretation, advice, and practical assistance, many thanks to: Aidan Foster-Carter, Ju Yeji, Jun Daeun, Ken Kaliher, Kaylee Kang, Alex Kim, Kim Hyun-jin, Kim Youngjin, Kim Young-il, Clare Lee, Bradley Martin, David Richardson, Simon Warner, and Jacco Zwetsloot. I would especially like to acknowledge my colleagues Andrew Salmon and John Burton for the many conversations during which they squashed my views and forced their own upon me. I don't know, but it's possible the book is better for it. Extra thanks to John Burton, who, after telling me how bad the history section was, gave it a thorough editing and declared himself pleased with the result.

For time with interviews, ideas and information, special thanks to: Peter Bartholomew, Beopryun, Brother Anthony, Chang Hahm-cheol, Bernie Cho, Cho Gab-je, Choe Sanghun, Mark Clifford, Daniel Davies, Hahn Dae-soo, Richard Hill, Jin Ick, Jo Young-su, Rodney Johnson, Jeffrey Jones, Kang Joong-hoon, Robert Kelly, Kim In-sook, Kim Jong-dae, Kim Joo-hyung, Kim Kang-ja, Kim Sang-hyun, Kim Yong-chul, Kim Young-hoon, Robert Koehler, Isa Kusumawati, Lee Charm, Lee Hyeonseo, Jin Lee, Lee Kie-hong, Kyu Lee, Lee Sang-don, Lee Tae-hoon, Lim Jie-hyun, Lim Tae-hoon, David Mason, Joe McPherson, Nathan Millard, Charles Montgomery, O Won-chul, Maureen O'Crowley, Oh Kyung-ja, Rob Ouwehand, Darcy Paquet, Park Jin-seng, Park Jongik, Park Jung-ah, Park Kyung-sin, Jonson Porteux, Pyo Wan-soo, Mark Russell, Todd Sample, Suzanna Samstag, Mark Setton, Song Sang-hyun, James Turnbull, Peter Underwood, Edgar Vaudeville, Ben Wagner, David Wood, and Yoo Seong-min.

NOTES

1. The reader will note that throughout this book I have used the normal Korean format for names with the surname coming first. The exceptions are in the bibliography and notes where some Korean authors have inverted their names for English-speaking readers. The only exception in the main text is with the first president who is so widely known as Syngman Rhee that it would be odd to turn his name around.

2. The detail in these pages is from newspaper reports and television footage. The quoted comments by students were from a video on a phone belonging to seventeen-year-old Park Du-hyeon released to the media by his father after his body was recovered. Ref: Choe Sang-hun, "Mom, This Looks Like the End of Me: Doomed Vessel's Last Minutes," *The New York Times*, April 30, 2014, ref: www.nytimes.com/2014/05/01/world/asia/korean-ferry-students-captured-sinking-on-video.html.

3. Aidan Foster-Carter column, "Give Credit Where It Is Due," *Korea JoongAng Daily*, February 27, 2015.

4. For the record, South Korea once had a thriving mining industry. There is

some local coal but most is now imported. Korea was the second graphite producer after China from the 1950s but this industry collapsed in the 1990s. Its
Sangdong tungsten mine was once the largest in the world but it, too, closed in
the 1990s. (As of this writing, a Canadian company is looking to revive it—
Ref: www.woulfemining.com/s/Sangdong.asp). There is also, interestingly,
uranium, which could be useful for the nuclear industry, but the government
lacks the will to address local opposition to its development.

5. James Cameron, *Point of Departure*, 116.

6. I googled this out of curiosity and found it taken, shaken, and slightly
stirred, from a poem called "The Example" by the Welsh poet William
Henry Davies:

Here's an example from
A Butterfly;
That on a rough, hard rock
Happy can lie;
Friendless and all alone
On this unsweetened stone.

Now let my bed be hard
No care take I;
I'll make my joy like this
Small Butterfly;
Whose happy heart has power
To make a stone a flower.

7. Seriously. It's here: Ju-min Park, " 'Well-Dying Course' in South Korea Includes Test Run in a Coffin," Reuters, July 7, 2011, ref: http://blogs.reuters
.com/faithworld/2011/07/07/well-dying-course-in-south-korea-includes-test
-run-in-a-coffin/.

8. See www.dmzforum.org.

9. The ministry of environment said in 2014 there were 1,043 bears on
forty-six farms.

10. Korea is the only developed country that treats inbound tourism receipts as revenue and outbound tourism as a cost. This goes back to the days when it made more sense for the government to stop valuable foreign currency being "wasted" on leisure.

11. *Tongil*, which was a long-grain nonsticky rice, itself became history in the 1980s when the yield of medium-and short-grain varieties caught up. It finally disappeared in 1992 when the government ended its purchase program.

12. After Bangladesh and Taiwan.

13. Figure cited in Chico Harlan, "After Decades of Economic Growth, South Korea is the Land of Apartments," *The Washington Post*, September 16, 2013.

14. This area under demolition had 456 homes and 434 stores. Here's a video of the police assault that led to the deaths: www.youtube.com/watch?v=gaE _KpBoFPE&feature=related.

15. The project is explained along with pictures of Gye-dong here: www .youtube.com/watch?v=JwjLbJhOBl0.

16. Ezra Vogel, *The Four Little Dragons: The Spread of Industrialization in East Asia (The Edwin O. Reischauer Lectures)*; Bernhard Seliger, *The Shrimp that Became a Tiger: Transformation Theory and Korea's Rise After the Asian Crisis*; Mark L. Clifford, *Troubled Tiger: Businessmen, Bureaucrats and Generals in South Korea*; Tariq Hussain, *Diamond Dilemma: Shaping Korea for the 21st Century*; Gregory Henderson, *Korea: The Politics of the Vortex*.

17. See "S. Korea Evokes National Image of Cutting-Edge Technology: Survey," *Yonhap News*, July 25, 2014. Ref: http://english.yonhapnews.co.kr/national /2014/07/25/7/0301000000AEN20140725003900315F.html

18. I was unaware of this as I had no dealings with these companies outside of Korea. I am grateful for the insight to Euh Yoon-dae who was the first head of the Presidential Commission for National Branding, a body created during the 2008–13 presidency of Lee Myung-bak.

19. Given the different Romanization systems, Joseon (South Korean system since 2000), Choson (North Korean), Chosun (South Korean before 2000), and Choson with a smiley diacritic mark over the second "o" (academic McCune-Reischauer system) are all the same word.

20. For full lists of what other countries call the two Koreas, see www.geonames.org/KR/other-names-for-south-korea.html and www.geonames.org/KP/other-names-for-north-korea.html.

21. I have suggested this a couple of times in columns in Korean newspapers, but the lack of response tells me that either nobody read those newspapers or that the country is not ready for such a revolutionary idea. See: "Korea Should Change Its Name," *The Korea Times*, June 3, 2010; ref: www.koreatimes.co.kr/www/news/opinon/2010/06/137_67039.html.

22. Peter Yapp, ed., *The Traveller's Dictionary of Quotations: Who Said What, About Where?* (London: Routledge Kegan & Paul, 1983).

23. After a visit to Asia in 1911.

24. James Kirkup, *Streets of Asia* (Worthing, UK: Littlehampton Book Services Ltd, 1969).

25. Peter Vay, *Empires and Emperors of Russia, China, Korea, and Japan: Notes and Recollections by Monsignor Count Vay de Vaya and Luskod* (First published in 1906. Reprinted by Nabu Press in 2010), 241.

26. Isabella Bird Bishop, *Korea and Her Neighbours* (first published 1898. Reprinted Seoul: Yonsei University Press, 1970), 27.

27. Ibid, preface.

28. Peter Vay, op. cit., 238–9.

29. For example, a developer may put a swimming pool in the basement of an apartment block if the tenants are foreigners, but not if he plans to lease to Koreans.

30. Figures from the ministry of security and public administration.

31. *The Economist*, "Farmed Out," March 24, 2014.

32. See "South Korea Redefines Multiculturalism," *The Diplomat*, July 18, 2014, ref: http://thediplomat.com/2014/07/korea-redefines-multiculturalism /; and Steven Denney, "Nature or Nurture: What Makes a Person 'Korean?'" *The Diplomat*, October 14, 2014, ref: http://thediplomat.com/2014/10/nature -or-nurture-what-makes-a-person-korean/.

33. For a better explanation than I can give, see Don Baker, *Korean Spirituality*, 8–10.

34. In October 2014, there were 597 men in prison according to the Jehovah's Witness site www.jw.org. Korea's record vis-à-vis other states is according to War Resisters' International, a UK-based advocacy group, quoted by Jason Strother and Malte Kollenberg in "S. Korean Conscientious Objectors Seek Alternative to Military Service," *VOA*, February 8, 2014, ref. www.voanews .com/content/south-korean-conscientious-objectors-seek-alternatives-to -military-service/1847516.html. For rulings in 2016, see Kim Se-jeong, "Court rulings over conscientious objections differ," *The Korea Times*, August 27, 2015, ref: http://koreatimes.co.kr/www/news/nation/2015/08/113_185691 .html.

35. In 2004, 49 percent of thirty-year-olds and 45 percent of twenty-year-olds said they were religious in 2004, but by 2014 those numbers had dropped to 38 and 31 percent respectively.

36. The reason Korean Jews have left, according to Seoul-based Rabbi Osher Litzman, who opened the Chabad House, are inconveniences such as the need to work on Friday, the inability to take off Jewish holidays, and the difficulty of obtaining kosher food.

37. For this story, see Ross Arbes, "How the Talmud Became a Bestseller in South Korea," *The New Yorker*, June 23, 2015.

38. Don Baker, op. cit., 30.

39. For more, see Hahm Pyong-choon, "Shamanism and the Korean World-view," in Chai-shin Yu and Richard Guisso, eds., *Shamanism: the Spirit World of Korea.*

40. Hyeonseo Lee, *The Girl with Seven Names: A North Korean Defector's Story*, 69.

41. William Franklin Sands, *Undiplomatic Memories*, 16. Sands, an American, was a diplomat in Korea from 1896–1904.

42. In 1991, 17.8 percent of the dead were cremated, but by 2012 this figure had increased to 74 percent. Government figures cited in "Burial Traditions Changing Fast," *Korea JoongAng Daily*, November 12, 2013.

43. Mason has written extensively on this theme. See *The Spirit of the Mountains: Korea's San-Shin and Traditions of Mountain Worship*, and his site, www .san-shin.org.

44. It is believed to be a US $2–4 billion industry with as many as 450,000 practitioners. See: Bae Ji-sook, "Curious Seek Destiny in New Year," *Korea Herald*, December 28, 2012, ref: www.koreaherald.com/common_prog/newsprint .php?ud=20121228000884&dt=2.

45. Henry Appenzeller, the first Methodist missionary, in a letter July 4, 1890, quoted in Martha Huntley, *Caring, Growing, Changing: A History of the Protestant Mission in Korea*, 131.

46. William Newton Blair and Bruce Hunt, *The Korean Pentecost and the Sufferings Which Followed*. See also "The Role of Robert Alexander Hardie in the Korean Great Revival and the Subsequent Development of Korean Protestant Christianity," a dissertation by Kim Chil-sung, Asbury Theological Seminary, Wilmore, Kentucky, 2012 (http://lib.scu.ac.kr/WebImg/data/pdf/3535011.pdf). For the early missionary experience see William Newton Blair, *Gold in Korea*, The Presbyterian Church of the USA, 1957, and for Protestant history, see Roy E. Shearer, *Wildfire: Church Growth in Korea* (Eerdmans, 1966), and Allen D. Clark, *A History of the Church in Korea* (Christian Literature Society of Korea, 1971).

47. Rev. Cho used to go by the Enligh name Paul. His Korean given name sometimes appears as Yonggi.

48. According to Lee Yo-han, a Unification Church minister tasked with approaching different groups in the 1950s and 1960s in an effort to convert them. It is possible there were many more he was unaware of. He told me the messianic groups began to decline in the sixties.

49. The Pyongyang branch of a group called the Holy Lord Church whose leader, Huh Ho-bin, and followers were jailed by communist authorities in 1946. Their fate thereafter is unknown. As told by Kim Won-pil, a close associate of Unification Church leader Moon Sun-myung who met some of this group's members in North Korea in the 1940s.

50. From a question-and-answer session with American followers during a U.S. tour in March 1965, published by the Unified Family, Washington, D.C, 1967. Ref. MS-1, p. 1.

51. This information is from Felix Moos, "Leadership and Organisation in the Olive Tree Movement" in *Transactions, Royal Asiatic Society, Korea Branch, Vol XLIII*, Royal Asiatic Society, 1967. Park's movement declined after his death.

52. From Korean government figures for 2014 and the CIA World Factbook 2014–15. The only places ranked less fertile than South Korea were, in descending order, Singapore, Japan, the tiny French territory Saint Pierre and Miquelon, and at the bottom, Monaco.

53. Ref: www.oecd.org/els/health-systems/MMHC-Country-Press-Note -Korea.pdf

54. Survey by the Korea Centers for Disease Control and Prevention cited by Annette Ekin in "South Korea's Elderly Suffer Most From Depression," Korea Realtime blog, *The Wall Street Journal*, Sept 15, 2014, ref: http://blogs.wsj.com /koreareatime/2014/09/15/south-koreas-elderly-suffer-most-from-depression/.

55. This was from one of several interviews during the 1980s. I became interested in Dr. Paek's ideas after learning that he was regularly called in by the

South Korean intelligence people to analyze the North Korean leader Kim Il-sung on the basis of TV and film footage.

56. Compared with, say, old BBC shows like *All Gas and Gaiters* and *The Vicar of Dibley* and in the U.S. ABC's *Scrubs* and NBC's *Night Court* and *Bad Judge*.

57. See Choe Sanghun, "By Lampooning Leaders, Talk Show Channels Young People's Anger," *The New York Times*, November 1, 2011, ref: www.nytimes .com/2011/11/02/world/asia/lampooning-leaders-talk-show-channels-young -peoples-anger-in-south-korea.html?_r=0. For Mr. Chung's case, see: Evan Ramstad, "Podcasting-Pol Chung Parts For Prison," *The Wall Street Journal*, December 26, 2011, ref: http://blogs.wsj.com/korearealtime/2011/12/26 /podcasting-pol-chung-parts-for-prison/

58. Jung Min-ho, "4 in 10 Apartment Guards Suffer from Verbal Abuse," *The Korea Times*, Nov 1, 2014. The survey was done after an apartment guard in Gangnam tried to immolate himself because of the abuse he was allegedly getting.

59. See Nam Hyun-woo, "'Salt Farm Slavery' Causes Uproar," *The Korea Times*, February 18, 2014, ref: www.koreatimes.co.kr/www/news/nation/2014 /02/116_151780.html; and Kelly Jung, "How the Homeless Became Salt Farm Slaves," Human Rights Monitor South Korea, February 25, 2014, which cites a report in the vernacular Donga Ilbo, ref: www.humanrightskorea.org/2014 /homeless-became-salt-farm-slaves/. See also note 193.

60. It got worse. "Not even one drop of ink must be allowed to fall into the Han River," the North Korean yelled. See "Two Koreas' Top Brass Resort to Racist Mudslinging," translated from *The Chosun Ilbo* on english.chosun.com, May 17, 2006, ref: http://english.chosun.com/site/data/html_dir/2006/05 /17/2006051761016.html.

61. Yoon Min-sik, "Saenuri chief apologizes for racist remark," *The Korea Herald*, December 18, 2015, ref: www.koreaherald.com/view.php?ud=2015 1218000803.

62. Excerpted from "The Nation I Desire," English translation on the Web site of the Kim Koo Museum & Library. Ref: www.kimkoomuseum.org/eng/kimkoo /mydesire03.html.

63. The memorial park outside Jeju City to the victims killed by government forces in 1948 is another exception. Although the American military was running the country when the killings started, the United States is not blamed.

64. Here's the proof: http://english.visitkorea.or.kr/enu/SI/SI_EN_3_4_1.jsp.

65. Joel P. Engardio, "Seoul Mayor Park Won-soon Wants Same-Sex Marriage in Korea as First in Asia," *San Francisco Examiner*, October 12, 2014, ref: http://archives.sfexaminer.com/sanfrancisco/seoul-mayor-park-won-soon -wants-same-sex-marriage-in-korea-as-first-in-asia/Content?oid=2908905.

66. See, for example, this story of Jonah Lee, a one-time gay bar owner who now campaigns against homosexuality: J. Lester Feder and Jihye Lee, "This Man's Story Explains the Emergence of South Korea's Anti-LGBT Movement," BuzzFeed News, July 31, 2015, ref: http:// www.buzzfeed.com/lesterfeder/meet -the-former-gay-bar-tycoon-now-trying-to-save-gay-people#.vhLPLWK5r.

67. See "Pity the Children," *The Economist*, May 23, 2015, ref: www.economist .com/news/asia/21651873-once-among-biggest-sources-infants-international -adoption-south-korea-stemming.

68. These numbers peaked at 262,465 students in 2011 and declined to 220,000 in 2014.

69. Ian Morris, *Why the West Rules for Now: The Patterns of History, and What They Reveal About the Future* (New York: Picador, 2011), 127–129.

70. This is pronounced "Dan-gun" not "Dang-un."

71. Peter H. Lee and Wm. Theodore de Bary, eds., *Sources of Korean Tradition Vol 1: From Early Times Through the Sixteenth Century*, 5–6, which offers a translation of the myth from *Samguk yusa* (Memorabilia of the Three Kingdoms), 1:33–34, written by the monk Ilyeon (1206–1289).

72. The *Kogi* (Old Record) and the *Wei shu*, by Pei Sung-chih (360–439), dates uncertain. The Dangun legend is also depicted on the Wu family shrine built in 147 in Shantung, China, according to the *Sources of Korean Tradition Vol 1*, op. cit., 5.

73. Even court documents were dated this way. I have a copy of a 1955 case in my files which is dated "Dangun Era 4288."

74. South Korean archaeologists believe this tomb, whomever it belongs to, to be from the tenth century AD.

75. Excerpt quoted from the New World Encyclopedia, ref: www.newworld encyclopedia.org/entry/Kim_Yushin#cite_note-1. Note also that Kim's name is often spelled Yushin to more accurately convey the pronunciation.

76. The actual modern border of North Korea and China was established in the fifteenth century.

77. Kyung Moon Hwang, *A History of Korea*, 37.

78. Note that we are using new South Korean spellings here. Jeong appears in academic texts as Chong Tojon and Yi Seong-gye may appear as Lee Song-gye or Sung-gye.

79. Other candidate sites were Muak valley in the Sinchon area of modem Seoul and a spot by Mt. Gyeryong near the city of Daejeon. Some construction began at Mt. Gyeryong.

80. John Man, *Alpha Beta: How 26 Letters Shaped the Western World* (New York: John Wiley & Sons, 2000).

81. In the late nineteenth century, parents of children in Christian Sunday schools protested the teaching of Western-style dancing because it was too similar to the butcher cringe.

82. Joseph H. Longford, *The Story of Korea*, 43.

83. Ibid., 355.

84. As the Taedong is a North Korean river I am using North Korean spelling of English as opposed to the South Korean version, which is Dae-dong.

85. Yi Kyu-tae, *Modern Transformation of Korea*, 258.

86. Carter J. Eckert, Ki-baik Lee, et al., *Korea Old and New*, 204.

87. In that year, for example, there were twenty mayors of Seoul, each in office for an average of two weeks. Ref. Yi Kyu-tae, op. cit., 28.

88. Ibid., 66.

89. Carter J. Eckert, Ki-baik Lee, et al., op. cit., 240.

90. See Kim Hyo-jin, "Lee Family Devoted to Korean Liberation," *The Korea Times*, February 2, 2015, ref: www.koreatimes.co.kr/www/news/nation/2015/11/180_172910.html; Shim Jae-yun, "Yi Si-young—Independence and Found-ing Leader," *The Korea Times*, June 13, 2012, ref: www.koreatimes.co.kr/www/news/issues/2015/11/363_113008.html; Yeh Young-june, "In praise of Kim San," *Korea JoongAng Daily*, August 18, 2008, ref: http://koreajoongangdaily.joins.com/news/article/Article.aspx?aid=2893745.

91. Nym Wales and Kim San (pseudonyms for Snow and Jang), *Song of Ariran: A Korean Communist in the Chinese Revolution*, 140. (Quote taken from this site: www.columbia.edu/~ey2172/kim.html).

92. Ibid., 320.

93. A Diet member and newspaper editor named Arakawa Goto, according to Peter Duus, *The Abacus and the Sword: The Japanese Penetration of Korea 1895–1910*, 397–8.

94. Ibid., 401. The gentleman quoted is called Okita Kinjo.

95. *Kyongsong Ilbo*, September 20, 1916, quoted in Yi Kyu-tae, *Modern Transformation of Korea*, 131.

96. Peter Bartholomew, "Choson Dynasty Royal Compounds: Windows to a Lost Culture," in *Transactions: Royal Asiatic Society, Korea Branch Vol. 68* (Seoul: Royal Asiatic Society, 1993). The colonial government building was used after independence by the Korean government and later turned into a museum before being demolished in a belated nationalistic gesture by President Kim Young-sam in the 1990s.

97. The Bank of Korea building remains, but the Chosun Hotel has been modernized beyond recognition.

98. A memorial hall to the assassin An Jong-geun was opened on the site of the former Shinto shrine in 1970.

99. Carter J. Eckert, Ki-baik Lee, et al., op. cit., 257, compares 1937 figures for bureaucrats in Korea (52,270 Japanese and 35,282 Koreans) with the similarly populated French colony of Vietnam (2,920 French officials, 10,776 French troops, and 38,000 Vietnamese officials).

100. Interviews with Kwak No-pil, a Christian who police suspected was a communist, and who was given the red pepper treatment by Korean policemen before being released without charge; and Lee Dae-young whose grandfather, Lee Myong-nyong, was one of the signers of the 1919 declaration of independence and told him about the fingernail torture.

101. This was the view of William Blair, a prominent American Presbyterian missionary at the time. See William Blair and Bruce Hunt, *The Korean Pentecost*, 84–5.

102. This was one item in Wilson's fourteen-point declaration which outlined the American agenda for the Versailles Peace Conference.

103. Details from *The Korean Situation: Authentic Accounts of Recent Events by Eye Witnesses*, compiled in 1919 from mission reports by the Federal Council of the Churches of Christ in America.

104. For her status in twentieth-century history, see: Mary Connor, "Famous Koreans: Six Portraits, Education about Asia," The Association for Asian Studies, Fall 2001. Ref: www.asian-studies.org/eaa/connor.htm. (Note her name is spelled Yu Kwan-Sun in this article.)

105. According to Korean figures. The Japanese government claimed 533 dead and 12,522 jailed.

106. Most white rice went to Japan. Ordinary Koreans ate rice mixed with other grains.

107. For a deep dive into the whole question of Korean business roots in this period, see Choong Soon Kim, *A Korean Nationalist Entrepreneur: A Life History of Kim Songsu, 1891–1955*; Carter J. Eckert, *Offspring of Empire: The Koch'ang Kims and the Colonial Origins of Korean Capitalism, 1876–1945*; and Dennis L. McNamara, *The Colonial Origins of Korean Enterprise: 1910–1945*.

108. Although not causes, the fact America and Australia had anti-Japanese immigration policies gives a sense of attitudes at that time.

109. "What the Japanese required after 1931 was active support and participation in their economic and military plans, not the indirect support of a portion of the elite and the grudging, sullen passivity of the Korean common man." Carter J. Eckert, Ki-baik Lee, et al., op.cit., 306.

110. Ironically, before the total assimilation period, a rule had been introduced to crack down on conmen posing as influential people that made it illegal for Koreans to take Japanese names.

111. Richard E. Kim, *Lost Names: Scenes from a Korean Boyhood*, 87–115.

112. See Brandon Palmer, *Fighting for the Enemy: Koreans in Japan's War, 1937–1945*, pp. 183–89.

113. Brandon Palmer (ibid., 3) draws on Korean and Japanese sources and puts the total at between four and seven million. A larger figure of 7.82 million

comes from a report by a Korean government committee. See Jang Hyeok-jin, "Study Provides New Look at Drafted Labor Workers," *Korea Joongang Daily*, January 2, 2015, ref: http://koreajoongangdaily.joins.com/news/article/Article.aspx?aid=2999184.

114. Among the number of studies, I have drawn on for this section are: Keith Howard ed., *True Stories of the Korean Comfort Women*; Yoshimi Yoshiaki, *Comfort Women*; and C. Sarah Soh, *The Comfort Women: Sexual Violence and Postcolonial Memory in Korea and Japan*.

115. As a measure that there is choice in how to treat prisoners, consider these death rates: 4 percent of Western prisoners in Nazi POW camps as opposed to 60 sixty percent of Soviet prisoners in Nazi camps; and 43 percent of American prisoners in the Korean War.

116. Twenty-three of these Koreans were executed. The 148 were charged with Class B (crimes against humanity) and C (planning of or failure to prevent such crimes) war crimes. (Class A criminals were those who conspired to wage war.)

117. Lee's story is told in three pieces here: Aiko Utsumi, Ikemi Nakamura, Heong-yun Gil (sic—should be Yun-hyung Gil), "Lee Hak Rae, the Korean Connection and "Japanese" War Crimes on the Burma-Thai Railway," *The Asia-Pacific Journal: Japan Focus*, 2007, http://japanfocus.org/-Gil-Heong_yun/2505/article.html. See also: Gil Yun-hyung, "The Lingering Issue of Korean Class B and C War Criminals," *The Hankyoreh*, April 2, 2015, ref: http://english.hani.co.kr/arti/english_edition/e_international/685183.html.

118. See "Failure of the Special Prosecution on pro-Japanese Collaborators: How, Who, Why," April 5, 2012, ref: https://mfalcon2011.wordpress.com/2012/04/05/failure-of-the-special-prosecution-committee-on-pro-japanese-collaborators-how-who-why/.

119. See Bae Ji-sook, "Park Chung-hee Leads List of Collaborators With Japan," *The Korea Times*, November 8, 2009, ref: www.koreatimes.co.kr/www/news/nation/2009/11/117_55107.html. The book, in Korean only, is: 친일인명사전 (*Encyclopedia of Pro-Japanese Figures*), published by 민족문제 연구소 (Institute for Research in Collaborationist Activities, 2009) ref: www.yes24

.com/24/goods/3655703?scode=029. For confiscation of assets and the chal-
lenge by some families, see: "Large plot of confiscated land returned to pro-
Japan collaborators' descendants," Yonhap News Agency, August 12, 2015,
ref: http://english.yonhapnews.co.kr/culturesports/2015/08/12/0701000000
AEN20150812003900315.html. For overall treatment of the subject, see Choe
Sang-hun, "Colonial-Era Dispute Agitates South Koreans," *The New York
Times*, April 4, 2010, ref: www.nytimes.com/2010/04/05/world/asia/05poet
.html. See also note 157.

120. See Yonson Ahn, "The Colonial Past in Post-colonial South Korea: Colonialism, Modernity, Gender," in Steffi Richter ed., *Contested Views of a Common Past: Revisions of History in Contemporary East Asia*.

121. For a very detailed analysis of this period between the end of World
War Two and the beginning of the Korean War, see Cumings, *The Origins of the
Korean War*.

122. "Inter-Korean Mt. Kumgang tourism meeting fails to produce agreement,"
The Hankyoreh, February 9, 2010, ref: www.hani.co.kr/arti/english_edition/e
_northkorea/403736.html.

123. The details in this section are from: author's interview in 1988 with
Moon Bong-jae, the youth group's president in 1948; other interviews on
Jeju Island; an interview in 2015 with Jeong Ham-cheol, spokesperson for
a revived form of the Youth Association; and "Internal Warfare in Korea,
1948–50: the Local Setting of the Korean War" by John Merrill in Bruce
Cumings, ed., *Child of Conflict: the Korean-American Relationship 1943–1953*,
133–68.

124. One refugee Protestant minister told me that his next-door neighbor became suspicious after seeing him pray with his eyes open and had to be dissuaded by his wife from reporting him as a communist. He learned this only
after they became close friends.

125. See Cumings, *The Origins of the Korean War*, 201–9.

126. Donald Stone Macdonald, *The Koreans: Contemporary Politics and Society*, 197.

127. Gen. Charles Helmick, cited in Mark L. Clifford, *Troubled Tiger: Businessmen, Bureaucrats and Generals in South Korea*, 29.

128. South Africa provided air units, and Denmark, India, Norway, and Sweden provided medical units. Italy, not a UN member at the time, provided a hospital.

129. These details from Joseph C. Goulden, *Korea: the Untold Story of the War*, 231.

130. Gregory Henderson, *Korea: The Politics of the Vortex*, 163–4.

131. Han had a copy of a contemporary U.S. 8th Army film which shows him at the site explaining in English to an American army chaplain what had happened. The film was discovered by a Korean TV researcher. Incredibly, one of the survivors had also survived the executions at sea the day before, after he'd concealed a razor in his mouth and cut the rope. He was Han's source for the information about the first effort to weigh bodies with rocks and dump them in the sea.

132. James Cameron, op. cit., 112.

133. Ref: www.usip.org/publications/truth-commission-south-korea-2005. See also: Choe Sang-hun, "Unearthing War's Horrors Years Later in South Korea," *The New York Times*, December 2, 2007, ref: www.nytimes.com/2007/12/03/world/asia/03korea.html?pagewanted=all&_r=0.

134. It is possible that some of these people went voluntarily, but their families may believe, or have found it wiser to assume, that they were unwilling.

135. Casualties from Macdonald, op. cit., 52. Other figures from Lee Ki-baik, *A News History of Korea*, 380, and Andrew C. Nahm, *Korea: Tradition and Transformation*, 481–2.

136. This was known as "climbing the barley ridge" The starvation came after the rice supplies ran out and before the winter barley crop ripened.

137. Macdonald puts the figure at $1.6 billion for three years after the war. Total U.S. aid to Korea from 1953 to the mid-1970s, when it ended, was $6 billion. Military assistance was said to be valued at $7 billion. Ref. Macdonald, op. cit., 198.

138. These were: a commando raid on the Blue House in 1968; a bomb at the National Cemetery in 1970 detonated as it was being planted, the day before Park Chung-hee was due to visit; an assassin in 1974 missed Park, but killed his wife; a bomb in Rangoon in 1983 missed president Chun Doo-hwan, but killed seventeen others. An intelligence official said there was an earlier, unpublicized attempt against Chun, but the author was unable to confirm this claim. It is not known if South Korea made attempts on Kim Il-sung. When asked about the known incidents, a North Korean told me that the 1968 attack was revenge against the alleged murder by Park of a go-between sent by North Korea to propose talks, and that the 1983 attack was revenge for some undisclosed incident in North Korea which authorities blamed on the South.

139. For her experience of this weeding out, see chapter 38 of Hyeonseo Lee, op. cit.

140. Chang was adopted by Amnesty International as a Prisoner of Conscience. Ref: file:///C:/Users/user/Downloads/asa250111993en%20(1).pdf

141. Ref: Kwak Byong-chan, "The NIS's long history of political interference," *The Hankyoreh*, July 12, 2013, ref: www.hani.co.kr/arti/english_edition/e _editorial/595495.html.

142. The movie was named *Silmido*, after the island near Incheon where the men were trained. For a portrait of such training methods, see: Brian Lee, "Headquarters Intelligence Detachment: 'The Military Unit from Hell,'" Joongang Daily, October 17, 2002, ref: http://fas.org/irp/world/rok/hid.htm. See also Andrew Salmon, "Fighting in the Shadows," *The South China Morning Post*, December 24, 2005, ref: www.andrewcsalmon.com/fighting-in-the -shadows/

143. See Sakie Yokota, *North Korea Kidnapped My Daughter*.

144. For an escape through China, see Hyeonseo Lee, op. cit.; for Tim Peters, see Bill Powell, "Long Walk to Freedom," *Time* Magazine, May 1, 2006; for others, see Yun Jung-min, "Reverend Helps North Koreans Defect to South," *Korea JoongAng Daily*, August 8, 2015, ref: http://koreajoongangdaily.joins .com/news/article/Article.aspx?aid=3007649; also, Anna Fifield, "This Journalist Didn't Just Interview North Korean Defectors, He Followed Them on Their Escape," *The Washington Post*, June 20, 2015, ref: www.washingtonpost.com /news/worldviews/wp/2015/06/20/this-journalist-didnt-just-interview-north -korean-defectors-he-followed-them-on-their-escape/.

145. Kang Chol-hwan became a reporter for the *Chosun Ilbo*. See his biography, Kang Chol-hwan and Pierre Rigoulot, *The Aquariums of Pyongyang: Ten Years in the North Korean Gulag*.

146. This story was told by the man's brother-in-law, a Korean-American who went to North Korea on a family reunion visit in 1991.

147. For more on this issue, see Chapter 21.

148. This was in response to a question about whether North Korea would open its economy as China had done.

149. See B.R. Myers, *The Cleanest Race: How North Koreans See Themselves and Why It Matters*.

150. James Cameron, op. cit., p. 105.

151. "The Gold Medalist," chapter 10 of Ruchir Sharma, *Breakout Nations: In Pursuit of the Next Economic Miracles*." (New York: Norton, 2013).

152. From conversations with Daniel Lee Kie-hong and from his autobiography, Daniel Lee, *Son of the Phoenix: One Man's Story of Korea*, 225–7. For the curious, the Dutch gentleman in this episode was Wouter Tims, who went on to teach at VU University in Amsterdam; the Japanese official was Asanuma Shinji, who later worked as an investment banker and then as a professor in Japanese universities; the Indonesian official was Emil Salim, one of a group of Indonesian economic planners educated in the United States known as the

"Berkeley Mafia." He became a government minister and presidential adviser. Refs: www.sow.vu.nl/Obituary%20Wouter%20Tims.htm; www.ipp.hit-u.ac .jp/appp/CVs/Asanuma.htm; http://en.wikipedia.org/wiki/Emil_Salim.

153. Mark L. Clifford, op. cit., 29. For detail on Park Chung-hee, several recent books are listed in the bibliography. There is, however, no full biography in English.

154. Such practices were not unusual for poor families, according to Cho Gab-je, author of *Nae mudum-e chimul baetora* (Spit on My Grave), a Korean-language biography of Park serialized in the *Chosun Ilbo* newspaper 1997–8.

155. Mark L. Clifford, op. cit., 35–7. Moon Chung-in and Jun Byung-joon note that, "Park was thoroughly militaristic in mentality, in the fashion of Japan of the 1930s and early 1940s." Ref: "Modernization Strategy: Ideas and Influences," chapter 4 of Byung-Kook Kim and Ezra Vogel, eds., *The Park Chung Hee Era: The Transformation of South Korea*, 118.

156. Ibid., 118–20.

157. The *Encyclopedia of Pro-Japanese Figures* (*chinil inmyeong sajeon*) was produced in 2009 by the Institute for Research in Collaborationist Activities (*minjok munje yeonguso*). Ref: www.minjok.or.kr/kimson/home/minjok/index .php. See also "Evidence of Park Chung-hee's military allegiance to Japan surfaces," *The Hankyoreh*, November 6, 2009. Ref: www.hani.co.kr/arti/english _edition/e_national/386277.html. See also note 119.

158. See "State Building: The Military Junta's Path to Modernity through Administrative Reforms," by Hyung-A Kim, chapter 3 of *The Park Chung Hee Era: The Transformation of South Korea*, op. cit.

159. O Won-chol, *The Korea Story: President Park Jung-hee's Leadership and the Korean Industrial Revolution*, 55–61. The following section is taken from this book and my interview with the author. (Note the different spelling of Park's given name in the title).

160. O Won-chol, ibid., 36.

161. Ibid., 21–2.

162. In 1983, Lee was the foreign minister and one of seventeen people in the entourage of President Chun Doo-hwan killed in Rangoon when a bomb was set off by North Korean commandos.

163. Kim Jae-ik, who was also killed in Rangoon, and Kim Ki-hwan, a former professor at the University of California at Berkeley. For a tribute to the former by the latter, see: Preface ("Kim Jae-ik: His Life and Contributions") to Lawrence B. Krause and Kim Ki-hwan, eds., *Liberalization in the Process of Economic Development* (Berkeley, CA: University of California Press, 1991).

164. Pyongyang blew up a South Korean airliner in 1987 on the eve of the meeting at which its allies were making this decision in what appears to have been a failed effort to create a pretext of poor security for an Eastern Bloc boycott.

165. SsangYong reeled under heavy debts during the regional financial crisis in 1997 and the family lost control. Many of its companies remain, but under new ownership.

166. Here's a portrait of that ownership web: "How to untangle Samsung group's ownership?" Credit Suisse Equity Research, June 18, 2014. Ref: https://doc.research-and-analytics.csfb.com/docView?sourceid=em&document_id=x574187&serialid=OrpldCkw5pCaYjZCCElk2xVOjbtbVIR7wckXF3W%2BiWE%3D.

167. Figures from the Korea Fair Trade Commission in June 2014. In that year, cross-shareholding was frozen by law at current levels, the result of an earlier election pledge by President Park Geun-hye.

168. Lee Jung-ae, "Top Four Chaebol's Value Added Accounts for Nearly 10% of GDP," *The Hankyoreh*, September 18, 2014. Ref: http://english.hani.co.kr/arti/english_edition/e_business/655761.html

169. In Japan, the *zaibatsu* were broken up by the American occupation immediately after World War Two. They regrouped in what are known as *keiretsu*, a looser association of companies with business relations.

170. Francis Fukuyama, *Trust: the Social Virtues and the Creation of Prosperity* (New York: Penguin Books, 1996).

171. Ibid., 127–8.

172. For a detailed account of Chung's story, see Donald Kirk, *Korean Dynasty: Hyundai and Chung Ju Yung*. Hyundai means "modern." The common foreign pronunciation of Hey-yoon-die may draw blank stares in Korea, where it is "hyondeh."

173. Mark L. Clifford, op. cit., 116.

174. Ibid., 67–75.

175. Kim Woo-choong, *Every Street Is Paved with Gold*, 62.

176. Clifford, op. cit., 118–9.

177. Author's interview with a North Korean consultant who said that in a 1993 visit, Kim had emptied his plate almost before the "Great Leader" Kim Il-sung had started. Later in the meal, the Daewoo chairman got into an argument with Kim Il-sung's son, Jong-il.

178. According to a former Daewoo executive who accompanied Kim on the trip.

179. Kim Tae-gyu, "Another Chaebol Chairman Given Jail Time," *The Hankyoreh*, February 1, 2013. Ref: www.hani.co.kr/arti/english_edition/e_national/572363 .html

180. The detail in this section is drawn from: Sam Byford, "King of Samsung: A Chairman's Reign of Cunning and Corruption," *The Verge*, November 30, 2012; ref: www.theverge.com/2012/11/30/3709688/samsung-25-years-lee-kun-hee; Chris Velazco, "How Samsung Got Big," *TechCrunch*, June 1, 2013, ref: http:// techcrunch.com/2013/06/01/how-samsung-got-big/; Kurt Eichenwald, "The Great Smartphone War," *Vanity Fair*, June 2014, ref: www.vanityfair.com/news /business/2014/06/apple-samsung-smartphone-patent-war.

181. These team members were Chung Jae-seok, who was Minister of the Economic Planning Board and Deputy Prime Minister from December 1993 to October 1994, and Choi Chang-nak, who was the Governor of the Bank of Korea from October 1983 to January 1986.

182. Daniel Lee, op. cit., 138–9.

183. Ibid., 142–3.

184. "What People Got for Christmas," December 25, 2009, *The Korea Times*. The column was subsequently removed by the newspaper, but is here: http://caseylartigue.blogspot.kr/2009/12/breens-column-that-outraged-samsung.html.

185. Kim Rahn, "Samsung Whistleblower Questioned," *The Korea Times*, November 28, 2007. Ref: www.koreatimes.co.kr/www/news/nation/2015/04/117_14552.html. See also: Choe Sang-hun, "Book on Samsung Divides Korea," *The New York Times*, April 25, 2010. Ref: www.nytimes.com/2010/04/26/technology/26samsung.html?_r=0.

186. The larger the chaebol, the lower the family ownership. For example, it is 0.4% for SK, 1.1% for Hyundai Heavy Industries, 1.25% for Hyundai, 1.28% for Samsung, and 1.9% for Hanwha. Average equity owned by affiliates and executives is 55.2%. These are Korea Fair Trade Commission figures for 2015 and cover the 41 of the 61 chaebol that have a family head.

187. Sweden is the exception, where the government accepts an enormous level of ownership of major firms by the Wallenberg family.

188. For this aspect of the story, see Jaeyong Song and Kyungmook Lee, *The Samsung Way: Transformational Management Strategies from the World Leader in Innovation and Design*.

189. These details from author's interviews, and from William Rylance, "Perspectives on Amway Korea's Soap Opera," *The Journal*, American Chamber of Commerce in Seoul, November/December, 1997, pp. 49–54.

190. For example, see Ser Myo-ja and Kim Jun-hyun, "Compensation Plan for New FTA Faces Backlash," *Korea JoongAng Daily*, December 2,

2015, ref: http://koreajoongangdaily.joins.com/news/article/Article.aspx?aid=3012263.

191. For perspective on this episode, see Adam Taylor, "Why 'Nut Rage' Is Such a Big Deal in South Korea," *The Washington Post*, December 12, 2014, ref: www.washingtonpost.com/blogs/worldviews/wp/2014/12/12/why-nut-gate-is-such-a-big-deal-in-south-korea/; and Alastair Gale, "'Nut Rage' Reignites Backlash Against South Korea's Family-Run Conglomerates," *The Wall Street Journal*, January 7, 2015, ref: www.wsj.com/articles/nut-rage-reignites-backlash-against-south-koreas-family-run-conglomerates-1420654954.

192. Room salons are expensive entertainment establishments where men are served by hostesses in private rooms. Services are sometimes sexual.

193. Foster Klug, Associated Press, story in *The Japan Times*, "Escaped Slave Recalls 'Living Hell' on remote South Korean islands," January 2, 2015, www.japantimes.co.jp/news/2015/01/02/asia-pacific/social-issues-asia-pacific/escaped-slave-recalls-living-hell-remote-south-korean-islands/#.VnUH8LZ96Ul. See also note 59.

194. Se-woong Koo, "Disposable Workers of Hyper-Capitalist Korea," *Korea Exposé*, November 24, 2014, ref: www.koreaexpose.com/voices/disposable-workers-of-hyper-capitalist-korea/.

195. Pyo is now the publisher of the popular news magazine *SisaIn*.

196. The elite manage to do this quite well. It may have even cost one presidential candidate the election in 1997. See: Nicholas Kristoff, "Sons' Military Weigh-In Pulls Korean Candidate from Lead," *The New York Times*, September 7, 1997, ref: www.nytimes.com/1997/09/07/world/sons-military-weigh-in-pulls-korean-candidate-from-lead.html; Joseph Kim, "Koreans Shun Military Service as Survey Shows Rich Dodge Draft," *Asian Correspondent*, March 18, 2014, ref: http://asiancorrespondent.com/120690/koreans-shun-military-service-as-survey-shows-rich-dodge-draft/

197. The academic was jailed for twelve years. See Jung Min-ho, "Professor Arrested for 'Torturing' Student," *The Korea Times*, July 14, 2015, ref: www.koreatimes.co.kr/www/news/nation/2015/07/116_182751.html.

198. For the fake resume story, see Su Hyun Lee, "Fake School Records Shame Korean Figures," *The New York Times*, August 28, 2007, ref: www.nytimes.com /2007/08/28/world/asia/28ihtkorea.1.7285800.html?pagewanted=all.

199. For the LG story, see interview with Didier Chenneveau by Korean Business Central, ref: www.koreabusinesscentral.com/free-content/korea-business -interviews/didier-chenneveau-global-expertise-within-the-korean-business -framework-at-lg-electronics/; for the story of Linda Myers at SK, see Sarah Green Carmichael, "Crucible: The Would-Be Pioneer," *Harvard Business Review*, April 2011, ref: https://hbr.org/2011/04/crucible-the-would-be-pioneer.

200. At this writing there are eighty-seven thousand foreign students at Korean universities, according to government figures. The goal is to increase to two hundred thousand by 2020.

201. According to OECD research in 2015, Koreans worked 2,163 hours a year, slightly shorter than Mexicans (2,237 hours) but way longer than Americans (1,788 hours) and Germans (1,388).

202. The points here are drawn from Michael Kocken, "Seven Reasons Why Korea Has the Worst Productivity in the OECD," *BusinessKorea*, March 17, 2014, ref: www.businesskorea.co.kr/article/3698/insider-perspective-seven -reasons-why-korea-has-worst-productivity-oecd.

203. George E. Ogle, *South Korea: Dissent Within the Economic Miracle*, 47.

204. Ibid.

205. Ibid., 52. The men were hanged and Ogle was deported.

206. Ibid., 87.

207. Government figures quoted in Mark L. Clifford, op. cit., 276.

208. Koreans would not consider PSY anti-American for doing this. He was just expressing his anger over something. See Bobby McGill, "Psy's Anti-America Protesting Past?" *BusanHaps*, November 28, 2012, ref: http://busanhaps.com /exclusive-psys-once-passionate-protesting-past/.

209. This section is based on the author's interviews with Daniel Lee Kie-hong and on the written account in chapter 7 "Aide to the U.S. Military Governor," of Daniel Lee, op. cit.

210. Robert T. Oliver, *The Truth About Korea* (Unwin Brothers Limited, 1951), 131. Oliver was an adviser to Rhee.

211. Ibid., 133.

212. Mark Gayn, *Japan Diary*, 359.

213. Ibid., 352.

214. From Hong Byung-gee, "Diplomat Says a Breakthrough in Korea-Japan Ties Is Needed," *Korea JoongAng Daily*, January 21, 2015, ref: http://koreajoongangdaily.joins.com/news/article/article.aspx?aid=2999921.

215. Daniel Lee, op. cit., chapter 35, "The Five-Year Plan."

216. In this period newspapers used Korean script and Chinese characters.

217. Figures from Hideo Kobayashi, "The Post-War Treatment of Japanese Overseas Nationals," chapter 10 of Philip Towle ed., *Japanese Prisoners of War* (London: Bloomsbury Academic, 2003). Some 250,000 Japanese were held in detention camps in Manchuria by the Soviets. For a fictionalized account of a Japanese family's experience in North Korea, See Yoko Kawashima Watkins, *So Far from the Bamboo Grove.*

218. By good fortune, Hyun was able to get a visa for Spain thanks to a new friend whose father just happened to be heading the team administering the Marshall Plan in that country. For more on his story, see Peter Hyun, *Darkness at Dawn: a North Korean Diary*. The other Peter Hyun was an intelligence officer in the U.S. Army in Korea who had been arrested and sent back to the States for unsanctioned meetings with Korean communists. For his story, see the two-volume autobiography *Man Sei: The Making of a Korean American* and *In the New World: The Making of a Korean American* (Honolulu: University of Hawaii Press, 1986, 1995). The two men eventually met in Seoul in 1988. For this: see "Case of mistaken identity leads to friendship," *The Telegraph,*

November 23, 1988, ref: https://news.google.com/newspapers?nid=2209&dat
=19881123&id=Jfg1AAAAIBAJ&sjid=E_wFAAAAIBAJ&pg=6975,6479579
&hl=en.

219. Richard C. Allen, *Korea's Syngman Rhee: An Unauthorized Portrait*, 40ff.

220. Sungjoo Han, *The Failure of Democracy in South Korea*, 178.

221. See "Kim Jong-pil Remembers: Election Fixing Provoked 'Revolution,'"
Korea JoongAng Daily, March 13, 2015, ref: http://koreajoongangdaily.joins.com
/news/article/article.aspx?aid=3001855; and, "Kim Jong-pil Remembers: Planning a 'Revolution' in Only 90 Days," *Korea JoongAng Daily*, March 11, 2015, ref:
http://koreajoongangdaily.joins.com/news/article/article.aspx?aid=3001738.

222. Through the 1960s, fifty-five of 125 ministerial posts went to people
with a military background. Only five went to civilian politicians. These figures compare with eleven military and fifty-eight civilian politicians out of
the 138 ministers under Rhee. For more on this, see Yang Sung-chul, *The
North and South Korean Political Systems: A Comparative Analysis*.

223. Park Chung-hee, *Our Nation's Path*, 199.

224. These details from Robert Boettcher, *Gifts of Deceit*, 78–98.

225. For more on this episode, see Robert Boettcher, ibid.

226. Author's interview with Kim Sang-hyun.

227. See "Kim Jong-pil Remembers: Old Connections Help Form a New
Administration," *Korea JoongAng Daily*, July 24, 2015, ref: http://korea
joongangdaily.joins.com/news/article/article.aspx?aid=3007002.

228. See "Kim Jong-pil Remembers: The Start of the Yushin Era Brings
Pushback with It," *Korea JoongAng Daily*, July 30, 2015, ref: http://korea
joongangdaily.joins.com/news/article/Article.aspx?aid=3007225.

229. As told to the author by a former aide to Chung Il-kwon who was the
prime minister when the incident happened.

230. Ref. Kim Byong-kuk, *Kim Dae-jung*, 89–97.

231. Media had been referring to Kim Dae-jung with the code "a person out of office."

232. These details are from Cheon Kum-sang, *Chun Doo-hwan: Man of Destiny*. Students of hagiography will find it a treasure.

233. "Baby Chun," as he was called, was appointed head of the Saemaul Movement by his brother. He later served several years in jail for corruption.

234. Cheon Kum-sang, op. cit., 77.

235. Ibid., 82.

236. The detail here is from "Yun Sang-won: the Knowledge in Those Eyes," a moving tribute to the militants' courage by American reporter Bradley Martin, in *Kwangju in the Eyes of the World*, a collection of reports written by foreign correspondents. Note that "Kwangju" became "Gwangju" in the new romanization system in 2000.

237. Ibid., 70–1.

238. Ibid., 92–3.

239. Elizabeth Shim, "South Korean Priests File Suit Against Gwangju Uprising Claims," UPI, August 31, 2015, ref: www.upi.com/Top_News/World -News/2015/08/31/South-Korean-priests-file-suit-against-Gwangju-Uprising -claims/7041441042773/. See English summary of Jee Man-won, Final Analysis Report on the May 18th Kwangju Riot (in Korean), here: www.ffnk.net /board/bbs/board.php?bo_table=free&wr_id=17769.

240. See Richard Holbrooke and Michael Armacost, "A Future Leader's Moment of Truth," *The New York Times*, 24 December 1997. Holbrooke and Armacost were the U.S. Department of State officials instrumental in saving Kim's life.

241. For an account of pro-North Korean students in this period, see excerpts in English of Han Ki-hong, 진보의 그늘 (*The Shade of Progressivism*), 시대정신

(Zeitgeist) Publishing House, 2012, on *Daily NK, 2014, ref:* www.dailynk
.com/english/sub_list.php?cataId=nk02502

242. Clyde Haberman, "Korean Opposition, Declaring Extensive Fraud, Pledges to Keep Fighting," *The New York Times*, December 18, 1987, ref: www
.nytimes.com/1987/12/18/world/korean-opposition-declaring-extensive
-fraud-pledges-to-keep-fighting.html. See also, chapter 3, "Seoul Brothers" of P. J. O'Rourke, *Holidays in Hell: In Which Our Intrepid Reporter Travels to the World's Worst Places and Asks, "What's Funny About This,"* (New York: Grove Press, 1988). It's a humorous take on this election.

243. Kim Dae-jung, "Is Culture Destiny? The Myth of Asia's Anti-Democratic Values" in *Foreign Affairs*, November/December 1994. This paper was a response to Lee Kuan Yew, the Singaporean leader, then the most prominent advocate of an Asian form of democracy.

244. The older man was Kwon Yang-sup, 78, a cab driver and former member of the communist South Korean Labor Party. He had been in prison since 1972.

245. This section is based on interviews in South Korea with former prisoners Lee Jong-hwan, Kim Sun-myung, Wang Yong-an, Suh Joon-sik, Li In-mo, Kwon Oh-hun, and human-rights officials. In North Korea, interviews with Li In-mo's wife, Kim Sun-im, and in 1994, after Li had been permitted to return north, with both together. For reference, see Suh Song, *Unbroken Spirits: Nineteen Years in South Korea's Gulag.*

246. In 2000, Kim Dae-jung allowed sixty-three former prisoners, including the two South Korean–born long-timers Lee Jong-hwan and Kim Sun-myung, to go to the North as part of a reconciliation agreement between the two countries.

247. The following biographical details for Kim Dae-jung are from author's interviews with relatives, friends, and staffers.

248. After Kim's mother's first husband, Jekal Song-jo, died, possibly of tuberculosis, her brother-in-law kindly offered to take her name off the

family book, allowing a posthumous divorce, and gave her some money to start a tavern. She had a daughter with a man named Yoon Chang-eon. It is not known how this relationship ended but she then met Kim Dae-jung's father. This information is based on interviews with Jekal Jang-chool from Kim's home island of Hawi-do, and Jekal Min, grandnephew of the first husband.

249. Kim Dae-jung, *A New Beginning: A Collection of Essays* (Cheng & Tsui, 1996), pp. 28–9. In this version, the teacher uses his Korean name, a decision, we may assume, that was a politically correct intervention by the author.

250. The official explanation for his wife's death was exhaustion. But the aide who claimed to have carried her on his back to the hospital told me she had gassed herself. See also Don Kirk, *Korea Betrayed: Kim Dae Jung and Sunshine*, 22.

251. For detail, see Kwon Tae-ho, "Former Ambassador Donald Gregg Discusses Park Chung-hee's Legacy," *The Hankyoreh*, May 13, 2011, ref: http://english.hani.co.kr/arti/english_edition/e_national/477813.html.

252. See Donald Kirk, *Korea Betrayed*, op. cit.

253. See "A Boy Politician, Smart and Stubborn," *Korea JoongAng Daily*, April 30, 2002, ref: http://koreajoongangdaily.joins.com/news/article/Article.aspx?aid=1903228.

254. Anthony Faiola, "Court Rejects S. Korean President's Impeachment," *The Washington Post*, May 14, 2004, ref: www.washingtonpost.com/wp-dyn/articles/A25441-2004May13.html.

255. Lee, like most achievers, has an inspiring rags-to-riches story. See, Lee Myung-bak, *The Uncharted Path: The Autobiography of Lee Myung-Bak*.

256. Kim Young-sam and Kim Dae-jung both conducted tax investigations as a way at getting back at the media. Roh was accused of pressuring the press when, in his last year, he tried to change the system of press clubs, whereby the journalists operate out of the government ministries they cover. This was actually not a bad idea and it was more the poor execution than any authoritarian intention that led to press criticism about his motives.

257. The report was "Promotion and Protection of All Human Rights, Civil, Political, Economic, and Culture Rights, Including the Right to Development," by Frank La Rue, then-U.N. Special Rapporteur for Freedom of Opinion and Expression. The program "Is American Beef Really Safe from Mad Cow Disease?" aired on MBC-TV on April 27, 2008.

258. See Freedom House, "South Korea Internet Freedom Report 2012," ref: https://freedomhouse.org/report/freedom-net/2012/south-korea.

259. See this story and two files with the breakdown of costs at the bottom: "'깜깜이 예산 집행' 부산시 광고예산은 눈먼 돈," ('Executing Budget in the Dark' Busan City's Publicity Budget is Money Blindly Thrown Away), OhmyNews, March 12, 2015, ref: www.ohmynews.com/NWS_Web/View/at_pg.aspx ?CNTN_CD=A0002089037&PAGE_CD=R0401&CMPT_CD=S0016.

260. Song Jung-a, "South Korea orders retrial of former spy chief Won Sei-hoon," *Financial Times*, July 16, 2015, ref: www.ft.com/intl/cms/s/0/ad223bca -2b95-11e5-8613-e7aedbb7bdb7.html#axzz3o8qpeCO6.

261. For an in-depth look at the businesses and artists in movies, TV dramas, music, and animation, see Mark James Russell, *Pop Goes Korea: Behind the Revolution in Movies, Music and Internet Culture*.

262. For more on this theme, see Song Woong-ki, "Artist's Death Highlights Indie Music's Problems," *The Korea Herald*, November 28, 2010, ref: www .koreaherald.com/view.php?ud=20101124000850.

263. Mark James Russell, *K-Pop Now: The Korean Music Revolution*, 6.

264. Julianne Escobedo Shepherd, "Pyro, Confetti and Deep Lust with BIGBANG, South Korea's Greatest Boy Band," *The Muse*, October 12, 2015, ref: http://themuse.jezebel.com/pyro-confetti-and-deep-lust-with-bigbang -south-koreas-1736131840.

265. For good insight into this, see Julianne Escobedo Shepherd, "Please Don't Go Girl," *Rookie Mag*, June 20, 2013, ref: www.rookiemag.com/2013/06/please -dont-go-girl-julianne/.

266. For detail and insights into Korean film history, see Kyung Hyun Kim, *Virtual Hallyu: Korean Cinema of the Global Era*; Jinhee Choi, *The South Korean Film Renaissance*; Darcy Paquet, *New Korean Cinema: Breaking the Waves*; and Mark Russell, *Pop Goes Korea*, op. cit. For a full list of titles, see Darcy Paquet's site, Koreanfilm.org.

267. Quotes are from author's interview and English drafts of two columns written by Paquet for publication in Korea.

268. See Joshua Hall, "How Not to Promote Korean Food," *The Wall Street Journal Asia*, May 21, 2013, ref: http://blogs.wsj.com/korearealtime/2013/05/21 /how-not-to-promote-korean-food/.

269. Jane Han, "'Bulgogi' ad makes Choo laughingstock," *The Korea Times*, March 19, 2014, ref: www.koreatimes.co.kr/www/news/nation/2014/03/116 _153711.html.

270. For example, see Daisy Buchanan, reatimes.co.kr/www/news/nation/*The Sunday Times*, April 12, 2015, ref: www.thesundaytimes.co.uk/sto/style/fashion /People/article1540561.ece.

271. Kate Wiltrout, "Korean War Vets Thanked by Little Angels in Norfolk," PilotOnline.com, June 8, 2010, ref: http://hamptonroads.com/2010/06/korean-war-vets-thanked-little-angels-norfolk.

272. For more on literature, see KTlit.com

273. The study was undertaken for UK Trade & Investment by Peter Underwood of IRC Ltd, a Seoul-based consulting firm. See "Korea's Growth Engines for the Future: Industries Likely to Emerge Over the Coming Decade," November 2014, ref: www.gov.uk/government/uploads/system/uploads /attachment_data/file/376851/Korea_s_Growth_Engines_for_the_Future .pdf.

274. The estimates are by the Korea Economic Research Institute.

275. Figures cited in this section are from the Bank of Korea.

276. In 1963, 25.8 percent of jobs were in shops, restaurants, hotels, and other services, and 11.1 percent were in mining, construction, and some form of manufacturing. These broad categories of services and industry contributed 36.3 and 14.7 percent, respectively, to the value of the economy back then.

277. Ruchir Sharma, op. cit., 157.

278. Korea lost 740,000 manufacturing jobs from 1995 to 2008. Source: "The resilient economy," essay by Stephen Roach and Sharon Lam in "South Korea: Finding its place on the world stage," McKinsey, 2010, ref: www.mckinsey .com/insights/winning_in_emerging_markets/south_korea_finding_its_place _on_the_world_stage.

279. See Lee Hyo-sik, "KOTRA to nurture 1,400 exporters," *The Korea Times*, January 28, 2015. Ref: www.koreatimes.co.kr/www/news/biz/2015/03/123 _172608.html

280. Ref: mes.co.kr/www/news/biz/2015/03/123_172608.htmlKo

281. These are government figures from 2013.

282. In 2014.

283. I am grateful to Charles Watson, the founder of the Financial Dynamics (now the Strategic Communications Division of FTI Consulting), for the "finders, minders and grinders" idea.

284. To chart the causes and course of the 1997 crisis, I have followed: Young-sun Koh, "The Growth of Korean Economy and the Role of Government," chapter 2 of Il SaKong and Youngsun Koh eds., *The Korean Economy: Six Decades of Growth and Development*; and Kim Ki-hwan, "The 1997–98 Korean Financial Crisis: Causes, Policy Response, and Lessons," an IMF conference paper, 2006, ref: /www.imf.org/external/np/seminars/eng/2006/cpem/pdf /kihwan.pdf.

285. The potential for disaster did not turn everyone off. One correspondent told me he was wined and dined during the crisis period by visitors from

several German regional banks, notorious then for their appetite for high risk, whose pressing question was whether the Korean patient was going to live long enough for them to safely issue another round of three-month loans.

286. From the March 2, 1998, Daily News Analysis of SsangYong Investment & Securities (which two name-changes later is now Shinhan Investment Corp.).

287. An unemployment benefit scheme was introduced in 1995 but when the crisis hit only ten percent of workers had been paying in long enough to be eligible to take advantage of it.

288. One *chaebol* chairman alleged in a speech that industrialized countries had, before the crisis, already finished "working out a program to punish Korea Inc. and waited until the time was ripe." I won't name him out of deep respect for Korea's defamation laws under which I could be sued for using his actual quote to make him look like an idiot.

289. For more, see *The Korean Economy: Six Decades of Growth and Development*, op. cit., chapter 2.

290. This case is argued in Jang-sup Shin, *The Global Financial Crisis and the Korean Economy*.

291. For insight into this underreported issue, see www.koreaandtheworld.org /jonson-porteux/ and http://hosei.academia.edu/JonsonPorteux.

292. See "Bitter Harvest: Exploitation and Forced Labour of Migrant Agricultural Workers in South Korea," October 2014, ref: www.amnesty.org/en /documents/ASA25/004/2014/en/; and Matt van Volkenburg, "CERD Rules That HIV Tests for Foreign Teachers in Korea Are Discriminatory," Gusts of Popular Feeling blog, May 23, 2015, ref: http://populargusts.blogspot.kr /2015/05/cerd-rules-that-hiv-tests-for-foreign.html.

293. From 46 cases in 2008, to 97 in 2010, 112 in 2012, and 129 in 2103, Park's first year in office.

294. See Park Ju-min, "South Korean Court-Martial Jails Soldiers in Hazing Death Case," Reuters, October 30, 2014, ref: www.reuters.com/article/2014/10/30/us-southkorea-military-idUSKBN0IJ0OH20141030

295. See this university publication for a good take on the expectations at the time: Jeon You-na, Kim Ji-yeon, "Ahn Chul-su, No Doubt a Great Leader, but a Great Politician?" *The Dongguk Post*, September 3, 2012, ref: www.dgupost .com/news/articleView.html?idxno=1292. (Despite the different English spelling, this article refers to Ahn Cheol-soo.)

296. Effectiveness of law-making bodies, World Economic Forum, Executive Opinion Survey 2014, ref: www3.weforum.org/docs/GITR/2014/GITR _DataTable1_2014.pdf.

297. The government owns or partially owns two of the three terrestrial channels, MBC and KBS, as well as the main news channels Yonhap News and YTN. Intellectuals now favor cable channels such as JTBC, which is owned by the JoongAng Ilbo Group.

298. Only the *Kyonghyang Shinum* and *The Hankyoreh* dailies and the news magazine, *SisaIn*, and the online publication *Pressian* routinely resist this pressure and suffer the advertising consequences.

299. A German ambassador to South Korea, talking to journalists in Seoul not long after Germany had reunified.

BIBLIOGRAPHY

General

Cumings, Bruce, *Korea's Place in the Sun: A Modern History*. (New York: W. W. Norton, 2005).

Henderson, Gregory, *Korea: The Politics of the Vortex*. (Cambridge, MA: Harvard University Press, 1968).

Kim, Choong Soon, *Kimchi and Information Technology: Tradition and Transformation in Korea*. (Seoul: Ilchokak, 2007).

Macdonald, Donald Stone, *The Koreans: Contemporary Politics and Society*. (Boulder, CO: Westview Press, 1996).

Salmon, Andrew, *Modern Korea: All That Matters*. (London: John Murray Learning, 2014).

Tudor, Daniel, *Korea: The Impossible Country*. (Rutland, VT: Tuttle Publishing, 2012).

Winchester, Simon, *Korea: A Walk Through the Land of Miracles*. (New York: Harper Perennial, 2005).

Pre-Twentieth-Century History

Bishop, Isabella Bird, *Korea and Her Neighbors*. (Seoul: Yonsei University Press, 1970).

Choe, Yongho, Peter H. Lee, and Wm. Theodore de Bary, eds., *Sources of Korean Tradition, Volume Two: From the Sixteenth to the Twentieth Centuries*. (New York: Columbia University Press, 2000).

Deuchler, Martina, *The Confucian Transformation of Korea: A Study of Society and Ideology*. (Cambridge, MA: Harvard University Press, 1992).

———, *Under the Ancestors' Eyes: Kinship, Status, and Locality in Premodern Korea*. (Cambridge, MA: Harvard University Asia Center, 2015).

Eckert, Carter J., Ki-baik Lee, et al., *Korea Old and New: A History*. (Seoul: Ilchokak, 1991).

Haboush, Jahyun Kim, *The Memoirs of Lady Hyegyong: The Autobiographical Writings of a Crown Princess of Eighteenth-Century Korea*. (Berkeley: University of California Press, 2013).

Hawley, Samuel, *The Imjin War: Japan's Sixteenth-Century Invasion of Korea and Attempt to Conquer China*. (Seoul: Conquistador Press, 2014).

Hwang, Kyung Moon, *A History of Korea*. (New York: Palgrave Macmillan, 2011).

Kim, Hyoung-chan, ed., *East Meets West (Korean Studies Series Vol. 1)*. (Seoul: The Korea National Commission for UNESCO and Hollym, 2014).

Kim, Sun Joo, and Jungwon Kim, trans., *Wrongful Deaths: Selected Inquest Records from Nineteenth-Century Korea*. (Seattle: University of Washington Press, 2013).

Lee, Peter H., and Wm. Theodore de Bary, eds., *Sources of Korean Tradition, Volume One: From Early Times Through the Sixteenth Century*. (New York: Columbia University Press, 1997).

Longford, Joseph H., *The Story of Korea*. (London: T. Fisher Unwin, 1911). (Accessed from the Martin Uden collection on the Royal Asiatic Society Web site, ref: http://raskb.com).

Palais, James B., *Confucian Statecraft and Korean Institutions: Yu*

Hyongwon and the Late Choson Dynasty. (Seattle: University of Washington Press, 2014).

———, *Politics and Policy in Traditional Korea.* (Cambridge, MA: Harvard University Asia Center, 1991).

Rutt, Richard, *James Scarth Gale and his History of the Korean People.* (Seoul: Royal Asiatic Society, 1972).

Sands, William Franklin, *Undiplomatic Memories.* (Seoul: Royal Asiatic Society, 1975).

Swope, Kenneth M., *A Dragon's Head and a Serpent's Tail: Ming China and the First Great East Asian War, 1592–1598.* (Norman: University of Oklahoma Press, 2009).

Turnbull, Stephen, *Samurai Invasion: Japan's Korean War 1592–1598.* (Oxford: Osprey Publishing, 2008).

Weems, Clarence Norwood, ed., *Hulbert's History of Korea Vol. II.* (New York: Hillary House, 1962).

Early Twentieth-Century History

Duus, Peter, *The Abacus and the Sword: The Japanese Penetration of Korea, 1895–1910.* (Berkeley: University of California Press, 1995).

Eckert, Carter J., *Offspring of Empire: The Koch'ang Kims and the Colonial Origins of Korean Capitalism, 1876–1945.* (Seattle: University of Washington Press, 1991).

Em, Henry H., *The Great Enterprise: Sovereignty and Historiography in Modern Korea.* (Durham, NC: Duke University Press, 2013).

Henry, Todd A., *Assimilating Seoul: Japanese Rule and the Politics of Public Space in Colonial Korea, 1910–1945.* (Berkeley: University of California Press, 2014).

Howard, Keith, ed., *True Stories of the Korean Comfort Women.* (London: Cassell Academic, 1996).

Kang, Hildi, *Under the Black Umbrella: Voices from Colonial Korea 1910–1945.* (Ithaca, NY: Cornell University Press, 2001).

Kim, Choong Soon, *A Korean Nationalist Entrepreneur: A Life History of Kim Songsu, 1891–1955.* (Albany: State University of New York Press, 1998).

Lankov, Andrei, *The Dawn of Modern Korea*. (Seoul: EunHaeng NaMu, 2007).

McNamara, Dennis L., *The Colonial Origins of Korean Enterprise: 1910–1945*. (Cambridge: Cambridge University Press, 1990).

Palmer, Brandon, *Fighting for the Enemy: Koreans in Japan's War, 1937–1945*. (Seattle: University of Washington Press, 2013).

Richter, Steffi, ed., *Contested Views of a Common Past: Revisions of History in Contemporary East Asia*. (Frankfurt: Campus Verlag, 2008).

Shin, Gi-Wook, and Michael Robinson, eds., *Colonial Modernity in Korea*. (Cambridge, MA: Harvard University Asia Center, 1999).

Soh, C. Sarah, *The Comfort Women: Sexual Violence and Postcolonial Memory in Korea and Japan*. (Chicago: The University of Chicago Press, 2008).

Uchida, Jun, *Brokers of Empire: Japanese Settler Colonialism in Korea, 1876–1945*. (Cambridge, MA: Harvard University Asia Center, 2011).

Wales, Nym, and San Kim, *The Song of Ariran*. (Menlo Park, CA: Ramparts Press, 1972).

Yi, Kyu-tae, *Modern Transformation of Korea*. (Seoul: Sejong Publishing Co., 1970).

Yoshiaki, Yoshimi, *Comfort Women: Sexual Slavery in the Japanese Military During World War II*. (New York: Columbia University Press, 2002).

Post-Occupation and Korean War

Cameron, James, *Point of Departure*. (London: Granta Books, 2006).

Clark, Eugene Franklin, *The Secrets of Inchon: The Untold Story of the Most Daring Covert Mission of the Korean War*. (New York: Berkley Books, 2002).

Cumings, Bruce, *The Korean War: A History*. (New York: Modern Library, 2010).

———, *The Origins of the Korean War: Liberation and the Emergence of Separate Regimes 1945–47*. (Princeton, NJ: Princeton University Press, 1981).

Cumings, Bruce, ed., *Child of Conflict: The Korean-American Relationship 1943–1953*. (Seattle: University of Washington Press, 1983).

Deane, Philip, *Captive in Korea*. (London: Hamish Hamilton, 1953). (Accessed from the Martin Uden collection on the Royal Asiatic Society Web site, ref: http://raskb.com).

Fehrenbach, T. R., *This Kind of War*. (Washington, DC: Potomac Books, 2001).

Gayn, Mark, *Japan Diary*. (Rutland, VT: Tuttle Publishing, 1989). (Accessed from the Martin Uden collection on the Royal Asiatic Society Web site, ref: http://raskb.com).

Goulden, Joseph C., *Korea: the Untold Story of the War*. (New York: Times Books, 1982).

Halberstam, David, *The Coldest Winter: America and the Korean War*. (New York: Hachette Books, 2008).

Hastings, Max, *The Korean War*. (New York: Simon & Schuster, 1988).

Kim, Hun Joon, *The Massacres at Mt. Halla: Sixty Years of Truth Seeking in South Korea*. (Ithaca, NY: Cornell University Press, 2014).

Lee, Daniel, *Son of the Phoenix: One Man's Story of Korea*. (Seoul: Voice Publishing House, 2008).

Meade, E. Grant, *American Military Government in Korea*. (New York: King's Crown Press, 1951).

Salmon, Andrew, *Scorched Earth, Black Snow: Britain and Australia in the Korean War, 1950*. (London: Aurum, 2009).

———, *To the Last Round: The Epic British Stand on the Imjin River, Korea, 1951*. (London: Aurum, 2007).

The Jeju 4.3 Incident Investigation Report. (Seoul: The National Committee for Investigation of the Truth about the Jeju April 3 Incident, 2003).

Postwar

Ahrens, Frank, *Seoul Man: A Memoir of Cars, Culture, Crisis, and Unexpected Hilarity Inside a Korean Corporate Titan*. (New York: HarperBusiness, 2016).

Allen, Richard C., *Korea's Syngman Rhee: An Unauthorized Portrait.* (Rutland, VT: Tuttle Publishing, 1960).

Amsden, Alice H., *Asia's Next Giant: South Korea and Late Industrialization.* (Oxford: Oxford University Press, 1989).

Boettcher, Robert, *Gifts of Deceit: Sun Myung Moon, Tongsun Park, and the Korea Scandal.* (New York: Holt, Rinehart and Winston, 1980).

Cheon, Kum Sang, *Chun Doo-hwan: Man of Destiny.* (Los Angeles: North American Press, 1982).

Clifford, Mark L., *Troubled Tiger: Businessmen, Bureaucrats and Generals in South Korea.* (Armonk, NY: M. E. Sharpe, 1993).

Eichengreen, Barry, Dwight H. Perkins, and Kwanho Shin, *From Miracle to Maturity: The Growth of the Korean Economy.* (Cambridge, MA: Harvard University Press, 2012).

Gleysteen Jr., William H., *Massive Entanglement, Marginal Influence: Carter and Korea in Crisis.* (Washington, DC: Brookings Institution Press, 1999).

Goldstein, Norm, *Kim Dae-jung.* (Philadelphia: Chelsea House, 1999).

Gregg, Donald P., *Pot Shards: Fragments of a Life Lived in CIA, the White House, and the Two Koreas.* (Washington, DC: New Academia Publishing, 2014).

Han, Sungjoo, *The Failure of Democracy in South Korea.* (Berkeley: University of California Press, 1974).

Hussain, Tariq, *Diamond Dilemma: Shaping Korea for the 21st Century.* (Seoul: Seoul Selection, 2008).

Kim, Byung-Kook, Ezra Vogel, eds., *The Park Chung Hee Era: The Transformation of South Korea.* (Cambridge, MA: Harvard University Press, 2013).

Kim, Byong-kuk, *Kim Dae-jung.* (Seoul: Ilweolseogak, 1992).

Kim, Dae-jung, *A New Beginning: A Collection of Essays.* (Boston: Cheng & Tsui, 1996).

Kim, Hyung-A, and Clark Sorensen, eds., *Reassessing the Park Chung Hee Era, 1961–1979: Development, Political Thought, Democracy, and Cultural Influence.* (Seattle: University of Washington Press, 2011).

Kim, Woo-choong, *Every Street Is Paved with Gold.* (New York: Morrow, 1992).

Kim, Yun Tae, *Bureaucrats and Entrepreneurs: The State and the Chaebol in Korea.* (Seoul: Jimoondang, 2008).

Kirk, Donald, *Korea Betrayed: Kim Dae Jung and Sunshine.* (New York: Palgrave Macmillan, 2009).

———, *Korean Dynasty: Hyundai and Chung Ju Yung.* (London: Routledge, 1995).

———, *Okinawa and Jeju: Bases of Discontent.* (London: Palgrave Pivot, 2013).

Lee, Byeong-Cheon, ed., *Developmental Dictatorship and The Park Chung-Hee Era: The Shaping of Modernity in the Republic of Korea.* (Paramus, NJ: Homa & Sekey Books, 2005).

Lee, Chong-Sik, *Park Chung-Hee: From Poverty to Power.* (Seoul: The KHU Press, 2012).

Lee, Jai-eui, *Kwangju Diary: Beyond Death, Beyond the Darkness of the Age.* (Los Angeles: UCLA, 1999).

Lee, Myung-bak, *The Uncharted Path: The Autobiography of Lee Myung-Bak.* (Naperville, IL: Sourcebooks, 2011).

Lee, Namhee, *The Making of Minjung.* (Ithaca, NY: Cornell University Press, 2007).

Michell, Anthony, *Samsung Electronics and the Struggle for Leadership of the Electronics Industry.* (Singapore: John Wiley & Sons, 2010).

Nahm, Andrew C., *Korea: Tradition and Transformation.* (Seoul: Hollym, 1988).

O, Won-chol, *The Korea Story: President Park Jung-hee's Leadership and the Korean Industrial Revolution.* (Seoul: WisdomTree, 2009).

Oberdorfer, Don and Robert Carlin, *The Two Koreas: A Contemporary History.* (New York: Basic Books, 2013).

Ogle, George, *South Korea: Dissent Within the Economic Miracle.* (London: Zed Books, 1990).

Oliver, Robert T., *The Truth About Korea.* (New York: Putnam, 1951).

Park Chung-hee, *Our Nation's Path.* (Seoul: Hollym, 1970).

SaKong, Il, and Youngsun Koh, eds., *The Korean Economy: Six Decades of Growth and Development.* (Seoul: Korea Development Institute, 2010).

Salmon, Andrew, *American Business and the Korean Miracle: US Enterprises in Korea, 1866–the Present.* (Seoul: AMCHAM Korea, 2002).

Seliger, Bernhard, *The Shrimp that Became a Tiger: Transformation Theory and Korea's Rise After the Asian Crisis*. (Frankfurt: Peter Lang International Academic Publishers, 2013).

Shapiro, Michael, *The Shadow in the Sun: A Korean Year of Love and Sorrow*. (New York: Atlantic Monthly Press, 1990).

Shin, Jang-sup, *The Global Financial Crisis and the Korean Economy*. (London: Routledge, 2013).

Song, Byong-nak, *The Rise of the Korean Economy*. (Oxford: Oxford University Press, 1990).

Song, Jaeyong, and Kyungmook Lee, *The Samsung Way: Transformational Management Strategies from the World Leader in Innovation and Design*. (New York: McGraw-Hill Education, 2014).

Steers, Richard M., *Made in Korea: Chung Ju Yung and the Rise of Hyundai*. (New York: Routledge, 1998).

Stephens, Michael, *Lost in Seoul and Other Discoveries on the Korean Peninsula*. (New York: Random House, 1990).

Straub, David, *Anti-Americanism in Democratizing South Korea*. (Stanford, CA: Shorenstein Asia-Pacific Research Center, 2015).

Studwell, Joe, *How Asia Works: Success and Failure in the World's Most Dynamic Region*. (New York: Grove Press, 2013).

Sung, Suh, *Unbroken Spirits: Nineteen Years in South Korea's Gulag*. (Lanham, MD: Rowman & Littlefield Publishers, 2001).

Thomas, Cullen, *Brother One Cell: An American Coming of Age in South Korea's Prisons*. (New York: Penguin Books, 2008).

Vogel, Ezra, *The Four Little Dragons: The Spread of Industrialization in East Asia (The Edwin O. Reischauer Lectures)*. (Cambridge, MA: Harvard University Press, 1993).

Weber, Amalie M., ed., *Kwangju in the Eyes of the World: The Personal Recollections of the Foreign Correspondents Covering the Kwangju Uprising*. (Seoul: Pulbit Publishing Co., 1997).

Wickham, John, *Korea on the Brink: From the "12/12 Incident" to the Kwangju Uprising, 1979–1980*. (Washington, DC: National Defense University Press, 1999).

Music, Movies, Food

Chang, Sun-young, *A Korean Mother's Cooking Notes.* (Seoul: Ewha Womans University Press, 2009).

Choi, Jinhee, *The South Korean Film Renaissance.* (Middletown, CT: Wesleyan, 2010).

Hepinstall, Soo Shin Hi, *Growing up in a Korean Kitchen.* (Berkeley, CA: Ten Speed Press, 2001).

Hong, Euny, *The Birth of Korean Cool.* (New York: Picador, 2014).

Hughes, Theodore Q., *Literature and Film in Cold War South Korea: Freedom's Frontier.* (New York: Columbia University Press, 2012).

Kim, Kyung Hyun, *Virtual Hallyu: Korean Cinema of the Global Era.* (Durham, NC: Duke University Press, 2011).

Maangchi, *Maangchi's Real Korean Cooking: Authentic Dishes for the Home Cook.* (New York: Rux Martin/Houghton Mifflin Harcourt, 2015).

McPherson, Joe, *Seoul Restaurant Expat Guide 2015.* (Seoul: Zen-Kimchi International, 2015).

Paquet, Darcy, *New Korean Cinema: Breaking the Waves.* (New York: Wallflower Press, 2009).

Park, Young-a, *Unexpected Alliances: Independent Filmmakers, the State, and the Film Industry in Postauthoritarian South Korea.* (Stanford , CA: Stanford University Press, 2014).

Pettid, Michael J., *Korean Cuisine: An Illustrated History.* (London: Reaktion Books, 2008).

Russell, Mark James, *K-Pop Now: The Korean Music Revolution.* (Rutland, VT: Tuttle Publishing, 2014).

———, *Pop Goes Korea: Behind the Revolution in Movies, Music and Internet Culture.* (Berkeley, CA: Stone Bridge Press, 2009).

Religion

Baker, Don, *Korean Spirituality.* (Honolulu: University of Hawaii Press, 2008).

Blair, William Newton, *Gold in Korea.* (Topeka, KS: The Presbyterian Church of the USA, 1957).

Blair, William Newton, and Bruce Hunt, *The Korean Pentecost and the Sufferings Which Followed*. (Edinburgh: The Banner of Truth Trust, 1977).

Chryssides, George D., *The Advent of Sun Myung Moon*. (London: Macmillan, 1991).

Chung, Edward Y. J., *The Korean Neo-Confucianism of Yi T'oegye and Yi Yulgok: A Reappraisal of the "Four-Seven Thesis" and Its Practical Implications For Self-Cultivation*. (Albany: State University of New York Press, 1995).

Clark, Allen D., *A History of the Church in Korea*. (Seoul: Christian Literature Society of Korea, 1971).

Guisso, Richard W.I., *Shamanism: The Spirit World of Korea*. (Fremont, CA: Jain Pub. Co., 1988).

Huntley, Martha, *Caring, Growing, Changing: A History of the Protestant Mission in Korea*. (New York: Friendship Press, 1984).

Kang, Wi Jo, *Christ and Caesar in Modern Korea: A History of Christianity and Politics*. (Albany: State University of New York Press, 1997).

Kendall, Laurel, *Shamans, Housewives, and Other Restless Spirits*. (Honolulu: University of Hawaii Press, 1987).

Mason, David A., *The Spirit of the Mountains: Korea's San-Shin and Traditions of Mountain Worship*. (Seoul: Hollym, 1999).

Setton, Mark, *Chong Yagyong: Korea's Challenge to Orthodox Neo-Confucianism*. (Albany: State University of New York Press, 1997).

Shearer, Roy E., *Wildfire: Church Growth in Korea*. (Grand Rapids, MI: William B. Eerdmans, 1966).

Young, Carl F., *Eastern Learning and the Heavenly Way: The Tonghak and Chondogyo Movements and the Twilight of Korean Independence*. (Honolulu: University of Hawaii Press, 2014).

Selected Fiction

Cho, Chang-rae, *The Land of the Banished*. (Seoul: Jimoondang International, 2001).

Cho, Se-hui, *The Dwarf*. (Honolulu: University of Hawaii Press, 2006).

Church, James, *Bamboo and Blood*. (New York: Minotaur, 2010).

————, *The Corpse in the Koryo*. (New York: Minotaur, 2007).

————, *A Drop of Chinese Blood*. (New York: Minotaur, 2012).

————, *Hidden Moon*. (New York: Minotaur, 2008).

————, *The Man with the Baltic Stare*. (New York: Minotaur, 2010).

————, *The Gentleman from Japan*. (New York: Minotaur Books, 2016).

Drabble, Margaret, *The Red Queen*. (Orlando, FL: Harcourt, 2004).

Han Kang, *The Vegetarian*, (London: Hogarth, 2016).

Hwang, Sok-yong, *The Guest*. (New York: Seven Stories Press, 2001).

Johnson, Adam, *The Orphan Master's Son: A Novel*. (New York: Random House, 2012).

Kang, Younghill, *The Grass Roof*. (River Grove, IL: Follett, 1966).

Kim, Richard E., *The Innocent*. (Boston: Houghton Mifflin, 1968).

————, *Lost Names: Scenes from a Korean Boyhood*. (Westport, CT: Praeger, 1970).

————, *The Martyred*. (New York: Braziller, 1964).

Kim, Won-il, *Evening Glow*. (Fremont, CA: Asian Humanities Press, 2003).

Kim, Young-ha, *Black Flower*. (Boston: Houghton Mifflin Harcourt, 2012).

————, *I Have the Right to Destroy Myself*. (Orlando, FL: Harcourt, 2007).

————, *Photo Shop Murder*. (Seoul: Jimoondang, 2003).

————, *Your Republic Is Calling You*. (New York: Mariner Books, 2010).

Lee, Jung-myung, *The Investigation*. (London: Mantle, 2014).

Lee, Krys, *Drifting House*. (New York: Viking, 2012).

————, *How I Became a North Korean*. (New York: Viking, 2016).

Li, Mirok, *The Yalu Flows: A Korean Childhood*. (Seoul: Hollym International Corporation, 1987).

Park, Sunyoung, *On the Eve of the Uprising and Other Stories from Colonial Korea*. (Ithaca, NY: Cornell University Press, 2010).

Park Wan-suh, *Who Ate Up All the Shinga?* (New York: Columbia University Press, 2009).

Shin, Kyung-sook, *I'll Be Right There*. (New York: Other Press, 2010).

————, *The Girl Who Wrote Loneliness*. (New York: Pegasus, 2015).

————, *Please Look After Mom*. (New York: Vintage, 2012).

Sung-hi, Lee Ann, *Yi Kwang-su and Modern Korean Literature: Mujong.* (Ithaca, NY: Cornell University Press, 2005).

Watkins, Yoko Kawashima, *So Far from the Bamboo Grove.* (New York: HarperCollins, 2008).

Yi, Mun-yol, *Our Twisted Hero.* (Seoul: Minumsa, 2012).

North Korea

Armstrong, Charles, *The North Korean Revolution, 1945–1950.* (Ithaca, NY: Cornell University Press, 2004).

———, *The Tyranny of the Weak: North Korea and the World 1950–1992.* (Ithaca, NY: Cornell University Press, 2013).

Cha, Victor, *The Impossible State: North Korea, Past and Future.* (New York: HarperCollins, 2013).

Demick, Barbara, *Nothing to Envy: Ordinary Lives in North Korea.* (New York: Spiegel & Grau, 2009).

Everard, John, *Only Beautiful, Please: A British Diplomat in North Korea.* (Stanford, CA: Shorenstein Asia-Pacific Research Center, 2012).

Fischer, Paul, *A Kim Jong-Il Production: The Incredible True Story of North Korea and the Most Audacious Kidnapping in History.* (New York: Flatiron, 2015).

Haggard, Stephan, and Marcus Noland, *Famine in North Korea: Markets, Aid, and Reform.* (New York: Columbia University Press, 2007).

Harden, Blaine, *Escape from Camp 14: One Man's Remarkable Odyssey from North Korea to Freedom in the West.* (New York: Viking Penguin, 2012).

Hyun, Peter, *Darkness at Dawn: A North Korean Diary.* (Seoul: Hanjin Publishing Company, 1981).

Kang, Chol-hwan, and Pierre Rigoulot, *The Aquariums of Pyongyang: Ten Years in the North Korean Gulag.* (New York: Basic Books, 2005).

Kim, Hyun Hee, *Tears of My Soul.* (New York: Morrow, 1993).

Kim, Il Sung, *With the Century (Volumes 1–8).* (Pyongyang: Foreign Languages Publishing House, 2014).

Kim, Yong, *Long Road Home: Testimony of a North Korean Camp Survivor.* (New York: Columbia University Press, 2009).

Jang, Jin-sung, *Dear Leader.* (London: Random House, 2014).

Kirkpatrick, Melanie, *Escape from North Korea: The Untold Story of Asia's Underground Railroad.* (New York: Encounter Books, 2012).

Lankov, Andrei, *North of the DMZ: Essays on Daily Life in North Korea.* (Jefferson, NC: McFarland, 2007).

———, *The Real North Korea: Life and Politics in the Failed Stalinist Utopia.* (Oxford: Oxford University Press, 2013).

Lee, Hyeonseo, *The Girl with Seven Names: A North Korean Defector's Story.* (London: William Collins, 2015).

Lintner, Bertil, *Great Leader, Dear Leader: Demystifying North Korea Under the Kim Clan.* (Chiang Mai, Thailand: Silkworm Books, 2005).

Martin, Bradley, *Under the Loving Care of the Fatherly Leader: North Korea and the Kim Dynasty.* (New York: St. Martin's, 2006).

Morris-Suzuki, Tessa, *Exodus to North Korea: Shadows from Japan's Cold War.* (Lanham, MD: Rowman & Littlefield, 2007).

Myers, B. R., *The Cleanest Race: How North Koreans See Themselves and Why It Matters.* (New York: Melville House, 2010).

———, *North Korea's Juche Myth.* (Busan: Sthele Press, 2015).

Natsios, Andrew S., *The Great North Korean Famine: Famine, Politics, and Foreign Policy.* (Washington, DC: United States Institute of Peace Press, 2001).

Suh, Dae-Sook, *Kim Il Sung: The North Korean Leader.* (New York: Columbia University Press, 1995).

Tudor, Daniel, and James Pearson, *North Korea Confidential: Private Markets, Fashion Trends, Prison Camps, Dissenters and Defectors.* (Rutland, VT: Tuttle Publishing, 2015).

Yang, Sung-chul, *The North and South Korean Political Systems: A Comparative Analysis.* (Boulder, CA: Westview Press, 1994).

Yokota, Sakie, *North Korea Kidnapped My Daughter.* (New York: Vertical, 2009).

Yoo, Young-bok, *Tears of Blood: A Korean POW's Fight for Freedom, Family, and Justice.* (Los Angeles: Korea War POW Affairs—USA, 2012).

INDEX